The Marketing Plan

Third Edition

William A. Cohen, Ph.D.

California State University
Los Angeles

John Wiley & Sons, Inc.

New York   Chichester   Weinheim   Brisbane   Singapore   Toronto

Acquisition Editor	Jeff Marshall
Marketing Manager	Jessica Garcia
Senior Production Editor	Patricia McFadden
Art Direction	Dawn L. Stanley
Illustration Coordinator	Anna Melhorn
Production Management	Hermitage Publishing Services
Illustration Editor	Gene Aiello
Cover Design	David Levy

This book was set in 10/12 Times Roman by Hermitage Publishing Services and printed and bound by Courier Companies. The cover was printed by Phoenix.

This book is printed on acid-free paper. ∞

Library of Congress Cataloging in Publication Data

ISBN 0-471-38412-7

Printed in the United States of America

10 9 8 7 6 5 4 3 2 1

Preface

Some have called this the era of marketing. Major articles not only in *Business Week,* but also in *Time, Newsweek,* and other popular magazines attest to this fact. Every organization needs marketing to be successful and the key to marketing is the marketing plan. Even on a personal level, high performance experts tell us we must have a plan to be successful. A good marketing plan is the difference between dreams and ideas and organized, tough-minded, financially accurate, bottom-line success.

Sometime after I incorporated marketing plans into the marketing course that I taught, a former student, Robert Schwartz, stopped by to tell me that he was interviewed for an article in *Entrepreneur Magazine.*[1] Robert had started a chain of pizza restaurants. His business was based on a marketing plan he developed in my class. His cash flow was an amazing $48,000 per month. Robert was an undergraduate student. Leon Abjian, a graduate student I taught, sold his marketing plan for $5,000.

A professional consultant had occasion to examine some of the plans prepared by my students. His verdict? The plans were the equivalent of those prepared by himself and other professionals. In his opinion, they were worth $25,000 each! Yet they all were developed by undergraduate and graduate students. Based on this, several former students have gone into the business of preparing marketing plans for businesspeople; some have used their marketing plans to get the funds to start their own businesses; others have used them in corporations where they were employed.

More than 20 years ago, I began to supervise marketing plans done for real businesses. Many were done under contract, and the businesses paid the university for the business plans the students developed. And why not? They were 100 percent professional, and were extremely valuable to the businesses that paid for their development. Yet, the businesses paid only a small fraction of that $25,000 which one professional consultant said they were worth,

The aim of this book is to give you the knowledge to be able to develop truly outstanding, professional marketing plans. Along with your professor's guidance, this book will explain marketing planning and give you step-by-step procedures to produce a professional plan. It also provides forms that can greatly assist you in your efforts. Actual student plans prepared in the classroom are included. You will see how students adapted the basic ideas in this book and translated them into marketing plans for particular products or services. When you complete the book, you will not only know what to do, but also how and why you are doing it. You will be able to develop an excellent and professional marketing plan.

Developing a marketing plan is not theoretical. It requires you to work hard, use your imagination, and integrate your knowledge of marketing with other disciplines such as accounting, finance, and management. It is worth the time and effort required. The method described in this book for producing a marketing plan has been action-tested in the classroom and in the real world by thousands of marketing students and professionals. If you work at it steadily over the time allocated, not only will you be successful, you'll have a lot of fun doing it. It works!

William A. Cohen

---

[1] "Entrepreneurship on Campus, A Panel Discussion on Teaching Entrepreneurship," *Entrepreneur Magazine* (November 1984), p. 49.

Acknowledgment

I want to acknowledge and thank the students who contributed sample marketing plans for this edition, as well as the hundreds of others who helped teach me to teach others while developing marketing plans in my classes.

Biographical Sketch

William A. Cohen, Ph.D.

Dr. William A. Cohen is Professor of Marketing and Leadership, Past Chairman of the Marketing Department and Director of the Small Business Institute at California State University, Los Angeles. He has also taught at the University of Southern California and the Peter Drucker School of Management at Claremont Graduate University.

Among his 36 books translated into 12 languages are *Winning on the Marketing Front, The Entrepreneur and Small Business Marketing Problem Solver, Building a Mail Order Business, The Stuff of Heroes: The Eight Universal Laws of Leadership, How to Make It Big as a Consultant,* and *The New Art of the Leader.* When in print, his marketing textbook, *The Practice of Marketing Management,* was adopted by more than 177 universities. His books have been recommended by Mary Kay Ash, Barry Goldwater, Peter F. Drucker, Jagdeth Sheth, Secretary of State Alexander Haig, Astronaut Frank Borman, General H. Norman Schwarzkopf, and Barry Gordon, longest-serving president of the Screen Actors Guild, numerous CEOs of major corporations, and marketing professors all over the world.

Professor Cohen has been a consultant to the government and Fortune 500 companies, as well as to numerous small businesses. He was series editor for the John Wiley Series on Business Strategy and has served on numerous boards of directors, government commissions, and editorial advisory boards. He has also served as spokesperson for AT&T, given more than 100 TV, radio, and print interviews, and made hundreds of speeches. He has been quoted or reviewed in *Harvard Business Review, USA Today, Business Week, Fortune, Success, Changing Times, Venture, Chicago Tribune, The Los Angeles Times, The Encyclopedia Britannica,* and many other publications.

Professor Cohen received the Outstanding Professor's Award at California State University, Los Angeles and the Freedoms Foundation at Valley Forge Honor Medal for Excellence in Economic Education. In 1996, he was named CSULA Statewide Professor, the first business professor from his university to be given this award. In 1999, the Academy of Marketing Science named him one of four "Great Teachers in Marketing." Professor Cohen has also received numerous awards for excellence in directing consulting activities from the U.S. Small Business Administration and has supervised the preparation of more than 1,000 student marketing plans which have won major awards in student competitions and have been successfully implemented by their authors.

Professor Cohen has a B.S. from the United States Military Academy at West Point, an M.B.A. from the University of Chicago, and an M.A. and Ph.D. in management from Claremont Graduate School. He is also a distinguished graduate of the Industrial College of the Armed Forces, National Defense University, and a former major general in the U.S. Air Force Reserve.

Contents

CHAPTER 6
STEP 6: FORECASTING FOR YOUR MARKETING PLAN   /81

CHAPTER 7
STEP 7: CALCULATING IMPORTANT FINANCIAL RATIOS FOR YOUR MARKETING PLAN   /96

PROLOGUE

THE POWER AND MYSTIQUE OF THE MARKETING PLAN

Not long ago a candidate for President of the United States was presented with a campaign plan developed by his staff. The plan helped get him elected. Meanwhile, two Harvard Business School students, Mike Wigley and Jerry De La Vega, planned how to promote audio recordings. Their idea was to enable people to order any recording they wanted— right from their own homes. Twelve months later they started their company. David Ishag, another Harvard classmate joined them. The three entrepreneurs advertised on a cable television network that aired rock 'n' roll videos 24 hours a day. They called their company Hot Rock, Inc. Hot Rock, Inc. received 50,000 inquiries in the first 17 days. Sales grew 10 to 14 percent a month. They expected sales of $6.7 million for the first year. Yet this was no surprise.

In another part of the country, Stouffers Lean Cuisine, a line of frozen food, suddenly boosted its market share by more than 30 percent in the $500 million frozen-entree food market. This caught the entire industry by surprise—but not those at Stouffers.

The Clorox Company had reached $1 billion in sales but profits were unimpressive. Shortly after that, half of the $1 billion revenue disappeared when a key division was sold. Yet only six years later Clorox again hit $1 billion in sales. Moreover, this time profits were double—and Clorox had predicted and fully expected these figures. Glenn R. Savage, Clorox's marketing dirtector noted: "There's power in giving people very clear objectives."[1]

Gordon Bethune is CEO of Continental Airlines, the fifth largest in the United States. In 1994, it was bankrupt. Then Bethune took over. Since it has become one of America's most admired corporations, winning prestigious awards, such as Airline of the Year in 1997, first in customer service for three out of four years in the J.D. Power Airline Customer Satisfaction study, and in 1999, *Fortune* magazine named Continental one of 100 Best Companies in America to work for. It goes almost without saying that the company has enjoyed record-breaking profits.[2]

---

[1] Joan O. C. Hamilton, "Brighter Days at Clorox," *Business Week,* (June 16, 1997), p. 62.
[2] Sheila M. Puffer, interview with Gordon Bethune, "Continental Airlines' CEO Gordon Bethune on Teams and New Product Development," *The Academy of Management Executive* (August 1999), pp. 28, 32.

What do these four vastly different types of companies in totally different industries have in common other than their success? The answer is the marketing plan. In each case a marketing plan played a major role in enabling the company to reach its goals and the success it planned. This surprised everyone else, but not those who did it. They had a marketing plan.

THE MARKETING PLAN IS ESSENTIAL FOR EVERY BUSINESS OPERATION

A marketing plan is essential for every business operation and for efficient and effective marketing of any product or service. This is true for a brand new business, or even for marketing a product, service, or product line within a company. Seeking success for any project without the use of a marketing plan is like trying to navigate a ship in bad weather, through stormy waters, while under torpedo attack, and with neither a compass nor a clear idea of where you are going. It does require time to develop a marketing plan. But this is time well spent. It will save you time overall. The marketing plan will allow you to visualize clearly both where you are going and what you want to accomplish along the way. At the same time, a marketing plan details the very important steps required to get you from where you are to where you want to be. An added benefit is that in compiling and developing the marketing plan, you will have thought through how long it will take to accomplish each step and what resources in money, time, and effort you will need. Without a marketing plan, you will not even know when or whether you have reached your objectives.

WHAT A MARKETING PLAN WILL DO FOR YOU

A properly developed marketing plan can accomplish a lot for a relatively small amount of focused effort. A marketing plan will:

- act as a road map.
- assist in management control and implementation of strategy.
- inform new participants of their roles in implementing the plan and reaching your objectives.
- assist in helping to obtain resources for implementation.
- stimulate thinking and the better use of limited resources.
- help in the organization and assignment of responsibilities, tasks, and timing.
- help you become aware of problems, opportunities, and threats in the future.

Let's look at each of these benefits in turn.

THE MARKETING PLAN ACTS AS A ROAD MAP

Perhaps the basic purpose of the marketing plan is to act as a road map to tell you how to get from the beginning of the plan to reach your objectives and goals. Like a road map, the plan describes the environment in which you are likely to find yourself along the way. A road map might describe the geographical terrain as well as the type and classification of the various road arteries, times, distances, and available stops for emergencies, gasoline, food, repair, or lodging. In the same fashion the marketing plan will describe the environment of the marketplace including your competitors, politics, laws, regulations, economic and business conditions, state of technology, forecast demand, social and cultural factors, and demographics of the target market, as well as the company's available resources.

THE MARKETING PLAN ASSISTS WITH MANAGEMENT CONTROL AND IMPLEMENTATION OF STRATEGY

If you're on a trip, your strategy is the route that you plan to take. Your road map shows it along with the expected physical and geographical environment. As you proceed, various problems may occur which could interfere with your planned strategy. You may need to detour due to unplanned circumstances. Perhaps there is road maintenance or severe weather that makes the most direct route or the planned route impossible to use. In fact, it is virtually certain that almost nothing will go exactly as originally planned. Yet, because your road map anticipates potential changes in your environment that may require detours, you can continue toward your destination with ease. In the same way, the marketing plan will allow you to spot and redirect your activities toward alternate paths in order to arrive at your objective with minimum difficulty. You will be able to see clearly the difference between what is happening during the implementation of your strategy and what you had planned to happen. This will give you control of the situation and allow you to take the corrective action necessary to put your project back on track and to keep it on track to reach your final objective.

THE MARKETING PLAN INFORMS NEW PARTICIPANTS OF THEIR ROLES AND FUNCTIONS

Successful implementation of a strategy requires integration of many actions, usually by many different people and departments both inside and outside the organization. Timing is frequently critical. And it is most important that all concerned individuals understand what their responsibilities are as well as how their tasks or actions fit into the overall strategy. Having a marketing plan enables you to describe "the big picture" in detail. It allows everyone to see how their actions fit in with the actions of others. New people may be assigned to activities involving your plan. They, too, can be brought immediately up-to-date regarding their responsibilities, what they must do, and how to adapt to the work of others. Thus, the marketing plan is a document that can be used to inform all participants of your objectives and how and why these objectives will be met: by whom, with what, and when.

THE MARKETING PLAN PLOTS THE ACQUISITION OF RESOURCES FOR IMPLEMENTATION

You will find that your resources to accomplish any project are far from unlimited. Resources are always limited. This is true whether you are an individual entrepreneur attempting to obtain money from a potential investor or you are working in a large corporation and seeking resources for your project within the firm. A marketing plan plays an important part in persuading those who have the authority to allocate limited resources— money, people, and other assets—to your project. And with resources scarce, you must convince these individuals that you are going to use capital, goods, and labor in the most effective and efficient manner. You must not only persuade them that your objectives are achievable, but that, despite competition and other potential threats, you will ultimately reach your goals. So, your marketing plan is also a sales tool. Even more, the marketing plan helps to prove your control over the project from start to finish. It shows that you not only can see the final objective, but that you know what you must do at every point along the way. This includes actions, costs, and alternatives. When you master the project on paper, you're already halfway there. Those who have the resources you need will be more likely to see the potential and give them to you.

THE MARKETING PLAN STIMULATES THINKING AND MAKES BETTER USE OF RESOURCES

Since your resources will always be limited, you must get the maximum results from what you have. A good marketing plan will help you make the most of what you have—to make one dollar do the work of ten. It will help you build on your strengths and minimize your weaknesses. It will also help you obtain a differential advantage over your competition. You can always do this by economizing where it doesn't count, and concentrating superior resources where it does. This leads to success. As you do the research for your marketing plan and analyze your strategic alternatives, your thinking will be stimulated. As the plan unfolds you will change and modify it as new ideas are generated. Eventually you will reach the optimum: a well-organized, well-integrated plan that will make efficient use of the resources available and will help you in anticipating most opportunities that can help or obstacles that can hinder your progress.

THE MARKETING PLAN ASSIGNS RESPONSIBILITIES, TASKS, AND TIMING

No strategy will ever be better than those who implement it. Therefore timing and the assignment of responsibilities are crucial. A marketing plan clearly outlines these responsibilities so there is no question where they lie. You also want to schedule all activities to maximize the impact of your strategy while taking full advantage of the environment that is expected to exist at the time of its execution. Hard thinking during development will preclude suboptimization. This occurs when one small element of the plan is optimized to the detriment of the overall project. Let's say that you are working on a marketing plan for a new personal computer. If the technical details alone are optimized, you may put the bulk of the funds on product development. This allocation may allow you to develop the best computer on the market, but insufficient funds to promote it. You may have a far superior product, but few will be able to buy it because they won't know about it. Because of suboptimization, the product will fail. Yet, a less grandiose technical solution might have satisfied the market and been better than your competition at a lower development cost. Funds would then be available to promote it properly. A good marketing plan will ensure that every task will be assigned to someone in the correct sequence, and that all elements and strategies will be coordinated synergistically to maximize their effect and ensure the completion of the project with the resources available. Is this important? Consider Zegna, an 85-year-old Italian company that sells men's suits for $1,000 and up. In a recent year, U.S. sales were $100 million, up 30 percent over the previous year. In Europe, Zegna's sales were $500 million. That made the company one of Europe's fastest-growing fashion groups. With Zegna, avoiding subobtimization is a major challenge. There are plenty of opportunities to err. Unlike its competitors, Zegna not only puts together its own clothes, but also spins the yarn. Zegna weaves the cotton, cashmere, and wool fabrics, everything that goes into its expensive garments. Not only that, Zegna has its own retail outlets. But according to experts, that's why Zegna is clobbering its competition.[3]

THE MARKETING PLAN PREDICTS PROBLEMS, OPPORTUNITIES, AND THREATS

You may intuitively recognize some of the problems, opportunities, and threats that can occur as you work toward your objectives. Your marketing plan will not only document

[3] John Rossant, "Is That a Zegna You're Wearing?" *Business Week* (March 4, 1996), pp. 84–85.

those of which you are already aware, but will help you identify others that you wouldn't see until you start working on your plan. It will enable you to think strategically and to consider what must be done about opportunities, problems, and threats that lie ahead. The more analysis and thinking you do as you plan, the more pitfalls you will see. That's not necessarily bad. Better to note them on paper before you get started than later when it's too late. These potential problems must never be ignored. Instead, construct your marketing plan to take maximum advantage of the opportunities, think up solutions to the problems you find, and consider how to avoid the threats.

GETTING IN A COMPETITIVE POSITION BEFORE YOU START

With a marketing plan you will be ahead of your competition even before you begin to execute your plan. You will have systematically thought it through from start to finish. You will already know where the future may lead. On paper, you will have coordinated all efforts to attain a specific objective. You will have developed performance standards for controlling objectives and goals and you will have sharpened your strategy and tactics to a much greater extent than would otherwise have been possible. You will be much better prepared than any of your competitors for sudden developments. You will have anticipated those that are potential problems and will know what to do when they occur. Finally, more than any competitor, you will have a vivid sense of what is going to happen and how to make it happen. Your competitors are going to react, but you will have already acted in anticipation.

TYPES OF MARKETING PLANS

Marketing plans tend to fall into a number of categories for different purposes. The two basic types are the new product and annual marketing plans.

THE NEW PRODUCT PLAN

The new product plan is prepared for a product, service product line, or brand that has not yet been introduced by the firm. It is wise to develop a complete new product plan even before you start the project. Granted the information at this stage may be sketchy, but it is still far better to start your thinking as early as possible before any major resources have been committed. In this way alternatives can be compared and analyzed. Moreover, you will have a general idea of the overall costs and timing of competitive projects. Naturally the marketing plan for a new product will have many more unknowns than the annual marketing plan. This is because the product will have little or no feedback from the marketplace and no track record with your firm. This last point is an important one to consider. It is not unusual for products that have achieved successful sales performance with one firm to fall far short of these goals in another. This is frequently due to certain strengths of the first firm that the second firm cannot duplicate and may not even know about. With a new product plan it is sometimes necessary to make assumptions based on similar products or services that the company has marketed or that have been introduced by other companies. But don't forget: if you use information based on other companies' experiences, you must assess your ability to duplicate their performance. Other sources of information may be necessary to modify data from other companies' experiences. This will be discussed later in this book. A marketing plan for a new product or service may also include development of the product from scratch. Of course if the product already exists, its technical development as a part of your plan is not needed.

6 PROLOGUE

ANNUAL MARKETING PLANS

Annual marketing plans are for those products, services, and brands that are already in your company's product line. Periodically, preferably once a year, this planning must be formally reviewed. Of course, the plan may be adjusted and modified in the interim as changes occur in the environment or in the company. But the review and annual creation of a new marketing plan for the coming year may help to identify emerging problems, opportunities, and threats that may be missed during day-to-day operations and the "fire fighting" associated with the management of an ongoing product or service. Again, however, notice that the plan is for the future; it's how you will get from your present position to some other position at a later time. Therefore, there will still be unknowns, for which information must be forecast, researched, or, in some cases, assumed. Although annual marketing plans are usually prepared for only one year, it is of course possible to plan for several years and to modify the plan annually. On the other hand, product plans generally cover the entire life of the project from initiation to its establishment in the marketplace. Establishment in the marketplace implies that the product is beyond the introductory stage and is growing, hopefully at a predicted rate.

SUMMARY

In this chapter we have discussed the importance of the marketing plan in satisfying objectives in the most efficient manner possible. We have noted the main benefits of a marketing plan:

- acting as a road map
- assisting in management control and implementing strategy
- informing new participants in the plan of their roles and functions
- obtaining resources for implementation
- stimulating thinking and making better use of resources
- assigning responsibilities and tasks and setting time limits
- being aware of problems, opportunities, and threats

Knowledge of the preparation of a marketing plan is not the option of a successful manager of marketing activities. It is a requirement. But beyond that, it is an effective and valuable tool that will enable you to work on a daily basis to accomplish the objectives that you have set for the particular project that you are going to market.

STEP 1

PLANNING THE DEVELOPMENT OF A MARKETING PLAN

A good marketing plan needs a great deal of information gathered from many sources. It is used to develop marketing strategy and tactics to achieve a specific set of objectives and goals. The process is not necessarily difficult, but it does require organization. This is especially true if you are not developing this plan by yourself and are depending on others to assist you or to accomplish parts of the plan. This frequently occurs both in the classroom and in the business world. Therefore, it is important before you start to "plan for planning." The time spent will pay dividends later. You will get back more than the time you invest up front.

To prepare for planning you must look first at the total job you are going to do and then organize the work so that things are done in an efficient manner and nothing is left out. If you do this correctly every element of your plan will come together in a timely fashion. This means that you won't be completing any task too early and then waiting for some other task to be finished before you can continue. It also means that no member of your planning team will be overworked or underworked. To accomplish this you must consider the structure of the marketing plan and all of its elements. Next you must organize your major planning tasks by using a marketing plan action-development schedule. This will give an overview of the entire marketing planning process, including who is going to do what and when each task is scheduled for completion. Managing the process is also important. You'll find some help with that in Appendix D, How to Lead a Team.

THE STRUCTURE OF THE MARKETING PLAN

Every marketing plan should have a planned structure or outline at the outset. This ensures that no important information is omitted and that everything is presented in a logical manner. One recommended outline is shown in the marketing plan outline in Figure 1-1. However, there are other ways to organize a marketing plan that are equally as good. You may be required to use a specific outline, or you may be able to use any outline you'd like. What outline you use is unimportant at this point. What is important is that your plan be

TABLE OF CONTENTS

Executive Summary (overview of entire plan, including a description of the product or service, the differential advantage, the required investment, and anticipated sales and profits).

I.   Introduction
      What is the product or service? Describe it in detail and explain how it fits into the market.

II.   Situational Analysis
      A. The Situational Environs
          1. Demand and demand trends. (What is the forecast demand for the product: Is it growing or declining? Who is the decision maker? The purchase agent? How, when, where, what, and why do they buy?)
          2. Social and cultural factors.
          3. Demographics.
          4. Economic and business conditions for this product at this time and in the geographical area selected.
          5. State of technology for this class of product. Is it high-tech state-of-the-art? Are newer products succeeding older ones frequently (short life cycle)? In short, how is technology affecting this product or service?
          6. Politics. Are politics (current or otherwise) in any way affecting the situation for marketing this product?
          7. Laws and regulations. (What laws or regulations are applicable here?)
      B. The Neutral Environs
          1. Financial environment. (How does the availability or unavailability of funds affect the situation?)
          2. Government environment. (Is current legislative action in state, federal, or local government likely to affect marketing of this product or service?)
          3. Media environment. (What's happening in the media? Does current publicity favor this project?)
          4. Special interest environment. (Aside from direct competitors, are any influential groups likely to affect your plans?)
      C. The Competitor Environs
          1. Describe your main competitors, their products, plans, experience, know-how, financial, human, and capital resources, suppliers, and strategy. Do they enjoy favor with their customers? If so, why? What marketing channels do the competitors use? What are their strengths and weaknesses?
      D. The Company Environs
          1. Describe your products, experience, know-how, financial, human, and capital resources, and suppliers. Do you enjoy the favor of your customers? If so, why? What are your strengths and weaknesses?

III. The Target Market
      Describe your target market segment in detail by using demographics, psychographics, geography, lifestyle, or whatever segmentation is appropriate. Why is this your target market? How large is it?

IV.   Problems and Opportunities
      State or restate each opportunity and indicate why it is, in fact, an opportunity.
      State or restate every problem. Indicate what you intend to do about each of them. Clearly state the competitive differential advantage.

V.   Marketing Objectives and Goals
      State precisely the marketing objectives and goals in terms of sales volume, market share, return on investment, or other objectives or goals for your marketing plan and the time needed to achieve each of them.

VI.   Marketing Strategy
      Consider alternatives for the overall strategy; for example, for new market penetration a marketer can enter first, early, or late, penetrate vertically or horizontally, and exploit different niche strategies.
      If the marketing strategy is at the grand strategy or strategic marketing management level, a market attractiveness/business capability matrix and product life cycle analysis should also be constructed.

VII. Marketing Tactics*
      State how you will implement the marketing strategy(s) chosen in terms of the product, price, promotion, distribution, and other tactical or environmental variables.

VIII. Implementation and Control
      Calculate the breakeven point and make a breakeven chart for your project. Compute sales projections and cash flows on a monthly basis for a three-year period. Determine start-up costs and a monthly budget, along with the required tasks.

IX.   Summary
      Summarize advantages, costs, and profits and restate the differential advantage that your plan offers over the competition and why the plan will succeed.

X.   Appendices
      Include all supporting information that you consider relevant.

* Note under the marketing strategy and tactics sections how your main competitors are likely to respond when you take the action planned and what you will then do to avoid the threats and take advantage of the opportunities.

FIGURE 1-1. Marketing plan outline.

presented in a logical way with nothing omitted. So, whether you are given a specific outline to follow, or are allowed to develop your own, keep these two goals in mind.

Let's examine each section of this marketing plan structure in Figure 1-1 in more detail. You will find many sections common to all marketing plans.

THE EXECUTIVE SUMMARY

The first part of the marketing plan structure or outline is the executive summary, which is a synopsis or abstract of the entire plan. It includes a description of the product or service, the differential advantage of your product or service over that of your competitors, the investment needed, and the results you anticipate. These can be expressed as a return on investment, sales, profits, market share, or in other ways.

The executive summary is especially important if your marketing plan is going to be used to help you to obtain the resources for implementation. Corporate executives are busy, and your marketing plan may be one of several they must consider. Sometimes several competing marketing plans are submitted simultaneously, but only one is given the green light to proceed. If you submit your marketing plan to a venture capitalist, there will be many competing plans. A venture capitalist receives hundreds of plans every year, but only funds a few. Therefore, it is hard to overestimate the importance of your executive overview.

The executive summary is a summary of the entire plan. It may range from a single paragraph to a few pages in length. From it a busy executive can get a quick overview of the project without reading the entire plan. Therefore, no matter how good the main body of your plan, your executive summary must be well thought out and succinct. It must demonstrate that you know what you're talking about and that your proposal has potential and a reasonable likelihood of success. If not, the executive judging your plan will probably read no further.

The executive summary usually is one of the last elements to be prepared, because it is impossible to summarize accurately until you complete every other part. But even though you save it for last, remember that it will appear at the beginning of the plan's documentation and must persuade the reader to read further.

THE TABLE OF CONTENTS

A table of contents sounds rather mundane and you may feel that it is unnecessary. You might be especially inclined to discard the idea if your marketing plan is short. But, let me tell you, a table of contents is absolutely necessary. It makes no difference whether your marketing plan is only a few pages or a hundred pages in length. It is required, never optional, because of a psychological factor that affects those who will evaluate your marketing plan for approval or disapproval.

If you are using your plan to acquire funding or other resources to implement your project, the table of contents is important because many individuals from many functional disciplines will be sitting on the review board. Some may be experts in the technical area, who will be interested primarily in the technical details of your product or service. Others will be financial experts, who will want to examine your breakeven analysis, the financial ratios you have calculated, and other financial information. In fact, every expert tends to look first at his or her own area. If you submit a table of contents, this will be fairly easy to do. The reader will scan the list of subjects and will turn to the correct page within a few seconds. But if you fail in this regard the evaluator of your plan will have to search for the information. If you are lucky, he or she will find it anyway. Unfortunately, you won't always be lucky. When many plans must be reviewed, the evaluator may spend only a few minutes or even a few seconds in the search. That's where the psychological factor comes in. If the information can't be found easily, the evaluator may assume it's not there. This not only raises questions of what you don't know, but may also give the competitive edge to a marketing plan done by someone who made the information easier to find.

The need for a table of contents is especially critical when your plan is being submitted to venture capitalists, who put up large sums of money to businesses that have an established track record and have a marketing plan for future growth.

You may have heard that venture capitalists only look at business plans. Marketing and business plans are identical, especially in smaller companies and with start-ups and new products. When you are trying to obtain resources from a venture capitalist, or any investor, the two plans are synonymous. Either the business plan must have a heavy marketing emphasis or the marketing plan must include complete financial, manufacturing, and technical data.

Typically, funds are available for investment in fewer than 1 percent of the plans that are submitted. One venture capitalist told me that he receives more than 1,000 marketing plans every month, each of which contains a minimum of 30 pages. Some exceed 100 pages. Under the circumstances, do you think that anyone could actually go over all of these plans in great detail? Of course not. Accordingly, this venture capitalist looks first at the executive summary, and, if it appears to be interesting, spot-checks the plan using the table of contents for items of particular interest. If he can't find the information he wants after a few seconds' search, he discards the plan. With so many plans to look at, he just doesn't have the time. In this initial screening most of the plans are dropped, leaving only a few for a more detailed reading and a final decision. So don't forget this mundane tool, and be certain that the contents table is an accurate list of all the important topics in your marketing plan.

INTRODUCTION

The introduction is the explanation of the details of your project. Unlike the executive summary, it is not an overview of the project. Its purpose is to give the background of the project and to describe your product or service so that any reader will understand exactly what it is you are proposing. The introduction can be a fairly large section. After reading it the evaluator should understand what the product or service is and what you propose to do with it.

SITUATIONAL ANALYSIS

The situational analysis contains a vast amount of information and, as the term indicates, is an analysis of the situation that you are facing with the proposed product or service. Because the situational analysis comes from taking a good hard look at your environment, many marketing experts refer to the process as environmental scanning.

I like to approach the situational analysis by dividing the analysis into four categories, which I call the environs of the marketplace. The four categories are situational environs, neutral environs, competitor environs, and company environs. Let's look at each in turn.

Situational Environs.   Situational environs include demand and demand trends for your product or service. Is this demand growing, is it declining, or has it leveled off? Are there certain groups in which the demand is growing and others in which demand is declining? Who are the decision makers regarding purchase of the product and who are the purchase agents? Sometimes the decision maker and purchase agent are the same, but often they are not. For example, one member of a family may be the decision maker with regard to purchasing a certain product, say a brand of beer. But the individual who actually makes the purchase may be another family member. Who influences this decision? How, when, where, what, and why do these potential customers purchase? What are the social and cultural factors? Are demographics of consumers important? If so, maybe you need to discuss educational backgrounds, income, age, and similar factors. What are the economic conditions during the period covered by the marketing plan? Is business good or is it bad? High demand can occur in both a good or bad business climate depending on the product or service offered. What is the state of technology for this class of product? Is your product high-tech state-of-the-art? Are newer products frequently succeeding older ones, thus indicating a shorter product life cycle? In sum, how is technology affecting the product or service and the marketing for this product or service? Are politics, current or otherwise, in any way affecting the marketing of this product? What potential dangers or threats do the politics in the situation portend? Or do the politics provide opportunities? What laws or regulations are relevant to the marketing of this product or service?

Neutral Environs. Neutral environs have to do with groups or organizations. Does government have an impact on this project? Is legislation on the state, federal, or local level likely to affect the demand or marketing of the product or service? What's happening in the media? Does current publicity favor your project or does it make any difference? Look at special interest groups. Might they have some impact? Are any influential groups (e.g., consumer organizations) likely to affect your plans for marketing this product or service?

Competitor Environs. Competitor environs are those competing against you. They are important because they are the only elements of the environment that will intentionally act against your interests. In this section of the situational analysis describe in detail your main competitors, the products they offer, their plans, experience, know-how, financial, human and capital resources, and suppliers. Most important, discuss their current and future strategies. Note whether or not your competitors enjoy favor with their customers, and why. Describe and analyze your competitors' strengths and weaknesses, what marketing channels they use, and anything else that you feel is relevant to the marketing situation as it will exist when you implement your project.

Company Environs. Company environs describe your situation in your company or company-to-be and the resources that you have available. Describe your current products, experience, and know-how, financial, human, and capital resources, suppliers, and other factors as you did environs. Do you enjoy favor with your customers or potential customers and why? Summarize your strengths and weaknesses as they apply to your project. In many respects this section covers many of the same items as the competitor environs section.

THE TARGET MARKET

The target market is the next major section in your plan. Describe exactly who your customers are and what, where, when, why, how, how much, and how frequently they buy.

You may think that everyone is a candidate for your product or your service. In a sense this may be true, but some segments of the total market are far more likely candidates than others. If you attempt to serve every single potential customer segment, you cannot satisfy those that are most likely to buy as well as you should. Furthermore, you will dissipate your resources by trying to reach them all. If you pick the most likely target market, or markets, you can devote the maximum amount of money to advertising your product or service in a message that your most likely customers can best understand.

Remember, the basic concept of strategy is to concentrate your scarce resources at the decisive points. Your target markets represent one application of this concept. Because you usually cannot be strong everywhere, you must be strong where it counts, in this case the markets you target.

You should also indicate why the target market you have selected is a better candidate for purchase than others. Of course, you will include the size of each market.

How will you define your target markets? First, in terms of (1) demographics (i.e., such vital statistics as age, income, and education); (2) geography (i.e., their location); (3) psychographics (i.e., how they think); and (4) lifestyle (i.e., their activities, interests, and opinions). There are of course other ways of describing, and perhaps segmenting your market. Knowing your customers is as important as knowing yourself (the company environs), your competitors (the competitor environs), and the other environs that you have analyzed.

PROBLEMS AND OPPORTUNITIES

The problems and opportunities section is actually a summary that emphasizes the main points you have already covered in preceding sections. As you put your plan together, developed your situational analysis, and described your target market, you probably implicitly covered many of the problems and opportunities inherent in your situation. Here you should restate them explicitly and list them one by one. Group them first by opportunities, then by problems. Indicate why each is an opportunity or a problem. Also indicate how you intend to take advantage of each opportunity and what you intend to do about each problem.

Many marketing planners do well in showing how they will take advantage of the opportunities, but they do not explain adequately what they will do about the problems. To get full benefit from your plan you must not only foresee the potential problems and opportunities, but also decide what actions you must take to overcome the problems.

This foresight will help you during implementation. It will also favorably impress those who will decide whether to allocate resources for your particular project. In most cases, those who evaluate your plans will know when you omit a problem; that instantly makes a bad impression. An evaluator will then get one of two perceptions: Maybe you are intentionally omitting a difficult problem because you didn't know what to do about it, or perhaps you didn't even recognize that you had a problem! Stating your problems and how you will solve them will give you a decided edge over others who submitted plans but did not take the time or trouble to consider the solutions to potential problems they might face in implementation.

Note that in the strategy and tactics sections, you will find additional potential problems. For example, when you initiate a particular strategy, a competent competitor isn't going to stand by and let you take his or her market. Competitor counteractions constitute a potential problem. You'll discuss these counteractions in those sections. You do not have to add these new potential problems and/or opportunities to this section. This is a summary section for your initial scan of your environment.

MARKETING GOALS AND OBJECTIVES

Marketing goals and objectives are accomplishments you intend to achieve with the help of your marketing plan. You have already prepared your reader by your earlier analysis of the target market. In this section you must spell out in detail exactly what you intend to do.

What is the difference between a goal and an objective? An objective is an overall goal. It is more general and may not be quantified. "To establish a product in the marketplace" is an objective. So is "to become the market leader" or "to dominate the market." Goals are quantified. "To sell 10,000 units a year" is a goal. Goals are also quantified in terms of sales, profits, market share, return on investment, or other measurements. There is one major cautionary note here: Don't get trapped into setting objectives or goals that conflict. For example, your ability to capture a stated market share may require lower profits. Make sure that all your goals and objectives fit together. You can do this by adjusting and reconfirming your goals and objectives after you have completed the financial portions of your plan.

MARKETING STRATEGY

In this section you will describe what is to be done to reach your objectives and goals. Your strategy may be one of differentiating your product from that of its competitors, of segmenting your total market, of positioning it in relation to other products, of carving out and defending a certain niche, of timing in entering the market, and so on. Marketing strategy is a what-to-do section.

One important part of the marketing strategy section that is frequently omitted is what your main competitors are likely to do when you implement your planned strategy, and what you will do to take advantage of the opportunities created, solve potential problems, and avoid serious threats. This strategy should be included, because this is another excellent opportunity for you to demonstrate what a terrific marketing strategist and planner you are.

MARKETING TACTICS

Just as strategy tells you what you must do to reach your objectives, tactics tell you how you will carry out your strategy. List every action required to implement each of the strategies described in the preceding section and the timing of these actions. These tactical actions are described in terms of what is called the "marketing mix," or the "4 Ps" of marketing: product, price, promotion, and place. Sometimes the 4 Ps are known as strategic variables. However, these variables are really tactical because they are actions taken to accomplish the strategy you developed in the preceding section.

IMPLEMENTATION AND CONTROL

In the implementation and control section you are going to calculate the break-even point and forecast other important information to help control the project once it has been implemented. You are also going to compute sales projections and cash flow on a monthly basis for a three-year period and calculate start-up costs in a monthly budget. After implementation you can use this information to keep the project on track. Thus, if the budget is exceeded you will know where to cut back or to reallocate resources. If sales aren't what they should be, you will know where to focus your attention to realize an improvement.

THE SUMMARY

In the summary you discuss advantages, costs, and profits and clearly state the differential advantage, once again, that your plan for this product or service offers the competition. The differential or competitive advantage is what you have that your competitors lack. Basically it says why your plan will succeed.

The summary completes your marketing plan outline. You now have a good idea of the information that you'll need for your marketing. As you go through this book, forms will be provided to assist in completing every section of the marketing plan that we've talked about. As you complete these forms you will automatically be completing your marketing plan.

Figure 1-2 is a sample marketing plan action development schedule that will assist you in planning to plan. Your schedule should be adjusted to your particular situation. It lists the actions that must be taken and shows you where to start and how long it should take to complete each action. The horizontal line begins when the action is to be initiated and continues until its scheduled completion. An adjusted date is provided by a dashed line; thus as you proceed you can use the action schedule to adjust dates when a certain action was not completed on time and the schedule must be modified. In this way you can develop and coordinate a planning process that fits your situation and any deadlines you might have for completing your plan.

If you are completing the plan on a team, names can be written within the spaces provided for the tasks to indicate who is responsible for every action. A blank development schedule (Figure 1-3) is provided on page 15 for your use in planning to plan.

Task	Weeks After Initiation											
	1	2	3	4	5	6	7	8	9	10	11	12
Secondary research into demographics, situational factors	↑———————↑ (through week 4)											
Market research regarding potential demand	↑———————————↑ (through week 5)											
Audit of competitors' and company environs	↑———————————————↑ (through week 6)											
Investigation of neutral environs	↑———————————————↑ (through week 6)											
Establishment of objective, goals, and overall strategy	↑———————————————————↑ (through week 7)											
Development and specification of tactics; additional marketing research as required	↑———————————————————————————↑ (through week 10)											
Development and calculation of implementation and control information	↑———————————————————————————————↑ (through week 11)											
Writing and development of marketing plan document	↑———————————————————————————————————↑ (through week 12)											

FIGURE 1-2.   Sample marketing plan action development schedule.

Task	1	2	3	4	5	6	7	8	9	10	11	12

FIGURE 1-3.   Blank marketing plan action development schedule.

KEEPING YOUR MATERIAL ORGANIZED

It is very important to keep your material together to guard against loss and for updating as new data are received. A loose-leaf notebook is a helpful tool. Each section can be marked: executive summary, introduction, situational analysis, target market, problems and opportunities, marketing goals and objectives, marketing strategy, marketing tactics, implementation and control, and summary. As additional information is received in its rough form it can be added to the appropriate section.

SUMMARY

In this chapter you have prepared yourself by planning to plan. You have examined the structure of the outline that will be used for developing your marketing plan, the information required in each of its sections, and a planning form that can be used to help you get organized and work efficiently. Finally, you have seen how to keep your material organized in a simple way by using a loose-leaf notebook.

2

STEP 2

SCANNING YOUR ENVIRONMENT

In this chapter you are going to decide what information you need for the introduction and situational analysis sections of your marketing plan and where you can obtain this information.

THE INTRODUCTION

In the introduction you must state what the product or service is, describe it in detail, and note why there is demand for it in the marketplace. To do this accurately and completely you need information that goes beyond product or service attributes and benefits. You must analyze the life cycle for your product or service. Every product and service class passes through a life cycle just as if it were a living thing. The shape of the curve as the product passes through the different stages of its life is called "the product life cycle."

The classic product life cycle is shown in Figure 2-1. Note that its stages are introduction, growth, maturity, and decline. Note also that sales and profits are plotted as a curve that changes shape from stage to stage. Different strategies work better for different stages. This is because conditions in each stage are different. The shape of the curve will have important strategic implications which are needed when you begin to develop a strategy. For now, notice that the sales and profit curves differ. For example, note that profits peak in the growth stage, whereas sales continue to rise and peak in the maturity stage.

You must decide whether your product is in the introductory, growth, maturity, or decline stage. You may think that if you are introducing a new product, it is automatically in the introductory stage. If it is sufficiently different from other products or services of its class, maybe it is. When personal computers first came on the market, they were so radically different from the mainframe models used by large corporations that these products were in the introductory stage of their own life cycle.

So this raises an important question. Do you analyze a new product in its own life cycle, or in the life cycle of its class of products or services? The answer is that you can gain useful insights in looking at your new product both ways. Which is more important depends on how different your product is from what is already in the marketplace. Let's contrast a couple of new products so you can see what I'm talking about.

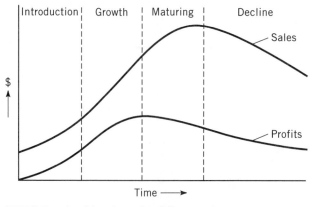

FIGURE 2-1.   Classic product life cycle.

Take the common, garden-variety marketing textbook. They've been around for a long time. As a class, marketing textbooks are definitely not in the introductory stage. But what if the entire textbook were on a CD ROM? Now you've got a class of new products that are in the introductory stage of their own product life cycle. That doesn't mean that the textbook doesn't have its own introductory stage also, only that it may make sense to consider where this product falls in the product class life cycle as well.

Perhaps your product is new, but its product class is in the growth stage of its life cycle. This could be confirmed if the product class had already been on the market for some time, but sales are still growing. A product that has been in the marketplace for some time and for which sales may still be increasing, but profits are not, is probably in the maturity stage. A typical product might be music recorded on a cassette tape. Finally, the product or service may be in the decline stage. A cigarette lighter might be toward the end of its product class life cycle and in the decline stage.

It may be unwise to introduce a new product that is approaching the end of its product class life—but not always. If your new product could immediately capture most of the declining market, it could still be very profitable.

You should also examine complementary products. These are products that do not directly compete with your product but in some way complement it or are used with it. If your new product is a computer, a complementary product could be a computer disk, peripheral equipment, or furniture built especially for computers. If your new product is a soft drink, complementary products could be the bottle, the bottle cap, or the package.

The next step is to investigate substitute products. These are products that are substitutes for the product you are introducing. These are not only direct substitutes through similar products made by a competitor, but substitutes in the sense that your target market can get similar benefits from them. If your new product is a video game, your direct substitutes for your product are other video games. But video games are actually a form of entertainment. What other entertainment might your potential customers buy with the money they could spend on your game? When the Wright brothers built the first airplane, no other airplanes existed, which meant there was only indirect competition from substitute products. What were these substitute products? Some were other means of short-range transportation. Others were probably large luxury items used by the very wealthy. And for the military market, they might have been observation balloons or even horse cavalry.

Now you are ready to describe your product or service: its size, weight, color, shape, the material of which it is made, its function, what it does, and its benefits to potential users.

THE SITUATIONAL ANALYSIS

As we noted in Chapter 1, the situational analysis is an extensive and important part of the marketing plan. On the basis of the situational analysis, you will develop an optimal strategy that you can use to reach your goals and objectives. To make a situational analysis you must answer questions about the environment you are facing. To help you with this challenge, let's go over the questions in Figure 2-2 individually.

TARGET MARKET

The first environmental question under the target market section has to do with location. You will want to describe this location and its special climatic and geographical features. Is it a hot, humid environment? A cold, dry one? A desert? Mountainous area? Oceanfront? Suburban? Urban? Or what? Every climatic or topographical feature should be noted and described in detail.

Now the buyer can be categorized into consumers and organizational buyers. Organizational buyers buy for their organizations rather than for their own consumption. We'll look at consumer buyers first and different ways of describing them.

Cultural, Ethnic, Religious, and Racial Groups.   It is important not only to identify the groups that are potential targets for your product or service, but also the size and characteristics of each group.

Years ago, marketers thought that they could maximize their profits by mass marketing. Under this concept, they tried to sell the identical product to everyone. Extensive research and practical experience found this to be an error. It was far more profitable to segment the market according to certain common characteristics and to concentrate on marketing to the particular segments that could be served best. This is consistent with the marketing concept of focusing on the customer rather than on the product. By focusing on characteristics of your customer, you can satisfy his or her needs more easily. This is also consistent with the basic principle of strategy of concentrating superior resources at the decisive point.

Obviously it would be difficult to succeed by selling food products containing pork to Jewish or Moslem groups. Also, different groups prefer certain types of products. Have you ever heard of peanut butter soup? In West Africa it is a delicacy. East Asians eat tofu or fermented soybean extract. You may drink only cow's milk, whereas others drink goat's milk. Some Chinese groups drink soybean milk. Among various nationalities insects, monkeys, and dogs are all considered culinary delicacies. Food we think of as "normal" would be shunned.

These preferences are crucial for the marketer, because they can spell the difference between success or failure. Cultural, ethnic, religious, and racial segmentation of the market is only the tip of the iceberg. As you will see, there are many other ways to segment. All of them will help you satisfy your customers better and more easily.

Social Classes.   The next environmental question involves social classes. The basic divisions are upper, middle, and lower, but you can categorize them more precisely as lower-lower (unskilled labor), upper-lower (basic wage earners and skilled workers), lower-middle (white-collar salaried), upper-middle (professionals and successful businesspeople), and upper class (the wealthy). Social classes are important as segments because people behave in different ways even though their income levels may be the same.

Some time ago, researchers surveyed three different social groups which had identical incomes. One group consisted of young attorneys just graduating from law school. They bought the best homes they could afford in prestigious neighborhoods. Naturally, these homes tended to be fairly small, because they couldn't afford large homes in prestigious neighborhoods. Next, the researchers surveyed small-business owners whose income was the same as the young attorneys. Do you think they spent their money the same way? After all, they were making the same salary. However, they didn't buy the same kind of homes. These small-business owners bought the largest homes they could in average neighborhoods. Finally, the researcher looked at groups in yet another class. Certain workers had been employed for years by large companies and were earning the same income as the

_____

TARGET MARKET

Geographical location _____

Special climate or topography _____

_____

CONSUMER BUYERS

Cultural, ethnic, religious, or racial groups _____

_____

_____

Social class(es) _____

Reference group(s) _____

Basic demographics: Sex _____ Age range _____

Education _____ Income _____

Household size and description _____

_____

Stage of family life cycle _____

Family work status: Husband _____ Wife _____

Occupation (husband and wife) _____

Decision maker _____ Purchase agent _____

Risk perception: Functional _____ Psychological _____

Physical _____ Social _____ Financial _____

Income for each family member _____

Disposable income _____

Additional descriptions, classifications, and traits of target market _____

_____

_____

Target market wants and needs 1. _____

2. _____ 3. _____

4. _____ 5. _____

Product general description _____

_____

Frequency of usage _____ Traits _____

_____

Marketing factor sensitivity _____

_____

FIGURE 2-2. Situational analysis: Environmental questions for the marketing plan. (Copyright © 1985 by Dr. William A. Cohen. _Note:_ This form is based on an earlier form designed by Dr. Benny Barak, then of Baruch College.)

Size of target market _____

Growth trends _____

MEDIA HABITS

	Hours/Week	Category
Television	_____	_____
Radio	_____	_____
Magazines	_____	_____
Newspapers	_____	_____
The Internet	_____	_____

ORGANIZATIONAL BUYERS

Decision makers _____

_____

_____

_____

Primary motivation of each decision maker _____

_____

_____

_____

_____

_____

Amount of money budgeted for purchase _____

_____

_____

Purchase history _____

_____

_____

_____

_____

_____

Additional descriptions, classifications, and traits of target market _____

_____

_____

Target market wants and needs 1. _____

2. _____   3. _____

4. _____   5. _____

Product general description _____

_____

FIGURE 2-2.   *Continued*

Frequency of usage _____ Traits _____

Marketing factor sensitivity _____

_____

_____

Size of target market _____

Growth trends _____

MEDIA HABITS

	Hours/Week	Category
Television	_____	_____
Radio	_____	_____
Magazines	_____	_____
Newspapers	_____	_____

	Number/Year	
Trade shows	_____	_____
Conferences	_____	_____

COMPETITION

Competitor	Products	Market Share	Strategy

FIGURE 2-2. *Continued*

RESOURCES OF THE FIRM

Strengths: 1. _____

2. _____

3. _____

4. _____

5. _____

Weaknesses: 1. _____

2. _____

3. _____

4. _____

5. _____

TECHNOLOGICAL ENVIRONMENT

_____

_____

_____

ECONOMIC ENVIRONMENT

_____

_____

_____

POLITICAL ENVIRONMENT

_____

_____

_____

LEGAL AND REGULATORY ENVIRONMENT

_____

_____

_____

SOCIAL AND CULTURAL ENVIRONMENT

_____

_____

_____

FIGURE 2-2. *Continued*

OTHER IMPORTANT ENVIRONMENTAL ASPECTS

_____

_____

_____

_____

_____

PROBLEMS/THREATS

1. _____

2. _____

3. _____

4. _____

5. _____

OPPORTUNITIES

1. _____

2. _____

3. _____

4. _____

5. _____

FIGURE 2-2. _Continued_

small-business owners and the young lawyers. This group didn't spend their money on homes in prestige neighborhoods or on larger homes. Their homes were smaller and in less affluent neighborhoods. Where did their money go? They had more expensive automobiles and household appliances (e.g., larger television sets) than the other two groups. Remember, all three groups had identical income.

If this research were conducted today, the findings might be different. Yet some kind of variation in buyer behavior among the social classes is still likely. Therefore this segmentation is important and the identification of the segments, which may constitute your target market, is useful.

Reference Groups.   Reference groups are those you turn to for information. They are especially important in the case of a general lack of information. Let's say that you are a member of a trade association that recommends a certain product. When other information is scarce or unavailable, this recommendation can be extremely influential in persuading you to use that product.

A reference group can also be a small number of trusted friends. Thus it is unimportant whether the reference group is large or small—only that you seek its advice in making purchase decisions.

Demographics.   The situational analysis question form now asks you to investigate certain fundamental attributes of your potential customers known as demographics. Of what sex is your target market? Are you trying to sell to both male and female or male or female only? What is the primary age range? How well educated are your prospects? Most products appeal primarily to certain demographic segments that can be defined by answering these questions. If your product is an encyclopedia, would it appeal primarily to college or noncollege graduates? In most cases the answer would probably be college graduates. Similarly, certain other types of product or service appeal to individuals with certain levels of education.

How much money is your prospect making? Can you sell a Rolls-Royce to someone whose annual income is less than $20,000 a year? Unless your prospect is independently wealthy, probably not.

How many people are in the household? Is it headed by a single parent? Male or female? Guardians? How many children are in the family and what are their ages? All of these demographic facts may result in different purchasing behavior.

Like a product, a family has also been described as having a life cycle, but the descriptive terms are different from those of the product life cycle. The family life cycle has been divided into nine stages:

1. The unmarried not living with parents.
2. A newly married couple; young with no children.
3. A full nest; the youngest child under six.
4. A full nest; the youngest child six or older.
5. A full nest; an older married couple with dependent children.
6. An empty nest; no children at home; head of family in the labor force.
7. An empty nest; family head retired.
8. A solitary survivor in the labor force.
9. A solitary survivor retired.

Can you see where different products or services would appeal to each group?

Family Work Status and Occupations.   If husband and wife are employed, both occupations should be listed. Or if one or both are retired or the family receives welfare, this is of interest to you as an astute marketer.

Decision Makers and Purchase Agents.   Note the spaces on the form in Figure 2-2 for decision maker and purchase agent. The decision maker is the one who actually decides to buy the product; the purchase agent buys it. A wife may prefer a certain brand of dishwasher detergent, but it may be her husband who actually buys the product if he happens to be doing the shopping. The implication is we may have to promote to both spouses for many products.

Consider also those who have influence on the decision maker and purchase agent. Children are subjected to a considerable amount of television advertising for many products, including toys and breakfast cereals. Children may not be decision makers or purchase agents, but their influence on other family members may be significant for your product. Many companies consider the millions of dollars invested in promoting to them as money well spent.

Risk Perception.   Risk perception concerns the chance your customer takes in buying a product. Any new product has a certain amount of risk associated with it. There are other types of risk to the customer. Functional risk refers to its dependability, that is, whether it will work. Psychological risks concern the possibility that the buyer may be disappointed or feel cheated if the product proves to be less than expected. Physical risk involves damage to the user. Social risk is taken if the buyer feels open to ostracism or ridicule for using the product or service. Finally, there is financial risk. This is the risk of money lost in buying a product that turns out to be worthless.

Risk is calculated as perceived by the customer. It may or may not actually exist in reality. A totally reliable product may be perceived as risky by the potential buyer and a less reliable one as safe. In marketing, the perception is the reality. So if you have a low-risk product perceived as risky, you have to plan for some kind of action.

Income for Each Family Member.   In this section of the form additional income that may come from other members of the family is documented. This income is of interest because the total may drastically alter what your prospect can afford and is likely to buy.

Disposable Income.   Disposable income is the amount left over after the bills for basic necessities such as food and shelter have been paid. Money left over is disposable income. It can be used for entertainment, a vacation, or luxuries like expensive clothes. The amount of disposable income will vary depending on geographical, cultural, ethnic, religious, and racial considerations.

Additional Descriptions, Classifications, and Traits of the Target Market.
This space in the form allows you to describe your potential buyers in any terms that have been omitted previously and that may be peculiar to the particular market you are targeting. For example, one segmentation system that has become extremely popular was developed at the Stanford Research Institute (SRI) in California. Its acronym is VALS, which stands for value and lifestyles. SRI divided consumers into nine different value and lifestyle groups. Other means of categorizing can provide valuable insights into your target markets so that you are not trying to be everything to everybody, and can concentrate on satisfying a well-defined target market.

Recently the firm of Roper Starch Worldwide conducted a survey to determine why one American brand succeeded globally while another comparable brand did not. In surveying consumers worldwide, based on answers, the researchers divided consumers into three groups holding strong feelings and making up almost half the populations surveyed:

- Nationalists, comprising 26 percent of the survey feel close to their own cultures, but not to others.

- Internationalists, comprising 15 percent feel somewhat close to three or more outside cultures.

- Disengaged, 7 percent of the sample consider themselves somewhat distant from their cultures.

These results can tell a company how to position its product in a foreign market, or even whether they should be there at all.[1]

Target Market Wants and Needs.   Wants and needs are both important, but they are not identical. A need is a requirement for basic subsistence, such as ordinary food and shelter. Wants are human desires that are nice to have, but not necessary for basic survival. You might want an expensive pair of shoes, but you don't really need them. Satisfying either represents opportunities for the marketer.

You've probably already heard about one of the most important theories of wants and needs. It originated with Abraham Maslow. Maslow's theory of human motivation involves a hierarchy of needs, beginning with basic physiological needs and progressing successively to safety or security, the need for love, for esteem or self-respect, and self-actualization. Also at a high level, but not fitting on a direct hierarchy with the others, are two more classes: aesthetic needs and the need to know and understand.

---

[1] Thomas A. W. Miller, "Cultural Affinity, Personal Values Factors in Marketing," *Marketing News* (August 16, 1999), p. H22.

Although there may be some overlap between needs, as one need is satisfied, the next higher need becomes more motivating. The basic physiological need is breathing. If someone suddenly began to choke you and you could no longer breathe, you would have no other immediate interest. No marketer offering an attractive product at a competitive price could gain your interest. Your immediate need would be for oxygen!

Once you had regained the ability to breathe, you might then have been interested in the next level. That's safety or security. Would you really be interested in buying an automobile at this point if you didn't know where your next meal was coming from?

You can see how needs are important to the motivation of customers to buy the products or services offered to them. No matter how good our product or service is, if some other major lower-level need has not been satisfied, your target customers may not be interested. In this section of the situational analysis form in Figure 2-2, identify specific target wants and needs that you intend to satisfy with the product or service you offer.

Product Description. The general description here is actually an abbreviated version of the more detailed material given in the introduction to the marketing plan. Be certain to note frequency of use; that is, how frequently will the customer use your product or service? Also, write down product traits. What are the attributes of your product or service? These may include price, size, quality, packaging, and service. Finally, you will want to rank the market factor sensitivity; that is, how sensitive are your customers to the traits of your product or service, from the most important to the least?

Size of the Target Market. State the total potential of each target market segment.

Growth Trends. Growth trends describe what is happening to your target market. Is it growing? Is it declining? Has it leveled off? Profits can be made under each of these conditions, but each will call for different marketing actions. Therefore you want to know what the trends are for your target market.

MEDIA HABITS

Media habits is a major classification on the form shown in Figure 2-2. It is significant because if you know the habits of your prospects, you will understand how to reach them most efficiently. Consider the basic media including television, radio, newspapers, and magazines. It would be helpful to know how many hours a week are devoted to each category.

ORGANIZATIONAL BUYERS

The basic information you need for organizational buyers is knowledge as to who are the decision makers. Within organizations, you must frequently market to more than one individual. Sometimes these decision makers will include engineers and their supervisors, purchase agents, and test and quality assurance groups. Each decision maker may have different motivations. The primary motivation of each decision maker involved in a purchase should be determined and written down on the form.

The Amount of Money Available or Budgeted for the Purchase. Obtain an estimate of the amount of money available for the particular purchase for which the marketing plan is being developed. This is necessary because significant differences in the amount charged lessen the chances of success in marketing the product and at the very least must be explained.

If a group is accustomed to paying $25 per unit in quantities of 1,000 a year, $25,000 will have been budgeted. If a greater amount is to be charged, the decision makers are going to ask why, because this will require an increase in the budget. Even a lower price must be explained lest it be viewed as representing a change to lower quality.

Purchase History.   The purchase history of the same or similar products will reveal buying patterns relating to the time of year in which the product was purchased and the quantities ordered.

Additional Industrial Buyer Information.   Additional industrial buyer information required is similar to what is needed about the consumer. The exception is media information about trade show and conference attendance.

COMPETITION

Competition is a critical element. It is an intelligent environmental factor that will act against your interests. Pay particular attention when you are targeting a stagnant or a declining market. If you are targeting the same market segment, your competitor can only succeed by taking sales from you. Therefore the more you know about your competition, the better. You should study your competitors, the products they are offering, the share of the market they control, and the strategies they are following. All of this information can be used in planning your optimal strategy for success in giving your customers better service or a better product.

RESOURCES OF THE FIRM

Indicate resources of the firm in terms of strengths and weaknesses. Few organizations are strong in everything. Perhaps you have technical strength like the "high-tech" firms in Silicon Valley. Or perhaps marketing know-how is your forte. Maybe you are strong in financial resources. Just as you have strengths, you have weaknesses. Jot these down on the form as well. Weaknesses don't become strengths by pretending they don't exist.

TECHNOLOGICAL ENVIRONMENT

Sometimes technology changes and expands rapidly. In a single year in the early 1970s, hand-held calculators declined in price by more than 50 percent, at the same time their performance increased. Computer technology is still growing by leaps and bounds. The largest memory computers of a few years ago can now be carried in the pocket. It can also work the other way around. The vinyl record industry, a $300-billion business, shrank to zero over a three-year period as CDs took over the entire market.

The Internet has revolutionized marketing in just a few years. Al Clemens, Chief Executive of Provident American, became successful as a medical insurer back in the 1970s by using television and celebrity endorsers to market direct to consumers. In this way, he bypassed insurance agents, a revolutionary idea at the time. Recently he formed a subsidiary with a new marketing plan, once again taking advantage of technology. His new subsidiary, called HealthAxis.com, will be the Web's first full-service on-line insurance agency.[2]

The technological environment may not be relevant to your particular situation, but if it is relevant, be sure to describe your situation completely.

ECONOMIC ENVIRONMENT

The economic environment involves the economy and business conditions that will exist as you enter the market. It is true that fortunes can be made in recessions and depressions,

---

[2] Marcia Stepanek, "Closed, Gone to the New," *BusinessWeek* (June 7, 1999).

during inflations, and in periods of economic well-being. However, the products and services with which you are most likely to be successful in these different economic conditions are not the same. Therefore a description of the economic and business conditions that you are likely to encounter during implementation is necessary.

POLITICAL ENVIRONMENT

The political environment must be considered because of the potential effect that politics may have on your project. There are certain countries to which the U.S. government will not permit you to export, just as there are certain products from certain countries that cannot be imported. Chinese imports are of major political interest at this time. So is preventing the unrestricted export of sophisticated weaponry and the knowledge and skills of former Soviet nuclear scientists. Politics affect the marketing of products and services. It is a part of the environment that you cannot ignore.

LEGAL AND REGULATORY ENVIRONMENT

The legal and regulatory environment can cause major headaches. One small company invested more than $100,000 in the development of a new bullet-resistant police helmet. Then it discovered that because of product liability the product could not be sold at a profit. Another firm invested thousands of dollars in a new wine cooler on the assumption that the alcoholic beverage tax would be the same whether or not they used another firm's wine to mix with their fruit juice. It wasn't, and the difference in tax made the product unprofitable. Be forewarned: Note the impact of the legal and regulatory environment before you complete your marketing plan.

SOCIAL AND CULTURAL ENVIRONMENT

Fifty years ago wearing a bikini on a public beach would have been cause for arrest. Sushi or raw fish has been a popular product in Japan for hundreds of years, yet only a few years ago sushi bars probably would have been unsuccessful in the United States. Today, sushi is extremely popular. Timing of your entry into a market may be the dominant factor. So a smart marketer investigates the social and cultural environment for a product or service before developing the rest of his or her marketing plan.

OTHER IMPORTANT ENVIRONMENTAL ASPECTS

In this section other important environmental aspects that are peculiar to your product or service not covered earlier should be listed and analyzed. An example might be a natural disaster such as a hurricane or an earthquake.

PROBLEMS AND OPPORTUNITIES

The problems and opportunities section of the form is actually a summary of all that has gone before. You should review your entire environmental situation and restate every problem and opportunity that you can anticipate. Naturally there may be more or less than five problems and five opportunities, so don't be restricted simply because the form allows space only for that number.

Many marketing planners who have no trouble recognizing their opportunities hesitate to discuss their problems. This is a mistake. First, it is important to identify the problems in order to avoid them once you have begun to develop your strategy. Second, if you have failed to include them and have listed only your opportunities, readers of your plan will suspect that you left them out intentionally or were not smart enough to acknowledge them. They would be more impressed if you described how you proposed to overcome them.

SOURCES OF INFORMATION FOR COMPLETING THE ENVIRONMENTAL QUESTIONS FORM

To answer environmental questions you must do research. This research may be primary or secondary. Primary research entails interviews, business surveys, and a personal search for the answers. In secondary research you consult other sources. Secondary research is generally preferable because it is already available. It should be examined before you spend the time and money to do primary research. What are some secondary research sources?

1. Chambers of Commerce. Chambers of Commerce have all sorts of demographic information about geographical areas in which you may be interested, including income, education, businesses and their size, and sales volume.

2. Trade Associations. Trade associations also have information regarding the background of their members and their industries.

3. Trade Magazines and Journals. Trade journals and magazines frequently survey their readership, and they also contain articles of interest that describe competitive companies, products, strategies, and markets.

4. The Small Business Administration. The U.S. Small Business Administration was set up to help small business. Whether you own a small business or are a marketing planner in a large company, the studies sponsored can be extremely valuable to anyone doing research in the situational analysis of a marketing plan. The many printed aids supplied include statistics, maps, national market analyses, national directories for use in marketing, basic library reference sources, information on various types of business (including industry average investments and cost), and factors to consider in locating a shopping center.

5. Databases. Databases are electronic collections of relevant data based on trade journals, newspapers, and many other public or private sources of information. They are accessed by computer, and companies sell the computer time to search the databases they have available.

6. Earlier Studies. Earlier marketing studies are sometimes made available to interested companies or individuals. These studies may have cost $40,000 or more when done as primary research. As a consequence, their results are not inexpensive—although in effect you are sharing the cost with other companies that purchase the results with you. Several thousand dollars for a short report is not atypical. Nevertheless, if the alternative is to do the entire primary research project yourself, it may be far less expensive to pay the price.

7. *The U.S. Industrial Outlook.* Every year the U.S. government publishes a document known as the *U.S. Industrial Outlook,* which contains detailed information on the prospects of more than 350 manufacturing and service industries.

8. *The Statistical Abstract of the United States.* This abstract is also an annual publication of the U.S. government. It contains a wealth of detailed statistical data having to do with everything from health to food consumption, to population, public school finances, individual income tax returns, mortgage debt, science and engineering, student numbers, and motor vehicle travel. It is published by the U.S. Department of Commerce, Bureau of the Census.

9. The U.S. Department of Commerce. If you are interested in export, the U.S. Department of Commerce has numerous sources of information, including amounts exported to foreign countries in the preceding year, major consumers of certain items, and detailed information on doing business in countries around the world. You can find the office of your local U.S. Department of Commerce in the U.S. government listings in your telephone book.

10. The U.S. Government. Because the U.S. government has so many sources of information, it is impossible to list them all here. But because so much information is available, and so much of it is free, you would be well advised to see what can be obtained from federal government sources. One recommended source that will give you access to this information is *Information U.S.A.* by Matthew Lesko (Viking Press). An additional listing of secondary-source information is contained in Appendix B of this book.

11. The Internet. The Internet is a relatively new but very important way to do research for your marketing plan. So much so, that the government became very concerned several years ago when instructions on how to build an atomic bomb appeared on the Internet! Start with the search engines provided on your browser. There are many search engines; some are specialized for certain areas of interest, some search the whole Web. Even with a 100 million or more entries, what one search engine can't locate for you, another can. You'll find major search engines listed in Appendix B. The Internet is relatively new compared with other means of doing secondary research. For an in-depth look, consult the following references:
    * *The Information Specialist's Guide to Searching and Researching on the Internet* by Ernest Ackermann and Karen Hartman (Abt Content)
    * *The 10 Minute Guide to Business Research on the Net* by Thomas Pack (Que Education and Training)
    * *The Internet Research Guide, Revised Edition* by Timothy K. Maloy (Watson-Guptill Pub.)

PRIMARY RESEARCH

In some cases you must do primary research yourself. Minimize the cost as much as possible by thorough planning. Time is also an important factor. Can you complete your primary research in time to be of use in preparing your marketing plan?

Three basic methods of gathering primary data are face-to-face interviewing and mail and telephone surveying. Each has its advantages and disadvantages; for example, in face-to-face interviewing more detailed information can usually be obtained and the interviewer can use verbal feedback and read body language or facial expressions to probe for answers. But face-to-face interviewing can be costly in time and money. Mail surveys are perhaps the quickest but most impersonal method. Their disadvantages are low return rate and lack of feedback. The telephone is an excellent means of surveying the country in the shortest time. Telephone calls, however, can also be expensive and will provide no visual feedback to your questions.

SUMMARY

In this chapter we explored the environmental questions, the answers to which are necessary to complete the situational analysis of your marketing plan. We have also recorded some of the sources of this information. The information will not be available by the time the marketing planning must be done, so you must make the best assumptions possible, based on the information you have already acquired. Don't forget to clearly state the assumptions you have made. You don't want anyone to confuse your assumptions as facts.

Having done the research and situational analysis required and knowing what environment you will face in the marketplace, you are now ready to establish your goals and objectives. We will do so in the next chapter.

3

STEP 3

ESTABLISHING GOALS AND OBJECTIVES

"Would you tell me, please, which way I ought to go from here?" asked Alice.

"That depends a good deal on where you want to get to," said the cat.
"I don't much care where," said Alice.

"Then it doesn't matter which way you go," said the cat.

Lewis Carroll, *Alice's Adventures in Wonderland*

You can't get *there* unless you know where *there* is. This chapter deals with establishing goals and objectives. They are the *there* of your marketing plan. Without them, you haven't got a marketing plan—you have a collection of facts and unrelated and partially related ideas. Moreover, research demonstrates that managers who make the need for action clear at the outset, set objectives, carry out an unrestricted search for solutions, and get key people to participate are more likely to be successful.[1] So establishing goals and objectives are not an insignificant part of developing your marketing plan.

ESTABLISHING OBJECTIVES

Your objectives answer the question: What are you trying to achieve? The following objectives are typical:

- To establish a product, product line, or brand in the marketplace.

- To rejuvenate a failing product.

- To entrench and protect a market under attack by competitors.

- To introduce a new product.

---

[1] Paul C. Nutt, "Surprising but True: Half the Decisions in Organizations Fail," *The Academy of Management Executive* (November 1999), p. 75.

- To harvest a product that is in the declining stage of its life cycle.
- To introduce a locally successful product nationally or overseas.
- To achieve maximum return on investment with a product or product line.

Normally, the statement of the objective should focus on a single task, but it is possible to have more than one objective or to specify additional conditions as long as they do not conflict with each other. If your objective is to introduce a new product, you might add: "To dominate the market, while achieving maximum sales."

In the same vein your objective might be worded: "To rejuvenate a failing product while maintaining high profitability and with minimum investment."

But in establishing more than one objective, or a main objective with additional conditions, care must be taken that the objectives do not conflict. It may be desirable to maximize the market share that you have been able to capture for a new product and at the same time achieve maximum profitability, but the two may not be achievable simultaneously. Capturing a maximum market share may require a penetration pricing strategy, and the low price and lower margins may result in something far less than maximum profitability. In fact, you may be lucky to reach the break-even point. Therefore, when you establish your objectives and add conditions to them, be certain that there is no conflict and that achievement of one condition will not make it impossible to achieve another.

Spend the necessary time to make sure that your objective statement is worded correctly and that all important conditions have been incorporated. Even after you have finished with it, however, it will not be complete until you have specified a time by which the objective must be achieved. Ask yourself the question, "By what time?" for every objective that you establish. Let's say that you want to introduce a new product, dominate the market, and build maximum sales. "By what time?" Three months? Six months? Nine months? A year? Longer than that?

If one of your objectives is to harvest a product that is in the decline stage of its product life cycle, how much time will you have? If you are going to introduce a nationally successful product overseas, how long will it take to complete this introduction?

Psychologists, time management experts, business researchers, and practitioners all tell us that specifying a time period is extremely important. Doing this will give you a target on which to focus and a guide that will tell you whether you're on schedule. It will also provide a date toward which everyone concerned with the marketing plan can coordinate their efforts.

In 1960 President John F. Kennedy set an objective for the United States. He said, "We're going to have a man on the moon by 1970." Note that he didn't just say, "We're going to put a man on the moon sometime." He said, "We're going to put a man on the moon by 1970." In actuality this goal was achieved in 1969. The fact that President Kennedy specified a date was of major significance, because it not only helped us to achieve this national objective, it helped us achieve it before the projected target date.

George A. Steiner, a man famed for his expertise in strategic planning, recommends 10 criteria to help in developing objectives.[2] Use them as guidelines to ensure that your objectives, whatever they are, will benefit the firm's overall mission:

Suitability. Your objectives must support the enterprise's basic purposes and help to move the company in that direction.

Measurability over Time. Objectives should state clearly what is expected to happen and when so that you can measure them as you proceed.

Feasibility. Your objectives must be feasible. If they cannot be fulfilled, they motivate no one. Be certain that they are realistic and practical even if they are difficult and require considerable effort.

---

[2] George A. Steiner, *Strategic Planning* (New York: Free Press, 1979), pp. 164–168.

Acceptability. The objectives you set must be acceptable to the people in your organization or to those who may allocate resources to implement your marketing plan. If your objectives are not acceptable, you will not receive the necessary funds. If someone besides yourself is working on the marketing plan and the objectives are not acceptable, you cannot expect to receive the same cooperation.

Flexibility. Your objectives should be modifiable in the event of unforeseen contingencies and environmental changes. This does not mean that they should not be fixed, only that, if necessary, they can be adapted to environmental changes.

Motivating. Objectives should motivate those who must work to reach them. If your objectives are either too easy or so difficult that they are impossible to achieve, they will not be motivating. If your objectives are difficult but achievable, they will challenge and motivate everyone to reach them.

Understandability. Your objectives should be stated in clear, simple language that can be understood by all. If they are not clear, they may be misunderstood and some individuals may unintentionally be working against them. You may also alienate those who allocate resources and capital. Your plan may be stopped midway through execution simply because your objectives were not clear to everyone.

Commitment. Make certain that everyone working on the development, planning, selling, and execution of the marketing plan is committed to your objectives. In today's real-life business world, senior managers seek to do this by getting as many managers as possible involved in determining what these objectives should be.

People Participation. Steiner points out that the best results are obtained when those who are responsible for achieving the objectives take some part in setting them. It is vitally important to consult with all who might participate in any way with the execution of the plan. If other staff members are committed to your objectives from the start, you will have much less trouble keeping them on track throughout the implementation of your plan. If you are working on your marketing plan as a team, you will find that ensuring everyone's participation and input will gain commitment to completing the plan. If one or two team members attempt to impose their ideas on the group, the opposite will occur. No matter how brilliant or "right" their ideas, they will be unable to gain the commitment of other team members.

Linkage. Naturally the objectives should be linked with the basic purposes of your organization. They must also be linked with the objectives of other collateral organizations in your firm. They must be consistent with and meet top management objectives. It's useless to set objectives that involve high sales if this runs counter to top management's overall philosophy of serving a small exclusive clientele. Ensure that the objectives you set are linked to other unique requirements of the environment of your firm.

After you have decided on the time frame for achieving your objectives, add it to the form in Figure 3-1.

GOALS

Goals are the specifics of the objectives. Let's look at one of the objectives we discussed: "Introduce a new product and dominate the market while achieving maximum sales. Time to achieve: one year."

Now the question is this: Does *introduce* mean to distribute it among 500 major retail outlets or at only one? Is maximum sales $100,000 in six months and then $1 million in one year? What are the figures that demonstrate introduction? What exactly do the words in your objectives mean? How about *dominating* the market? Is dominating the market

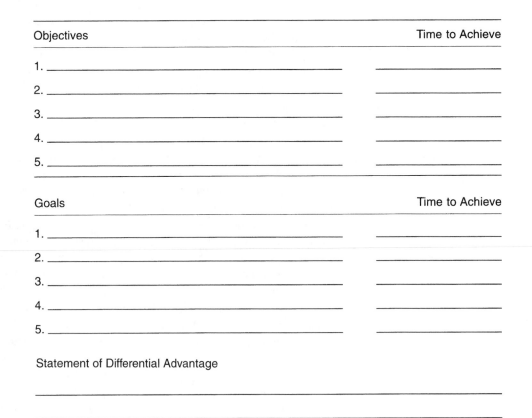

FIGURE 3-1.   Objectives, goals, differential advantage statement. (Copyright © 1985 by Dr. William A. Cohen.)

having a market share of 100, 90, or 50 percent? When the market is fragmented, you may dominate the market by taking a 25 percent share (or less).

Objectives can also be broken down into smaller intermediate units within the overall time period specified. These shorter-term objectives are also goals. Thus maximum sales may be defined at the end of the period indicated (one year) as well as at shorter intervals, say six months. The same can be done to define *dominating the market.*

Let's look at another example: "Rejuvenate a failing product with minimum investment while maintaining high profitability."

First, what does *rejuvenate* mean? In this case let's say that it means increasing sales by 30 percent over the preceding year. How about *minimum investment*? Let's say that the maximum amount that your company is ready to invest is $100,000. If you think this is the minimum amount that you need to get the job done, then your *minimum investment* may be $100,000. And *high profitability*? Well, profitability is related to the margin, that is, your costs compared with the selling price that was set. Let's say that the definition of high profitability is a margin of 60 percent. You can use this figure to define high profitability.

Again, you must consider the time for achieving these goals. You may want to indicate quarterly sales increases over the preceding year combined with a total sales increase of 30 percent at the end of the coming year. Both the final and intermediate figures are goals.

You can now complete the goals section in Figure 3-1. Specifying your goals and writing them down makes sense, because it allows you to concentrate your efforts on achieving what is really important in order to obtain the objectives that were set earlier.

Specificity also affects vision. Vision has to do with the future as the leader or manager sees the outcome of the project. One study of leaders discovered that groups were far more likely to follow leaders and were much more enthusiastic about doing so when the leaders set specific objectives and goals.[3]

In another study more than 200 combat leaders who subsequently went on to very successful careers in civilian pursuits listed "declare your expectations," which included promoting vision, goals, and objectives as one of the eight major principles of leadership.[4]

When goals and objectives are made specific, it is much easier to avoid conflict between individuals and groups that must assist in carrying out the required tasks. Also, individuals will work together to coordinate their efforts in a synergistic way. This makes their efforts far more effective than if their actions were simply to achieve movement in a general direction toward a less specific goal.

THE CONCEPT OF COMPETITIVE OR DIFFERENTIAL ADVANTAGE

In all cases, you must direct your efforts toward satisfying the customer by achieving a competitive or differential advantage over your competitors. That's one reason organizations are constantly trying to improve their services. As they get better and better at what they do, the customer wins by getting better products at lower prices.

Some call this competitive advantage, others differential advantage, and still others use all three words. This is unimportant. What is important is what the words stand for. They mean not only that your product or service has one or more advantages, but that these are more important than the advantages that your competitors may have.

Also, do you seek one competitive advantage, or can there be more than one? There may be one overriding competitive advantage that is so significant, that others are not as important. At other times, your statement of competitive advantage may actually encompass a number of advantages over your competitor. The number is less important than the total strength of your advantage or advantages over your competitors.

In addition, you should consider sustainability of your competitive advantage. That is, not only must you be able to attain a competitive advantage, but you must be able to sustain it as well. But for how long? Certainly not indefinitely. The environment will change sooner or later and you will lose your competitive advantage, regardless of what you do. Rolles in England once held the monopoly on the self-shapening razor for men, the sustainable competitive advantage being the patents on their unique self-contained sharpening system. Then in the 1960s, advanced steel manufacturing processes produced razor blades sharper than any manufactured previously. The Rolles' advantage became irrelevant and the Rolles razor was withdrawn from the market. Your competitive advantage needs to be sustainable over the life of your planned strategy, not forever.

Include the concept of competitive advantage in your marketing plan. Once established, you must think about, develop, and find ways to promote your competitive advantage. If you have no competitive advantage you will not succeed. Why should customers

---

[3] Warren Bennis and Burt Nanus, *Leaders* (New York: Harper & Row, 1985).

[4] William A. Cohen, *The Stuff of Heroes: The Eight Universal Laws of Leadership* (Marietta, GA: Longstreet Press, 1998).

buy your product or service if it is identical to a competitor's product with which they are satisfied? Therefore the key question is, "Why should anyone buy from us as opposed to one or more of our competitors?"

Although your objectives and goals focus on what *you* want, the differential competitive advantage focuses on what your customer wants. What is the advantage of the customer buying your product or service? Think this through to determine how the two are linked. Your competitive advantage is derived from an eventual customer benefit.

Let's look at an example of this linkage. Why have so many Americans bought Japanese cars in the past? Americans recognized a benefit over American-made cars. It may be stated as "quality at an affordable price," or "value for the price." This quality was made possible by a combination of factors. First was the notion that much higher quality than had previously been achieved was possible. Also, the Japanese automobile industry was automated to a far greater extent than its American competitors, which meant its labor force was more productive. Finally, the Japanese had a lower cost of labor. Assuming this to be correct, these factors were competitive advantages over American automobile manufacturers. Together they resulted in the benefit of "high quality at an affordable price."

This is not to say that American manufacturers may not also have competitive differential advantages that benefit customers, which may exceed those offered by Japanese companies. As a matter of fact, that is exactly what American manufacturers have been doing in recent years—capitalizing on their own differential advantages to achieve a link to customer benefits in addition to raising quality.

Competitive advantages can be derived from a number of widely varying factors. A competitive differential advantage could be the ability to buy in quantity from special sources not enjoyed by others. The resulting benefit to the customer: low price. You may have a great number of Ph.D.'s in your research and development department. The resulting benefit to the customer: advanced state-of-the-art technology. You may own a restaurant for which you have employed the best chef in your entire geographical area. The resulting benefit to the customer: the best gourmet food. Knowledge can also be a competitive differential advantage that will result in customer benefits; for example, marketing know-how translates into better satisfied customer needs.

You can even find competitive advantages in what you might think are disadvantages. When Mercedes-Benz first introduced the diesel models, they didn't sell. At that time diesel fuel sold for almost the same price as gasoline. Also, diesel fuel wasn't sold at many gasoline stations, so it was not as convenient to use. Finally, if you've ever heard a diesel engine, you know that it's much louder and noisier than one burning gasoline.

Mercedes-Benz saved the product line by turning these disadvantages into competitive advantages. They promoted the fuel as exotic and exclusive, "not available at every gasoline station." As for the noisy engine? Mercedes-Benz said it was unique too. "It wasn't like gasoline–burning engines that were so quiet you couldn't even tell if they were running or not. When you started up a diesel engine, you can hear its power." Mercedes-Benz knew that to the wealthy segments at which these products were targeted, uniqueness and exclusivity were major benefits.

Make sure that any competitive advantages have the following characteristics:

They must be real. Wishes will not make it so. Some retail stores claim that their prices are lower than those of all their competitors. Sometimes even a cursory inspection will prove this to be untrue or that they are lower only in certain circumstances or with certain products. Thus their advantage will *not* be translated into a benefit for the customer. They must be important to the customer. Note the words *the customer,* and not *to you.* Freeman Gosden, Jr., who was once president of the largest direct response agency in the world, says, "It's not what you want to sell, but what your customer wants to buy." This principle is directly applicable to the competitive advantage. It's not the competitive advantage that you seek but rather the benefits as the customer sees them.

A major supplier of U.S. Air Force helmets once considered getting into the motorcycle helmet market. This company believed it could make a better protective motorcycle helmet than its competitors because of its experience with pilot helmets. And it did make these more protective helmets. However, they were priced at approximately 30 percent more than the preceding top-of-the-line motorcycle helmets. This pricing was not arbitrary, merely based on higher manufacturing costs for a more protective product. If that was not enough, this expensive helmet was 15 percent heavier than competitive models. Despite all this, the company actually thought it had a competitive edge because of the greater protection. Within a year this manufacturer learned a hard lesson when the product failed. The customer did not want a more protective helmet—at least, not to the degree that the customer would pay 30 percent more, and accept a 15 percent weight penalty. When the perception of competitive differential advantage differs between marketer and customer, the customer always wins.

Lee Iacocca says that in 1956, Ford decided that safety was of primary interest to the consumer and emphasized it in all the advertising of its 1956 models. Ford's sales plummeted and the competition won on all fronts. Ford's claims were questionable. Quickly realizing that he lacked a competitive differential advantage, and needed one fast, Iacocca hit on what was really the main issue: ability to purchase the car. The year 1956 was one of mild recession. Therefore Iacocca instituted a policy by which customers could purchase new cars for only $20 down and $56 a month. This made it easier to buy a Ford than competitive cars. Iacocca hit on the correct differential advantage, as perceived by his potential customers. His district went from last place to number one in sales.[5]

They must be specific. Whatever your competitive differential advantages, they must be specific, just as objectives and goals must be specific. It is not enough to say, "We're the best." The question is, the best what? And why? To the customer nonspecificity translates into mere puffery and is not a competitive differential advantage.

They must be promotable. Whatever your competitive differential advantages are, they must be promotable to the customer. The Edsel was a great failure in the marketplace and is frequently cited as a prime example of poor marketing. Yet Ford did extensive market research to determine what the customer wanted before introducing the Edsel line. This research indicated that power was an important competitive differential advantage. The Edsel was designed to be one of the most powerful cars ever built for its price range. Unfortunately in the same year that the Edsel was introduced a new government regulation limited automobile advertisers from promoting the high horsepower of engines. As a result this competitive differential advantage, although it existed and may have been desired by the customer, could not be promoted. If you are planning on a specific differential advantage, it is essential that your customer know it; otherwise it might as well not exist.

When you have thought through this challenge, return to Figure 3–1 and enter your statement of competitive differential advantage in the space provided on the form. What is it that you have that others haven't, and how does it translate into benefits to your potential customers?

SUMMARY

In this chapter we have examined objectives and goals: objectives being what you are trying to achieve, and goals the specifics of your objectives. In both cases it is very important to indicate the time frame within which these objectives and goals should fall. Remember, there is a sound psychological basis for both specificity and time frame that will help you to organize your efforts. Although your objectives and goals are what *you* want, you must also be aware of what is wanted by your potential customers. Thus you must build and emphasize a concept of competitive differential advantage. This should be something unique that you will have but your competition will not. Otherwise there

---

[5] Lee Iacocca, *Iacocca* (New York: Bantam, 1984), p. 39.

is no reason for your customers to buy from you, and they won't. And your competitive differential advantages must translate into benefits and satisfaction as perceived by your customers.

Develop strong objectives, goals, and competitive advantages and you will be well on your way to success. You will be in a position to develop strategy to reach your objectives and goals building on the competitive advantages you have formulated.

CHAPTER 4

STEP 4

DEVELOPING MARKETING STRATEGY

The word *strategy* stems from the Greek *strategos,* which means the art of the general. Many of the concepts that we use in marketing strategy evolved from early use in military strategy. The very top level of military strategy is sometimes called grand strategy. It entails many other elements besides that of military force, including economic power and diplomacy. At the next level down is military strategy itself. Military strategy involves all actions taken by military forces up to the point of reaching the battlefield. Finally, according to the military concept of strategy, we have tactics, which are those actions taken on the battlefield. In all cases there are objectives: national objectives that are achieved by grand strategy, military objectives achieved by military strategy, and tactical objectives achieved by tactics. The basis of all strategy is the concentration of superior resources at the decisive point. For example, over the last few years, Procter & Gamble Company adopted a strategy of simplification. It trimmed its product line, slashing items in hair care alone by more than half. It also standardized packaging and promotions worldwide. As one P&G executive said, "There is a real push in the company to do fewer, bigger things." By simplfying, P&G could concentrate resources where it counted. The results? P&G sales grew by a third in five years.[1]

THE STRATEGY PYRAMID

In marketing we have a similar concept, called the strategic pyramid (see Figure 4-1). At the very highest level of the pyramid is strategic marketing management (SMM). SMM seeks to achieve the mission of the firm. To do this, SMM decides what businesses, product lines, and products to pursue. One level down is marketing strategy. This is the strategy that is implemented in support of the businesses, product lines, and products decided on in SMM.

---

[1] Zachary Schiller, Greg Burns, and Karen L. Miller, "Make It Simple," *BusinessWeek* (September 9, 1996), pp. 96–104.

FIGURE 4-1.   The strategic pyramid.

Let's say that at the corporate or top organizational level a decision had been made to exploit the capability that your company has for manufacturing certain products. This would be an SMM decision. Moving one level down to the marketing strategy level, how might this be accomplished? Penetrating new markets might be one way. Expanding the share of the market that you already have for this product might be another. If you select the option for new market penetration, you might consider a niche strategy, which whereby you market to a definable segment that you can dominate. If you have sufficient resources, you might consider a vertical marketing strategy. You would try to control more of the marketing functions between production and selling to the customer. You might also consider entry strategy in which you would weigh the advantages against the disadvantages of being first, early, or late in the market with your new product.

If you decide on a strategy of market share expansion, you might choose product differentiation or market segmentation—that is, you could consider emphasizing a product that is considerably different from other products and target the entire market. Or you could segment your market into smaller markets and enter each with a slightly different product. You might also consider a limited share expansion versus a general share expansion.

The lowest level in your strategic pyramid is marketing tactics, which are the actions you take to support the marketing strategy decided on at the preceding level. To do this you manipulate certain marketing variables having to do with the product, price, promotion, or distribution. You can manipulate all of these variables, or only one, depending on your overall tactical plan.

Maybe the marketing strategy you decide on is market share expansion. One tactic for accomplishing this may involve modifying your product to increase its performance. It may involve a lower price to make your product more affordable. It may involve increased advertising, or advertising in new media or new media vehicles. Finally, your tactics may include different distribution channels, or more emphasis on the distribution channels you are currently using.

Because resources are always limited, its usually not possible to take all of these actions, so you allocate your resources—including your money, time, personnel, facilities, capital goods, and equipment—where they can have the most effect. The resulting tactical mix, known as a marketing mix, is what finally implements the decision that started at the very top of the corporate ladder with the mission of the firm.

Now let's look at the details of making these strategy decisions.

STRATEGIC MARKETING MANAGEMENT

To make the decisions that are necessary for developing strategy at the SMM level and then incorporate them into your marketing plan you will need a method for deciding to what businesses, product lines, or products the firm should allocate its resources.

To do this, we will use a portfolio matrix and the product life-cycle curve. The portfolio matrix is a box with four cells. The vertical axis represents business strength; the horizontal axis represents market attractiveness. We will locate candidate businesses, product lines, or products in the matrix.

The product life cycle graphically shows what happens to product sales and profits as a new business, product line, or product passes through the phases of introduction, growth, maturity, and decline.

Let's look at the four-cell portfolio matrix first.

THE FOUR-CELL PORTFOLIO MATRIX FOR DECISION MAKING IN SMM

The first step in using the four-cell matrix is to decide whether you are going to work with individual products, product lines, or even an entire business. If you have or are developing strategy for only a few products, you will plot their individual product positions in the matrix. If you have several different product lines, you will plot them in the matrix. If you are doing SMM for a large corporation with many businesses, you will plot businesses in the matrix.

If you are plotting products or product lines, what you plot are called strategic product units (SPUs). If you are working with businesses, you plot strategic business units (SBUs). If you have many different types of products, always combine products into product lines, or even product line groupings to form SPUs. Do the same if you have many businesses to form SBUs. This will greatly simplify your work, and it will also enable you to take advantage of economies of scale where possible. To establish SPUs or SBUs, look for similarities in customers served, product lines under a single manager, or products having identical competitors.

Once you have your SPUs established, calculate the values of the SPUs for both business strength and market attractiveness. Now let's see how to do this.

Calculation of SPU Value for Business Strength.   The first step in calculating the SPU value for business strength is to list the criteria important to the SPU being analyzed. Typical business strength criteria that may be relevant include:

Current market share	Raw materials cost
Growth rate	Image
Sales effectiveness	Product quality
The proprietary nature of the product	Technological advantages
Price competitiveness	Engineering know-how
Advertising or promotion effectiveness	Personnel resources
Facilities' location or newness	Product synergies
Productivity	Profitability
Experience curve effects	Distribution
Value added	

You may think of even more. The question is, which of these criteria are relevant to you in your situation?

Once you've established which criteria of business strengths are relevant, relative importance weightings should be established. This isn't difficult to do; you just need to remember that all the weightings of the different relevant criteria must total 100 percent.

Look at this simple example: Let's say that only four business strength criteria are considered important to you. We will assume that these are engineering know-how, size of your organization, organizational image, and productivity. Now, the question is, what is the relative importance of each of these four criteria to your business strength? After some thought, you decide that the most important is engineering know-how. You assign it a relative importance to the whole of 40 percent. You decide that the next most important criterion is organizational image. You give it 30 percent. Next you decide that the size of your organization and productivity are worth about 15 percent each. The addition of 40, 30, 15, and 15 percent equals 100 percent. If they didn't add up, you'd go back and adjust your weightings.

The weightings you establish will be used to rate all of your products, or SPUs against the same criteria. The only thing that will vary is how well each SPU does when measured against each. We'll use a point assignment to do this: 1 point means very weak; 2 points is weak; 3 points means fair. If the SPU looks good on this criterion, we'll give it 4 points if it's strong and 5 points if it's very strong.

Let's say for the specific SPU that you are analyzing you award a point rating of 5 for engineering know-how, 4 for organizational image, 2 for size of the organization, and 3 for productivity. You must now multiply the point rating for this particular SPU by the weightings you have established for the SPU (Figure 4-2) to arrive at a weighted rank for business strength of 3.95. Repeat this process for every SPU you are analyzing on the business strength computation sheet (Figure 4-3). Duplicate this figure and use a separate sheet for each SPU.

Market Attractiveness.   Next you are going to calculate market attractiveness to plot along the horizontal axis of your matrix. Typical market attractiveness criteria include:

Size of the market segment	Ease of entry
Growth of the market segment	Life-cycle position
Market pricing	Competitive structure
Strength of demand	Product liability
Vulnerability to inflation and depression	Political considerations
Government regulation	Distribution structure
Availability of raw materials	

Again, you may think of additional market attractiveness factors that are important to your company.

Let's assume that only four marketing attractiveness criteria are considered important. These are the size of the market, the growth rate of the market, the ease of entry, and the life-cycle position. You estimate that the relative importance of the size of the market is 40 percent, growth rate of the market is 30 percent, ease of entry is 25 percent, and life-cycle position, 15 percent.

	Weight × Rating
Engineering know-how	0.40 × 5 pts = 2.00
Size of the organization	0.15 × 2 pts = 0.30
Organizational image	0.30 × 4 pts = 1.20
Productivity	0.15 × 3 pts = 0.45
	Total = 3.95

FIGURE 4-2.   Calculation of SPU value for business strength.

SPU # _____ Date _____

Business Strength Criteria	Weights	× Rankings	= Weighted Rank
	1.00	× Rank	=

FIGURE 4-3. Business strength computation sheet. (Copyright © 1983 by Dr. William A. Cohen.)

Note that once again the relative importance of all the market attractiveness criteria must equal 100 percent. If it doesn't, we'll go back and reestimate our percentages until it does.

You must rate each market attractiveness criterion for the SPU being analyzed on a scale of 1 point for very unattractive, 2 points for unattractive, 3 points for fair, 4 points for attractive, and 5 points for very attractive.

Let's assume that you assign the following ratings: size of market, 4 points; growth of market, 4 points; ease of entry, 1 point; and life-cycle position, 5 points.

You then calculate the rating for each market attractiveness criterion by multiplying the weight times the point rating. Add it up it to find the total (Figure 4-4). Note that the total value is 3.40. Now we repeat the process for each of your SPUs. You can use Figure 4-5 and duplicate it to use a separate sheet for each SPU.

You are now able to plot the location of your SPU on the matrix (Figure 4-6). Note that in this matrix business strength increases from bottom to top and market attractiveness increases from right to left. The position of the SPU is located at the coordinates of business strength, 3.95 and market attractiveness, 3.40.

	Weight × Rating
Size of market	0.30 × 4 pts = 1.20
Growth of market	0.30 × 4 pts = 1.20
Ease of entry	0.25 × 1 pts = 0.25
Life-cycle position	0.15 × 5 pts = 0.75
	Total = 3.40

FIGURE 4-4.   Calculation of SPU value for market attractiveness.

SPU # _____   Date _____

Market Attractiveness Criteria	Weights	× Rankings	= Weighted Rank
	1.00	× Rank	=

FIGURE 4-5.   Market attractiveness computation sheet. (Copyright © 1983 by Dr. William A. Cohen.)

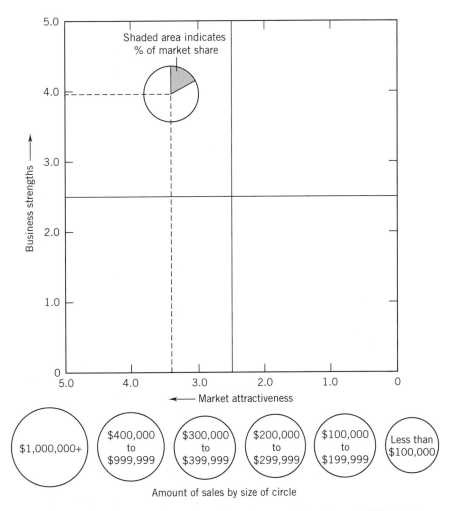

FIGURE 4-6. Matrix showing sales, size of market, and location of SPU: business strength versus market attractiveness.

You can illustrate the amount of current sales for this SPU by the size of the circle illustrated and can indicate the percentage of the market share that this SPU represents with a shaded portion of the circle.

You can plot other SPUs in the same manner (see Figure 4-7). Each is calculated and compared with the criteria for business strength and market attractiveness, using the same relative importance percentages. Only the point ratings for each market attractiveness or business strength criterion differ. This causes the SPU to be located in different positions in the matrix.

The location of the SPU in the matrix suggests a number of strategic moves. Those in the upper left quadrant imply additional investment priority, which is logical because that quadrant contains SBUs that have attractive markets and for which the firm has considerable business strength. The names for the SPUs in each quadrant come from the names given to the original four-celled matrix designed by the Boston Consulting Group back in 1960. The measurements in that matrix were different, but the names still fit. The SPUs in the upper left-hand quadrant are known as *stars.*

SPUs that fall in the upper right-hand quadrant of the matrix imply selective investment. You have the business strength, but the market just isn't all that attractive. Still, SPUs can be profitable in this quadrant. SPUs that fall in this quadrant in the matrix are called *question marks* or *problem children.*

The lower left quadrant of the matrix contains SPUs for which you must apply selective investment to move to star status or to manage for earnings. These SPUs can be moved

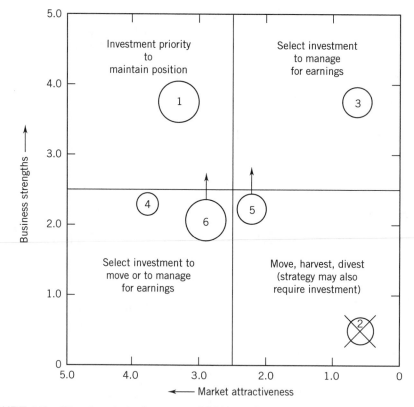

FIGURE 4-7.   Planning strategic moves of SPUs on four-cell.

by increasing your business strength and are known as *cash cows*. That's because if this SPU exists you are already in an attractive market even though your business strength is low. You don't have to use resources to get into the market, yet are benefiting from the market's attractiveness.

Finally you have *dog* SPUs located in the lower right-hand quadrant of the matrix. They can be moved; usually, however, they are harvested or divested. You don't have the business strength, so why would you want to invest resources to move yourself into a less attractive market? In Figure 4-7, SPU 5 does indicate possible movement into the question-mark quadrant. However, note that SPU 5 is a borderline SPU, already close to the star and the question-mark quadrants.

If your SPUs are potential ones, it makes little sense to invest in them unless they are stars, the exceptions being if you have more opportunities than resources (rare) and they are close to the star quadrant.

Decisions as to which SPUs to invest in and possible SPU movements must be made considering other factors—such as sales, percentage of market share, and so on—after the graphic analysis using the four-celled portfolio matrix is complete. SMM is complete only when this has been accomplished.

PRODUCT LIFE-CYCLE ANALYSIS

Each product has a cycle of life that contains different stages: introduction, growth, maturity, and decline. This is called the product life cycle or PLC. During each stage of the PLC, the product exhibits characteristics and performances that favor the use of different marketing strategies.

There is also an important overall trend for products to proceed more rapidly through the PLC. The mechanical watch was invented hundreds of years ago and over the centuries proceeded very slowly through its life cycle. Yet over the last 15 years electronic watches have exhibited life cycles that are sometimes measured in months, not years. Electronic watches with features that once sold for several hundred dollars may sell today for less than $50.

Finally, if possible, it is best to maintain a portfolio of products in different stages. You don't want to get caught with all of your products in the maturity or decline stage. You can also have trouble with a large number of products in the introduction stage because of the considerable expense of introduction for each new product. With a number of new products in the introduction stage at the same time, there is a heavy negative cash flow. The solution is to know what stages in the PLC your products are in.

THE INTRODUCTORY STAGE

In the introductory stage of the product life cycle the organization experiences high costs due to marketing. Manufacturing is generally involved in short production runs of highly-skilled labor content and there is an overcapacity. These factors lead to high production costs. Furthermore, buyers have not yet been persuaded to purchase the product on a regular basis. Many buyers may be totally unaware of the product. Generally, the only good news in the introductory stage of a new product is that competitors are few or nonexistent. Profits, of course, are also nonexistent or negligible. The basic strategy during this stage is generally to establish market share and to persuade early adopters to buy the product.

GROWTH

In the growth stage the situation begins to change. The product has established itself and is successful. Sales are continuing to increase and, as a result, other companies are attracted and new competitors will probably be entering the market with their own version of the product. Marketing costs are still high, but manufacturing costs are reduced somewhat. An undercapacity develops because of a shift toward mass production. Distribution channels were probably limited in the introductory stage simply because of limited resources, but not anymore. In the growth stage distribution tends to become intensive and multiple channels may be used. All other things considered, profits tend to reach peak levels during this stage because of the increased demand and the fact that most companies take advantage of this demand with high pricing. Strategies followed during the growth stage are new market penetration and market share expansion. Tactical support of these strategies includes product improvement, development of new channels of distribution, and a manipulation of price and quality.

MATURITY

The product in the maturity stage has changed its situation again. Although many competitors may remain from the growth stage, they are now competing for smaller and smaller market shares. As a result the competition heats up and what is known as a shake-out begins to occur. Less efficient competitors go under or withdraw from the market. Buyers who have been purchasing the product exhibit repeat buying, and although sales continue to increase during this stage, profits begin to fall. Manufacturing costs are much lower during this stage, but the increased competition for a smaller market share ultimately forces prices down. This stage encourages a strategy of entrenchment, yet a search for new markets is still possible. Typical tactics include reducing some channels to improve profit margins, low-pricing tactics against weaker competitors, and increasing emphasis on promotion.

DECLINE

In the decline stage, as in the introductory stage, there are few competitors. Buyers who are purchasing the product are now sophisticated and much more selective. Production has problems again because there will be an overcapacity caused by reduced demand. Marketing expenditures will probably be reduced. In this stage both profits and sales are declining. At some point this will force a liquidation of inventory. The most logical strategy for the decline stage is some form of withdrawal, although entrenchment may also be followed in selective markets over the short term. Tactics in support of this strategy include reduction of distribution channels to those that are still profitable, low prices, and selective but quick spurts of promotion when rapid liquidation is needed. You've got to consider immediate liquidation versus a slow milking and harvesting of all possible benefits over a period of time. In any case, you must now be prepared for ultimate product removal.

LOCATING THE PRODUCT IN ITS PRODUCT LIFE CYCLE

Before you can analyze the PLC for strategy implications, you must locate the product in its life cycle. This requires considerable judgment. Although the general shape of the product life cycle shown in Figure 2-1 is true in many cases, it is not true in all. As a matter of fact many other shapes for product life cycle have been calculated, such as those shown in Figure 4-8. So before you can determine what position the product has taken in its life cycle, you must know what the life-cycle shape looks like. To do this, first look at what has happened to the product so far. Use Figure 4-9 to help you do this. Write down approximate sales, profits, margin, market share, and prices for varying periods over the product's life so far. You don't need exact figures, only whether your sales are high, low, or average or very high or very low. The same is true for profits, margins, and the other elements. You will also want to look at the trends and characterize them as declining steeply, declining, on a plateau, ascending, or ascending steeply.

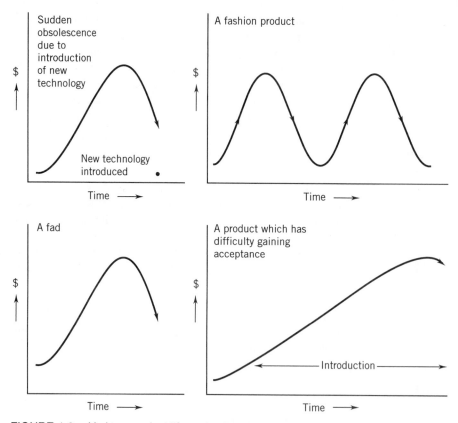

FIGURE 4-8. Various product life-cycle shapes.

Product _____   Date _____

	Period 1	Period 2	Period 3	Period 4	Trend
Sales					
Profits					
Margins					
Market share					
Prices					

Complete matrix with following information:	Characterize trends as:	
Very low or very small	Declining steeply	↓
Low or small	Declining	↘
Average	Plateau	→
High or large	Ascending	↗
Very high or very large	Ascending steeply	↑

FIGURE 4-9.   Historical trend analysis matrix. (Copyright © 1983 by Dr. William A. Cohen.)

Next, you will use the form in Figure 4-10 to analyze the recent trends in competitors' product share and their strengths. These can be characterized as very weak, weak, medium, strong, or very strong.

Now you will take a closer look at recent trends in competitive product quality, performance characteristics, shifts in distribution channels, and their relative advantages. Write down this information on the form in Figure 4–11.

Finally you will accomplish an analysis of your competitors' short-term tactics using Figure 4-12. Be sure to note the probable meaning of each action.

Leave the analysis of the product and its competition and scan the historical information on product life cycles of similar or related products. The best way to do this is to take a product that is similar to the one you are analyzing and determine what happened to it during its introduction, growth, maturity, and decline. Get as much information as you can regarding the number and strength of competitors, profits, pricing, strategies used, and the length of time in each stage. Use the form in Figure 4-13 for this.

With this information turn to Figure 4-14, which is a matrix that contains sales and profits on the vertical axis and time in years or months on the horizontal axis. Use the other information to help determine the shape of the curve. Sketch a rough sales curve and a rough profit curve for the similar or related product you have just analyzed.

The next step is to project sales of your current product over the next three to five years based on information from the first part of your analysis of your own and competing products. You can use the form in Figure 4-15 to estimate sales, total direct costs, indirect costs, pretax profits, and profit ratio, which is the estimate of total direct costs to pretax profits.

By comparing this information with the historical product information that you have already documented, you can make an estimate of the profitable years that remain for your product. You can plot your product in its PLC using Figure 4-16.

Your Product _____ Date _____

Strength code: VW = very weak   M = medium   VS = very strong
                W = weak   S = strong

Competitor	Market Share	Strength	Products

FIGURE 4-10.   Recent trends of competitor's products, share, and strength. (Copyright © 1983 by Dr. William A. Cohen.)

Your Product _____ Date _____

Company	Product	Quality and Performance Characteristics	Shifts in Distribution Channels	Relative Advantages of Each Competitive Product

FIGURE 4-11.   Recent trends in competitive products. (Copyright © 1983 by Dr. William A. Cohen.)

Your Product _____ Date _____

Competitor	Action	Probable Meaning of Action	Check Most Likely

FIGURE 4-12. Analysis of competitors' short-term tactics. (Copyright © 1983 by Dr. William A. Cohen.)

Product _____	Similar or Related Product _____			
Product stage	Introduction	Growth	Maturity	Decline
Competition				
Profits				
Sales (units)				
Pricing				
Strategy Used				
Length of Time in Each Stage				

FIGURE 4-13.   Developing life cycle of similar or related product. (Copyright © 1983 by Dr. William A. Cohen.)

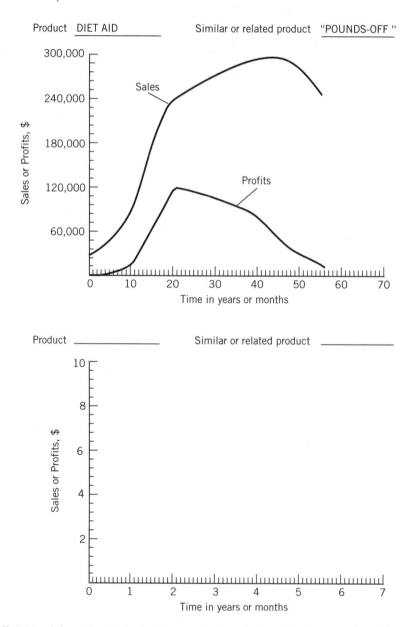

FIGURE 4-14.   Life-cycle curve of similar or related product. Sketch a rough sales curve and a rough profit curve for a similar or related product.
(Copyright © 1983 by Dr. William A. Cohen.)

Product _____ Date _____					
Year	1	2	3	4	5
Estimated sales					
Estimated total direct costs					
Estimated indirect costs					
Estimated pretax profits					
Profit ratio (est. total direct costs to pretax profits)					

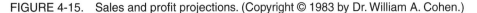

FIGURE 4-15.   Sales and profit projections. (Copyright © 1983 by Dr. William A. Cohen.)

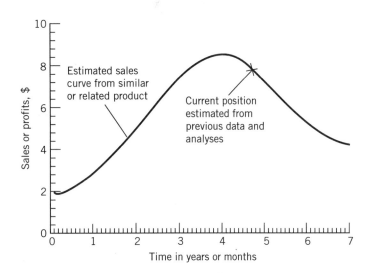

FIGURE 4-16.   Position in product life cycle curve (Copyright © 1983 by Dr. William A. Cohen.).

DEVELOPING STRATEGIES FOR THE PRODUCTS IN EACH STAGE OF THE PRODUCT LIFE CYCLE

To develop strategies for products in each stage of the product life cycle you must consider industry obsolescence trends, the pace of new product introduction, the average lengths of product life cycles of all the products that are in your product line, growth and profit objectives, and the general situation you are facing because of the present stage of the product's life cycle. You can use the alternative marketing strategies discussed in the next section. However, before you leave the PLC, you must understand that there may be changes that will alter the anticipated shape of the PLC. What can cause this to happen?

A need may disappear. Demand for the buggy whip is close to zero today, not because the buggy whip itself was replaced but because the buggy was replaced by the automobile. Thus there is no longer a need for the product. In the same vein, demand for the iron lung, once essential to the breathing of many polio victims, is very low because the main disease for which it was used has been eradicated.

A better, less expensive, or more convenient product may be developed to fill a need. All engineers once carried a device known as a slide rule, which was a mechanical device used for making mathematical and other scientific calculations. When the electronic calculator was introduced in the early 1970s, it replaced hundreds of thousands of slide rules virtually overnight.

A competitive product may, by superior marketing strategy, suddenly gain an advantage. Adam Osbourne's second generation of computers failed and suddenly had its product life cycle terminated not because of technological inferiority but by IBM's superior marketing strategy when it introduced the famous PC.

There may be an intentional change in the shape of the curve by product repositioning, innovation, or extension. Arm and Hammer baking soda was once used only as an additive for home cooking. As the product went into the decline stage, its life was extended by its use as an odor absorbent in refrigerators. In the same way, the DC-10 became an advanced cargo tanker for the Air Force.

Any of these occurrences will cause the anticipated life-cycle curve to change. Under these circumstances, a new marketing plan and marketing strategy must be developed.

ALTERNATIVE STRATEGIES FOR THE MARKETING PLAN

As pointed out by marketing consultant Jay Abraham, there are really only three basic ways to increase business. You can increase the number of customers, you can increase the average size of the sale per customer, and you can increase the number of times customers return to purchase again.[2] The major alternative strategies that you might pursue are new market penetration, market share expansion, entrenchment, and withdrawal.

NEW MARKET PENETRATION

There are four classes of new market penetration strategy. They may be pursued simultaneously, although they need not be. They involve entry, niche, dimension, and positioning. Let's look at each in turn.

Entry. In new market penetration you can be first, early, or late. A company that chooses a strategy of being first is the first to benefit from its learning curve—that is, as it gains experience in manufacturing and marketing of the product it is using for new market penetration, its cost goes down. This means that as competitors attempt to enter the market, the company that was there first has a cost advantage that can be passed on to the customer in the form of a lower price. Alternatively, the company can use this advantage against competitors by using their higher profits for additional promotion, to establish new channels of distribution, and so forth. Those customers who have been persuaded to buy the first product on the market and whose needs have been satisfied may be reluctant to switch because of inertia. Also, the firm that enters first picks up a certain momentum. Firms that enter later must catch up. Thus the first firm has an advantage. It can continue to innovate to maintain a lead over its competition. The first firm to enter a market also has an edge in dominating that market.

Being first is not without its risks, however. As Peter F. Drucker said in his book *Innovation and Entrepreneurship,* to reap the benefits of being first requires an extreme concentration of effort on a clear-cut goal. Once a firm is successful in entering the marketplace first, it must expend considerable effort to maintain leadership or everything that has been invested will be lost to one of the later-entering competitors. Being first does not

---

[2] Jay Abraham, *Getting Everything You Can Out of All You've Got* (New York: St. Martin's Press, 2000), p. 5.

automatically ensure victory. This firm must react and react strongly to later-entering competitors to maintain its lead.

A second possibility is that of entering the market early but not first. This early entry may be intentional or unintentional. Perhaps the firm intended to be first but was edged out by another firm. When this happens, the firm that is edged out may suffer all of the disadvantages of being first, but reap none of the advantages. Early, rather than first entry can be advantageous if the firm has sufficient resources to fight the firm ahead of it. It has somewhat reduced risk because risk in demand, technological obsolescence, and other areas of business have been absorbed by the first entry. Some knowledge will be gained of what works and what does not. This was all paid for by the firm that enters first. Finally, coincident with lower risk, much of the opportunity in the marketplace still exists. It is not a case of a product being in the mature stage of its life cycle, with many competitors fighting for reduced shares, or even of the later growth stages, with many competitors entering the market. This product is usually still in the very early stage of its introduction.

The major disadvantages of being early but not first are the barriers to entry set up by the first entry. Also, the market opportunity may be somewhat reduced. IBM overcame these disadvantages and captured a good share of the market for personal computers even though Apple got there first.

Finally, we have a late entry. Believe it or not, there are a number of advantages to entering the market after it is already established. For example, the fact that earlier entrants are usually committed to the previous direction of their products means that late entrants can include the latest technological improvements without penalty. The Japanese entered the American car market with brand new plants and manufacturing processes that competed against older, established American competitors that were tied to their obsolescent capital equipment and facilities. Late entrants may be able to achieve greater economies of scale because all entrants have a better idea of the actual size and demand of the market and can produce optimal facilities. Late-entry firms may also be able to get better terms from suppliers, employees, or even customers because earlier entrants may be locked into negotiations or fixed ways of doing business. Late entrants will enjoy reduced costs of research and development because they have been borne by earlier competitors. Finally, the late entrant can attack a perceived soft spot in the market, whereas a defending firm may have to defend everywhere.

Of course, a late entrant has some obvious disadvantages. At this stage several competitors have become established in the market and there are reduced opportunities.

Niche.   A niche strategy simply means finding a distinguishable market segment, identifiable by size, need, and objective, and to dominate it. This is done by concentrating all resources on fulfilling the needs of this particular niche and no other. This strategy can work because a niche may not be large enough to be worthwhile to larger competitors. This is a real advantage because the organization that practices a niching strategy may be smaller, yet be a king in its niche. It becomes a "big frog" in its chosen small pond. But even very large companies can employ a niche strategy. For example, the Canadian company Bombardier, Inc. is the world's number-three builder of civilian aircraft and has captured 56 percent of the global market of aircraft for regional airlines. According to Bombardier's CEO Robert Brown, Bomardier's strategy is to enter only select market niches in which it can be the number-1 or number-2 player.[3] Drucker identified three separate niching strategies: the tollgate, the specialty skill, and the specialty market.

A company attempting to dominate a particular niche with the tollgate strategy seeks to establish itself so that potential buyers cannot do without its product. This means that the product must be essential, that the risk of not using it must be greater than the cost of the product, and that the market must be eliminated so that whoever controls the niche preempts others from entrance.

---

[3] William H. Miller, "After 33 Years, a New Leader," *Industry Week* (July 5, 1999).

One maker of a small valve needed in all oxygen masks for fliers had strong patents protecting it. Although many companies manufactured oxygen masks, all had to use that particular valve. The niche was too small for other companies to pay the price to get in.

The specialty skill strategy can be used when a company has a particular skill that is lacking in other organizations. A management consultant who has acquired a particular skill in locating venture capital through contacts, knowledge, or other expertise usually has developed a particular niche that others cannot enter.

Then there is the specialty market strategy. This is somewhat akin to the specialty skill strategy; however, rather than a unique skill, it capitalizes on a unique market. One of my students was general manager of a mail-order company selling unique products to physicians. The company followed this niche strategy, selling to this specialty market.

Drucker notes that the danger is that the specialty market will become a larger market and therefore more attractive to larger competitors. This is what happened to Osbourne and some of the early computer manufacturers. The market grew rapidly from a limited number of business and professional users. This encouraged larger manufacturers like IBM to develop strategies that overcame the nicher's leads.

Dimension.   Another alternative for new market penetration is vertical versus horizontal expansion. Vertical penetration involves combining two or more stages of the production or marketing processes under a single ownership. Thus a farm that formerly sold its chickens to a food processor, buys a processor and sells prepared chickens to a retail store.

In a sense, vertical integration can be a type of niching. It also has the advantage of a narrow focus that can make marketing activities easier and more effective by the concentration of resources in a certain class of market. There may also be advantages in economies of scale of combined operations. One example might be lower transaction costs owing to the purchase of a greater supply of raw materials. This could lead to bigger profits.

But vertical market penetration also has its disadvantages. There is a potential loss of specialization due to different management requirements for different types of operation in the vertical integration. Capital investment requirements and higher fixed costs will increase. Methods of management, marketing, and production may have little in common. Raising chickens doesn't require the same skills or equipment as processing them. Instead of an overall net reduced cost there may be an overall increase in costs.

Horizontal expansion means expansion into new markets. The risk here is that the new markets may not be well understood, even though the supplier is well acquainted with the product and its marketing. Horizontal expansion may have an additional advantage in greater potential for sales than in vertical integration. It is a workable strategy in those markets that are as yet untapped. It is more difficult when competitors are already established in those markets in which penetration is sought.

Both vertical and horizontal new market penetration require an investment in resources. Therefore an assessment of the investment and the potential payoff, as well as the risks and uncertainties, must be considered before a decision can be made.

Positioning.   Positioning refers to the position of the product in relation to those of competing products in the minds of the customers. The position of your product is always important. The position occupied by Rolls-Royce is different from Volkswagen's. A Brooks Brothers suit does not occupy the same position as a suit purchased at K Mart. But there are differences more subtle than these extremes. You should always have a particular position in mind and strive to achieve it with your other marketing strategy objectives.

Sometimes the positioning of the product can be the center of gravity in the whole situation and it should receive emphasis equal to those of entry, niche, and dimension strategy.

MARKET SHARE EXPANSION

There are two basic market share expansion strategies. One is product differentiation versus market segmentation. The other involves a limited versus general expansion.

Product Differentiation versus Market Segmentation.   Product differentiation and market segmentation are sometimes considered alternatives. Basically, product differentiation promotes product differences to the target market. Market segmentation is a strategy which emphasizes that subgroups of buyers may have common characteristics that can best be served individually.

Although product differentiation and market segmentation can be employed simultaneously, a company usually chooses one or the other. This is partly because successful product differentiation results in giving the marketer a horizontal share of a broad and generalized market, whereas successful market segmentation tends to produce greater sales to the market segments that have been targeted. Both involve coordinating the market with the product offered.

Product differentiation is used to gain greater sales in a large market by differentiating the product so that it is superior to its competition. In market segmentation, a product is optimized for the target markets selected. Because the product is optimal for the market segments, it is superior to its competitors' products in these markets. The strategies may occur simultaneously when two or more competitors target the same segments. Then, both may pursue a product differentiation strategy in addition to market segmentation in the segments in which they are competing.

Varying conditions tend to call for one strategy or the other; for example, marketing scientist R. William Kotruba developed the strategy selection chart shown in Figure 4-17, which illustrates the alternatives that must be considered.

Consider the size of the market. If the market segment served is already small, additional segmentation may not be possible because the financial potential is insufficiently attractive.

In some cases the consumer or buyer may be insensitive to product differences. This would also argue for a market segmentation strategy.

The stage of a product life cycle may also have an effect. As noted earlier, a new product priority is to become established in as large a market segment as possible. This would argue against a market segmentation strategy and for product differentiation.

The type of product may also be important. Oil, butter, salt, and gasoline are commodity products, which means that if these products are differentiated the variation will stand out and can be readily promoted to potential customers.

The number of competitors can affect which strategy is selected. With many competitors in the marketplace it is far more difficult to differentiate the product. Thus market segmentation strategy may be required.

Of course, we must also consider competitive strategies. If many competitors are using the strategy of market segmentation, it will be difficult to counter with a product differentiation strategy because attempting to sell to all segments simultaneously means becoming all things to all people. That's a difficult proposition. Your best strategy may be to do a little market segmenting of your own and to select your target market, along with your competitors, carefully. Conversely, if many of your competitors are using a product differentiation strategy, you probably could counter with a market segmentation strategy.

Limited versus General Expansion.   Depending on resources, objectives, and the competition, a firm can also initiate a limited or a general market share expansion. More than 100 years ago, according to Confederate General Nathan Bedford Forrest, strategy was a matter of getting there "furstest with the mostest." Thus a new product intended for introduction on a national basis had better pursue a general market share expansion rather than alert its competitors to its intentions and give them the opportunity to preempt with a general market share expansion of their own.

On the other hand, sometimes limited resources force a company to adopt a limited market share expansion strategy, or perhaps a limited market share expansion into certain areas or segments of the market. This may be because a general expansion is not possible owing to the strength of the competition.

Use product differentiation												Use market segmentation
Emphasis on Promoting Product Differences	**Strategy Selection Factors**											**Emphasis on Satisfying Market Variations**
Narrow	Size of market											Broad
							Ⓐ		Ⓑ			
	1	2	3	4	5	6	7	8	9	10		
High	Consumer sensitivity to product differences											Low
			Ⓑ					Ⓐ				
	1	2	3	4	5	6	7	8	9	10		
Introduction	Stage of product life cycle											Saturation
							Ⓐ		Ⓑ			
	1	2	3	4	5	6	7	8	9	10		
Commodity	Type of product											Distinct
	Ⓑ							Ⓐ				
	1	2	3	4	5	6	7	8	9	10		
Few	Number of competitors											Many
		Ⓑ					Ⓐ					
	1	2	3	4	5	6	7	8	9	10		
Product differentiation	Typical competitor strategies											Market segmentation
			Ⓑ	Ⓐ								
	1	2	3	4	5	6	7	8	9	10		

FIGURE 4-17.   Strategy selection chart. Ⓐ —home computers; Ⓑ —salt. Adapted from R. William Kotruba, "The Strategy Selection Chart," *Journal of Marketing* (July 1966), p. 25.

ENTRENCHMENT

Entrenchment means digging in. It is not a withdrawal strategy, nor is it one of new market penetration or market share expansion. Entrenchment may be necessary when a product is in its mature or even somewhat declining stage of the life cycle. In any case, the market is no longer expanding. Two different entrenchments are possible: repositioning and direct confrontation.

Repositioning.   Repositioning means changing the position of your product in the mind of the buyer relative to competitive products. A repositioning strategy means that you will no longer position the product where it was before, but will position it somewhere else.

Some years ago a successful men's aftershave called Hai Karate was introduced. After several years of successful sales, the market contracted. There was a general shakeout, after which few competitors were left. Hai Karate was positioned first as a brand of after-shave that was more expensive than older brands like Old Spice, Aqua Velva, and Mennen, but less expensive than the prestige brands. When the market collapsed, marketing strategy options included withdrawal and entrenchment. One alternative for entrenchment was to reposition. The product could be repositioned as a cheap brand with a lower image than that of the old brands or as a prestige brand. In this case the brand survived by being repositioned against Old Spice and other similar brands.

Did you know that Marlboro, the macho man's cigarette, was once a woman's cigarette and that Parliament, repositioned as a cigarette for all classes, was once a prestige cigarette, the Rolls-Royce of its product category?

The advantage of repositioning is finding a position in which competition is less or can be overcome more easily. Disadvantages include the cost of repositioning, promotion to make the consumer aware of the brand's new position in relation to its competitors, and possibly repackaging and establishing new distribution channels.

Direct Confrontation.   Direct confrontation means that you're going to fight it out toe-to-toe against the competition. Obviously this should never be attempted unless you are certain you are going to win. Direct confrontation usually means that you have superior resources or the ability to use your resources better than your competitors.

Reentrenchment by a direct confrontation is actually a power strategy. If you lack power that exceeds that of your competition, you shouldn't attempt it.

WITHDRAWAL

Withdrawal means that you are going to take this product out of the market. The only question is when and how. The mildest type of withdrawal is risk reduction, in which you don't withdraw the entire product or service from all geographical areas, but merely try to limit the risk of profit loss.

Going up the scale, you may consider harvesting. Harvesting implies an eventual total withdrawal but at a planned rate. You will harvest this particular product for maximum profits even as you are withdrawing from the marketplace.

Finally there is liquidation or sellout. In liquidation you are leaving the marketplace now. This strategy is adopted when there are no advantages to harvesting over a period of time and an immediate use can be found for the resources that you acquired by getting out of the marketplace immediately. Repositioning can also be a part of this strategy. Certain alternative marketing strategies tend to be more effective at different stages of the product life cycle. This is shown in Figure 4-18. A summary of the alternative strategies is contained in Figure 4-19.

SUMMARY

In this chapter you've seen the three different levels of strategy. These are strategic marketing management, marketing strategy, and marketing tactics. We examined ways of developing SMM strategies by the use of a four-cell portfolio matrix that measures factors involving business strengths and marketing attractiveness. We looked at developing marketing strategies using the product life cycle. We also considered other alternative marketing strategies, including new market penetration, market share expansion, entrenchment, and withdrawal. In preparing your market plan, it is helpful to indicate exactly what strategies you plan to use to meet the goals and objectives set. You will implement your strategies with the tactics discussed in Chapter 5.

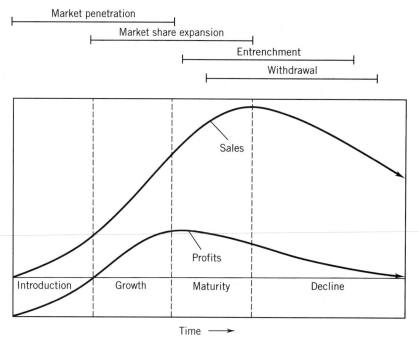

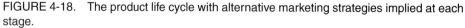

FIGURE 4-18.   The product life cycle with alternative marketing strategies implied at each stage.

I. New Market Penetration
    A. Entry
        1. First
        2. Early
        3. Late
    B. Niche
        1. Toll gate
        2. Specialty skill
        3. Specialty market
    C. Dimension
        1. Vertical
        2. Horizontal
    D. Positioning

II. Market Share Expansion
    A. Product differentiation versus market segmentation
    B. Limited versus general expansion
    C. Repositioning

III. Entrenchment
    A. Direct confrontation
    B. Repositioning

IV. Withdrawal
    A. Harvesting
    B. Risk reduction
    C. Liquidation
    D. Repositioning

FIGURE 4-19.   Marketing strategies.

CHAPTER 5

STEP 5

DEVELOPING MARKETING TACTICS

Tactics tell you how to implement the strategy you have developed. There are two general classes of tactics. The first includes marketing variables that you can control fairly easily. The second involves manipulating marketplace environs. Let's look at each in turn.

MANIPULATING THE CONTROLLABLE VARIABLES

Professor E. Jerome McCarthy in Michigan conceptualized many controllable tactics under only four categories, each beginning with the letter "p": product, price, promotion, and place. These four categories of controllable marketing variables are known as "the four Ps."

PRODUCT

Three basic things can be done with any product. It can be introduced into the marketplace, it can be modified or changed, and it can be withdrawn. Each alternative can be the best in different conditions.

A product may be introduced into the market to support a strategy of new market penetration. A tactic of product withdrawal may also support the same strategy. This is because the resources that were used to market the withdrawn product can be put to use elsewhere.

A product can also be changed or modified to alter the shape of the product's life cycle. When a product has been effectively rejuvenated in this fashion, there are a number of benefits. Goodwill toward the product and product awareness that is already established are retained. As a consequence, promotional costs for introducing and familiarizing consumers with a brand new product are unnecessary.

Other actions can be taken that will also affect your ability to implement a marketing strategy. These actions include decisions related to product quality, branding, and packaging.

Research has shown that product quality not only affects the image and the price that can be charged but also the product's profitability. This does not necessarily mean that the highest-quality product is always desired by customers. Rather that for a particular class of product or service, customers want the highest quality that they can get.

Some marketers mistakenly reduce quality to lower production costs, because they think that this increases profitability. This is incorrect. The customer wants the best that he or she can get for the money, and will reward marketers that provide it.

You must also analyze the situation carefully. During a depression or recession, when money is short, you generally expect less expensive products to be more successful, which isn't always true. During the Great Depression in 1929, cigar smokers proclaimed, "What this country needs is a good 5-cent cigar." Yet a company selling premium cigars was started right in the middle of the depression. It grew into a multimillion-dollar company while many makers of 5-cent cigars failed.

Branded products sell for much more than products that are not branded. You may have heard of Chiquita bananas and Sunkist oranges and Dole pineapples. But have you heard of TomAhtoes? TomAhtoes sell at about 30 percent per pound more than unbranded tomatoes. Clearly this is an exclusive brand.

Higher profit margins are only one reason for branding a product. Another is image and identification. Once a product's name has been planted in the mind of the consumer, it can be as important as any functional aspect of the product.

In general, there are four branding possibilities:

1. A company can use a new brand with a product or service in a category that is completely new to the company.

2. A company can introduce a new brand in a category in which the firm is already selling products.

3. A company can use a line-extension tactic in which the company's brand name is used to cover a new product as well as others already in the product line.

4. A firm can adopt a franchise extension in which a brand name familiar to the consumer is applied to products in a category that the firm has never marketed.

A new get-well card in Hallmark's line of greeting cards or a new ice-cream flavor are examples of line extension, whereas franchise extension may include Ivory shampoo and conditioner developed from Ivory soap.

There are advantages and disadvantages to each of these tactics. A brand-line extension attempts to capitalize on some of the company's valuable assets in the form of goodwill, brand name, and brand awareness. The expectation is that a synergistic effect will help to promote the old and new products under the same label.

There are disadvantages to brand extension in some situations. An inexpensive Cadillac may increase sales over the short run for individuals who wish to own a prestige car but cannot afford to pay a lot of money for it. Over the long run this tactic may cause the loss of buyers in Cadillac's traditional market segment of affluent consumers because Cadillac's high-priced, exclusive brand image would be less distinct. In the extreme, using a brand name for everything like Cadillac greeting cards or Cadillac gasoline could destroy the old brand name with no benefit to the new product.

Packaging is important to protect the product, to help promote it, and to make it stand out when displayed among many other products. In a recent year more than 5,000 new items appeared on grocery shelves. In this new-product clutter, many experts have shown that simple repackaging can increase brand identification and awareness significantly.

PRICE

Three basic pricing tactics may be followed in introducing a new product: penetration pricing, meet-the-competition pricing, and price skimming.

Penetration pricing involves entering the market with a low price that will capture as large a share of the market as possible. The lower price is emphasized as a competitive differential advantage over the competition. Once the product is well established in the marketplace, the price may be raised to be level with or even higher than the competition.

When the Nissan was introduced to the United States as a sports car under the Datsun brand name in the early 1970s, it carried a lower price than other similar sports cars. Then, as the market responded and the car became an established brand, the price was slowly raised. Now it is on the high end of the price scale for its product class.

Of course, low-price tactics may always be introduced in support of an overall strategy. Five years ago Procter & Gamble reduced its supermarket specials and replaced these promotional tactics by lower list prices on all its products. Retailers weren't pleased. They lost income due to the loss of discounts and special deals, and they responded by cutting back on purchases. However, customers bought more at the lower prices, and P&G has held steady or increased volume market-share for 38 months in a row.[1]

Meet-the-competition pricing involves introducing a product or service at about the same level as that of its competitors. When this tactic is used, you must differentiate your product in some other way. Some marketers that adopt this tactic offer higher quality or better service. Some bundle the product with several other products or benefits to increase the overall value. An entertainment system containing a TV, an AM–FM stereo, and a CD player may be priced at the price sum of the individual components. The bundling into a system provides a differential advantage. If you do not offer some competitive advantage, there is no reason for a consumer to switch from a competitive product or service.

Price skimming involves pricing a new product relatively high. Skimming is frequently done when the product or service is first in the marketplace. Computers, when first introduced, were frequently priced high, not only because of the cost of components and labor, but also because competition was almost nonexistent.

As competitors enter the market the price is usually reduced to meet their lower prices or to make it more difficult for other competition to enter the market. Moreover, additional financial resources have been accumulated because of the higher profit margin. These resources can be used to fight the competition with other tactics. A company that used the skimming tactic can spend more on promotion when competitors enter the market, and can open additional channels of distribution.

However, the price can also be raised in the face of competition. Marketing genius Joe Cossman introduced a plastic-hose, lawn-sprinkling device, consisting of a single flexible plastic tube with many holes in it. Although highly innovative, this product was easy to copy and manufacture and could not be protected by patent.

Even though the first season's market was all his, Cossman knew that competition would enter the following year at a lower price. Cossman's tactics were creative. He raised his recommended selling price and decreased the wholesale price to the retailer. Because of the larger margins offered to the retailers, Cossman shut his competitors out and maintained a market share through a second season with a higher retail price.

Other Tactical Pricing Tactics.   Other pricing tactics should also be considered. There is always the alternative of promotional versus baseline pricing. P&G decided on lower baseline prices as we saw earlier. The question is should you introduce a lower price to promote the product or maintain a standard price? Although promotional pricing can increase sales, you've got to make certain that your customers don't get confused by the two prices. If customers think of the promotional price as your standard price, you're in trouble. It will be difficult to sell at the baseline price once the promotional period has ended.

Various psychological pricing tactics are also useful and should be considered. Have you ever wondered why numbers such as $3.99 and $6.98 are used in selling products

---

[1] Zachary Schiller, Greg Burns, and Karen L. Miller, "Make It Simple," *BusinessWeek* (September 9, 1996), p. 96.

rather than $4.00 and $7.00? Psychologists have discovered that $3.99 is frequently seen as $3.00 rather than $4.00, and $6.98 as $6.00 rather than $7.00.

There are other important psychological considerations. At relatively low prices, a 10 percent difference may be perceived as significant by a potential buyer or prospect. So dropping your price 10 percent can make a real difference in sales. But if you have a higher-priced product, a 10 percent difference may not make any impact at all. So dropping a $1 product to 90 cents makes a difference. But knocking off $3 from a product selling for $30 makes no difference. Yet the $3 is 30 times the 10-cent reduction! A 10 percent price difference is simply not perceived by the prospect as significant at higher prices.

Any markdowns must be examined from the customer's viewpoint. The way to do this is to make certain that the premarkdown price is perceived as a real value for the product. You might even explain why it is in your promotion before you reveal the markdown price. Then a markdown will increase sales and the baseline price can also be restored more easily if that is your plan.

You must also consider discount pricing. Most buyers expect that the greater the quantity purchased, the lower the price. This expectation is so pervasive that if you do not discount on larger quantities, you must have valid reasons that are acceptable to the buyer.

Finally, never forget the psychological aspect of pricing's effect on image. In 1999, the children's book market exploded over a British export with an 11-year-old wizard who can cast spells as the hero. The hero's name? Harry Potter. The first two titles in a planned series of seven books have been published in 25 languages in 130 countries. Warner Bros., which controls most of the merchandising rights, and Scholastic, Inc., which controls U.S. publishing rights, were faced with a marketing problem: how to turn this incredible popularity into sustainable long-term sales. They key, they felt, was a high-class image. So the books were released initially in hard cover, and were priced at $18 a copy. And even at this price, books disappeared rapidly from bookstores.[2]

A high price denotes an expensive image and a low price, a cheaper one. The same is true of quality. In many situations where buyers must make a choice among products, many will pick the product costing the most. They may feel that this increases their chances of getting a higher-quality product.

PLACE

Place has to do with channel and distribution tactics to support. There are six basic channel alternatives to consider:

1. Direct or indirect channels
2. Single or multiple channels
3. Length of channel
4. Type of intermediaries
5. Number of distributors at each level
6. Which intermediaries to use

A direct channel means selling directly to the consumer. Perishables may spoil if they must pass through many channels. Specialty products may require a great deal of explanation and demonstration that can best be done by the manufacturer.

Sometimes the limited resources of a smaller firm may prohibit the use of a direct channel, especially when a large number of customers are widely scattered. But because reaching widely scattered customers or organizational buyers is so beneficial, larger firms may choose this alternative as well.

---

[2] Kerry Capell, Larry Light, and Ann Therese, "Just Wild About Harry Potter," *BusinessWeek* (August 9, 1999), p. 54.

The use of indirect channels includes retailers, wholesalers, industrial supply houses, manufacturer's representatives, and agents. The fact that your profit margin on each item is far lower when sold through these intermediaries may be outweighed by the fact that you can reach many more customers than would otherwise be the case. Thus your overall profit could be much greater than if you attempted to sell direct.

The choice of multiple channels means working more than one simultaneously. Because an additional channel would seem to involve more outlets for sales and more chance for selling, you may wonder why multiple channels are not always selected. There are several reasons. First, additional channels are more expensive, and this additional capital may not be available to you. Small companies with limited resources sometimes start with a single channel and expand to a greater number as more money becomes available. The same is true regarding where to distribute. A company may begin distribution locally and later expand to national distribution as more capital becomes available.

Interchannel rivalry is another reason for not always using multiple channels. Let's say you sell to retail outlets. These outlets will not be enthusiastic about your selling to other channels, particularly discount houses. Similarly, a mail-order catalog house won't want to see its product in retail stores and vice versa. So even if you decide to operate with multiple channels, you should recognize that one or more channels may not push your product aggressively. A channel could even boycott your product and refuse to handle it. Veterinarians did this to the Upjohn Company years ago when Upjohn refused to grant them exclusive use of a drug intended to cure an illness in cattle. Eventually, the company was forced to create a special product exclusively for veterinarians.

The length of the channel is based on the number of intermediaries along a single line of distribution. You don't have to sell to a retailer; you can sell to a wholesale distributor who, in turn, sells to a retailer. But your channel could be even longer. You can employ an agent or sell to a jobber who sells to a wholesaler. There is no single answer to the length of a channel. Factors to be considered include your strength as a manufacturer, the average order size, the geographic concentration of customers, seasonality of sales, geographical distance from producer to market, and the perishability of the product.

Types of intermediaries to use must also be considered. A wholesaler may be desirable when greater distribution is required over a larger area. When this is unnecessary, retailers may be preferred. A small company with limited resources may choose to work with manufacturers' representatives or agents who do not take title to the goods even though their profitability would be far greater with a sales force of their own. Why? To recruit, train, and maintain a sales force takes a lot of money and a lot of other resources. As noted earlier, many small companies lack these resources. Also, established manufacturers and agents who take a percentage of the sales price may also have the contacts and know-how to sell the product better than you could, at least in the near term.

You also need to decide on the number of distributors at each level of distribution. More distributors at each level are needed when the unit value of the product is low, the product is purchased frequently, the technical complexity of the product is high, service requirements and inventory investment are high, product differentiation is significant, the total market potential is high, geographic concentration is low, the manufacturer's current market share is high, competition is intense, and the effect on the customer's production process owing to lack of availability is significant. When these factors are absent, you'll need fewer distributors at each level.

The selection of specific intermediaries does not depend only on their track records, although this certainly is a major consideration. You must also consider the market segment served, how well the intermediary knows and understands this market, how you and the intermediary fit together in policy, strategy, and image, and whether you and the distributor understand the roles each of you play in marketing the product.

Place tactics also require decisions in regard to physical distribution of the product. These include what physical distribution services are needed, how they should be provided, and what resources are required. Warehousing, packaging for transportation, the form of transportation, and distribution points must be considered. These all involve serious trade-offs among alternatives. Only in this way can you develop the best tactical "place" decisions.

PROMOTION

Most marketers divide promotion into additional categories of face-to-face selling, sales promotion, advertising, and publicity. Face-to-face selling requires decisions involving your own sales force or using the services of an agent to sell for you. We may have considered this decision previously under distribution. If so, you need not repeat your analysis. But if you haven't considered the alternatives, now is the time.

This decision can be especially important in the early stages of a firm's growth, when limited resources may prohibit investing large sums to operate your own sales force.

Sometimes you must weigh this means of promotion against others. Never forget that you have limited resources for implementing your marketing plan. So you must weigh face-to-face selling against other ways of gaining sales.

The advantages of personal selling over other promotional methods include:

More flexibility (your salesperson can tailor the sales presentation to fit a customer's needs, behavior, and motives in special situations)

Immediate feedback from the customer (this will let you know when your appeal isn't working and must be adjusted)

Instant receipts for sales

Additional services to be rendered at the time of the sales call

Flexible time to make the sale

In developing tactics for face-to-face selling, decisions must be made regarding recruitment, compensation, and training of your sales force, the allocation of exclusive or nonexclusive sales territories and, perhaps most important, motivation of your salespeople to maximum performance.

Use of Sales Promotion Tactics.   Sales promotion is one of the hottest areas of the promotional tactic variable. Companies spend more than $60 billion annually on this tactic. And no wonder—it can be extremely effective in boosting sales. A single display at the front of a store can increase a product's sales 600 percent.

Sales promotion techniques can involve sampling, coupons, trade allowances, price quantity promotion, premiums, contests and sweepstakes, refund offers, bonus packs, stamp and continuity plans, point-of-purchase displays, and participation in trade shows. Naturally, each of these options has a cost associated with it. Therefore testing is essential to determine which work best in different situations. It is doubtful that any firm would be strong enough financially to employ all of these techniques simultaneously or even most of them. Therefore resources should be concentrated where they will have the greatest payback in implementing the mix of sales promotion tactics selected.

Sales promotion tactics are especially useful for new product introduction and during periods of high competition, when additional stimulation is necessary to increase sales.

Advertising and Publicity Tactics.   Advertising and publicity tactics are usually required. Why? Because no matter how good the product or service, there will be no sales if the potential buyer or prospect has never heard of it and therefore cannot buy. So your main objective is to make the product or service known to the market and to present it in its most favorable light in comparison with competitive products.

Some marketers believe that advertising and publicity works automatically and should be used in every marketing situation, which is not true. For one thing, advertising can be extremely expensive. No company has unlimited resources to spend on advertising everywhere simultaneously just as no firm has unlimited resources to spend on many tactics. In some cases advertising may be only marginally beneficial; in others, it may not work at all.

Cigarette advertising on television and radio came to an end on January 2, 1971. Many cigarette manufacturers claimed that sales would drop drastically. Yet sales over the next few years actually increased without the TV and radio advertising. The forced move from radio and television uncovered the amazing fact that other types of advertising were more effective. Some TV and radio advertising may have been hurting sales. Too much advertising by different manufacturers was probably canceling out the value of each others' promotion.

Publicity is sometimes touted as free advertising, with the added advantage of greater credibility because promotion seems to come from a third party. But publicity is expensive. Even a simple release involves preparation and mailing costs.

Some years ago, the promotion of a science fiction book, *Battlefield Earth,* by L. Ron Hubbard, cost a staggering $750,000. Therefore, although it definitely makes sense to consider a publicity campaign in addition to advertising, it is not "free" in the true sense of the word.

One final point about advertising and publicity: Advertising can never force a consumer to buy products or services that are not really wanted or are believed to have low value. Of course various governmental and nongovernmental regulatory agencies forbid misleading and inaccurate advertising. But the product or service must live up to its advertising or publicity claims or the customer will not buy it again. Even raising the expectations of the consumer by too much hype may cause a product to be returned or ignored in the future, even though it has technically met all the claims in its advertising.

Five key issues will determine whether your use of advertising and publicity will be successful:

1. Where to spend.
2. How much to spend.
3. When to spend.
4. What to say.
5. How to measure results.

The answers to these questions depend on your overall advertising and publicity objectives, your target market, and certain broad alternatives for reaching the advertising objective.

The broad alternative objectives you should consider are to stimulate primary demand for the product or service; to introduce unknown or new advantages or attributes; to alter the assessed importance of an existing product or service attribute; to alter the perception of a product or service; or to change the perception of competing products. Keep focused on what you are trying to accomplish.

In advertising, *media* refers to TV, radio, print, or whatever carries your message; *vehicle* is the particular TV channel and spot, magazine, or newspaper. In every case you must not only outline the cost of advertising in the media and vehicles chosen but also the expected benefits. These benefits should be quantified by sales or market share increases over a specific time period. In other words, an acceptable publicity or advertising objective would be to sell 500,000 units in three months or to capture 1 percent of the market in six months. Only in this way can you reconcile costs and benefits or determine whether results have met your expectations in your advertising and publicity tactical campaign.

Note the similarity in describing these benefits and objectives for your marketing plan.

INTERNET MARKETING TACTICS

Because the Internet has grown so much in recent years, especially as a marketing tool, incorporating it into marketing tactics should always be considered. For example, in the summer of 1999 a movie that cost $50,000 to make was more successful than *Star Wars Episode I* in per screen average sales, taking in an average of $26,500 at every screening. The movie was *The Blair Witch Project.* Made by Hollywood "nobodies" with no name actors and actresses, the movie became a blockbuster and grossed millions of dollars. What was the secret? You can find it at http://www.blairwitch.com, the Web site, and their excellent use of Internet marketing tactics.

THE PRIMARY INTERNET MARKETING TACTICS

At the present time, there are three main Internet marketing tactics. These are:

1. The World Wide Web
2. The Usenet
3. E-mail

Let's look at each in turn.

THE WORLD WIDE WEB

The World Wide Web is a giant freeway of home pages, catalogs, electronic stores, and such. It is in color, has graphics, sound, and even video is a possibility.

To place a color advertisement of multiple pages in a magazine, and run it on a month-to-month basis, is very expensive. A magazine does not have the flexibility of sound or video; but on the World Wide Web, you can do this for under three hundred dollars a year.

ESTABLISHING A WEB SITE

Although there are companies that charge several thousand dollars or more to build a Web site, software with templates allows anyone to establish a Web site. Many universities also conduct courses in this subject. Some companies maintain templates on the Web to allow you to build your own site. (One that recently came across my desk was at www.usits.com.)

I have a Web site, http://www.stuffofheroes.com, which was was developed to help promote my book *The Stuff of Heroes: The Eight Universal Laws of Leadership* (Longstreet Press, 1998). A student, who was also an instructor in the subject at a community college, developed the site. My plans are to convert the site to help promote my seminars and workshops.

MARKETING AT THE WEB SITE

Once a Web site has been established, it can be used for many purposes:

• To sell a specific product or service directly
• To maintain a catalog
• To open up a dialogue and communicate directly with customers
• To build an image as an expert in a certain field

- To conduct surveys and marketing research of your customers or prospects
- To build an e-mail list of prospects interested in certain products or services
- To announce monthly specials or sales promotions
- To provide new product information

CYBERMALLS

Cybermalls or virtual malls have been heavily promoted to potential marketers of products or services with full-page weekend newspaper advertisements, free seminars, videotapes, and other methods. They promise the ability to cash in on the "Internet marketing bonanza." This promise is rarely kept. Why not? The idea sounds good on the surface. Just like regular shopping malls, you open a store on a cybermall. The cybermall develops your site and you pay yearly "rent" for it. Most offer some sort of "training"—actually consulting to help you with marketing questions. And most cybermalls bundle various services together: e-mail boxes, free virtual banners advertising your service, and so on. Costs are high in comparison with a regular Internet service provider or ISP to put up your site—as much as $1,000 or more a year, compared with $100 to $200 for an ISP.

Is it worth the additional costs? For most marketers, I would say no. The mall theory is that (1) people come to visit the mall and stop in and buy your services just like a regular shopping mall, and (2) customers come for one thing and see your listing and go to visit your site, too. This is called "spillover."

However, the psychology of visiting a "brick and mortar" shopping mall, is not the same as the virtual mall. People go to a regular mall partly for a good time. They go to see what's new, they socialize, they have lunch, and may even go to a movie. For many it's a "day at the mall" and they "shop until they drop." Those who visit a cybermall are usually looking for something specific. Few have time to spend all day at a cybermall without the socialization with friends, spouse, or girl friend/boy friend that goes along with it. So even though the cybermall may be well promoted (and most are not), you're not going to get much business due to "walk-in customers" and the fact that you are in "a mall." Spillover in most cybermalls is limited.

HOW TO MARKET ON THE WORLD WIDE WEB

The key to World Wide Web marketing is promotion, both on-line and off-line. You've got to get prospects to your Web site. You can't rely on any search engine to do it for you. There is so much competition on the Web for any business or service, that trying to build a business based on a search engine is ludicrous. So, off-line publicity for your Web site is your primary ally.

Hot!Hot!Hot! was a Web site that sold salsa over the Internet. The owners sold out a couple of years ago. They began in 1994, so Hot!Hot!Hot! was one of the first businesses to attempt to sell anything on-line. It became hugely successful and is one of the folk heroes of the Internet. Now as it happens, the salsa business was located in Old Town, Pasadena, near my home, and I participated in some consulting for the owners of Hot!Hot!Hot! in their new business. They told me that half of their salsa business came from their Web site, the other half from their storefront.

The key even back in 1994 was not a search engine—it was publicity. One of the owners had majored in public relations in college. She tirelessly promoted the business and the Web site through articles she wrote and interviews she gave to newspapers and magazines about the uniqueness of the business and what was then the uniqueness of the Web site marketing. So any Web site marketing tactics must be in conjunction with other marketing efforts and the Web site must be promoted heavily off-line.

USING BANNERS

Banners are the color advertisements you can see floating around all over the World Wide Web. You click them, and they send you to the associated Web site. Spend advertising dollars for banners only where prospective clients hang out.

Amazon.com, the on-line bookseller, places banners all over the Web. But each banner is specific to the topic of the Web site in which it appears. Even so, probably much of their advertising dollar is wasted because frequenters of some Web sites are probably not readers or book buyers.

Banner advertising can be free by allowing a noncompetitor to exchange banner advertising privileges. In fact, there are banner exchange services. Here are a few:

- http://www.linkexchange
- http://www.smartage.com
- http://www.worldbannerexchange.com

Banners can be created at www.worlddesignservices.com or using programs at the sites listed above.

CYBERLINKS

Cyberlinks are electronic links connecting one Web site to another. You "point" using your mouse at a particular link and "click" the button on the mouse. You are immediately taken to that Web site. Like much of marketing on the World Wide Web, this a case of using proven marketing tactics in another environment. Links can be exchanged with noncompetitors.

GIVE INFORMATION AWAY

The concept of giving information away seems to confirm the belief that whatever you give away comes back to you many times over. You can put articles you have published or even a newsletter on your Web site.

One interesting twist for articles and the like is not to put the article or newsletter on your Web site directly, but to put a link whereby your client or prospect can download this information to his or her computer.

By giving information away, prospects will be attracted to return again and again, and many will become customers.

USENET MARKETING

The Usenet consists of interactive discussion groups, also called newsgroups. People participate by reading "postings" done by others, and possibly by adding their own in response. Some Usenets are screened for what is allowed to be posted and what is not. For others, it's a complete free-for-all. Each newsgroup has its own protocol and etiquette that you need to master before you market on them. A mass marketing of your services through postings would be ill-advised. That's called "spamming," and it can get you banned by some ISPs, and many won't do business with you once you do it. It's important to know the culture of the newsgroup you're dealing with before you begin to market through it.

You can reach the newsgroup through your browser. Here are a few:

- Internet Newsgroup Directory   http://internetdatabase.com/usenet.htm
- Liszt's Usenet Newsgroup Directory http://liszt.com/news/
- Newsgroup Index   http://ben-schumin.simplenet.com/newsindex/

E-MAIL MARKETING

E-mail is electronic mail. You type in a message, press a button, and your message is instantly sent anywhere in the world. With the e-mail addresses of 1,000 or 10,000 potential customers, anyone can send a message to these 1,000 or 10,000 potential customers instantly and it doesn't cost you a cent. There is one cautionary note, however. If the message is unwelcome, that's "spamming" just as with the newsgroups, and can get the marketer in a lot of trouble.

So, it looks like catch-22. There is this wonderful method of direct marketing that is instantaneous and costs nothing, but if you use it you're in trouble. There are several solutions to this problem. All depend on sending the advertisement only to someone who wants it. How can we know this?

1. Do research, offer something free, and make certain it is something the recipient will be interested in.

2. Ask visitors to the Web site if they would like to receive additional information about special offers periodically.

3. Rent e-mail lists of people who have specifically requested information about the kinds of products or services offered. These names are collected by others and rented to us.

4. Search programs are available that will search usenets for keywords and construct a mailing list from the results. These lists must be used with care. In most cases, it is better to use the e-mail to invite them to a Web site where you can advertise the product or service.

If you use either options 2 or 3, you should note in your advertisement that this was information they specifically requested. It's just a little reminder to them and lets them know that you are not "spamming."

Following are some sources and description of e-mail lists you can take a look at:

- http://www.catalog.com/vivian/
- http://www.copywriter.com/lists
- http://www.listz.com

USING E-MAIL FOR PUBLICITY

You can get a lot of mileage through publicity to media using e-mail. However, again you must be careful to avoid "spamming" or your publicity will backfire. Paul Krupin publishes *The U.S. Media E-Mail Directory* and can be reached at http://www.owt.com/dircon. He wrote a very useful article on getting news coverage, published on the Web by Hanson Marketing. Their Web site carries a lot of useful information for consultants at http://www.hansonmarketing.com.

Krupin says that the "Golden Rule" for e-mail promotion to the media is to target and personalize. He gives 10 commandments for sending e-mail to the media:

1. Think, think, think before you write. What are you trying to accomplish. Will a media professional publish it or toss it?

2. Target narrowly and carefully. Go for quality contacts, not quantity.

3. Keep it short—no more than three to four paragraphs filling one to three screens.

4. Keep the subject and content of your message relevant to your target.

5. If you are seeking publicity for a product or service, or want to get reviews for a new book or software, use a two-step approach. Query with a "hook" and news angle before transmitting the entire news release or article.

6. Tailor the submittal to the media style or content.

7. Address each e-mail message separately to an individual media target.

8. Reread, reread, and reread and rewrite, rewrite, rewrite before you click to send.

9. Be brutally honest with yourself and your media contacts—don't exaggerate or make claims you can't prove.

10. Follow-up in a timely manner with precision writing and professionalism.[3]

MANIPULATING MARKETPLACE ENVIRONS

For many years manipulating the environs for marketing tactics was largely ignored. Of course, it was recognized that demand, social and cultural factors, state of the technology, and politics and laws could be influenced. In general, however, marketing experts believed that it was far easier and less demanding for firms to attempt to manipulate the variables of product, price, promotion, and place. Thus environmental variables were assumed to be uncontrollable.

More recently the possibility of changing the context in which the organization operates, in terms of constraints on the marketing function and limits on the marketing organization, were investigated. Researchers found that these conditions can be used effectively and less expensively than was imagined.

The bottom line is that you should consider environmental marketing tactics as a possible alternative. Consider a company engaging in a private legal battle with a competitor on the grounds of deceptive advertising, or efforts to lobby for a particular political action before Congress to ensure a more favorable business environment or to limit competition. Two marketing scientists, Carl P. Zeithaml and Valerie A. Zeithaml, did a great deal of work in this field and prepared a framework for environmental management tactics. Their division of these tactics into independent, cooperative, and strategic subcategories is shown in Figure 5-1.

TACTICAL QUESTIONS FOR THE MARKETING PLAN

The form shown in Figure 5-2 contains questions in each of the areas discussed in this chapter—product, price, promotion, and place as well as in the use of the marketing environs to develop tactics. Completing this form will assist you in considering the trade-offs to develop powerful marketing tactics for your marketing plan.

SUMMARY

In this chapter you have learned how to develop marketing tactics to implement the strategies that you selected in Chapter 4. Marketing tactics have to do with your manipulation of product, price, promotion, and place and the marketing environs. In Chapter 6 you will learn how to determine the total potential available for any given market, and to forecast sales that will result from the strategy and tactics that you selected.

---

[3] Paul J. Krupin, "Ten Tips for Using E-Mail to Get News Coverage for Business," http://www.hansonmarketing.com/guest2-ahtml.

Environmental Management Tactic	Definition	Examples
Independent Tactics		
Competitive aggression	Focal organization exploits a distinctive competence or improves internal efficiency of resources for competitive advantage.	Product differentiation. Aggressive pricing. Comparative advertising.
Competitive pacification	Independent action to improve relations with competitors.	Helping competitors find raw materials. Advertising campaigns which promote entire industry. Price umbrellas.
Public relations	Establishing and maintaining favorable images in the minds of those making up the environment.	Corporate advertising campaigns.
Voluntary action	Voluntary management of and commitment to various interest groups, causes, and social problems.	McGraw-Hill efforts to prevent sexist stereotypes. 3M's energy conservation program.
Dependence development	Creating or modifying relationships such that external groups become dependent on the focal organization.	Raising switching costs for suppliers. Production of critical defense-related commodities. Providing vital information to regulators.
Legal action	Company engages in private legal battle with competitor on antitrust, deceptive advertising, or other grounds.	Private antitrust suits brought against competitors.
Political action	Efforts to influence elected representatives to create a more favorable business environment or limit competition.	Corporate constituency programs. Issue advertising. Direct lobbying.
Smoothing	Attempting to resolve irregular demand.	Telephone company's lower weekend rates. Inexpensive airline fares on off-peak times.
Demarketing	Attempts to discourage customers in general or a certain class of customers in particular, on either a temporary or a permanent basis.	Shorter hours of operation by gasoline service stations.
Cooperative Tactics		
Implicit cooperation	Patterned, predictable, and coordinated behaviors.	Price leadership.
Contracting	Negotiation of an agreement between the organization and another group to exchange goods, services, information, patterns, etc.	Contractual vertical and horizontal marketing systems.
Co-optation	Process of absorbing new elements into the leadership or policymaking structure of an organization as a means of averting threats to its stability of existence.	Consumer representatives, women, and bankers on boards of directors.
Coalition	Two or more groups coalesce and act jointly with respect to some set of issues for some period of time.	Industry association. Political initiatives of the Business Roundtable and the U.S. Chamber of Commerce

FIGURE 5-1. A framework of environmental management strategies. From "Environmental Management: Revising the Markets Perspective," by Carl P. Zeithaml and Valerie A. Zeithaml, *Journal of Marketing* (Spring 1984), pp. 50–57. Used with permission.

Environmental Management Tactic	Definition	Examples
	Strategic Maneuvering	
Domain selection	Entering industries or markets with limited competition or regulation coupled with ample suppliers and customers; entering high growth markets.	IBM's entry into the personal computer market. Miller Brewing Company's entry into the light beer market.
Diversification	Investing in different types of businesses, manufacturing different types of products, vertical integration, or geographic expansion to reduce dependence on single product, service, market, or technology.	Marriott's investment in different forms of restaurants. General Electric's wide product mix.
Merger and acquisition	Combining two or more firms into a single enterprise; gaining possession of an ongoing enterprise.	Merger between Pan American and National Airlines. Philip Morris's acquisition of Miller Beer.

FIGURE 5-1.   *Continued*

PRODUCT

Product description _____

_____

_____

Life cycle stage _____

Characteristics of stage _____

_____

_____

_____

Complementary products   1. _____   2. _____

3. _____   4. _____   5. _____

Substitute products   1. _____   2. _____

3. _____   4. _____   5. _____

Package: Message _____

Size _____ Shape _____ Color _____

Function _____ Material _____

Brand: Name _____

Type of branding _____

Forecast sales volume _____

Forecast production volume _____

_____

Basic product strategy _____

_____

_____

PRICE

Objectives 1. _____   2. _____

3. _____   4. _____

Basic per unit cost of acquisition _____

Other relevant costs _____

_____

_____

_____

_____

FIGURE 5-2. Tactical questions for the marketing plan. (Copyright © 1985 by Dr. William A. Cohen. Note: This form is based on an earlier form designed by Dr. Benny Barak, then of Baruch College.)

Discount policy _____

_____

_____

Pricing strategy _____

_____

_____

Unit pricing _____

_____

_____

Forecast revenue _____

Forecast profit _____

DISTRIBUTION

Channels to be used and timing _____

_____

_____

_____

Alternative strategies: Push/pull _____

Intensive/selective/exclusive _____

PROMOTION

Positioning _____

_____

Advertising: Objectives 1. _____

2. _____ 3. _____

Campaign theme _____

_____

Copy theme _____

_____

_____

_____

Graphics and layout_____

_____

_____

_____

FIGURE 5-2. *Continued*

Media plan	Description	Length/size	Freq/dates	Cost
Newspapers	_____	_____	_____	_____
	_____	_____	_____	_____
	_____	_____	_____	_____
Magazines	_____	_____	_____	_____
	_____	_____	_____	_____
	_____	_____	_____	_____
Television	_____	_____	_____	_____
	_____	_____	_____	_____
	_____	_____	_____	_____
Radio	_____	_____	_____	_____
	_____	_____	_____	_____
	_____	_____	_____	_____
Other	_____	_____	_____	_____
	_____	_____	_____	_____
	_____	_____	_____	_____

Budget for advertising _____

Publicity: Objectives 1. _____ 2. _____

3. _____ 4. _____

Action/cost/timing

Description of action	Timing	Cost
_____	_____	_____
_____	_____	_____
_____	_____	_____
_____	_____	_____
_____	_____	_____
_____	_____	_____
_____	_____	_____
_____	_____	_____
_____	_____	_____
_____	_____	_____
_____	_____	_____
_____	_____	_____

Budget for publicity _____

Personal selling: Objectives 1. _____

2. _____ 3. _____

_____

FIGURE 5-2.   *Continued*

Sales force size and type _____

_____

_____

Sales territories _____

_____

_____

Method of compensation _____

_____

_____

Budget for personal selling _____

Sales promotion: Objectives 1. _____

2. _____ 3. _____

Methods and costs
_____

Method	Timing	Cost
_____	_____	_____
_____	_____	_____
_____	_____	_____
_____	_____	_____
_____	_____	_____
_____	_____	_____
_____	_____	_____

Budget for sales promotion _____

Summary of overall goals/costs/time to achieve of project

Goals 1. _____ 2. _____

3. _____ 4. _____

Overall cost _____ Timing _____

_____

_____

_____

_____

 FIGURE 5-2.   *Continued*

CHAPTER 6

STEP 6

FORECASTING FOR YOUR MARKETING PLAN

When you forecast, you attempt to predict the future. To a significant extent you will do this by analyzing the past. Of course, this does not necessarily mean that whatever happened in the past will continue to happen in the future, but it is here that the process of forecasting begins. Forecasting enables you to establish more accurate goals and objectives for your marketing plan. But forecasting does even more: It will help you to do all of the following:

- Determine markets for your products.
- Plan corporate strategy.
- Develop sales quotas.
- Determine whether salespeople are needed and how many.
- Decide on distribution channels.
- Price products or services.
- Analyze products and product potential in different markets.
- Decide on product features.
- Determine profit and sales potential for products.
- Determine advertising and sales promotion budgets.
- Determine the potential benefits of various elements of marketing tactics.

Sales forecasting involves decisions made in all sections of your marketing plan. As you proceed, you will see that forecasting may involve some guesswork and a great deal of managerial judgment. Nevertheless, even guesswork becomes far more valuable when supported by facts and careful analysis.

If you simply pull facts out of thin air and construct a marketing plan based on them without a logical method of proceeding, many of your basic assumptions are as likely to be wrong as right. Succeeding under these conditions would be largely a matter of luck.

In this chapter you will learn how to optimize your hunches through forecasting techniques. This will make the figures in your marketing plan far more credible. It will also greatly increase your chance of success should you actually implement your plan.

THE DIFFERENCE BETWEEN MARKET POTENTIAL, SALES POTENTIAL, AND SALES FORECAST

Market potential, sales potential, and sales forecast all mean different things. *Market potential* refers to the total potential sales for a product or service or any group of products being considered for a certain geographical area or designated market, over a specific period. Market potential relates to the total capacity of that market to absorb everything that an entire industry may produce, whether airline travel, lightbulbs, or motorcycle helmets.

Let's say that there are one million new motorcyclists every year, and that one million old motorcycle helmets wear out every year and must be discarded. The market potential for motorcycle helmets in the United States is two million helmets every year. If helmets sell for $100 each, that would be a market potential of $200 million a year.

Sales potential refers to the ability of the market to absorb or purchase the output of a single company in that industry, presumably yours. Thus, if you are a motorcycle helmet manufacturer, the ability of the market to purchase that output might be only $50 million, even though the market potential is $200 million.

The term *sales forecast* refers to the actual sales you predict your firm will realize in this market in a single year. In using our motorcycle helmet example, perhaps your sales forecast will be only $20 million, even though the market potential is $200 million for the entire industry and the sales potential $50 million for your company.

Why the difference? Why can't you reach the full market potential in sales? Sales potential may not exceed market potential because of your production capacity. You can produce only $50 million in helmets, not $200 million.

There may be many reasons for not trying to achieve 100 percent of the sales potential of which you are capable. Perhaps selling to the entire market would require more money than you have available for your marketing campaign.

Maybe the return on your investment to reach your full sales potential is insufficient to make this a worthwhile objective. To achieve 100 percent of anything requires consideration of the law of diminishing returns. This means that the marginal cost of each additional percentage point becomes greater and greater as you try to achieve the full sales potential. Therefore it may be better to stop at 90, 80, or even 70 percent of your sales potential, because the significantly higher costs of achieving those final percentage points to get to 100 percent make the goal less desirable. There may be far better uses for your resources because the return on each dollar you invest elsewhere may be greater.

Finally, there may be some other reason that will discourage you from achieving 100 percent. Maybe competition is particularly strong. Perhaps there is an unfavorable factor in the marketing environment, such as a state law that requires cyclists to wear helmets being repealed.

Nevertheless, we must know the market potential and sales potential before we can calculate our sales forecast.

FINDING MARKET POTENTIAL

Sometimes it is possible to find the market potential for a specific product through research already done by someone else. Such research may have been previously done by the U.S. government, a trade association, or an industry magazine. At other times it is necessary to derive the market potential for your products by using a chain of information. This latter method is called a chain ratio and involves connecting many related facts to arrive at the total market potential you are seeking.

Some years ago, I wanted to explore the market potential for body armor used by foreign military forces for an export project. Because only a few countries used this equipment at that time, this number had to be determined by a chain ratio method.

First, I calculated the number of units of body armor used by U.S. military forces. I used a government publication called the *Commerce Business Daily,* which lists contracts awarded for most government purchases. An average number of body armor units per year was derived from a look at purchases over several years.

Next I researched the size of the U.S. Army during that period. From the total annual sales of body armor to the U.S. Army and the average size of the ground forces during the same period, a ratio of body armor units per soldier could be developed.

Then, I consulted the *Almanac of World Military Power,* which listed the strength of military forces for all countries. Because the body armor was an export military item, the sale of it is controlled by the U.S. government. Therefore only those countries for which sales were likely to be approved by the U.S. government were included.

I added the figures for each country and calculated the total. Next, I took the ratio of body armor units per soldier developed earlier from U.S. data and applied it to this figure. The result was a total market potential of military body armor for export from the United States to foreign armies.

Note that this was not the sales potential for the sale of body armor by any single company for this market, nor was it a forecast of what body armor would be sold. It was the market potential for sales from the United States.

As another example, let's say that a dance studio wishes to know the market potential for dance students in its geographical area. The first step would be to note the total population in the area served by the studio. If the area has a 5-mile circumference, you will want to know its population. These population figures can be obtained from the census surveys of the Department of Commerce. Your local Chamber of Commerce may have this information, or surveys may have been done by local or state governments.

Once you know the population, the next step is to arrive at the per capita expenditure for dancing lessons. Again, government statistics may be helpful. Industry associations of dance studios may be able to provide this information. You might also look for trade magazines geared toward professional dance and studio management. Naturally you must be sure that the geographical information furnished corresponds closely with the geographical area you are analyzing. Per capita expenditure can differ greatly, depending on the region of the country, its culture and climate, and the habits and interests of its people.

By multiplying the population in the 5-mile area by the per capita expenditure for dance lessons, you will end up with a total annual expenditure.

As you can see, the market potential for any product or class of product or service can be determined by doing a little detective work. Think about how you might get the market potential that is not readily available by linking other available information.

THE INDEX METHOD OF CALCULATING MARKET POTENTIAL

An alternate way of calculating market potential is by the use of indexes that have already been constructed from surveys and basic economic data. One example is the survey published by *Sales and Marketing Magazine,* which publishes a survey of buying power indexes every year. They develop commercial indexes by combining estimates of population, income, and retail sales. This results in a positive indicator of consumer data demand according to regions of the U.S. Bureau of Census by state, by its organized system of metro areas by counties, or even by cities with larger populations. Multiply the resulting buying power index (BPI) by national sales figures to obtain the market potential for any local area.

Let's say that you sell a certain brand of national television but only in the local area in your own city store. The manufacturer claims that 10 million units are sold every year. Now you want to calculate the market potential for your city. By taking the listed BPI and multiplying it by 10 million, you get market potential for your city. *Sales and Marketing Magazine's* methodology also permits you to calculate the market potential with a custom BPI depending on demographics of your target market and your geographical area.

The BPI can also be used as a relative indicator to compare the potential buying power of the market you have targeted for your product. You can calculate a custom BPI for each market targeted.

Once you have the market potential, you can calculate sales potential by deciding how much of this market potential "belongs" to your firm. With no competition, perhaps it's all yours. But again, you must consider your capacity for satisfying the entire market. Once you have sales potential, you can turn to forecasting.

BOTTOM-UP AND TOP-DOWN SALES FORECASTING

There are two basic ways to forecast sales: the bottom-up and top-down methods. With the bottom-up method the sequence is to break up the market into segments and forecast each separately. You sum the sales forecast in each segment for the total sales forecast. Typical ways of doing this are by sales-force composites, industry surveys, and intention-to-buy surveys. We'll look at each of these later in the chapter.

To accomplish top-down forecasting the sales potential for the entire market is estimated, sales quotas are developed, and a sales forecast is constructed. Typical methods used in top-down surveys are executive judgment, trend projections, a moving average, regression, exponential smoothing, and leading indicators. Let's look at each of these forecasting methods first.

EXECUTIVE JUDGMENT

Executive judgment is known by a variety of names, including "jury of executive opinion," "managerial judgment," and even "gut feeling." With this method you just ask executives who have the expertise. This could be many individuals or one single person who may be responsible for the program. This method of forecasting is fairly easy to use, but it is not without risks. Experts on anything have differing biases and differing opinions.

To overcome individual bias, some unusual methods have evolved. Perhaps the best known is the Delphi method, in which experts are assembled and their opinion asked. Instead of stating this opinion verbally, it is written down anonymously, along with the reasons behind it. A facilitator analyzes the results and calculates the range of answers, the frequency of each answer, the average, and indicates the reasons given. This summary is returned to the group of experts. A second round is then conducted and the same questions are asked. This process may be repeated several times until a group consensus emerges to result in the final forecast.

This method is effective because it enables expert opinion and reasoning to be shared without many of the psychological "hang-ups" of a public debate or alteration of opinion. It eliminates many psychological barriers inherent in roundtable discussions that might block legitimate input, such as relative power. The Delphi method has been a useful and accurate method of using executive judgment in forecasting.

SALES FORCE COMPOSITE

A sales force composite can be obtained by assigning each of your salespeople the duty of forecasting sales potential for a particular territory. These territorial estimates are then summed to arrive at an overall forecast. The dangers in obtaining a forecast this way are based on the possibility that customers may not be entirely truthful in giving information to the salesperson. Also, the salesperson may overstate or understate the area's potential.

Why would a salesperson do this? Perhaps fear of being assigned sales quotas that are difficult to reach may cause the potential to be understated. Or the salesperson may overstate the potential to prevent the area from being eliminated.

If you have a new business, you may be unable to use this method because you have no sales force.

TREND PROJECTIONS

A trend projection in its simplest form is an analysis of what has already happened, extended into the future. Your recorded observations of past sales may reveal that they have increased on an average of 10 percent every year. A simple trend projection would assume that sales will increase by 10 percent for the coming year as well.

If sales two years ago were $100,000 and last year, $300,000, and you projected the trend into the future by percentage, you would estimate $900,000 for next year. You might also estimate an increase in sales in absolute terms. If you did, you would estimate an increase of $200,000 each year. So next year's sales would be $500,000. The type of linear projection to be used depends on your circumstances. You need to find out why you achieved the previous increase. If the reason can be related more to a percentage, then that's the way to do your trend analysis projection. If not, an absolute dollar increase may provide a more accurate forecast.

A moving average is a more sophisticated trend projection. With this approach the assumption is made that the future will be an average of past performance rather than a linear projection. This minimizes the danger of a random event or element that could create a major impact on the forecast and cause it to be in error. Possibly a salesperson made a huge, unusual sale.

I met a young real estate salesman who sold an $18 million property three months after he started in the business. He was even written up in the local newspapers. It would have been unwise for his organization to create a sales forecast for the following year without some consideration that this type of event was unusual and unlikely to be repeated.

What can we do to take care of unusual events like this? Let's look at what would happen to our forecast using a moving average. The average of $100,000 and $300,000 for two years is $200,000—you would forecast $200,000 for the coming year. The moving average is simply summing up the sales in a number of periods and dividing by that number.

Which is the "correct" method of trend projection? That's what makes marketing and forecasting so much fun. There isn't a correct method. You've got to consider other factors to help you decide which is best for your situation.

Again, if you have no track record, you can't use this method.

INDUSTRY SURVEY

In the industry survey method companies that make up the industry for a particular product or service are surveyed. The industry survey method has some of the characteristics of the bottom-up method, rather than the top-down, and some of the advantages and disadvantages of executive opinion and sales-force composites. Representatives of companies may give inaccurate answers. One way to minimize this is to make certain you talk to the right people. Some employees who want to help may not have access to accurate information, but will try to give you some answer anyway. At other times, companies consider information highly proprietary. However, sometimes you can gather useful information or you may get helpful data from industry associations or trade magazines.

Naturally, no one is going to do your forecasting for you, but you may be able to obtain information regarding the norm for salespeople in the industry and geographical area you're interested in. You then apply this or similar information to work out your forecast.

REGRESSION ANALYSES

A regression analysis may be linear or it may involve multiple regression. With linear regression, relationships between sales and a single independent variable are developed to forecast sales data. With multiple regression, relationships between sales and a number of independent variables are used. Computer programs are available to assist you in doing these calculations.

Sales predictions are made by estimating the values for independent variables and incorporating them into the multiple regression equation. Thus, if a relationship can be found among various independent variables—for example, units of computers sold, number of males between the ages of 36 and 55, average family income, rate of inflation, and per capita years of education—a multiple regression equation based on this information can be developed to predict sales for the coming year.

INTENTION-TO-BUY SURVEY

The intention-to-buy survey is done before the introduction of a new product or new service or for the purchase of any product or service for some future period. The main problem with these surveys is that individuals may not always give accurate information regarding their intention to buy products or services in the future. So what's new? you may ask. What is it this time?

Inaccurate responses may be due to an inadequate explanation, a misunderstanding on the part of the respondent, or to other psychological factors, such as the individual's unwillingness to offend or a desire to respond in a socially acceptable way.

Face-to-face surveys regarding sexually explicit reading matter frequently indicate almost no intent to purchase. Yet, *Playboy* magazine is a multimillion-dollar business with a large number of readers and subscribers.

Also, there is something about actually making the purchase that distinguishes it from intending to do so. The respondent may have truly believed he or she would buy if the product were available. When it comes to the moment of truth, however, there may be reasons that this person never thought of to interfere with the sale.

EXPONENTIAL SMOOTHING

Exponential smoothing is a timed series approach similar to the moving average method of trend analysis. Instead of a constant set of weights for the observations, however, an exponentially increasing set of weights is used to give the more recent values more weight than the older values.

This is exponential smoothing in its most basic form. More sophisticated models include adjustments for factors like trend and seasonal patterns, and such. Forecasting techniques based on exponential smoothing are available on various computer programs. So you don't need to be a mathematical wizard; just be able to put the disk in your computer and follow the directions.

LEADING INDICATORS

Leading indicators to predict recessions and recoveries are used by the National Bureau of Economic Research. Typical leading indicators reported by this bureau include the prices of 500 common stocks, new orders for durable goods, an index of net business formation, corporate profits after taxes, industrial material prices, and changing consumer installment credit.

The problem of forecasting sales with these leading indicators is in relating them to specific products or services. When relationships are found, a multiregression model can be constructed. In fact, leading indicators are incorporated into some computer programs available for forecasting.

You can make rudimentary guesses based on leading economic indicators and apply them to your forecast. Many times this will have as good a chance of being correct as an expensive computer model.

Method	Regular Use (%)	Occasional Use (%)	Never Used (%)
Jury of executive opinion	52	16	5
Sales force composite	48	15	9
Trend projections	28	16	12
Moving average	24	15	15
Industry survey	22	20	16
Regression	17	13	24
Intention-to-buy survey	15	17	23
Exponential smoothing	13	13	26
Leading indicators	12	16	24

FIGURE 6-1. Utilization of sales forecasting methods by 175 firms. Adapted from Douglas J. Dalrymple, "Sales Forecasting Methods and Accuracy," *Business Horizons, 18* (December 1975), p. 71.

WHICH METHOD TO USE

Some methods are more popular in forecasting than others. A survey of 175 firms conducted some time ago indicated that the jury of executive opinion and sales force composite were the two most popular. (This is shown in Figure 6-1.) Another study, which confirms that the executive opinion method is still the most popular, found that the two quantitative methods, time-series smoothing and regressional analysis, were in second and third place, respectively, with sales force composite following.

Consideration of a sales forecasting method for your particular situation and for your marketing plan should not be based merely on popularity of the method, but on situational factors that affect you. These factors include the resources that you have available, the time available, accuracy required, your estimation of the accuracy that can be attained by different methods given to your sales force, your customers, the individuals surveyed, and the cost of the forecast. Thus your judgment in choosing a sales forecasting method, or a combination of methods, is of primary importance.

Alvin Toffler, author of *Future Shock* and *The Third Wave,* probably said it best: "You can use all the quantitative data you can get, but you still have to distrust it and use your own intelligence and judgment."

YOU NEED MORE INFORMATION FOR YOUR FORECAST

Forecasting sales alone is insufficient. You must also forecast the costs involved and when they occur. This is done with a project development schedule, a break-even analysis, a balance sheet, a projected profit-and-loss statement, and cash-flow projections. Let's look at each in turn.

THE PROJECT DEVELOPMENT SCHEDULE

The project development schedule, or PDS, shown in Figure 6-2, lists every task necessary to implement the project and the money spent during each period. These periods can be months or, in the case of the example indicated, weeks. Note that you need not know the exact date you will begin in order to develop an accurate PDS. All you need to do is describe the timing as "weeks or months after project initiation." If many different departments or individuals are involved, you can include them all to see who is doing what. By incorporating the amount of money spent by each, you will see totals spent by each department, totals spent for each task, and when money is needed for each task.

Task	Months After Project Initiation											
	1	2	3	4	5	6	7	8	9	10	11	12
Manufacture of units for test manufacturing	$5,000 →											
Initial advertisement in test area	$10,000	$10,000	$10,000 →									
Shipment of units in test market area	$300	$200 →										
Analysis of test		$500	$700	$200 →								
Manufacture of units—1st year				$5,000	$10,000	$10,000	$10,000	$10,000 →				
Phase I advertising and publicity				$10,000	$30,000	$30,000	$15,000 →					
Shipment of units					$1,000	$1,000	$1,000	$1,000	$500 →			
Phase II advertising								$10,000	$10,000	$5,000	$5,000	$5,000 →

FIGURE 6-2. Project development schedule.

The project development schedule shows your entire plan financially and graphically. It will reveal problems in timing, financing, and coordination before you start. Once you begin to implement the plan, it will help you to monitor and control the project.

THE BREAK-EVEN ANALYSIS

A break-even analysis is used for evaluating relationships among sales revenues, fixed costs, and variable costs. The break-even point is the point at which the sales from a number of units sold cover costs of developing, producing, and selling the product. Prior to this point, you will be losing money. Beyond it you will make money. Break-even analysis is an excellent means for helping you forecast both the success of the product and what you need to succeed before the project is actually initiated because it will tell you the following:

- How many units you must sell in order to start making money.

- How much profit you will make at any given level of sales.

- How changing your price will affect profitability.

- How cost increases or reductions at different levels of sales will affect profitability.

Combining your sales forecasts with break-even analysis will tell you how long it will take you to reach break-even.

To accomplish a break-even analysis, separate the cost associated with your project into two categories: fixed costs and variable costs.

Fixed costs are those expenses associated with the project that you would have to pay whether you sold one unit or 10,000 units or, for that matter, whether you sold any units at all.

If you need to rent a building to implement your project and the owner of the building charges you $50,000, this would be a fixed cost. You would have to pay the $50,000 whether you sold no units or millions of units. Research and development costs for a project or a product are also considered fixed costs. You have to spend this money whether or not you sell any of the product.

Variable costs are those that vary directly with the number of units you sell. If postage for mailing your product to a customer is $1, then $1 is a variable cost. If you sell 10 units, then your postage is 10 times $1, or $10. If you sell 100 units, your total variable costs for postage would be 100 times $1 or $100.

It is sometimes difficult to decide whether to consider costs as fixed or variable, and there may not be a single correct answer. Use judgment, along with the advice of financial or accounting experts if they are available. As a general guideline, if there is a direct relationship between cost and number of units sold, consider the cost as variable. If you cannot find such a relationship, consider the cost fixed. The total cost of your project will always equal the sum of the fixed costs plus the variable costs.

Here's an example of an item that you are going to sell for $10. How much profit would you make if you sold 1,000 units?

Fixed Costs

Utility expense at $100 per month for 36 months	$3,600
Telephone at $200 per year for three years	600
Product development costs	1,000
Rental expense	2,500
Total fixed costs	$7,700

Variable Costs

Cost of product	$1.00 per unit
Cost of postage and packaging	0.50 per unit

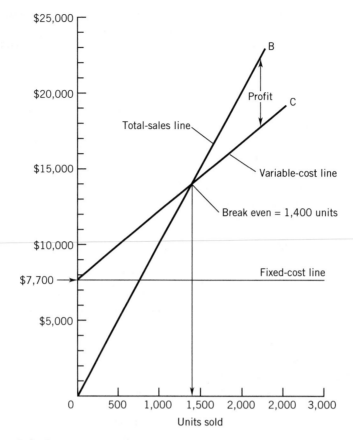

FIGURE 6-3.   Break-even analysis chart.

| Cost of advertising | 3.00 per unit |
| Total variable costs | $4.50 per unit |

To calculate the break-even point, start with the equation for profit. Total profit equals the number of units sold times the price at which they are being sold, less the number of units sold multiplied by the total variable cost, less the total fixed cost.

If P stands for profit, and p for price, and U equals the number of units sold, V equals variable costs, and F equals fixed costs, then our equation becomes

$$P = (U \times p) - (U \times V) - F$$

You can simplify this to

$$P = U(p - V) - F$$

Substituting the values given in your example, you have

$$P = \$1,000 (\$10 - \$4.50) - \$7,700$$
$$= \$5,500 - \$7,700 = -\$2,200$$

The significance of the minus is that instead of making a profit at the particular number of units you have estimated, you have lost $2,200.

If you want to know how many units you must sell in order to reach the break-even point, you can again use the equation for profit:

$$P = U(p - V) - F$$

Because profit at the break-even point is by definition zero, you can transpose terms and let $P = 0$. Then the break-even point equals F divided by $p - V$.

Because you know that $F = \$7,700$, $p = \$10.00$ and $V = \$4.50$, the break-even point must equal \$7,700 divided by \$10.00 $-$ \$4.50. That's \$7,700/5.50 or 1,400 units.

This means that if you don't change price or reduce expenses, you must sell 1,400 units of the product before you can start realizing a profit.

You can calculate this graphically by using the chart in Figure 6-3. A break-even chart has an advantage over using the break-even equation. It shows you the relationship between profits and sales volume graphically. It is therefore easier to see how cost and other factors affect the results.

Even though there are advantages to break-even analysis, keep in mind that there are some limitations. First, break-even analysis shows profit at various levels of sales, but does not show the return for investment and other measures of financial efficiency. Because there are always alternative uses for a firm's financial resources, it is impossible to compare return on investment solely on the basis of break-even analysis. Also, break-even analysis does not allow you to examine the cash flow. One way to compare investment or capital budgeting alternatives is to consider the value of the cash flows over a period of time and to discount the cost of capital by an appropriate percentage. You can't do this with a break-even analysis alone because the time to reach the various levels of sales is not indicated.

Despite these shortcomings, break-even analysis is a useful technique and should always be included as a part of your marketing plan.

THE BALANCE SHEET, PROJECTED PROFIT-AND-LOSS STATEMENT, AND CASH-FLOW PROJECTIONS

Although a balance sheet is usually calculated for businesses, it can also be calculated for a project. Basically, it consists of financial snapshots of two or more different points in your project. Most people select start-up and at least one other important milestone in the project.

In Figure 6-4, a balance sheet form is shown for Year 1 and Year 2. Current assets, fixed assets, other assets, current liabilities, and long-term liabilities are calculated to arrive at a total net worth.

The projected profit-and-loss statement is shown in Figure 6-5. It is broken down on a monthly basis. Total net sales, the cost of sales, and gross profit must be documented. Also note controllable expenses and fixed expenses and develop a net profit or loss before taxes for every month. This may be done only for a single year or it can be done for up to five years into the future, depending on the project.

The profit-and-loss statement along with the cash-flow projections in Figure 6-6 will show what happens between balance sheets. The latter displays cash, income, and expenses on a monthly basis from start-up. Do these cash-flow projections for the same number of years that you did the profit-and-loss statement.

A cash-flow projection shows the availability of cash on a monthly basis. If you need additional cash to keep your project going, it will show when the money will be needed. Obviously this will not only be of great interest to you, but also to your potential investors or company finance officers. They will want to know not only how much is needed, but when.

SUMMARY

In this chapter you have seen how to forecast everything you need for your marketing plan. You have seen how to calculate market potential, sales potential, and sales forecasts. You have seen how to forecast costs to develop a project development schedule with costs recorded periodically as needed, how to complete a break-even chart to determine how

BALANCE SHEET

	Year 1	Year 2
Current Assets		
Cash		
Accounts receivable		
Inventory		
Fixed Assets		
Real estate		
Fixtures and equipment		
Vehicles		
Other Assets		
Licenses		
Goodwill		
Total Assets		
Current Liabilities		
Notes payable (due within 1 year)		
Accounts payable		
Accrued expenses		
Taxes owed		
Long-Term Liabilities		
Notes payable (due after 1 year)		
Other		
Total Liabilities		
Net Worth (Assets minus Liabilities)		

Total Liabilities plus Net Worth Should Equal Assets

FIGURE 6-4. Balance sheet.

PROJECTED PROFIT AND LOSS STATEMENT

	Month 1	Month 2	Month 3	Month 4	Month 5	Month 6	Month 7	Month 8	Month 9	Month 10	Month 11	Month 12
Total Net Sales												
Cost of sales												
Gross profit												
Controllable expenses: salaries												
Payroll taxes												
Security												
Advertising												
Automobile												
Dues and subscriptions												
Legal and accounting												
Office supplies												
Telephone												
Utilities												
Miscellaneous												
Total Controllable Expenses												
Fixed expenses: depreciation												
Insurance												
Rent												
Taxes and licenses												
Loan payments												
Total Fixed Expenses												
Total Expenses												
Net profit (loss) (before taxes)												

FIGURE 6-5.   Projected profit and loss statement.

CASH-FLOW PROJECTIONS

	Start-up or prior to loan	Month 1	Month 2	Month 3	Month 4	Month 5	Month 6	Month 7	Month 8	Month 9	Month 10	Month 11	Month 12	TOTAL
Cash (beginning of month)														
Cash on hand														
Cash in bank														
Cash in investments														
Total Cash														
Income (during month): Cash sales														
Credit sales payments														
Investment income														
Loans														
Other cash income														
Total income														
Total Cash and Income														
Expenses (during month): Inventory or new material														
Wages (including owner's)														
Taxes														
Equipment expense														
Overhead														
Selling expense														
Transportation														
Loan repayment														
Other cash expenses														
Total Expenses														
Cash Flow Excess (end of month)														
Cash Flow Cumulative (monthly)														

FIGURE 6-6. Cash-flow projections.

many units you need to sell to be profitable, how to determine how much money you earned at any level of units sold, how to complete a balance sheet that indicates the status of your project at the end of various periods of time, and how to calculate a profit-and-loss statement and cash-flow projections on a monthly basis.

No marketing plan can be implemented without financial resources. The forecasts discussed in this chapter will enable you to know what financial resources are necessary, as well as the benefits that will accrue as a result of investing these resources.

You are now in a position to calculate important financial ratios and to use them to help determine how efficient your plan is and how beneficial it is to the firm compared with other alternatives. Knowledge of these financial ratios will help you to get resources from those in authority in your company or from outside lenders. They will add tremendous credibility to your plan. We will learn how to calculate them in the next chapter.

STEP **7**

CALCULATING IMPORTANT FINANCIAL RATIOS FOR YOUR MARKETING PLAN

The financial ratios in this chapter will help provide the information so that you, or others, can compare your plan with competing plans on a financial basis. They will enable you to better understand the financial efficiency of your plan and will help you to win support for your project. To do this your planned figures must be analyzed. If you implement your marketing plan, you can analyze what is actually happening, in part by using these financial ratios.

Some of these ratios are used primarily to measure the financial condition of an entire business, rather than a single project. However, with many marketing plans, especially start-ups, the project and the business are one and the same. You must decide which ratios are applicable to your situation and which are not.

MEASURES OF LIQUIDITY

Liquidity is the ability to use the money available. In general, the more liquid, the better the state of financial health. The ratios intended to measure liquidity will tell you whether you have enough cash on hand, plus assets that can be readily turned into cash, to pay debts that may fall due during any given period.

THE CURRENT RATIO

The current ratio is possibly the best-known measure of financial health. It answers this question: Does your business have sufficient current assets to meet current debts with a margin of safety for possible losses due to uncollectible accounts receivable and other factors?

The current ratio is computed by using information on your balance sheet. Divide current assets by current liabilities. Look at the sample balance sheet in Figure 7-1. Current assets are $155,000 and current liabilities are $90,000; $155,000 divided by $90,000 equals a current ratio of 1.7.

Is 1.7 a "good" current ratio? You cannot determine this from the numerical value of 1.7 by itself. There is a popular rule of thumb which says that a current ratio of at least 2.0 is wanted. However, a desirable current ratio is very dependent on your business and the specific characteristics of your current assets and liabilities. That's why a comparison with other current ratios is a better indication. Sources for this information appear in the section "Sources of Ratio Analyses from All Industries" later in the chapter.

If after analysis and comparison you decide that your current ratio is too low, you may be able to raise it by the following actions:

1. Increase your current assets by new equity contributions.

2. Try converting noncurrent assets into current assets.

3. Pay some of your debts.

4. Increase your current assets from loans or other types of borrowing which have a maturity of at least a year in the future.

5. Put some of the profits back into the business.

December 31, 20_____

BALANCE SHEET

Current assets:		
Cash	$ 35,000.00	
Accounts receivable	55,000.00	
Inventory	60,000.00	
Temporary investments	3,000.00	
Prepaid expenses	2,000.00	
Total current assets		$155,000.00
Fixed assets:		
Machinery and equipment	$ 35,000.00	
Buildings	42,000.00	
Land	40,000.00	
Total fixed assets		$117,000.00
Other assets:		
None		
Total other assets		0
Total assets		$272,000.00
Current liabilities		
Accounts payable	$ 36,000.00	
Notes payable	44,000.00	
Current portion of long-term notes	4,000.00	
Interest payable	1,000.00	
Taxes payable	3,000.00	
Accrued payroll	2,000.00	
Total current liabilities		$ 90,000.00
Long-term liabilities:		
Notes payable	$ 25,000.00	
Total long-term liabilities		$ 25,000.00
Equity:		
Owner's equity	$115,000.00	
Total equity		$115,000.00
Total liabilities and equity		$272,000.00

FIGURE 7-1.   Sample balance sheet for the XYZ Company.

THE ACID TEST, OR "QUICK," RATIO

The acid test, or "quick," ratio is also a measurement of liquidity. This ratio is calculated as follows: cash plus government securities plus receivables divided by current liabilities.

The company shown in Figure 7-1 has no government securities. Therefore the numerator of this figure becomes $35,000 cash plus $55,000 in accounts receivable, or $90,000. This is divided by current liabilities on the same balance sheet of $90,000 to result in an acid test ratio of 1.0.

The quick ratio concentrates on extremely liquid assets whose values are definite and well known. So the quick ratio answers this question: If all your sales revenue disappears tomorrow, can you meet current obligations with your cash or quick funds on hand? Usually an acid test ratio of approximately 1.0 is considered satisfactory. However, you must also make this decision conditional on the following:

1. There should be nothing to slow up the collection of your accounts receivable.
2. The receipt of accounts receivable collections should not trail the due schedule for paying your current liabilities. In checking out this timing, you should consider payment of your creditors sufficiently early to take advantage of any discounts which are offered.

If these two conditions are not met, you will need an acid test ratio higher than 1.0. It is a mistake to believe that the current or the acid test ratio should always be as high as possible. Only those from whom you have borrowed money would agree. Naturally, they are interested in the greatest possible safety of their loan. However, you do not want to have large sums of money lying idle and not earning additional profits. If you do have idle cash balances and receivables and inventories that are out of proportion to your needs, you should reduce them.

Be conservative enough to keep a safety pad and yet bold enough to take advantage of the fact that you have these resources that can be used to earn additional profits. Before making the decision about the right amount of liquidity, consider the next two ratios: average collection period and inventory turnover.

AVERAGE COLLECTION PERIOD

The average collection period is the number of days that sales are tied up in accounts receivable. This number can be calculated by using your profit-and-loss statement or income statement as shown in Figure 7-2. Divide net sales by the days in your accounting period.

In Figure 7-2 net sales are $1,035,000, and your accounting period 365 days, which equals $2,836. This is the average sales per day in the accounting period.

Next, look at the accounts receivable you obtained from the balance sheet, Figure 7-1. Accounts receivable are $55,000. Divide $55,000 by the average sales per day in the accounting period; $55,000 divided by $2,836 equals 19.

The result (19) is the average number of days sales are tied up in receivables. It is also your average collection period. This tells you how promptly your accounts are being collected, considering whatever credit terms you are extending. It also provides other important insights. First, the quality of your accounts and notes receivable—that is, whether or not you are getting paid on time. It also shows you how good a job your credit department is doing in collecting these accounts. Now the question is whether the figure of 19 days is good or not good. A rule of thumb says the average collection period should not exceed one and one-third times the credit terms offered. Therefore, if you offer terms of 30 days to

For the year ended December 31, 20_____

INCOME STATEMENT

Sales or revenue	$1,040,000.00	
Less returns and allowances:	5,000.00	
Net sales		$1,035,000.00
Cost of sales:		
Beginning inventory, Jan. 1, 20 ___	250,000.00	
Merchandise purchases	500,000.00	
Cost of goods available for sale	750,000.00	
Less ending inventory, Dec. 31, 20 ___	225,000.00	
Total cost of goods sold		525,000.00
Gross profit		$ 510,000.00
Operating expenses:		
Selling and general and administrative		
Salaries and wages	180,000.00	
Advertising	200,000.00	
Rent	10,000.00	
Utilities	5,000.00	
Other expenses	10,000.00	
Total operating expenses		405,000.00
Total operating income		$ 105,000.00
Other revenue and expenses		0
Pretax income		$ 105,000.00
Taxes on income	50,000.00	
Income after taxes but before extraordinary gain or loss		$ 55,000.00
Extraordinary gain or loss		0
Net income (or loss)		$ 55,000.00

FIGURE 7-2.   Sample income statement for the XYZ Company.

pay and the average collection period is only 19 days, you are doing very well. On the other hand, anything in excess of 40 days ($1^{1}/_3 \times 30 = 40$) would indicate a problem.

INVENTORY TURNOVER

Inventory turnover will show you how rapidly your merchandise is moving. It will also show you how much capital you have tied up in inventory to support the level of your company's operations for the period you are analyzing. For your marketing plan, you can analyze planned inventory turnover.

To calculate inventory turnover, simply divide the cost of goods sold that you obtain from your income statement by your average inventory. From Figure 7-2, your income profit-and-loss statement, the cost of goods sold equals $525,000. You cannot calculate your average inventory from Figure 7-1. You only know that for the period for which the inventory is stated, it equals $60,000. Let's assume that the previous balance sheet indicated that your inventory was $50,000. Then the average inventory for the two periods would be $60,000 plus $50,000 divided by 2, or $55,000. Now, let's see what inventory turnover is: Cost of goods sold of $525,000 divided by average inventory of $55,000 equals 9.5.

This means that you turned your inventory 9.5 times during the year. In other words, through your business operations you used up merchandise that total 9.5 times the average inventory investment. Under most circumstances, the higher the inventory turnover, the better, because it means you are able to operate with a relatively small sum of money invested in this inventory.

Another implication is that your inventory is the right inventory. You know this because it is salable and has not been in stock too long. But even here you must consider that too high a figure may signify a problem. Very high inventory turnover may mean that you have inventory shortages. Inventory shortages soon lead to customer dissatisfaction. This, in turn, may mean a loss of customers to the competition in the long run.

Is 9.5 a satisfactory inventory turnover? Again, the desirable rate depends on your business, your industry, your method of valuing inventories, and numerous other factors that are unique to your situation. Once again, it is helpful to study and compare your turnover rate with that of similar businesses of your size in your industry. After you have been in operation for some time and have a track record, past experiences with inventory turnover will indicate what is good and what is not with less reliance on industry comparisons.

Of course, you can analyze specific inventory turnover for different products or even groups of products or product lines in your marketing plan. This will show you which items are doing well and which are not. You may also prepare turnover analyses for much more frequent periods than a year. Even monthly or weekly periods may be necessary or required for perishable items or items that become obsolete very quickly. You will know that "hot" items should be reordered early and which items should not be ordered. You will also know which items you must order before their value decreases to a point at which you can no longer sell them.

PROFITABILITY MEASURES

Measures of profitability are essential for knowing how much money you are making, whether you are making as much as you can, or whether you are making money at all. There are several different ratios that will assist you in determining this. These are the asset earning power, return on owner's equity, net profit on sales, investment turnover and, finally, return on investment (ROI).

ASSET EARNING POWER

Asset earning power is determined by the ratio of earnings before interest and taxes to total assets. From the income statement in Figure 7-2 we can see that total operating profit or income is $105,000. Total assets from the balance sheet (Figure 7-1) are $272,000. $105,000 divided by $272,000 equals 0.39, or 39 percent.

RETURN ON THE OWNER'S EQUITY

Return on the owner's equity shows the return that you received in exchange for your investment in your business. To compute this ratio you will usually use the average equity for 12 months. If this isn't available, use the average of figures from two different balance sheets, your latest and the previous one.

Return on the owner's equity equals net profit divided by equity. Net profit from Figure 7-2 is $55,000. Equity from Figure 7-1 is $115,000. Assuming the equity from the previous period is also $115,000, use this as an average. Therefore, return on the owner's equity equals $55,000 divided by $115,000. That equals 0.48, or 48 percent.

A similar ratio can be calculated by using tangible net worth in lieu of equity. Tangible net worth equals equity less any intangible assets, such as patents owned and goodwill. If no intangible assets exist, the two will be equal.

NET PROFIT ON SALES

The net profit on sales ratio measures the difference between what you take in and what you spend in the process of doing business. Again, net profit was determined to be $55,000. Net sales from Figure 7-2 are $1,035,000. Therefore net profit on sales equals 0.053, or 5.3 percent. This means that for every dollar of sales the company has earned a profit of 5.3 cents.

The net profit on sales ratio depends mainly on operating costs and pricing policies. If this figure goes down, it could be because you have lowered prices or it could be because costs have been increasing while prices have remained stable.

Compare this ratio with those from other similar businesses. Also consider trends over a period of time. By comparing net profit on sales ratios for individual products, you will know which products or product lines need additional emphasis and which should be eliminated.

INVESTMENT TURNOVER

The ratio of investment turnover is annual net sales to total assets. In this case net sales of $1,035,000 divided by total assets of $272,000 from Figure 7-1 equal 3.8. Once again, compare with other similar businesses and watch for trends.

RETURN ON INVESTMENT (ROI)

ROI is an excellent way of measuring profitability of your investment or proposed investment. There are several different ways of calculating return on investment.

One simple way is to take net profit and divide it by total assets. In this case (Figure 7-1) the net profit equals $55,000. Total assets are $272,000. Therefore, $55,000 divided by $272,000 equals 0.20, or 20 percent. You want the highest net profit for the smallest amount of total assets invested. You can use this rate of return on investment for intercompany and interindustry comparisons, as well as pricing costs, inventory, and investment decisions, and many other measurements of efficiency and profitability. No matter how you use it, always be sure that you are consistent in making your comparisons—that is, be sure that you use the same definitions of net profit and assets invested.

Here are some additional measures of profitability using ROI:

1. Rate of Earnings on Total Capital Employed Equals Net Income Plus Interest and Taxes Divided by Total Liabilities and Capital. This ratio serves as an index of productivity of capital as well as a measure of earning power in operating efficiency.

2. Rate of Earnings on Invested Capital Equals Net Income Plus Income Taxes Divided by Proprietary Equity and Fixed Liabilities. This ratio is used as a measure of earning power of the borrowed invested capital.

3. Rate of Earnings on Proprietary Equity Equals Net Income Divided by Total Capital Including Surplus Reserves. This ratio is used as a measure of the yield on the owner's investment.

4. Rate of Earnings on Stock Equity Equals Net Income Divided by Total Capital Including Surplus Reserves. This ratio is used as a measure of the attractiveness of common stock as an investment.

5. Rate of Dividends on Common Stock Equity Equals Common Stock Dividends Divided by Common Stock Equity. This ratio is used to indicate the desirability of common stock as a source of income.

6. Rate of Dividends on Common Stock Equity Equals Common Stock Dividend per Share Divided by Market Value per Share of Common Stock. This ratio is used as a measure of the current yield on investment in a particular stock.

SOURCES OF RATIO ANALYSES FROM ALL INDUSTRIES

In order to compare your business with other businesses in your industry it is necessary to obtain pertinent data on other businesses. The following are sources of this information:

1. Dun & Bradstreet, Inc., Business Information Systems, 99 Church Street, New York, NY 10007. This firm publishes key business ratios on 125 lines annually. Copies can be obtained free upon request.

2. Accounting Corporation of America, 1929 First Avenue, San Diego, CA 92101. This organization publishes *Parameter of Small Businesses,* which classifies its operating ratios for various industry groups on the basis of gross volume.

3. National Cash Register Company, Marketing Services Department, Dayton, OH 45409. This firm publishes *Expenses in Retail Businesses,* which examines the cost of operations in more than 50 kinds of businesses obtained from primary sources, most of which are trade associations.

4. Robert Morris Associates, Philadelphia National Bank Building, Philadelphia, PA 19107. Robert Morris has developed and published ratio studies for more than 225 lines of business.

5. The Small Business Administration. The SBA has a series of reports that provide expenses as a percentage of sales for many industries. Although the reports do not provide strict ratio information, a comparison of percentage expenses will be very useful for your financial management.

6. Trade Associations. Many national trade associations publish ratio studies, including the following:

    Air Conditioning & Refrigeration Institute (ARI), 4301 N. Fairfax Dr., Ste. 425, Arlington, VA 22203, 703-524-8800, Fax: 703-528-3816, E-mail: ari@ari.org, Web site: ari.org

    Air Transport Association of America (ATA), 1301 Pennsylvania Ave., Ste. 1100, Washington, DC 20004-7017, 202-626-4000, Fax: 202-626-4166, E-mail: ata@air-transport.org, Web site: air-transport.org

    American Bankers Association, 1120 Connecticut Ave. NW, Washington, DC 20036, 202-663-5000, Toll free: 800-338-0626, Fax: 202-663-7543, Web site: aba.com

    American Booksellers Association, 828 S. Broadway, Tarrytown, NY 10591, 914-591-2665, Toll free: 800-637-0037, Fax: 914-591-2720, E-mail: info@bookweb.org, Web site: bookweb.org

    American Electronics Association (AEA), 5201 Great American Pky., Ste. 520, Santa Clara, CA 95054, 408-987-4200, Toll free: 800-284-4232, Fax: 408-986-1247, Phone: 202-682-9110, Web site: aeanet.org

    American Forest & Paper Association (AF&PA), 1111 19th St. NW, Washington, DC 20036, 202-463-2700, Fax: 202-463-2785, Web site:, afpa.org

    American Furniture Manufacturing Association (AFMA), PO Box HP-7, High Point, NC 27261, 336-884-5000, Fax: 336-884-5303

    American Meat Institute (AMI), 1700 N. Monroe St., Ste. 1600, Arlington, VA 22209, 703-841-2400, Fax: 703-527-0938, Web site: meatami.org

    American Society of Association Executives (ASAE), 1575 I. St. NW, , Washington, DC 20005-1168, 202-626-2723, Fax: 202-371-8825, E-mail: asae@asaenet.org, Web site:, asaenet.org

    American Supply Association (ASA), 222 Merchandise Mart, Ste. 1360, Chicago, IL 60654, 312-464-0090, Fax: 312-464-0091, E-mail: asaemail@interserv.org, Web site:, asa.net/tech

American Wholesale Marketers Assoc. (AWMA), 1128 16th St., Washington, DC 20036, 202-463-2124, Toll free: 800-482-2962, Fax: 202-463-6456, E-mail: davids@awmaner.org, Web site: awmanet.org

Association of American Publishers (AAP), 71 5th Ave, New York, NY 10003-3004, 212-255-0200, Fax: 213-255-7007, Web site: publishers.org.

Automotive Service Industry Association (ASIA), 25 Northwest Point, Elk Grove, IL 60007-1035, 847-228-1310, Fax: 847-228-1510, E-mail: asia@aftmktusa.org, Web site:, aftmkt.com/asi.

Bowling Proprietors' Association of America, Inc. (BPAA), 615 Six Flags Dr., Arlington, TX 76011, 817-649-5105, Fax: 817-633-2940, E-mail: bpaainc@aol.com.

Building Owners & Managers Association International (BOMAI), 1201 New York Ave. NW, Ste. 300, Washington, DC 20005, 202-408-2662, Fax: 202-371-0181, E-mail: soppen@boma.org, Web site: boma.org.

Business Products Industry Assoc. (BPIA), 301 W. Fairfax St., Alexandria, VA 22314, 703-549-9040, Toll-free: 800-542-6672, Fax: 703-683-7552, Web site: bpia.org

Carpet & Rub Institute (CRI), 310 Holiday Ave., PO Box 2048, Dalton, GA 30722, 706-278-3176, Toll-free: 800-882-8846, Fax: 706-278-8835.

Door & Hardware Institute (DHI), 14170 Newbrook Dr., Chantilly, VA 20151-2232, 703-222-2010, Fax: 703-222-2410, Web site: dhi.org.

Food Marketing Institute (FMI), 800 Connecticut Ave. NW, Washington, DC 20006, 202-452-8444, Fax: 202-429-4519, E-mail: fmi@fmi.org, Web site: fmi.org.

Food Service Equipment Distributors Association (FEDA), 223 W. Jackson Blvd., Ste. 620, Chicago, IL 60606, 312-427-9605, Fax: 312-427-9607.

Independent Insurance Agents of America (IIAA), 127 S. Peyton, Alexandria, VA 22314, 703-683-4422, Toll-free: 800-221-7917, Fax: 703-683-7556.

Institute of Management Accountants (IMA), 10 Paragon Dr., Montvale, NJ 07645-0000, 201-573-9000, Toll-free: 800-638-4427, Fax: 201-573-8483, E-mail: ingo@imanet.org, Web site: imanet.org.

International Association of Plastic Distributors (IAPD), 4707 College Blvd., Ste. 105, Leawood, KS 66211, 913-345-1005, Fax: 913-345-1006, E-mail: iapd@iapd.org, Web site: iapd.org.

International Fabricare Institute (IFI), 12251 Tech Rd., Silver Spring, MD 20904, 301-622-1900, Toll-free: 800-638-2627, Fax: 301-236-9320, E-mail: wecare@ifi.org, Web site: ifi.org.

International Hardware Distributors Assoc. (IHDA), 401 N. Michigan Ave., Ste. 2200, Chicago, IL 60611-4267, 312-644-6610, Fax: 312-527-6640, E-mail: ihda@sba.com, Web site: ihda.

Kitchen Cabinet Manufactures Assoc. (KCMA), 1899 Preston White Dr., Reston, VA 20191-5435, 703-264-1690, Fax: 703-620-6530, E-mail: dtitus@kcma.org, Web site: kcma.org.

Material Handling Equipment Distributors Assoc. (MHEDA), 201 Rte. 45, Vernon Hills, IL 60061, 827-680-3500, Fax: 847-362-6989, E-mail: connect@mheda.org, Web site: mheda.org

Mechanical Contractors Association of America (MCAA), 1385 Piccard Dr., Rockville, MD 20850-4329, 301-869-5800, Toll free: 800-556-3653, Fax: 301-990-9690, E-mail: john@mcaa.org, Web site: mcaa.org.

Motor & Equipment Manufacturers Association (MEMA), 10 Laboratory Dr., PO Box 13966, Research Triangle Park, NC 27709-3966, 919-549-4800, Fax: 919-549-4824, Web site: mema.org.

National Association of Electrical Distributors (NAED), 1100 Corporate Square Dr., Ste. 100, St. Louis, MO 63132, 314-991-9000, Fax: 314-991-3060, E-mail: info@naed.org, Web site: naed.org.

National Association of Music Merchants, Inc., 5790 Arnada Dr., Carlsbad, CA 92008, 760-438-8001, Toll-free: 800-767-6266, Fax: 760-438-7327.

National Automatic Merchandising Association (NAMA), 20 N. Wacker Dr., Ste. 350, Chicago, IL 60606, 312-346-0370, Fax: 312-704-4140, Web site: vending.org.

National Beer Wholesalers Assoc. (NBWA), 1100 S. Washington, Alexandria, VA 22314, 703-683-4300, Toll-free: 800-300-6417, Fax: 708-683-8965, Web site: nbwa.org.

National Electrical Contractors Assoc. (NECA), 3 Bethesda Metro Ctr., Ste. 1100, Bethesda, MD 20814, 301-657-3110, Fax: 301-215-4500, E-mail: neca@necanet.org, Web site: necanet.org.

National Electrical Manufacturers Association (NEMA), 1300 North 17th St., Ste. 1847, Arlington, VA 22209, 703-841-3200, Fax: 703-841-5900.

National Grocers Association (NGA), 1825 Samuel Morse Dr., Reston, VA 20190, 703-437-5300, Fax: 703-437-7768, Web site: Nationalgrocers.org

National Home Furnishing Association (NHFA), PO Box 2296, High Point, NC 27261, 336-883-1650, Toll-free: 800-888-9590, Fax: 336-883-1195, E-mail: mail@nhfa.org, Web site: nhfa.org.

National Lumber & Building Material Dealers Assoc. (NLBMDA), 40 IVY St. SE, Washington, DC 20003, 202-547-2230, Fax: 202-547-8645.

National Paper Trade Association (NPTA), 111 Great Neck Rd., Great Neck, NY 11021, 516-829-3070, Fax: 516-829-3074.

National Paperbox Assoc. (NPA), 801 N. Fairfax St., Ste 211, Alexandria, VA 22314-1757, 703-684-2212, Fax: 703-683-6920, E-mail: boxmoore@paperbox.org, Web site: paperbox.org.

National Parking Assoc. (NPA), 1112 16th St. NW, Ste. 300, Washington, DC 20036, 202-296-4336, Toll free: 800-647-park, Fax: 202-331-8523, Web site: npapark.org.

National Restaurant Association (NRA), 1200 17th St. NW, Washington, DC 20036, 202-331-5900, Fax: 202-331-2429, E-mail:isal@restaurant.org, Web site: restaurant.org.

National Retail Federation (NRF), 325 7th St. NW, Ste. 1000, Washington, DC 20004-2802, 202-783-7971, Toll-free: 800-nrf-how2, Fax: 202-737-2849, E-mail: nrf@nrf.com, Web site: nrf.com.

National Retail Hardware Association (NRHA), 5822 W. 74th St., Indianapolis, IN 46278, 317-290-0338, Toll-free: 800-772-4424, Fax: 317-328-4354, E-mail: nrha@iquest.net, Web site: nrha.org.

National Shoe Retailers Association (NSRA), 9861 Broken Lady Pkwy, Ste. 255, Columbia, MD 21046-1151, 410-381-8282, Toll-free: 800-673-8446, Fax: 410-381-1167, E-mail: ingfo@nsra.org, Web site: nsra.org.

National Sporting Goods Association (NSGA), Lake Center Plaza Bldg, 1699 Wall St., Mt. Prospect, IL 60056-5780, 847-439-4000, Fax: 847-439-0111, E-mail: nsga 11699@aol.com, Web site: nsgachicagoshow.com.

National Tire Dealers & Retreaders Association (NTDRA), 11921 Freedom Dr., Ste. 550, Reston, VA 20190-5608, Toll-free: 800-876-8372.

National Wholesale Druggists' Association (NWDA), 1821 Michael Faraday Dr., Ste. 400, Reston, VA 20190, 703-787-0000, Fax: 703-787-6930, Web site: nwda.org.

North American Equipment Dealers Assoc. (NAEDA), 10877 Watson Rd., St. Louis, MO 63127, 314-821-7220, Fax: 314-821-0674, E-mail: naeda@naeda.com, Web site: naeda.com.

North American Heating, Refrigeration, & Air-Conditioning Wholesalers Assoc. (NHRAW), PO Box 16790, 1389 Dublin Rd., Columbus, OH 43216, 614-488-1835, Fax: 614-488-0482, E-mail: nhramail@nhraw.org, Web site: nhraw.org.

North American Wholesale Lumber Association, 3601 Algonquin Rd., Ste. 400, Rolling Meadows, IL 60008, 847-870-7470, Fax: 847-870-0201.

Optical Laboratories Assoc., PO Box 2000, Merrifield, VA 22116-2000, 703-359-2830, Fax: 703-359-2834.

Paint & Decorating Retailers Assoc., 403 Axminster Dr., St. Louis, MO 63026, 314-326-2636, Toll-free: 800-737-0107, Fax: 314-326-1823, E-mail: info@pdra.org, Web site:, pdra.org.

Petroleum Equipment Institute (PEI), PO Box 2380, Tulsa, OK 74101, 918-494-9696, Fax: 918-491-9895, E-mail: pei@peinet.org, Web site: pei.org.

Printing Industries of America (PIA), 100 Daingerfield Rd., Alexandria, VA 22314, 703-519-8100, Toll-free: 800-742-2666, Fax: 703-548-3227, E-mail: jsass@printing.org, Web site: printing.org.

Robert Morris Assoc./Assoc. of Lending & Credit Risk Professionals, 1 Liberty Pl., 1650 Market St. Ste. 2300, Philadelphia, PA 19103-7398, 215-446-4000, Fax: 215-446-4101.

SAMA Group of Assoc., 225 Reineker, Ste. 625, Alexandria, VA 22314, 703-836-1360, Fax: 703-836-6644.

Shoe Service Institute of America (SSIA), 5024-R Cambell Rd., Baltimore, MD 21236, 410-931-8100, Fax: 410-931-8111, Web site: shoeservice.com/shoemarts.

Textile & Cleaners Allied Trades Association (TCATA), 271 U.S. Highway 46, No. 203-D, Fairfield, NJ 07004-2458, 973-244-1790, Fax: 973-244-4455, E-mail: tcata@ix.netcom.com.

United Fresh Fruit & Vegetables Assoc. (UFFVA), 727 N. Washington. St., Alexandria, VA 22314, 703-836-3410, Fax: 703-836-7745, E-mail: uffva@uffva.org.

Urban Land Institute (ULI), 1025 Thomas Jefferson St. NW, Ste. 500W, Washington, DC 20007-5201, 202-624-7000, Toll-free: 800-321-5011, Fax: 202-624-7140, E-mail: joinuli@uli.org, Web site: uli.org.

Wine & Spirits Wholesalers of America (WSWA), 805 15th St. NW, Ste. 430, Washington, DC 20005, 202-371-9792, Fax: 202-789-2405, E-mail: juanita.duggan@wswa.org, Web site: wswa.org.

SUMMARY

In this chapter we've looked at many financial ratios that can be used to measure the financial efficiency of what we plan to do. These ratios can be used by comparing our planned figures with alternative approaches, and also by comparing our planned ratios with others that are published for the same industry. If your marketing plan is implemented, you will want to return to this chapter to use actual rather than planned information. In this way the ratios enable us to monitor our implementation and to make adjustments as we proceed.

Now we have all the information needed to put together an outstanding presentation of your marketing plan. You'll see how to do that in the next chapter.

CHAPTER

8

STEP 8

PRESENTING THE MARKETING PLAN

By the time you have reached this chapter you should have all the information necessary to put together a first-rate marketing plan. But now you have another problem. You've done all necessary research and assembled your material. You've completed the situational analysis and scanned your environment. You've established goals and objectives and developed marketing strategy and tactics. You've peered into the future and forecasted sales and costs. You've developed extensive financial information and measured its efficiency. Now it is important not to trip up. You must present your marketing plan to those who have the authority to approve it or give you the resources needed to implement it. You must do this in the most professional manner possible. The purpose of this chapter is to show you how to present your plan.

THE MARKETING PLAN AS A PRODUCT

Your marketing plan is a sales document, but it is also a product representing your concept for the project or business. It must be as professional a product as you can make it. There is an old saying, "You can't judge a book by its cover." It may be true, but it is irrelevant. A professional-looking plan has a far better chance of success than one that is highly creative with accurate information, but put together in a haphazard fashion with grammatical or spelling errors. So, your marketing plan must look as good as it is. If it does, the psychological advantage is yours. The reader will proceed from the premise that your plan is accurate and that you know what you are talking about.

On the other hand, if your marketing plan doesn't look professional, the contents must overcome a significant negative bias. Let's see what you can do to make your plan look more professional.

The first thing is to have your plan typed by one person, so the printing will have a consistent style and format throughout the document. It should be neat and free from typographical errors and obvious corrections. In this day of computerization, this shouldn't pose any problem.

A standardized method of typing and collating the different sections of the plan should be used. Which method you choose is usually not critical, unless specified by whoever has asked you to prepare the plan. Standardization also means a single way of doing footnotes, bibliography, and so forth. Several different style manuals are available, so pick one and stick with it.

Sometimes, when several different people work on a single marketing plan, different sections of the plan are assigned to each of the participants. Although there is nothing inherently wrong with this, one individual should be assigned the task of assembling the overall product to ensure that its writing, styling, typing, and formatting are consistent. If one coordinator is not assigned, it is not unusual to find sections that do not fit together.

I'm sad to report I have seen a conclusion in one section nullified by a statement in another section. I have also seen terminology that is inconsistent among different sections.

If the typing or printing is done by different individuals, the marketing plan may have an inconsistent appearance owing to different styles of type, darkness of imprint, margins, fonts, and paper. This guarantees a shoddy-looking product, so don't let this happen to you!

Illustrations and charts should be included as a part of your marketing plan. You must never, however, include illustrations or any unnecessary information merely to pad the marketing plan and make it appear more substantial. Information that may distract from the presentation can be added as an appendix. The survey form used to gather research might be an example. But even information in the appendix should be necessary and relevant and not added simply to increase the size of the document.

There is no minimum length for a marketing plan. Many venture capitalists prefer shorter plans, say 50 pages or less, because they review so many marketing and business plans that they prefer to have the essential facts in the plan and to request additional information only if needed. This is usually not the case if you are preparing the marketing plan in the classroom, someone else is paying you to prepare it, or you are preparing one as a member of a large corporation. Then, it is best to ensure that all the information is available right from the start. This will require at least 50 pages and possibly more.

Make your plan long enough to tell your entire story, always considering what your readers will want to know. If you need more pages to cover essential information, use them. On the other hand, if you have covered all the information you think is necessary for your reader, then stop. Don't pad.

The final point to consider is binding. Some excellent plans are typed neatly and compiled with correct and complete information, yet they still fail to give a professional appearance simply because a cheap binding is used. Even though it is easy and inexpensive to get a really top-of-the-line binding, many fail to get it for their plans.

Hardcover binding, bound like a book, is available from many printers for less than $10. One cautionary note. In their enthusiasm, one of my student teams got their marketing plan bound in leather to the tune of $70! I don't recommend needless expense, even for a professional plan.

If you are unable to obtain hardcover binding, consider spiral binding. A mechanical means of doing rapid spiral binding is available at many printers. Check the Yellow Pages of your telephone book for additional sources. Again, the point here is to make your marketing plan look as professional as you can. Your marketing plan should be good and it should look good.

THE FORMAL PRESENTATION

In most cases, simply preparing the marketing plan is insufficient. You must also make a formal presentation of your marketing plan to someone else. This may be to individuals who may be interested in funding your plan or to higher management in your company who must give the approval to implement it. Your professor may ask you to do a formal presentation of your plan in the classroom.

In all cases you must first consider the object of your presentation. Usually the object of a marketing plan is to persuade management or investors to allocate funds to enable you to implement your project. Remember that no one is going to give you money for your plan unless they are convinced that it will succeed and will make money for them.

What will these people want to know? They'll want to know how much money can be made, how much money will be needed from them and when, how long it will be before they will get their money back, exactly what you will do with the money, and why you will succeed with your project. Therefore, although the outline of your marketing plan can be used as described in preceding chapters, some minor changes may be needed to maximize the impact of your presentation.

Here is one outline for a formal presentation:

I. Introduction. In the introduction the information in your executive summary is covered, including the opportunity and why it exists, the money to be made, the money that's needed, and some brief financial information, such as return on investment, to support the extent of the opportunity as you see it.

II. Why You Will Succeed. In this section you will cover your situational analysis and environmental scanning and the research you did to support it. You conclude the section with problems, opportunities, and threats, as well as the project's goals and objectives. Finally, you spell out your differential competitive advantage. The essential message in this part of the presentation is why you will succeed even though others may fail.

III. Strategy and Tactics. In this section you will cover the strategy you are going to follow as well as the tactics used to implement that strategy.

IV. Forecast and Financial Information. In this section you will discuss your forecast, project development schedule, profit-and-loss statement, and financial ratios and data. This section will contain a detailed description of what you need and when you need it. Sometimes, because of the limited time available for the presentation, you may have to edit this section and present only the main points. The important financial information should always be available so that in the question-and-answer session that follows you can provide the additional data, if required.

V. Conclusion. In this final part of your formal presentation you will restate the opportunity and why you will succeed with it, the money that is required, and the expected return on the investment. You told 'em. Now tell 'em what you told 'em.

PREPARING FOR YOUR PRESENTATION

Your first step in preparing for your presentation is obtaining the answers to several important questions. These include the time and date of your presentation, where it is to be held, the time allowed, who the audience is, who is in the audience, and the purpose of your presentation. You should also think about the audience's attitude, their knowledge and preconceived notions, and anything that requires particular care. After getting this information, you can write down the main points to cover.

Probably 99 times out of 100 the purpose of presenting your marketing plan will be to obtain resources. This holds true whether you are an entrepreneur presenting a marketing plan to the loan officer of a bank, a venture capitalist, or someone else who is going to lend you money, or whether you are an employee of a company and have been asked to prepare a plan as a potential investment. The exception is a plan that you have prepared as a consultant to an entrepreneur or larger corporation interested in implementing it. In this case your main object is to demonstrate that you have done your job by preparing a plan that your client can use to get resources and eventually to implement.

Think through and write down the answers to these questions, because they can affect what you are going to cover and how you are going to do it.

Your next step is to make an outline of your main and supporting points. To develop this outline you need not follow the outline of the written marketing plan report. Remember that you may wish to change your order in presenting different elements depending on your audience and their backgrounds, interests, and concerns. With different audiences, different sections or topics must be emphasized. If the audience is primarily financial, don't omit any financial information from your presentation. On the contrary, you should emphasize it.

On the other hand, an engineering audience will probably be more interested in the technical aspects of your product, its manufacture, and so forth. Some financial data can be excluded in order to allow room for more technical information. Now, you are probably doing this for your marketing class at the direction of your marketing professor. Need I say what emphasis your plan should have?

The following technique is sometimes useful in helping you prepare your outline and its supporting points. Obtain a number of 3- × 5-inch file cards and, without stopping to think, write down everything you think should be emphasized in your presentation, one item to a card. Don't try to coordinate or organize anything at this point. If you have statistics that you think should be included, or anecdotes, quotes, or even jokes, write each on a separate card.

Once you have written down as many ideas as you can, begin to organize the cards into your main points and supporting points. Statistics will be supporting points to some main points. So will anecdotes, jokes, and quotes. By using this system you will soon have a stack of cards for each major element of your presentation. They will automatically be organized in a logical fashion.

After you complete your presentation by arranging your ideas using these cards, you can prepare a complete written outline. Notice that this is a flexible system. You can move cards around, as well as add cards and points to your presentation as new ideas occur.

Note that I have not said to write a speech. Your presentation should never be written out word-for-word. If it is, you will probably present it that way. Marketing plan speeches are dull and boring. You want your marketing plan presentation to reflect the work, the accuracy, and the potential it represents for whoever implements it. But above all, you want it to be exciting. This cannot be done with a written speech, so leave your presentation as an outline.

Once you have completed your outline you can begin planning for your visual aids.

PLANNING FOR VISUAL AIDS

Visual aids can greatly enhance the impact of your presentation and should always be used in making a presentation of a marketing plan. Your basic options are the use of 35-mm slides, overhead transparencies, charts, handouts, videos, computer presentations, or chalkboards. All have their advantages and disadvantages. Let's look at each of them.

Slides (35-mm).   A 35-mm projector and 35-mm slides are easy to carry around. Furthermore, the slides can be done in color, look quite professional, can be manipulated by the presenter, and yield an extremely professional appearance. The disadvantages are the lead time to prepare the slides, the cost, and the difficulty of changing a particular slide once it has been developed. New systems are now available by which 35-mm slides are constructed by computer and then enhanced, in color or otherwise, rapidly and at relatively low cost per unit. However, the equipment costs several thousand dollars. This system will not be readily available to everyone.

Overhead Transparencies.   Overhead transparencies are as portable as 35-mm slides. Most of these projectors are heavier, more cumbersome, and less transportable, although some models available today are as portable and only slightly larger than slide projectors. There is a lead time associated with the preparation of overhead transparencies, if you have them done professionally. However, if camera-ready artwork is available, duplicating machines located at many printing shops can make instant overhead transparencies from your camera-ready copy. Also, desktop publishing programs available for many computers allow you to make professional quality transparencies yourself. Another advantage of an overhead transparency is that you can write on it as you talk. As a result, you can also make changes in the transparency if required. This cannot be done with a 35-mm slide. Although you can talk and operate a projector with overhead transparencies at the same time, this is more difficult than with a 35-mm projector because the latter can be operated remotely.

Videos.   A videotape presentation allows a lot of flexibility and can add interest to your presentation. However, there are drawbacks. First, don't get so carried away with your presentation on film that you make the video your entire presentation, unless this has been requested. Practice with the tape to ensure the timing fits with the rest of your presentation. Of course, a television and videocassette player or other means to show your video must be available. Most presenters work with equipment furnished by someone else. Frequently, the first time they see the equipment is when they make their presentation. As a result, many times presenters struggle with getting unfamiliar equipment to work. This distracts from your presentation and can irritate your audience.

Computer Presentations.   The state-of-the-art of computer technology has advanced to the point where some very sophisticated multimedia presentations can be easily developed and used with a portable computer and a device linking it to an overhead projector. *Power Point* is perhaps the most popular. Here again, there is a danger of getting carried away with sound effects and visuals possibilities. While entertaining, this can distract from your basic purpose in making the presentation. Again, be careful of equipment. Practice with the actual equipment you will use. I have seen presenters start their presentation only to discover that the equipment available is not compatible with what they have put together and that no one can see the presentation except in complete darkness—under which conditions they cannot see their notes. Veteran presenters of multmedia always have standard overheads as backup.

Handouts.   Handouts are easy to make. They can be reproduced in quantity, even in color if required. Handouts can be changed and new information substituted for the old. But handouts suffer from two major disadvantages. First, if the information is extensive and the audience large, a considerable amount of material must be carried around and distributed. Second, audiences may read ahead in your handout and miss the points you are covering. At the same time, a dramatic sequence of events that you've built into your presentation may be spoiled as the audience reads ahead to your "punch line." Handouts that are exact duplicates of transparencies or multimedia programs are excellent as backup should some electronic means fail. They are also useful when members of the audience ask for copies of your transparencies.

Charts.   Charts can be the flip variety or they can be large cardboard or plastic devices that are used in conjunction with your other visual aids. Charts are much less portable than 35-mm slides, transparencies, or handouts. One advantage of a chart, however, is that those with artistic bent can prepare them on their own and thus need not allow as much lead time as with professionally prepared overhead transparencies or 35-mm slides. This places them in the same category as handouts as far as this particular attribute goes. However, if you prepare your own charts, it is important that it *not* be done the night before. Always allow enough time to check them for accuracy, typographical errors, and so forth. If you do them the night before, you are almost certain to make errors.

Chalkboards.   Chalkboards, or plastic boards on which you can write with colored pencils, can also be useful during presentations. The major disadvantage is that you cannot prepare your material ahead of time. In this case, the advantage is also the disadvantage, because there is much more drama and spontaneity in having your audience see the point you wish to get across as you write it. However, there are usually so many disadvantages with chalkboards that, at best, they can be used only as an adjunct to your other systems. These include the facts that they are not readily transportable, the material is not permanent, you cannot use the material to jog your memory (an advantage with all four other visual systems), and chalkboards may not always be available where you give your presentation.

Whatever system of visual aids you plan to use, you should prepare your visual aids immediately, even before you begin to practice for the first time, and not wait until the last moment. I recommend that you attempt a presentation in the time you have been allocated at least once. When you are reasonably confident that the major points of your presentation will not change, have your visual aids constructed. One reason is the long lead time—it is always a lot longer than you anticipate. Also, you want to allow time to proofread the material that is done for you by someone else.

After having given hundreds of presentations using all of these methods, I have found that in 90 percent of the cases typographical errors appear. If your visual aids are prepared at the last minute, you may find that insufficient time is available to correct the errors. So once you know what you want on your visual aids, have them made at once. You can practice with dummy visual aids while the real ones are being prepared.

Use of Products as Visual Aids.   Sometimes the product that is the subject of your marketing plan is available. These products can be very useful for adding interest to your presentation. However, if you use products as part of your visual aids, make sure they are relevant. If your product is interesting and the particular twist or unique advantage you have in your product is worth seeing, then it's worth showing. On the other hand, if your marketing plan concerns a product that everyone is familiar with, don't use it as a visual aid unless there is some unique aspect that should be seen or demonstrated. Do something else with the time you have available.

To summarize our discussion on visual aids, I'd like you to consider the following points as you prepare for your presentation.

Make sure you use aids that contain material that is easy to read, without too much information on each. They must make an impact on the audience and reinforce what you say, or make what you say more easily understood. If there is too much information in a single view, your audience may get lost. If the type is too small, your audience will not be able to read what you have prepared.

Even your pointing techniques may be important. If you are going to use a pointer, be careful not to turn your body so as to cut off the view of someone in your audience. The best way to avoid this is to follow this rule: If you are standing to the right of the view of your presentation, have the pointer in your left hand. This will keep you from turning your back on the audience and cutting off the view of members of the audience who are to your right front. On the other hand, if you are standing to the left of the view, use the pointer in your right hand. In this way, you will not turn your back and cut off the view of individuals in the audience who are on your left front.

Keep your visual aids covered until you use them. Displaying many visual aids simultaneously only causes distractions. It may cause your audience to become more interested in your visuals than in you. So show one visual. Then, only when you're ready, show the next.

THE PRACTICE SEQUENCE

I want to emphasize that you must never memorize anything. If you try to memorize your presentation, you may forget it. Memorization simply isn't necessary. Nor is it necessary to read your presentation. I learned this lesson the hard way.

As a young Air Force officer, I was once asked to make a presentation to 300 science and math teachers on space navigation, a topic in which I had great interest at the time. I prepared superb 35-mm full-color slides and spent considerable time writing and honing a one-hour speech. I wrote down every single word. I memorized this speech perfectly, word for word, and coordinated it with my excellent multicolor slides.

When the day came I looked out at 300 science and math teachers, gulped once, and could barely remember my name. After several stumbling attempts to try to remember the speech I thought I had memorized perfectly, I reached in my pocket and read my speech word for word.

What a mistake! Hours of work wasted unnecessarily for a boring speech. After all, I knew the subject matter. By simply flipping through my slides, I could have talked to my audience and told them about each. That really was all that was required for an excellent presentation.

The same is true for you. To give an outstanding presentation of your marketing plan, you don't have to memorize anything. You need not bore your audience by reading a speech, either. You know your subject better than anyone else. Once you are prepared, just going through your presentation as you use your visuals to support what you say will enable you to communicate with your audience for maximum impact. In this way, you can give an outstanding presentation.

If your visual aids are complete while you practice, use them during your practice. If not, write the content of your visual aids on $8 \times 10^1/_2$-inch sheets of paper and practice with them. You can use the cards that you prepared earlier to help remember the main points. I recommend going through your presentation three times and making adjustments as necessary in order to complete the presentation and get your points across in the time you have been allotted.

If you use cards to supplement what you have displayed on your visual aids to help you remember the main points, do not write more than a few words on the cards. If you do, you will read them. And once you begin to read your cards, you will probably continue to read them. Then you are back to reading a speech. So write just a few words on each and use them only as cues. Of course, the same is true of the visual aids. They should be sparsely worded for maximum impact. Simply look at the visual aid and speak about it to your audience.

As I fine-tune my presentations, I may add statistics, I may take out a point here or add one there, and I may modify other parts of what I originally intended to discuss. One element is fixed: I concentrate on staying within whatever time constraints have been given me. Time is crucial.

THE IMPORTANCE OF CONTROLLING YOUR TIME

You must always control your time, and practice giving your presentation within the allotted time. This is true whether you are making a 15-minute presentation or one lasting several hours. Why is this so? The individuals in your audience, no matter how critical and important they feel your presentation will be to them, allot a certain amount of time for it in their schedules. If you exceed this time, even by a few minutes, you will make it more difficult, even impossible, to achieve the objective of your presentation. If you exceed your allotted time by only a few minutes, it may be annoying. If you go over by more than that, it could set up a negative reaction due to its impact on the schedules of audience members.

Let me give you a couple of examples to illustrate just how important controlling your time can be. A few years ago a large aerospace corporation was competing for a major government contract with the Air Force. Fifty representatives from the Air Force flew in to receive what was to be a full day's presentation to end no later than 4 P.M. The presentation, however, was not well planned by the presenters. By 3:30 P.M. it was obvious their full presentation could not be completed within the allotted time. The audience was not given a choice. The presenters forged ahead, determined to cover every single one of their overhead transparencies. The presentation was completed more than an hour late. As a result, most of these government representatives had to reschedule their return flights. While the presentation was sufficiently important that these representatives listened to the full presentation, they were definitely unhappy with the poor planning on the part of the prospective contractor. Maybe this was only one factor among many, but this company did not win the contract.

Mistakes like this in time control are not limited to industry. One practice generally followed in hiring university professors is to require the candidate to make a presentation to the department. Typically this presentation is on the candidate's research. This presentation is critical because the membership of the department has a say in whether or not to hire the candidate.

Several years ago, a major university reviewed the credentials of a candidate who had graduated from a well-known university. This individual's background was so outstanding that the members of the department were in favor of hiring the candidate even before he made his face-to-face appearance.

They asked the candidate to limit his presentation to 25 minutes owing to the prior commitments of his audience. All 14 members of this department listened attentively as the candidate began. His presentation was interesting and relevant. However, 25 minutes after he started he was still speaking. At 30 minutes professors in the audience began to fidget; several had other meetings scheduled. A few had classes and excused themselves. Thirty-five minutes went by, then 40. The candidate finally concluded at 45 minutes.

This candidate was still hired as a professor by the institution involved. However, the candidate had interviewed for a position leading to tenure and promotion, but because of just 20 minutes, he was offered only a one-year appointment. After one year, he might be considered for the original position that was offered. Twenty minutes cost this professor one year in time toward a promotion to the next rank, including pay, allowances, and other fringe benefits.

The lesson is clear. Ask if there is a certain time allotted for your presentation. If there is, do not exceed this time. Practice to make sure that you stay within this time limit. Give yourself a slight pad. And when you make your presentation, control your time.

Once you have practiced three times and have good control over your presentation, I recommend that you do the presentation twice more, only this time in front of other people. This can mean a spouse, friend, brother, sister, or whomever. The important thing is not to look for a pat on the back but for a real critique. This includes the answers to a number of questions:

Should I talk louder or softer?

Did I use eye contact?

Did I talk in a conversational fashion, or did I simply start reading from my cards or visual aids?

Did I have a good opener that grabbed the interest of my audience?

Did I close my presentation with impact?

Did I use supporting matter such as anecdotes or statistics?

Was there something particular I said that was liked?

Something not liked?

If available, were my visual aids written large enough, and could they be read? Do they need to be changed or improved in some way?

Was there anything in my presentation that could not be understood, and, if so, what could I do to make it understandable?

Are there any other points or comments or advice that may be relevant?

QUESTIONS AND ANSWERS AND HOW TO PREPARE FOR THEM

Questions and answers are going to be a part of every marketing plan presentation you make. The first thing you must do is prepare ahead of time. Research has shown that approximately 85 percent of the questions asked can actually be anticipated. So once you have prepared your presentation, think about what questions might be asked by your audience, and prepare for them. You might also have your practice audience ask questions, both to test your preparation for answering them and your ability to think on your feet.

Next have your facts, figures, quotes—all of this information—available. Many astute presenters who cannot fit all the information they would like into their presentation because of time restrictions, have other visual aids ready and waiting. That way when this information is requested, it can be immediately used to good advantage.

An example might be financial information such as cash flow on a monthly basis. You may not have time to cover this in your formal presentation, but it would not hurt to have an overhead transparency or some other visual aid available so that when you are asked a question about these details, you can immediately use it. This will not only demonstrate your knowledge, but your preparation for any eventuality.

Remember to keep cool no matter how embarrassing the question or even if you're not sure you can answer it. I recommend a four-step procedure in answering questions. First, restate the question that has been asked. This ensures that the entire audience has heard the question and that you understand it. It also gives you additional time to think about your answer. Second, state your position or your answer to the question. Third, state the supporting reasons for your position. Finally restate your position to make it clear to everyone.

In general, keep your answers brief. If you know the individual who asked the question, use his or her name. If the individual is right and you are wrong about something, admit it. Or, if you don't know something, admit that also. Simply say, "I don't know." Of course, if every other answer is, "I don't know," the audience is likely to believe that you have done a poor job in preparing your marketing plan, and that you lack the necessary expertise to discuss the material.

Never get sidetracked or argue with someone who has asked a question. Always be tactful, even with individuals who attack you or your position. Harshly correcting a questioner can turn others in your audience against you even if they agree with your point of view. This is because the audience may be members of the same firm or group. Also, they may resent the manner in which you respond to an innocent question, even if it is not asked in a tactful way.

USE OF THE MENTAL VISUALIZATION TECHNIQUE

I've always worried about speeches before I made them. As I lay in bed thinking about what I was to do the next day, I would go over the entire speech in my mind. I rehearsed it again and again. I never thought much about this. Then, on January 13, 1982, *The Wall Street Journal* published an article entitled, "Why Do Some People Out-Perform Others?" It mentioned a psychologist by the name of Charles Garfield who had investigated top performance among business executives. Garfield said that he was most surprised by a trait that he called mental rehearsal, which had meanwhile caught on as a popular concept in sports. According to Garfield, top chief executives would imagine every aspect and feeling of a future presentation, including a successful ending, while less effective executives would prepare their facts and the presentation agendas, but not their psyches.

Now I teach this technique to others to help them prepare for presentations, and they report outstanding success with it. All that is necessary is that you take a few minutes before falling asleep the night before your presentation. Visualize everything from greeting your host and your audience to going through your presentation to a successful conclusion. See your conclusion in detail, with smiles and vigorous applause. Repeat this again and again, each time with a favorable conclusion. You will find that you can go through an entire hour's presentation in a few seconds, and thus you can have as many as 30 or more repetitions of success even before you go before your audience to make your presentation for the first time.

I believe this technique has several benefits. First, because you visualize a success again and again, you come to expect that success and, more frequently than not, that is exactly what you will receive. Second, mental rehearsal seems to eliminate excessive anxiety. While all of us may be a little nervous when we make a presentation, this is probably good. If we weren't nervous at all, we probably would come across as rather dull and uninteresting. But too much nervousness can cause us to stumble, and may make our audience nervous as well. With mental visualization, you have made your presentation so many times before that when you stand and look at your audience, the sting is gone. It is "old hat." After all, didn't you make the same presentation before the same audience 30 or more times the night before?

I highly recommend that you try this technique. From my own experience and the experience of so many others, I know that it will work wonders in helping you to present your marketing plan in an interesting, self-confident manner.

THE KEYS TO SUCCESS FOR MARKETING PLAN PRESENTATIONS

The number-one key for making your marketing plan presentation a success is to be enthusiastic about your project. If you aren't enthusiastic, you certainly cannot expect anyone else to be. What happens when you don't have a great deal of enthusiasm for a project? Perhaps it was not your idea at all. In the classroom, it is your professor who decides that you must make this presentation. At work, it is probably your boss who instructed you to prepare this marketing plan presentation for top management. It really makes no difference. My recommendation is that if you really aren't interested in the project, then you must act; you must pretend that you are highly interested. This is crucial.

Whenever I discuss acting or pretending, I think about the movie *Patton*. George C. Scott played the famous World War II general. In one scene depicting an event during the Battle of the Bulge, things were not going well for American forces. General Patton suddenly turned to an aide and exclaimed, "If any of our commanders retreat, shoot them!" The aide was shocked. In disbelief, he asked, "You really don't mean that?" Patton answered, "It really is not important whether you know whether I really mean it or not. It's only important that I know." In other words, Patton was acting.

Now, in fact, Patton was a tremendous actor. I know this for a fact because Patton's diaries have been published. During World War I, Patton was 29 years old and the commander of the first U.S. tank forces in France. He wrote to his wife, saying, "Every day I practice in front of a mirror looking mean." He called this his "war face." Patton felt that his mean-looking "war face" saved lives, because it meant his men were more afraid of him than they were of the enemy.

But Patton isn't the only one who recommends acting in order to achieve success. Mary Kay Ash, who developed a $100 million cosmetic company, recommends that her salespeople "Fake it till you make it." In other words, until you actually have a good day, pretend you're already having one. Or, until you have success, pretend that you are already achieving it. If you do this, if you pretend to be enthusiastic about your product and your project even though you are not, I promise you that this enthusiasm is contagious, and that your audience will be enthusiastic as well.

You must dress professionally. You represent your marketing plan. Appearance does count. As pointed out previously, although you may not be able to judge a book by its cover, psychologically people will do so. The same goes for your presentation. If you have any doubts about how to dress, the most famous book on this subject is called *Dress for Success* by John T. Molloy. Another important book is *Power Dressing* by Victoria Seitz, a professor at California State University San Bernardino. I highly recommend both of these books.

If you have any kind of test to do, or something that must work as a part of your presentation for your marketing plan, it is advisable to practice this test fully, and not just go through the motions.

Several years ago, a Navy project engineer made a presentation about an important Navy project. When Navy aviators must eject from aircraft over water, they have a serious problem in getting rid of their parachutes once in the water. The normal procedure is to climb into a small, one-person life raft, which is attached to a nylon line attached to the parachute harness that extends 15 feet below the pilot. It opens automatically at ejection.

However, the pilot must climb into the raft while wearing heavy flight equipment, including boots, helmet, and survival gear. Obviously this is difficult. Worse, the parachute canopy can fill with water. But even if it doesn't, its water-soaked weight may drag the aviator straight down to the bottom.

The Navy teaches its aviators to use an emergency release to get rid of the parachute canopy just as their feet touch the water. Naturally, most pilots cheat a little in case the quick release gets stuck. They actually start dumping their "chute" a few feet before they hit.

There is a serious problem, however. Because the ocean appears flat, it is very difficult to judge height. As a result, many aviators who think they are a few feet above the water release their parachutes while they are still several hundred feet in the air. This practice can be dangerous.

In order to overcome this problem, the Navy developed a special squib. This is a light explosive charge that automatically releases the canopy when a sensor attached to the life raft contacts water; it hangs 15 feet below the pilot and thus comes in contact with the water first. In this way, the parachute is jettisoned safely without endangering the pilot.

The Navy project manager did an outstanding job of presenting. His presentation included films of how the system worked, 35-mm slides, and handouts illustrating the project. For the grand finale, he donned a parachute himself and held up a jar of seawater. He told his audience of several hundred that he would introduce the sensor into the seawater. He told them that they would hear a loud crack as the squib exploded, and that the parachute canopy trailing behind the harness he had donned would immediately separate.

The audience prepared themselves, some holding their hands over their ears, and others waiting expectantly for the loud report of the exploding squib. The presenter inserted the probe into the seawater with high drama. There was a loud silence. Nothing happened. He extracted the sensor and inserted it again, and again, and again. Nothing happened. Finally, red-faced as the audience began to snicker, he examined the harness. He discovered that someone had forgotten to replace a discharged battery. With no current there was nothing to ignite the squib.

Here was an important and outstanding presentation ruined by a demonstration that went awry. It was a mistake that need not have happened if a full demonstration had been done during the practice stage.

Try to establish empathy with your audience throughout your presentation. You can do this by being friendly. Remember, the audience is not your enemy, so enjoy yourself, and think of yourself as the host of your presentation.

The presentation and your written marketing plan report go together. They support one another, and will support your achieving whatever objectives you have set.

SUMMARY

In this chapter we have seen that presenting the marketing plan has two main elements: the written report and the formal presentation. This is not the frosting on the cake. Both are necessary for success. You will be successful by focusing on preparation and ensuring that your plan is presented with a high degree of professionalism.

With professionalism, your excellent content will be supported by an excellent package. I hope that you have learned that professional is not accidental. If you implement the techniques outlined, you cannot fail. In the classroom, your professionalism in presenting your plan will lead to a high grade. In the "real world" it will help to get you the resources to implement your marketing plan. You may not implement your plan in the classroom, but when you graduate and begin to use your marketing skills, you will. You are now ready to see how this is done in the next chapter.

CHAPTER 9

STEP 9

IMPLEMENTATION

No matter how good your marketing plan is, or how well you have presented it, once you have received the go-ahead you must actually carry out the actions you have planned. Implementation is the final stage in the marketing planning process. During implementation, you can and should use your plan to help you. But the execution of your plan is not automatic. Your plan is not a light switch which, simply turned on, automatically completes every task, tactic, and strategy in exactly the manner you planned. To implement your marketing plan successfully, you must exercise control to ensure that you will reach your planned objectives and goals. To accomplish this you must monitor the implementation of your plan on a periodic basis. Use your project development schedule and measure planned resource allocations against those actually used, together with the time frame in which they were to be used. Measure expected results against actual results. Calculate your financial ratios.

Once implementation has been initiated, things never go exactly as planned. This may be because your planning was not perfect (and what planning ever is?), or it may be because of a change of one or more marketplace environs. Perhaps your competition responded in a way that you never expected. All of this is normal. It simply means that you must make adjustments to get back on track to achieve the objectives and goals you have set.

Conceptually, certain actions are always required in implementation:

1. If you are the one responsible for the plan's implementation, or some subsection of the plan, take complete responsibility for implementation. This does not only mean responsibility for initiating the actions contained in the plan but responsibility for reaching the goals and objectives contained in the plan.

2. Track all tasks, tactics, and strategies and measure what is planned against what actually happens. Make adjustments as required and do not blindly continue any action simply because it is in your plan.

3. Track the changes in the environs as the implementation of your marketing plan progresses. Changes will sometimes tell you that actions planned for the future should not be taken, or should be altered. And just as an ounce of prevention is worth a pound of cure, an ounce of change taken now may be well worth a pound of change at a later

date, when a foreseeable or predictable threat grows and causes a major problem in implementation.

No marketing plan, regardless of how good it is, with brilliant strategies and clever tactics, can succeed without being implemented. You cannot realize your objectives by implementing a poor marketing plan. But you cannot realize your objectives by poorly implementing a good marketing plan either.

Therefore I wish you the development of an outstanding marketing plan. And if you implement it, I wish you an outstanding implementation as well.

APPENDIX

SAMPLE MARKETING PLANS

The marketing plans that follow were done by students as a part of regular courses in marketing. They range from plans for entrepreneurial start-ups to plans for a division of a large corporation. They involve different products and varied services. They were accomplished by teams consisting solely of marketing majors, and mixed teams from other disciplines. They were done by students taking the entry-level undergraduate course in marketing, and students at the graduate level. They were developed by native-born American students, and mixed teams of American and foreign students. One plan was done by Australian students in an Australian university.

These students sometimes used different approaches. They applied the concepts and techniques of marketing to develop the best plans they could. These plans are not perfect, but they are good.

My purpose in including them is to show you what can be done as well as to give you some new ideas. Sometimes the students used a different approach than you might want to use. They saw things differently than you might today. They came up with different solutions to what might even be different problems than you may find. This is true even if you were to develop a plan for the identical product and industry. I hope their efforts will challenge and motivate you to develop the most professional marketing plan that you can. Only by stretching to your limits can you grow to your potential for mastering this important marketing skill.

A1

PROMOTING HEALTHY FAMILIES

Developed by
ANNETTE R. DAVIDSON
SAIM KEFELI
JONATHAN RO
EMY YULIATY

Contents

EXECUTIVE SUMMARY

This marketing plan was constructed to promote a health plan called Healthy Families, which is underwritten by the state of California and designed for children of the working poor. Enrollees to this program must select a physician for primary care services, who is often times affiliated with at least one Independent Physician's Association (IPA) such as Superior IPA. Superior IPA was established six years ago. Among its competitive advantages, Superior IPA is a physician-owned entity. It has a very strong infrastructure that prevents mistrust between the physicians and the IPA, which has historically plagued many IPAs. In the wake of folding IPAs, it became known as a reliable and stable entity in the health care business. Superior keeps the physicians involved in all the aspects of the IPA including some management tasks and financial decision making. Another competitive advantage for Superior IPA is that it is launching an aggressive marketing effort to increase its member (patient) base which is something their competitors have yet to do. Superior also has a contract with CAP Management Systems (CMS). CMS is responsible for helping Superior IPA market their services to the public.

The product CMS is marketing is the Healthy Families Program which amounts to low-cost insurance that provides health, dental and vision coverage to children one to 18 years old. The cost of the care is low but the quality of health care provided by Superior IPA is the same as the care provided for those individuals paying in full. Healthy Families is a state funded health care program and the state of California is eager to provide health care to all its children.

California's effort to provide health care insurance to more uninsured children was made possible last year when Congress passed and President Clinton signed the State Children's Health Insurance Program (CHIP). This is the largest expansion of children's health coverage since the adoption of Medicaid in 1965. CHIP is a $4 billion-a-year national initiative to help states provide health insurance for uninsured children in low-wage working families. California created the Healthy Families Program to use its share of these funds to cover low-income, uninsured children.

CMS, after reviewing extensive demographic and psychographic data, has chosen to market this program to a specific demographic sector in its surrounding geographic market. Specifically, the characteristics of our target market are as follows: one to 18 years of age, primarily Hispanic, household of 3–4 members, household income level ranging from $32,387–$35,524, no current health insurance coverage, and a U.S. citizen or legal immigrant.

According to the breakeven analysis, CMS will have to enroll 264 new members in the Healthy Families Program at Superior IPA. The marketing budget after all expenses is $320 per month for the first year. Since this program was started by the state, the majority of the printed material needed to promote, explain, and enroll in the program is provided by the state free of charge. Money allotted for marketing will be spent only on supplemental materials needed and/or the vehicle used to get the materials in the hands of the target market. The state of California will allocate additional funds to CMS as they have been issued $6 million from the federal government to promote this program and the funds must be spent each year or the funds will be transferred to another state. CMS will apply each year for a portion of the allocated funds to supplement its marketing efforts. CMS will request a minimum of $100,000 per year.

INTRODUCTION

A time traveler from three decades ago would not recognize the current health care industry. Up until approximately a decade ago, health insurance in the United States operated primarily under an "indemnity" or "fee-for-service" (FFS) model. Under that system, a holder of a health insurance policy was free to visit any physician of his or her choosing. In turn, the physician would bill the policyholder's insurance company for whatever services were provided.

In effect, the FFS model was a self-referral model to health care and it had one major weakness in that it did not provide any incentives for the medical community to control costs. Although there are other contributing factors, lack of control was a primary contributing element that fueled extraordinary inflation in medical costs.

The managed care approach to health care delivery differs most significantly from the FFS model in that it provides strong incentives for the medical community to control costs. Under managed care, physicians and other providers of medical services generally enter into written agreements with health insurance companies, in which the physician agrees to accept a set dollar amount per member for primary care services. This system of prefunding a provider for a given number of patients who enroll with that provider is also called "capitation" in health care lingo.

As you can see, a capitated provider has strong incentive to carefully manage the utilization of services of his or her patients because that has a direct impact on the bottom line. Ultimately, the theory is that captitated providers will be less likely to prescribe unnecessary procedures and will instead try to instill "wellness" in the patient's health regimen. Wellness is generally used in the health care community to describe an overall approach to health care in which the focus is to keep members at a generally good level of health. Presumably, this helps to minimize severe episodes of illness that require more expensive and invasive medical intervention.

In the western United States, managed care plans have gained wide acceptance with the public and many managed health care companies have become powerful regional businesses as a result of it. In response to this, physicians formed alliances among themselves and these affiliations are commonly called "Independent Physician Associations" or IPAs. By pooling their membership, physicians of an IPA are in a better position to negotiate with health care companies for more favorable terms than if each were to go it alone.

Superior IPA is one such affiliation of family practice and specialist physicians. There are approximately 163 physicians affiliated with Superior IPA and their practices are located in various parts around west San Gabriel Valley. The physicians of Superior IPA treat Medicare, Medi-Cal, and Commercial patients who are members of most major health plans such as Blue Cross, UHP, and Universal Care.

Currently, Superior IPA has a very low number of Healthy Families enrollees and it desires to grow that membership primarily through an informational and educational blitz in its service area. Healthy Families is a federal and state funded health care plan that is intended for children ages one to 18 who come from families loosely defined as "working poor."

Our marketing plan studies demographic and other relevant data to determine whether Superior IPA's service area is suitable for the Healthy Families health plan and, if so, how that market can be reached.

SITUATIONAL ANALYSIS

Situational Environment

People, for many years, have had a vested interest in the health care industry. They use health services not only when they need urgent medical attention but also for preventative purposes such as regular checkups. The enormous width of the industry encompasses many specializations and services that range from tetanus vaccination for small scars to artificial heart transplantation surgeries. Furthermore, the unpredictable manner of people's medical needs along with the requirement of fast response for these needs, make health care a dynamic industry. The need for fast and accurate medical response for the numerous medical needs makes it imperative for the various components of the health care delivery system to work in concert. Since people's health is at stake, high-quality service is paramount. It is quite a challenge to provide quality service in today's environment of increasing managed care.

As managed care plans gained wider popularity and acceptance with the public, physicians discovered it to be to their advantage to pool their resources and form affiliations. These affiliations are often called Independent Physicians Associations (IPA) and there are some advantages to forming this alliance. Perhaps the most notable one is that pooling their membership gives them greater bargaining strength when negotiating with health plans on rates.

Of course, not all IPAs are alike. They come in all shapes and sizes, in that, some IPAs are actively managed by their affiliated physicians while others have delegated day-to-day management to outside management firms.

Unfortunately, some IPAs have encountered fiscal trouble despite the apparent merits of affiliation, primarily because "they lacked a solid financial base, a clear approach to governance and a strong infrastructure" (Finger, 1999). As a result, many IPAs throughout the country have filed for bankruptcy. These failures do not help engender trust between physicians and health plans. Even without failures, physicians sometimes complained about losing some autonomy and being told what types of treatments they can or cannot apply. Moreover, having no financial control over the IPA, many physicians felt like outcasts.

IPAs face many external and internal challenges, perhaps much more than they can handle. In fact, some experts do not expect many of them to continue as viable businesses. Industry observers think that most of them will file bankruptcy within the next 18 to 24 months due to "the combination of poor management and inadequate payment from health plans" (Bernstein, 1999).

It is in the interest of the health plans, physicians, and patients that IPAs remain financially viable and solvent. Health plans need a stable network of contracted physicians to provide health care to their members in select service areas. Conversely, a member wants to have confidence that his or her primary care physician will be around when medical attention is needed. In the purest Darwinian sense, the current existence of some IPAs might signal the end of unfit IPAs and the start of a period of domination by a group of fewer, but better managed, IPAs.

Neutral Environment

Special agencies of the state and federal government normally regulate the health care industry, and their work has become more involved with the growth of managed care plans. The complexity of the issue, the number of parties involved, and the fact that all the parties have been hurt in some way, renders the whole issue hard to solve with temporary or minor regulations that are applied by local or state governments. The solution seems to be a health care reform that is introduced by the federal government.

Fortunately, economic and political conditions enable the federal government to focus on health care. After decades of struggling with issues such as the Cold War, budget deficit, and nuclear threats, the U.S. government finally has the resources to deal with issues such as environmental protection, health care, and social security. Despite favorable conditions and the general expectation that the federal government will start health care reform, the elections that will be held next year reduce the chances for such reforms to take place over the next two years. However, with so many industry observers, it seems certain that everything will change, and will change dramatically.

Another strong influence on health care is the new health consciousness that started to affect lives for the last two decades. Increasing general welfare, favorable economic conditions along with stable political conditions help not only governments but also the public focus on different issues. Naturally, the health care industry benefits considerably from this trend. Increasing awareness will result in an increasing number of people covered by the managed care plans that provide health care at a low price. In particular, the number of children enrolled in managed care plans is expected to grow even higher due to the tendency of parents to seek better care for their children. Managed care plans for children are expected to benefit most from this trend of health consciousness, compared with other types of managed care plans.

In addition to all these, the California state government is placing a special emphasis on managed care plans for children, called the Healthy Families Program. The state promotes this managed care plan by publishing and distributing brochures and booklets. This actually provides free advertising for the IPAs. In addition, the government has passed laws in favor of the managed care program such as the one that makes legal immigrant children eligible for the program. The current changes are expected to be followed by some major changes that will increase the overall eligibility levels of families (Heath, 1999). The increase in market size along with an increase in the number of applications being filed will dramatically increase the number of people enrolled in Healthy Families, creating a promising future for the IPAs providing Healthy Families to their members.

Competitor Environment

The competitor environment of Superior IPA consists of IPAs and medical groups that accept the Healthy Families members and are located within the target market area.

When we consulted the Healthy Families Hot Line, Web sites, and studied its geographic locations, we learned that two other IPAs in Superior IPA's service area were direct competitors. These two IPAs are considered competitors because of the overlap in service areas, the number of physicians in those IPAs currently serving the community, the variety of languages spoken by bilingual physicians, and the choice of contracted health plans they currently have that qualify for the Healthy Families Program. The two competitors are:

- *Allied Physician IPA,* which has a network of more than 600 physicians and has contracted health plans with Blue Shield, UHP Healthcare, Health Net, and LA Care Health Plan. Bilingual physicians can speak languages such as: Chinese Mandarin, Tagalog, Cantonese, Fookien, Spanish, Taiwanese, Burmese, Vietnamese, Korean, Hindi, Urdu, Armenian, Arabic, Japanese, Farsi, French, German, and Italian.
- *Pacific IPA,* which has a network of 200 physicians, contracted health plans with Blue Cross, Blue Shield, and Health Net. The bilingual physicians can speak in languages such as: Chinese Mandarin, Cantonese, Spanish, Taiwanese, Vietnamese, Korean, Hindi, and Japanese.

The competitors' strength is that they have more physicians than Superior IPA (which has a network of 163 physicians). In addition, they have many varieties of bilingual physicians, which will be more favorable for the large Asian population living in the San Gabriel Valley and neighboring cities. Convenient location and a beautiful building may attract more walk-in customers to the Allied Physicians IPA. Furthermore, the Allied Physicians IPA is affiliated with more hospitals than Superior IPA, giving their patients more alternatives for further treatments.

The major weakness of these competitors is their lack of promotions. Since the Healthy Families Program is considered a new managed care plan, promotional materials and further information will be helpful in building awareness within the community. Strategies used by competitors depend on interested customers, word of mouth, current patient lists, and promotion by the Healthy Families Program itself. Among other weaknesses are the lack of an established image and reputation, and market presence of the competitors.

To counteract the strength of the competitors, our marketing plan for Superior IPA will emphasize building customer awareness of the presence of the Healthy Families Program. By doing so, CMS will also emphasize the existence of Superior IPA as their image provider for this program, so that every prospective customer will be more likely to choose physicians associated with Superior IPA.

Company Environment

Superior IPA is an independent physician association with a network of 163 physicians. It is a nonprofit mutual benefit corporation that is owned by physicians. The physicians are scattered throughout the west San Gabriel Valley and neighboring cities. Superior IPA also has physicians at distant places such as Glendora, Santa Monica, and San Clemente.

Superior IPA was established six years ago. It has now become a corporation that is identified as reliable and stable in the health care industry. This success depends on two major elements. First, it has always had good business management. Since 1995, Superior IPA has been under contract with a professional management services organization, CAP Management Systems (CMS). Since then, CMS has been handling the management of Superior IPA, and this contract is expected to be kept valid for the oncoming years. Second, Superior IPA is a nonprofit corporation that is owned by the physicians themselves. Therefore, all physicians have unlimited access to the financial records and they all participate in the decision-making processes. This establishes a feeling of trust within the organization, which is then reflected in the physician-member and health care company relationships.

With the physicians currently specializing in a total of 38 areas, Superior IPA can provide a wide range of services. It has contracts with all major health care companies, and although it provides service for most managed care plans, most of the members are covered by Medi-Cal managed care plan. Currently, it has 3,486 members, 3,083 of whom are Medi-Cal members. But when these members' incomes increase they will be able to join the Healthy Families Program instead of Medi-Cal. Superior IPA also established a good relationship with a nearby hospital, Garfield Medical Center, and it provides Superior its facilities as needed. Overall, it has good contracts with all parties, and it established a superior network of health care providers to provide premium health care service.

Competitive Advantages

Probably the most important competitive advantage of the company is that unlike many IPAs, it is owned by the physicians themselves. It has a very strong infrastructure that prevents mistrust between the physicians and the IPA, and it keeps the physicians involved in all aspects of the IPA including management, providing a primary motivation for solving many problems that resulted in disasters for many IPAs such as staff layoffs or postponing payments.

A second advantage has been that the majority of the physicians are Asian. Considering that the immediate target market within the two-mile radius primarily consists of Asians (46 percent to be accurate), this has been a fairly important advantage over the other IPAs, because Asians feel more comfortable with Asian physicians, and make their decisions on this issue accordingly. This issue was more important in cases where the patients are younger than 18 and feel more comfortable communicating with the physician in his/her own language. Market expansion efforts will come from achieving this synergy from the Hispanic market too (see Target Market).

Another important advantage is that Superior IPA has been in the market for six years, and during this time it has managed to establish a trustworthy name. Unlike many other IPAs, Superior IPA does not suffer from management problems and it has good relationships with the health care companies. The members and the health care companies are confident that Superior IPA will be in the market for a long time, and this provides a considerable advantage in a market full of uncertainty and discomfort.

In addition to all that, Superior IPA has a distinctive future that separates it from the rest: It provides high coordination among the members, the health care company, and physicians. It uses procedures that clearly state the actions to be taken in any given situation. This makes all the interactions easy and clear, eliminates the confusion, and makes the health care company-IPA-physician-member relationships comfortable. Since every party knows what it can expect and what it is expected to do, everything runs smoothly and problems become easy to detect and solve.

Finally, Superior IPA has a strong relationship with a nearby hospital, Garfield Medical Center. Because both parties know each other well and recognize what to expect from each other, they managed to establish specific procedures that help them work in harmony. The members of Superior IPA benefit from this relationship, since they can use facilities of the Garfield Medical Center. This increases the quality of the service, and provides a major advantage over other IPAs.

Each of these points not only furnishes Superior IPA with necessary features to survive and stay in the market for an extended period of time, but also provides a distinctive advantage, making it unique among many other IPAs. It provides high-quality service, and establishes strong relations with all other parties; Superior IPA ensures a healthy and stable future.

TARGET MARKET

Demographics

This is the most common basis for segmenting consumer markets because markets are strongly related to demand and are relatively easy to measure. The characteristics that are used in segmentation are age, gender, median income, and ethnicity of the population in each service area.

- **Age and gender:** In each service area, the segment markets are divided into three groups: population of females and males whose ages are below 6, population of females and males whose ages are between 6 and 13, and population of females and males whose ages are between 13 and 18 years of age. This category is based on the eligibility age to apply for the Healthy Families Program, which is between one and 18 years of age.
- **Median income:** Using the median income for each segment, we can determine the number of members in each household and determine if they fall between the federal Poverty Levels.
- **Ethnicity:** Market segmentation of the market based on ethnicity is used to determine the market behavior (which will be used in the Psychographic Segmentation section), and therefore will be used to determine the best ways to approach this market.

Although CMS would prefer to target the entire population surrounding Superior IPA, a market segmentation strategy will be implemented. This will allow CMS to develop an optimal, cost- and time-efficient strategy to reach its goal to increase the number of patients using Superior IPA. CMS will accomplish this by promoting the Healthy Families Program at Superior IPA to the Hispanic population in the San Gabriel Valley and surrounding cities.

The characteristics of our target market were derived from a demographic analysis using population statistics provided by The MEDSTAT Group (MEDSTAT, 1999). The characteristics are as follows:

- 1–18 years old
- Primarily Hispanic
- Household of 3–4 members
- Household Income Level Ranging from $32,387–$35,524
- No Current Health Insurance Coverage
- U.S. Citizen or Legal Immigrant

The above target market is eligible for the Healthy Families Program at Superior IPA. We chose to promote Healthy Families to the Hispanic market for a multitude of reasons. First, when reviewing the previously stated population data, we found that approximately 64 percent of the population in the Combined Service Area is Hispanic (MEDSTAT, 1999).

Second, Healthy Families is a state funded managed care program and the state of California is eager to provide health care to all children. California's effort to provide health care insurance to more uninsured children was made possible last year when Congress passed and President Clinton signed the State Children's Health Insurance Program (CHIP). This is the largest expansion of children's health coverage since the adoption of Medicaid in 1965. CHIP is a $4-billion-a-year national initiative to help states provide health insurance for uninsured children in low-wage working families (100% Campaign, Web Site). California created the Healthy Families Program to use its share of these funds to cover low-income, uninsured children (*Healthy Families Handbook,* 1999).

Psychographics

Demographic data are used to segment markets because these data are related to behavior and are relatively easy to gather. However, demographics are not in themselves the cause of behavior. CMS realizes that it should go beyond demographic attributes in an effort to better understand why consumers behave the way they do, which involves examining attributes related to how a person thinks, feels, and acts.

The Hispanic community may have some apprehension about the health care system or no awareness of the benefits of preventative care (*La Opinion,* Interview). For this reason, *La Opinion,* a well-respected Hispanic newspaper, has published supplements to their newspaper focusing on health and well-being. These highly targeted supplements focus on the health issues that affect and interest Latinos most (*La Opinion,* Brochure). CMS may take advantage of this venue in the November issue. *La Opinion* also offers assistance in targeting the ad specifically to the audience needed. It will be important to focus on educating the Hispanic community that obtaining health services through the Healthy Families Program will in no way affect their status with Immigration and Naturalization Services (INS), and that the Healthy Families Program does not share any information with the INS. This topic will be reviewed in the Marketing Tactics section.

According to *La Opinion,* the following facts may be useful in selecting venues for advertising Superior IPA and the Healthy Families Program:

- Hispanic adults accounted for 42 percent of all adults who attended rock/Spanish rock concerts in Los Angeles and surrounding cities
- 55 percent of Hispanic adults attended one or more movies in the past 12 months
- 46 percent have purchased CD's in the past three months
- Hispanic adults accounted for 39 percent of all adults attending dance/nightclubs in the past 12 months
- Hispanic adults accounted for 84 percent of all adults who attended an international soccer game in the past 12 months
- Hispanic adults accounted for 83 percent of all adults who attended a Galaxy soccer game in the past 12 months
- Hispanic adults accounted for 40 percent of all adults who attended a Dodgers baseball game in the past 12 months
- Hispanic adults accounted for 40 percent of all adults who attended a Lakers basketball game in the past 12 months
- 2.2 million Hispanics travel on L.A. Freeways every weekend
- 72 percent of Hispanic adults in the Los Angeles area and surrounding cities are involved in community, church and school events (*La Opinion,* Brochure)

Geographics

CMS divided its markets also based on the service area definitions. The service area definitions are based on actual facility discharges by zip code. To determine the areas, actual inpatient and outpatient cases for the most recent fiscal year were ranked by zip code in descending order. Once ranked, the areas were defined on a basic formula. These areas are:

 – 2-mile radius: inpatients and outpatients residing within a 2-mile radius.

– *Primary Service Area (PSA):*	top 70 percent of combined inpatients and outpatients by zip code.
– *Secondary Service Area (SSA):*	next 15 percent (71–85 percent) of combined inpatient and outpatients by zip code.
– *Combined Service Area (CSA):*	combination of PSA and SSA equaling 85 percent of combined inpatient and outpatient cases by zip code.

Thus, the target market is the west San Gabriel Valley and neighboring cities (see Appendix A for map of service area). This includes, but is not limited to, the following cities: Alhambra, Montebello, Rosemead, San Gabriel, Monterey Park, West Covina, Baldwin Park, Los Angeles, Temple City, El Monte, Covina, Pasadena, La Puente, and Arcadia. Superior IPA provides a complete network of general practitioners and specialists in this service area. Approximately 488,847 people are eligible based on our analysis.

STRENGTHS, WEAKNESSES, OPPORTUNITIES, AND THREATS

Strengths

Nonprofit, Mutual Benefit Organization.   As previously stated, Superior IPA is a nonprofit, mutual benefit organization, which is dedicated to fully serving its physicians and members. Accordingly, financial statements are disclosed and trust among physicians is established. This creates an environment that will enable physicians and their staff to work well and provide the best service for members of the community.

Bilingual Physicians.   Superior IPA provides the community with a variety of bilingual physicians who can communicate in numerous languages such as: Chinese Mandarin, Cantonese, Vietnamese, Korean, Japanese, Tagalog, Spanish, Taiwanese, Arabica, Italian, French, Portuguese, Armenian, Turkish, and Cambodian. The majority of Superior IPA physicians can speak Chinese, which gives them an edge over the competition because there is a significant Chinese population living within its primary service area.

Trustworthy Physicians.   Most of the physicians associated with Superior IPA have been serving the Asian community in the San Gabriel Valley and neighboring cities for many years. They are among the most qualified physicians in the area to ensure the finest level of medical excellence. Each of them is affiliated with the most respected hospitals and medical centers, such as: Garfield Medical Center, Alhambra Hospital, San Gabriel Valley Medical Center, Monterey Park Hospital, Whittier Hospital Medical Center, and Greater El Monte Community Hospital.

Private Practice.   Superior IPA provides health services to its patients through a variety of local and private practice offices, not in a clinic. This enables patients to choose and visit the closest one of the many offices that are scattered throughout many cities, including: Monterey Park, Alhambra, Rosemead, San Gabriel, El Monte, West Covina, Montebello, Temple City, Pasadena, Arcadia, Covina, Baldwin Park, La Puente, and Los Angeles.

Partnership. Superior IPA has partnered with Garfield Medical Center and Tenet Health Systems to better serve its community by enabling patients to receive further treatments easily. Furthermore, the partnership with CMS as its management services organization provides Superior IPA with the best management for smooth relations between its physicians and patients.

Direct Referral Program. Superior IPA provides direct referral to specialists; this enables patients to get better treatment conveniently, while benefiting the specialists as well.

Weaknesses

Limited Number of Spanish-Speaking Physicians. The demographic and ethnic analysis indicates that our target market is children who come from Hispanic families or communicate in Spanish as their first language. In fact, of all the primary care physicians in Superior IPA, only 36 percent speak Spanish. This number may be considered low since our target market consists of a large number Hispanic families. Besides, one of the main competitors, Allied Physicians IPA, has a large number of Spanish-speaking physicians (60 percent of the primary care physicians speak Spanish). Our strategy will be to attract more Spanish-speaking physicians to join Superior IPA in the future in order to establish better communication channels between physicians and patients.

Limited Contracted Health Plan. In the Los Angeles area, there are numerous health care companies offering the Healthy Families Program, such as: Community Health Plan, Blue Cross HMO, Blue Shield HMO, Health Net, Kaiser Permanente, L.A. Care Health Plan, Molina, Dental Plan (Superior Dental Plan, Delta Dental, Denticare), and vision services plan.

However, Superior IPA has limited contracts with health care companies such as Blue Cross, Molina, and UHP. Limiting the number of contracts with health care companies may hinder Superior IPA from attaining the market share it strives for since our consumers will not be able to choose from a wide variety of health care companies. To counteract this weakness, we will attract more health care companies to contract with in order to provide our potential members with a large variety of health plans.

Opportunities

Large Numbers of Prospective Customers. Based on our analysis in the target market section, there is a large number of prospective customers who are potentially eligible (approximately 488,847 people are eligible based on our analysis in the Target Market section). This means that Superior IPA faces an important opportunity for growth. Therefore, our marketing strategy will be based on introductory and growth models (which will be explained in more detail in the Marketing Strategy section).

Future State Regulation. Currently, children who are eligible for the Healthy Families Program are those whose family income level falls between 133 percent and 200 percent of the Federal Poverty Level (FPL) for ages 1 to 6, and between 100 percent to 200 percent for ages 6 to 18.

As of November 1999, children between 200 and 250 percent of the FPL (and more with income deductions) will be eligible. The budget expanded coverage for children by increasing eligibility from 200 percent to 250 percent of the Federal Poverty Level (see Table A1–1 below). For example, if a child comes from a family of two and the family's

Table A1-1. Percent of Federal Poverty Levels

Percent of Federal Poverty Level	Number of Family Members				
	2	3	4	5	6
100	10,850	13,650	16,450	19,250	22,050
200	21,700	27,300	32,900	38,500	44,100
225	24,413	30,713	37,013	43,313	49,613
250	27,125	34,125	41,125	48,125	55,125
275	29,838	37,538	45,238	52,938	60,638
300	32,550	40,950	49,350	57,750	66,150

Source: The Federal Register.

annual income is $27,000 then the child is qualified for the Healthy Families Program based on the new regulation. In the past, the child would not qualify for the program if the annual income falls at more than 200 percent of FPL. Therefore, prospective families for this program will increase if the new regulation is activated.

The budget also allows the income deductions that are used in Medi-Cal to be applied to Healthy Families, such as child-care or work-related expenses. That means children with family incomes above 250 percent of poverty may also be eligible in the near future.

Threats

Strong Competitors. Two main competitors will be somewhat of a threat for Superior IPA in terms of their large numbers of physicians, the variety of languages spoken by physicians, and their contracted health plan, as we stated earlier in the competitor environment. However, Superior IPA is located in an area where the target market is quite large, so that there will be enough room for all the IPAs. Furthermore, these two main competitors do not promote Healthy Families; therefore, people are not fully aware of their market presence. Our strategy will be to provide prospective customers with the most updated information regarding Healthy Families, and through our marketing tactics, we will try to attract them to join the program with Superior IPA as their provider.

Limited Numbers of Physicians Associated with Superior IPA. As our marketing plan becomes more successful, a possible problem will be the limited number of physicians associated with Superior IPA. If the number of physicians remains the same and the number of members increases in the future, then the physician-to-member ratio will go up. This will be a problem for providing the best service to our patients/members. Therefore, in the future, we will be working on increasing our number of physicians, especially Spanish-speaking physicians, since our target market largely consists of Hispanic families.

MARKETING OBJECTIVES AND GOALS

Marketing Objectives

Because it was introduced in June 1998, the Healthy Families Program is considered a new health care program and many people are not fully aware of its existence. Therefore, our marketing objectives in this project are:

1. Being the first to promote this concept, we will be able to penetrate the market and attract more patients to sign up with the Healthy Families Program with Superior IPA as their provider. Our objective is to increase the number of Healthy Families' memberships within Superior IPA.

2. By increasing the number of memberships, we will be able to increase the overall capitation revenue, which is our ultimate objective.

3. To introduce Healthy Families to prospective audiences who have little or no awareness about health plans for children.

4. Educate prospective members that Healthy Families has not collected information regarding immigration status. The program will not provide information on the immigration status of such parents to the INS or use immigration information to demand repayment information from recipients for services lawfully provided.

Marketing Goals

Our marketing goals are:

1. To introduce the Healthy Families Program to at least 50 percent of all prospective customers within the west San Gabriel Valley area.

2. To increase the number of members in the Healthy Families Program by 81 percent from year 2000 to year 2002 (see Table A1-2 below).

3. To increase the capitation revenue by 196 percent from year 2000 to year 2002 (see Table A1-2 below).

The details regarding the number of target members and capitation revenue are as follows:

Table A1–2. Number of Members and Related Capitation Revenues per Year

	2000	*2001*	*2002*
Number of members	698	1,003	1,265
Capitation revenue	$116,226	$259,242	$343,956

MARKETING STRATEGY

For promoting Healthy Families, it is crucial to focus on the fact that the product is still in the introductory phase. Many of the potential members are still unaware of the Healthy Families Program and that Superior IPA offers it. It will be a focus of CMS to educate the local population about the existence of Healthy Families at Superior IPA and stimulate more demand for its services. Typically this phase, as it relates to the product life cycle (see Figure A1-1 below), is risky and plagued with expensive marketing dollars (Etzel et al. 1997).

CMS is at an advantage since the Healthy Families Handbooks, which are provided by the Department of Health Services, are free of charge and contain the majority of the information that CMS seeks to share with the local community. Since this handbook would be costly to print, this represents a considerable cost advantage for CMS.

FIGURE A1-1. Product Life Cycle

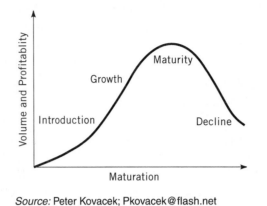

Source: Peter Kovacek; Pkovacek@flash.net

Our marketing philosophy will be based on two basic strategies, information strategy and image strategy. Consumers purchase a product because it provides satisfaction. The thing that makes a product capable of satisfying wants is its utility, and it is through marketing that much of a product's utility is created. Healthy Families is considered a new program that was introduced by the state in June 1998, so most people are not fully aware of its presence. Unless you know a product exists and where you can get it, the product has no value. Therefore, informing the prospective buyers that a product exists needs information utility. Through information strategy, we are trying to build awareness that there is a new type of children's health plan in addition to Medi-Cal for Children. Normally, people only know about Medi-Cal for Children, which was designed for low-income families and provides no-cost medical service for their children under 21. Healthy Families is a low-cost insurance that provides health, dental, and vision coverage to children who do not currently have insurance or whose family income is too high to qualify for no-cost Medi-Cal. As people are informed of the existence of the Healthy Families Program, we will, through image strategy, deliver the message that Superior IPA is their main provider. Image strategy is the emotional or psychological value that a person attaches to a product or brand because of its reputation or social standing. Superior IPA's brand image must be a gateway for all prospective customers as they decide to enroll in the program. The overall strategy can be summarized as follows:

- **Information Strategy:**

1. CMS will deliver the message to the community and build or increase their awareness of the existence of the Healthy Families Program as low-cost health coverage besides no-cost Medi-Cal.

2. CMS will educate families of the importance of having health care coverage for their children and help them understand the benefits of regular and preventive health care.

3. CMS will motivate them to take the actions necessary to apply and obtain health coverage for their uninsured children.

4. CMS will inform families that information and free enrollment assistance is available in their neighborhood in seven languages.

5. CMS will add special services to differentiate its product. All new enrollees will be called to see if all of their needs are being met.

6. CMS will issue a newsletter to repeat customers informing them of important medical issues.

- **Image Strategy:**

1. CMS will continue delivering the message and build awareness in the community while introducing Superior IPA as a primary provider in Healthy Families Program.

2. CMS will create a brand identity for Superior IPA as "their local doctor's office who cares about its community."

3. CMS will emphasize the benefits of enrolling with Superior IPA. Benefits include bilingual physicians and service provided to all prospective customers.

4. CMS will stress the easy application process for the Healthy Families Program and that there is free assistance in filling out the application form. Healthy Families will help them choose the right plan and the right physician and drive the target population or all eligible customers to enroll. Superior IPA will also have a certified application assistant in each office so that they may help potential clients fill out the application in the office. This will dramatically increase the probability that patients will stay with Superior IPA for their medical needs.

- **Promoting the Image:**

1. CMS will use vehicles such as special events, partnerships, promotional opportunities, on-site marketing, local advertising, community marketing, grass-roots collateral materials, mass media, media relations as well as both traditional and nontraditional forms of marketing simple in form and image. More detail will be provided in the Marketing Tactics section.

Another crucial focus for CMS will be to mitigate the fears of potential clients regarding the INS. Although federal guidelines were recently issued clarifying that the use of Healthy Families will not affect a family's immigration status, the fear by Hispanic families is so entrenched that it will be essential to educate families about the issue (100% Campaign, Web site). Materials provided by the state at no cost will be distributed by CMS to the potential members explaining that the use of the Healthy Families Program will in no way affect their status. The material is available in English and Spanish, and phone numbers are provided for those who have more questions. The state will also provide funding to assist CMS in this campaign. This is explained further in the following section on Marketing Tactics.

MARKETING TACTICS

Product

Technically, the company to be promoted is Superior IPA. One vehicle to promote Superior IPA is to promote one of the products they offer, called Healthy Families. CMS's primary goal is to increase the number of patients who utilize Superior IPA when they join the Healthy Families Program. Superior IPA has 163 general practitioners and specialists in the previously stated service area.

Superior will be providing the Healthy Families services to clients who meet the criteria established by the state of California. The qualifications are as follows:

- Children ages 1–18
- Families with incomes at or below 250 percent (as of November 1, 1999) of the Federal Income Guidelines
- Children without employer-sponsored health insurance in the last 3 months
- Children not eligible for Medi-Cal
- Children who are U.S. citizens, nationals or eligible immigrants
- Children who live in California

The Healthy Families Program amounts to low-cost insurance that provides health, dental and vision coverage to children who meet the above stated criteria. It is important to mention that even though the cost of the care is low, the quality of health care provided by Superior IPA is the same as the care provided for those individuals paying in full. This is a crucial point and will be stressed in our advertising campaign since low-cost health care is typically thought of as a low-quality care.

Price

Family size, family income level, and the health care company chosen determine the monthly premium for Healthy Families. The monthly premiums range from $4 to $9 a month for each child up to a maximum of $27 for all children within the household. Incentives are provided to pay premiums in advance, to receive one month free. Specifically, for every three months paid in advance the fourth month is free. In addition to the monthly premiums, a co-payment of $5 is required at the time of service. However, this co-payment is not required if the service is of a preventative nature (such as immunization shots) rather than regular health care. The total expenditure per family is $250 per year. Once this limit is reached, all services provided thereafter are free to the family. (See Appendix B for a Healthy Families Handbook.)

Promotion and Place

There are numerous low-cost vehicles to promote Healthy Families and Superior IPA to our target market. If CMS dedicated one full-time, bilingual marketing person, CMS could accomplish the goal of increasing the number of patients for Superior IPA. This person would utilize a combination of marketing techniques, such as person-to-person selling, sales promotion, advertising, and publicity.

This marketing person could find out about all of the local trade shows and community events that are reaching similar audiences. A booth would be set up to distribute the Healthy Families Handbooks and Superior IPAs physician roster to individuals who fit the target market criteria. This method is extremely cost effective since the Healthy Families Handbooks are free and will have all of the information the potential member will need, including phone numbers to call if they have difficulty filling out the forms. The methods are as follows:

Establishing Key Alliances and Community Involvement: Creating strategic alliances with other nonprofit organizations that are targeting the Hispanic community. This will help share and thereby lower the cost of promotions. CMS will request help from public and private organizations.

Current Members: In an effort to keep existing customers, a newsletter could be sent out to promote Healthy Families and discuss medical issues related to the Hispanic market. If the newsletter were a folded 11×17, 2-sided, 2-color process, the cost to print 10,000 units would be $675 plus tax (Lambert Printing Company, Interview). Postage for this newsletter would cost $1,200 according to the U.S. Post Office (U.S. Post Office, Interview).

Private Sector: In the private sector, small businesses can help promote Superior IPA by allowing us to provide materials for their employees that explain the Superior IPA and the Healthy Families Program. The focus of the promotion will be to explain that when your children have preventative health care, the parents decrease their absentee rates from work and their children will be happier and more productive in school. Also, those children will receive critical preventative care they need to prevent or detect illness before it becomes more serious.

Public Sector: In the public sector, CMS will create allies with schools, childcare organizations, religious congregations, advocacy groups, grass-roots organizations, the local Chamber of Commerce, Community Based Outreach, the PTA, and many others.

Community Based Outreach (CBO), for instance, is sensitive to culture and language and intimately familiar with the populations it serves. It has the ability to work well directly with the low-income, hard-to-teach target audience. CBO conducts demographic research and assists in developing coalitions and networks. Its success is based on how well it connects various causes in an effort to share resources. CBO will have extensive public relations campaigns, which will help CMS reach as many prospective families as possible. CBO also maintains connections with corporations and will enlist their help as well as the media's help to portray the benefits of a healthy lifestyle.

According to Yahoo.com Yellow Pages, there are five Catholic churches in our target area (Yahoo Yellow Pages, Web Site). Most of these churches were willing to allow the information to be distributed to their parishioners. Many of the churches were also willing to make announcements during Spanish and English services informing the parishioners that the information was available and where to find it. There are also approximately 15 junior high schools and approximately 17 high schools to which CMS could target its effort of informing the public.

Ads will be displayed in theaters and on buses as well. When advertising in a theater, the cost is based on an 18-week minimum and a 10-screen theater. It costs $20 per screen, times 18 weeks and 10 screens for a total of $3,600 (Edwards Cinema Corporate Office, Interview). Many of the cities in our target market vary in their approach to advertising on bus benches and city buses. All of the cities provide ways for CMS to advertise free of charge, since Superior IPA is a nonprofit organization.

Local Cable: Another vehicle is the local cable channel, which allows nonprofit organizations to run ads for free. Information could be projected in English and in Spanish promoting the need for adequate health care for children. The ad could

Table A1-3. Analysis of Advertising Costs

Description	Basic cost	Remark	Year 2000	2001	2002	Total
Movie Theaters	$20/screen/week	Minimum of 18-week commitment required. Average theater in Alhambra has 7 screens. $20 × 7 × 18 = $2,520. Run two times a year at 18 weeks each. $2,520 × 2 = $5,040.	$5,040	$5,040	$5,040	**$15,120**
10-Minute Promotional Video	$1,500	$1,500 is cost of producing the promotional video. It is free to run it on local cable.	$1,500	$0	$0	**$1,500**
Monterey Park, Bus Shelter Advertising	$300	$300 is cost of preparing and producing the poster to be placed in bus shelter advertising. The city of Monterey Park does not charge for advertising in bus shelters as long as it serves a clear public benefit.	$300	$0	$0	**$300**
Spanish Language Newspaper	$3,870	Cost of half-page ad per year in *La Ola*. Circulation is 100,000.	$3,870	$3,870	$3,870	**$11,610**
Newsletter Quarterly	$1,875/quarter	$1,875 × 4 = $7,500 per year	$7,500	$7,500	$7,500	**$22,500**
		Total Cost	**$18,210**	**$16,410**	**$16,410**	**$51,030**

explain how Superior IPA has everything they need to keep their family healthy and that they have been serving the local community for many years. Superior IPA will provide the phone numbers and contacts of certified application assistants to help potential members in signing up for the Healthy Families Program. Ads for the local cable channel may be in two forms; they may be all text or in video form. A professional, eight-to-ten-minute video may be provided for $1500 (Gary Center, Interview).

Spanish Media: There are local Spanish newspapers and radio stations available also for a fee. Wave Community Newspapers are geared for multicultural audiences. *La Ola* is a Spanish newspaper published by Wave Communications, which is doorstep delivered in our target region. The cost varies depending on the length of the ad and whether or not color is used. A full-page ad with 100,000 circulation is $7,740 per year. A half-page ad with the same circulation is $3,870 per year.

La Opinion is another newspaper in the area, but its circulation is beyond our geographic scope and the cost is much higher. *La Opinion* provides a large variety of services at varying prices. The cost will be determined by the breath and depth of the proposed advertising campaign. However, due to our nonprofit status, we may advertise in their supplement Health section in the November issue free of charge. *La Opinion* will also provide assistance in writing and developing the material prior to printing.

State Financial Assistance: As previously stated, there is a $4-billion-a-year national initiative to help states provide health insurance to uninsured children in low-wage working families. Of these funds, California has been allocated $6 million. CMS will file the proper paperwork in an effort to receive a portion of these funds to offset the advertising expenses. Grants may be written to receive funds in the amount of $100,000 or more depending on the remaining funds available. All funds allocated to the state of California must be designated by the end of the calendar year or the funds will become available for another state to utilize. CMS will apply for funds each year to supplement its campaign.

ORGANIZATION, EVALUATION, CONTROL, AND IMPLEMENTATION

1. Organization Chart for Project

In terms of the outreach initiative, the Marketing Coordinator must necessarily take a central role in ensuring that critical steps be executed at the appropriate time. Due to the newness of the Healthy Families program, our marketing plan calls for an approach to advertising that is educational and informational in nature. To help realize that vision, we have identified some important action items that need to be followed through on. Those action items, and related parties, are also summarized in the following chart.

Organization chart for Project

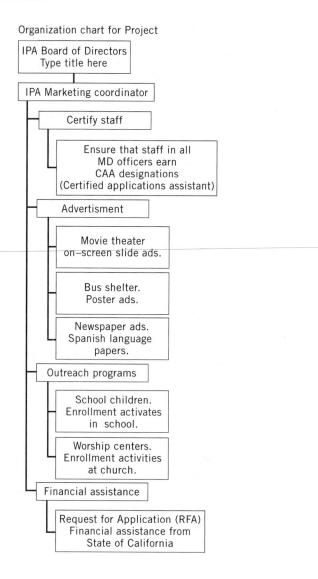

2. Project Development Schedules

The following schedule summarizes the timing of action steps that need to be taken as prescribed in this marketing plan.

Due Date	Action Step	Affected Party(ies)
2/2000	Meet with account executive of Spanish language newspapers, *La Ola,* to discuss costs and other issues related to running advertisement for Health Families and the IPA.	• Marketing Coordinator • *La Ola* account executive
2/2000	Initiate contact with leadership of local area churches (Protestant and Catholic) to discuss possibility of disseminating information and application forms about the Healthy Families program.	• Marketing Coordinator • Leadership of local area churches
3/2000	Get at least one front office staff person at every physician's clinic certified as Certified Application Assistance. (CAA)	• Marketing Coordinator • Front office manager at each physician's office.

Due Date	Action Step	Affected Party(ies)
3/2000	Meet with account executive at Edwards Theater Corporate office to discuss and plan pre-movie slide advertisement. Continue contact with account executive on as-needed basis until advertisement begins run in movie theaters.	• Marketing Coordinator • Edwards Theater account executive
5/2000	Initiate contact with council members of the city of Monterey Park and prepare presentation to convince city that Healthy Families presents a clear benefit to a significant number of city residents.	• Marketing Coordinator • City of Monterey Park council members
5/2000	Meet and discuss costs and other issues related to the preparation and production of poster suitable for bus shelter advertising. These posters will be used in the event that the city of Monterey Park votes to permit advertisement of Healthy Families in conjunction with the IPA's name in city bus shelters.	• Marketing Coordinator • Outdoor advertising account executive
6/2000	Make presentation to Monterey Park council members as planned.	• Marketing Coordinator • City of Monterey Park council members
7/2000	Meet and discuss costs and other issues related to the professional production of informational/promotional videos. These videos to be run on local cable television free of charge and will be designed to strongly associate Healthy Families with the IPA.	• Marketing Coordinator • Video production company
7/2000	Initiate contact with officials of local school districts to discuss possibility of conducting Healthy Families presentation in conjunction with back-to-school activities.	• Marketing Coordinator • School district officials
8/2000	Obtain and complete the Request for Application (RFA) forms from the state of California. These documents to be completed so that IPA considered when state awards funds for outreach programs.	• Marketing Coordinator • Upper management (CEO, COO, CFO, Director of IPA Operations)
9/2000	Meet with applicable representatives to discuss scheduling of IPA's professionally produced informational videos on local cable television. Continue communication as appropriate until videos begin airing on local cable.	• Marketing Coordinator • Representatives of local cable television
9/2000	Conduct presentation at local schools to teachers and students to identify and sign up eligible enrollees.	• Marketing Coordinator • School officials
11/2000	Contact state representative to follow up on status of the RFA that was submitted in consideration of possible financial assistance for outreach programs.	• Marketing Coordinator • State of California representatives
1/2001	Finalize written agreement with city of Monterey Park regarding the nature and duration of the advertisements to be placed in bus shelters.	• Marketing Coordinator • City of Monterey Park council members
1/2001	Finalize with the outdoor advertising company the poster to be used in Monterey Park bus shelters.	• Marketing Coordinator • Outdoor advertising account executive
3/2001	Meet with Edwards Theater account executive to extend on-screen advertising for 2001.	• Marketing Coordinator • Theater account executive
3/2001	Contact all physicians' offices to ensure that at least one person is a CAA and conduct followup procedures as necessary.	• Marketing Coordinator • Front office manager at each physician's office.
5/2001	Meet with Monterey Park council members to present report on effectiveness of advertisement campaign and express desire to continue in second half of the current year.	• Marketing Coordinator • City of Monterey Park council members
5/2001	Meet with outdoor advertising agency to discuss updating or adjusting the ad poster as necessary.	• Marketing Coordinator • Outdoor advertising account executive

Due Date	Action Step	Affected Party(ies)
7/2001	Contact school district officials to express desire to conduct back-to-school Healthy Families enrollment in similar fashion as last year.	• Marketing Coordinator • School officials
8/2001	Obtain and complete RFA for state assistance in financing outreach programs.	• Marketing Coordinator • Upper management (CEO, COO, CFO, Director of IPA Operations)
9/2001	Conduct presentation at local schools to teachers and students to identify and sign up eligible enrollees.	• Marketing Coordinator • School officials
10/2001	Meet with local cable representative to extend airing of informational video.	• Marketing Coordinator • Cable television representatives
11/2001	Contact state representative to follow up on status of the RFA that was submitted in consideration of possible financial assistance for outreach programs.	• Marketing Coordinator • State of California representatives
1/2002	Meet with Monterey Park council members to present report on the effectiveness of bus shelter advertising last year and express desire to continue some form of advertising in current year.	• Marketing Coordinator • City of Monterey Park council members
1/2002	As necessary, meet with outdoor advertising agency to discuss adjustments to poster or other issues related to bus shelter advertising.	• Marketing Coordinator • Outdoor advertising account executive
3/2002	Meet with Edwards Theater account executive to extend on-screen slide advertising for 2002.	• Marketing Coordinator • Theater account executive
5/2002	Conduct Healthy Families information and enrollment fairs at area churches.	• Marketing Coordinator • Church leadership
7/2002	Contact school officials to plan for back-to-school enrollment drive in September.	• Marketing Coordinator • School officials
8/2002	Complete and submit RFA to state for consideration of financial assistance in outreach efforts.	• Marketing Coordinator • Upper management (CEO, COO, CFO, Director of IPA Operations)
9/2002	Conduct back-to-school informational meeting at area schools and enroll eligible children.	• Marketing Coordinator • School officials

IPA
Breakeven Analysis

	Per Member							
Number of Members	Revenue	Fee to PCP	Fee to Specialist	Net Income (Before Fixed Costs)	Fixed Cost	Number of Members	Total Revenue	Total Costs
0	25.25	8.00	12.00	5.25	1,388.60	0	0.00	1,388.60
10	25.25	8.00	12.00	5.25	1,388.60	10	252.50	1,588.60
20	25.25	8.00	12.00	5.25	1,388.60	20	505.00	1,788.60
30	25.25	8.00	12.00	5.25	1,388.60	30	757.50	1,988.60
40	25.25	8.00	12.00	5.25	1,388.60	40	1,010.00	2,188.60
50	25.25	8.00	12.00	5.25	1,388.60	50	1,262.50	2,388.60
60	25.25	8.00	12.00	5.25	1,388.60	60	1,515.00	2,588.60
70	25.25	8.00	12.00	5.25	1,388.60	70	1,767.50	2,788.60
80	25.25	8.00	12.00	5.25	1,388.60	80	2,020.00	2,988.60
90	25.25	8.00	12.00	5.25	1,388.60	90	2,272.50	3,188.60
100	25.25	8.00	12.00	5.25	1,388.60	100	2,525.00	3,388.60
110	25.25	8.00	12.00	5.25	1,388.60	110	2,777.50	3,588.60
120	25.25	8.00	12.00	5.25	1,388.60	120	3,030.00	3,788.60
130	25.25	8.00	12.00	5.25	1,388.60	130	3,282.50	3,988.60
140	25.25	8.00	12.00	5.25	1,388.60	140	3,535.00	4,188.60
150	25.25	8.00	12.00	5.25	1,388.60	150	3,787.50	4,388.60
160	25.25	8.00	12.00	5.25	1,388.60	160	4,040.00	4,588.60
170	25.25	8.00	12.00	5.25	1,388.60	170	4,292.50	4,788.60
180	25.25	8.00	12.00	5.25	1,388.60	180	4,545.00	4,988.60
190	25.25	8.00	12.00	5.25	1,388.60	190	4,797.50	5,188.60
200	25.25	8.00	12.00	5.25	1,388.60	200	5,050.00	5,388.60
210	25.25	8.00	12.00	5.25	1,388.60	210	5,302.50	5,588.60
220	25.25	8.00	12.00	5.25	1,388.60	220	5,555.00	5,788.60
230	25.25	8.00	12.00	5.25	1,388.60	230	5,807.50	5,988.60
240	25.25	8.00	12.00	5.25	1,388.60	240	6,060.00	6,188.60
250	25.25	8.00	12.00	5.25	1,388.60	250	6,312.50	6,388.60
260	25.25	8.00	12.00	5.25	1,388.60	260	6,565.00	6,588.60
270	25.25	8.00	12.00	5.25	1,388.60	270	6,817.50	6,788.60
280	25.25	8.00	12.00	5.25	1,388.60	280	7,070.00	6,988.60
290	25.25	8.00	12.00	5.25	1,388.60	290	7,322.50	7,188.60
300	25.25	8.00	12.00	5.25	1,388.60	300	7,575.00	7,388.60
310	25.25	8.00	12.00	5.25	1,388.60	310	7,827.50	7,588.60
320	25.25	8.00	12.00	5.25	1,388.60	320	8,080.00	7,788.60
330	25.25	8.00	12.00	5.25	1,388.60	330	8,332.50	7,988.60
340	25.25	8.00	12.00	5.25	1,388.60	340	8,585.00	8,188.60
350	25.25	8.00	12.00	5.25	1,388.60	350	8,837.50	8,388.60
360	25.25	8.00	12.00	5.25	1,388.60	360	9,090.00	8,588.60
370	25.25	8.00	12.00	5.25	1,388.60	370	9,342.50	8,788.60

Breakeven point = 264 enrollees

IPA
Projected Statement of Cash Flows – 2000 to 2002

	FYE 12/31/2000	FYE 12/31/2001	FYE 12/31/2002
Net Income From Operations	7,503	144,496	167,193
Less:			
Capitation Receivable	116,226	259,242	343,956
Total Receivable	116,226	259,242	343,956
Plus:			
Accounts Payable	16,663	14,539	14,539
Accrued Expenses – IBNR	92,060	200,207	262,224
Total Payables and Accrued Expenses	108,723	214,746	276,763
Positive/(Negative) Cash Flow From Operations	0	100,000	100,000

IPA
Income Statement – 2000
Product Line – Healthy Families

	Jan	Feb	Mar	Apr	May	Jun	Jul	Aug	Sep	Oct	Nov	Dec	YTD	PMPM	% Gross
Member Months	174	201	225	240	279	325	375	423	498	553	612	698	4,603		
Capitation Revenue	$4,394	$5,075	$5,681	$6,060	$7,045	$8,206	$9,469	$10,681	$12,575	$13,963	$15,453	$17,625	$116,226	$25.25	100.00%
PMPM	25.25	25.25	25.25	25.25	25.25	25.25	25.25	25.25	25.25	25.25	25.25	25.25			
MEDICAL EXPENSES															
Capitated Fees – PCP	1,392.00	1,608.00	1,800.00	1,920.00	2,232.00	2,600.00	3,000.00	3,384.00	3,984.00	4,424.00	4,896.00	5,584.00	36,824.00	8	31.68%
Capitated Fees – Lab													0.00	0	0.00%
Capitated Fees – Other													0.00	0	0.00%
Specialist Fees	2,088.00	2,412.00	2,700.00	2,880.00	3,348.00	3,900.00	4,500.00	5,076.00	5,976.00	6,636.00	7,344.00	8,376.00	55,236.00	12	47.52%
Reinsurance Expense													0.00	0	0.00%
Total Medical Expenses	3,480.00	4,020.00	4,500.00	4,800.00	5,580.00	6,500.00	7,500.00	8,460.00	9,960.00	11,060.00	12,240.00	13,960.00	92,060.00	20	79.21%
Income Before Non-Medical Expenses and Other Revenue	913.50	1,055.25	1,181.25	1,260.00	1,464.75	1,706.25	1,968.75	2,220.75	2,614.50	2,903.25	3,213.00	3,664.50	24,165.75	5	20.79%
NON-MEDICAL EXPENSES															
Management Fees	600.00	600.00	600.00	600.00	600.00	600.00	600.00	600.00	600.00	600.00	600.00	600.00	7,200.00	2	6.19%
Insurance Expense	300.00	300.00	300.00	300.00	300.00	300.00	300.00	300.00	300.00	300.00	300.00	300.00	3,600.00	1	3.10%
Interest Expense													0.00	0	0.00%
Marketing Expense	320.00	320.00	320.00	320.00	320.00	320.00	320.00	320.00	320.00	320.00	320.00	320.00	3,840.00	1	3.30%
Purchases Services													0.00	0	0.00%
Legal & Accounting	166.00	166.00	166.00	166.00	166.00	166.00	166.00	166.00	166.00	166.00	166.00	166.00	1,992.00	0	1.71%
Dues & Subscriptions													0.00	0	0.00%
Taxes & Licenses													0.00	0	0.00%
Bank Charges	2.60	2.60	2.60	2.60	2.60	2.60	2.60	2.60	2.60	2.60	2.60	2.60	31.20	0	0.03%
Total Non-Medical Expenses	1,388.60	1,388.60	1,388.60	1,388.60	1,388.60	1,388.60	1,388.60	1,388.60	1,388.60	1,388.60	1,388.60	1,388.60	16,663.20	4	14.34%
Income (Loss) Before Other Revenue	(475.10)	(333.35)	(207.35)	(128.60)	76.15	317.65	580.15	832.15	1,225.90	1,514.65	1,824.40	2,275.90	7,502.55	2	6.46%
OTHER REVENUE															
Participation Fees													0.00	0	0.00%
Interest Revenue													0.00	0	0.00%
Other Revenue/Other Expense													0.00	0	0.00%
Total Other Revenue	0.00	0.00	0.00	0.00	0.00	0.00	0.00	0.00	0.00	0.00	0.00	0.00	0.00	0	0.00%
NET INCOME	(475.10)	(333.35)	(207.35)	(128.60)	76.15	317.65	580.15	832.15	1,225.90	1,514.65	1,824.40	2,275.90	7,502.55	2	6.46%

IPA
Income Statement – 2001
Product Line – Healthy Families

	Jan	Feb	Mar	Apr	May	Jun	Jul	Aug	Sep	Oct	Nov	Dec	YTD	PMPM	% Gross
Member Months	712	734	757	789	803	839	879	898	913	957	983	1,003	10,267		
Capitation Revenue	$17,978.00	$18,533.50	$19,114.25	$19,922.25	$20,275.75	$21,184.75	$22,194.75	$22,674.50	$23,053.25	$24,164.25	$24,820.75	$25,325.75	$259,241.75	$25.25	100.00%
PMPM	25.25	25.25	25.25	25.25	25.25	25.25	25.25	25.25	25.25	25.25	25.25	25.25			
MEDICAL EXPENSES															
Capitated Fees – PCP	5,696.00	5,872.00	6,056.00	6,312.00	6,424.00	6,712.00	7,032.00	7,184.00	7,304.00	7,656.00	7,864.00	8,024.00	82,136.00	8	31.68%
Capitated Fees – Lab														0.00	0.00%
Capitated Fees – Other														0.00	0.00%
Specialist Fees	8,188.00	8,441.00	8,705.50	9,073.50	9,234.50	9,648.50	10,108.50	10,327.00	10,499.50	11,005.50	11,304.50	11,534.50	118,070.50	12	45.54%
Reinsurance Expense														0.00	0.00%
Total Medical Expenses	13,884.00	14,313.00	14,761.50	15,385.50	15,658.50	16,360.50	17,140.50	17,511.00	17,803.50	18,661.50	19,168.50	19,558.50	200,206.50	20	77.23%
Income Before Non-Medical Expenses and Other Revenue	4,094.00	4,220.50	4,352.75	4,536.75	4,617.25	4,824.25	5,054.25	5,163.50	5,249.75	5,502.75	5,652.25	5,767.25	59,035.25	6	22.77%
NON-MEDICAL EXPENSES															
Management Fees	600.00	600.00	600.00	600.00	600.00	600.00	600.00	600.00	600.00	600.00	600.00	600.00	7,200.00	1	2.78%
Insurance Expense	300.00	300.00	300.00	300.00	300.00	300.00	300.00	300.00	300.00	300.00	300.00	300.00	1,511.00	0	0.58%
Interest Expense														0.00	0.00%
Marketing Expense	143.00	143.00	143.00	143.00	143.00	143.00	143.00	143.00	143.00	143.00	143.00	143.00	1,716.00	0	0.66%
Purchases Services														0.00	0.00%
Legal & Accounting	166.00	166.00	166.00	166.00	166.00	166.00	166.00	166.00	166.00	166.00	166.00	166.00	1,992.00	0	0.77%
Dues & Subscriptions														0.00	0.00%
Taxes & Licenses														0.00	0.00%
Bank Charges	2.60	2.60	2.60	2.60	2.60	2.60	2.60	2.60	2.60	2.60	2.60	2.60	31.20	0	0.01%
Total Non-Medical Expenses	1,211.60	1,211.60	1,211.60	1,211.60	1,211.60	1,211.60	1,211.60	1,211.60	1,211.60	1,211.60	1,211.60	1,211.60	14,539.20	9.20	5.61%
Income (Loss) Before Other Revenue	2,882.40	3,008.90	3,141.15	3,325.15	3,405.65	3,612.65	3,842.65	3,951.90	4,038.15	4,291.15	4,440.65	4,555.65	44,496.05	4	17.16%
OTHER REVENUE															
Participation Fees														0.00	0.00%
Interest Revenue														0.00	0.00%
Other Revenue/ Other Expense	100,000.00												100,000.00		
Total Other Revenue	100,000.00	0.00	0.00	0.00	0.00	0.00	0.00	0.00	0.00	0.00	0.00	0.00	100,000.00	10	38.57%
NET INCOME	102,882.40	3,008.90	3,141.15	3,325.15	3,405.65	3,612.65	3,842.65	3,951.90	4,038.15	4,291.15	4,440.65	4,555.65	144,496.05	14	55.74%

IPA
Income Statement – 2002
Product Line – Healthy Families

	Jan	Feb	Mar	Apr	May	Jun	Jul	Aug	Sep	Oct	Nov	Dec	YTD	PMPM	% Gross
Member Months	1,012	1,036	1,050	1,066	1,087	1,109	1,138	1,176	1,199	1,235	1,249	1,265	13,622		
Capitation Revenue	$25,553.00	$26,159.00	$26,512.50	$26,916.50	$27,446.75	$28,002.25	$28,734.50	$29,694.00	$30,274.75	$31,183.75	$31,537.25	$31,941.25	$343,955.50	$25.25	100.00%
PMPM	25.25	25.25	25.25	25.25	25.25	25.25	25.25	25.25	25.25	25.25	25.25	25.25			
MEDICAL EXPENSES															
Capitated Fees – PCP	8,096.00	8,288.00	8,400.00	8,528.00	8,696.00	8,872.00	9,104.00	9,408.00	9,592.00	9,880.00	9,992.00	10,120.00	108,976.00	8	31.68%
Capitated Fees – Lab													0.00	0	0.00%
Capitated Fees – Other													0.00	0	0.00%
Specialist Fees	11,385.00	11,655.00	11,812.50	11,992.50	12,228.75	12,476.25	12,802.50	13,230.00	13,488.75	13,893.75	14,051.25	14,231.25	153,247.50	11	44.55%
Reinsurance Expenses													0.00	0	0.00%
Total Medical Expenses	19,481.00	19,943.00	20,212.50	20,520.50	20,924.75	21,348.25	21,906.50	22,638.00	23,080.75	23,773.75	24,043.25	24,351.25	262,223.50	19	76.24%
Income Before Non-Medical Expenses and Other Revenue	6,072.00	6,216.00	6,300.00	6,396.00	6,522.00	6,654.00	6,828.00	7,056.00	7,194.00	7,410.00	7,494.00	7,590.00	81,732.00	6	23.76%
NON-MEDICAL EXPENSES															
Management Fees	600.00	600.00	600.00	600.00	600.00	600.00	600.00	600.00	600.00	600.00	600.00	600.00	7,200.00	1	2.09%
Insurance Expense	300.00	300.00	300.00	300.00	300.00	300.00	300.00	300.00	300.00	300.00	300.00	300.00	3,600.00	0	1.05%
Interest Expense													0.00	0	0.00%
Marketing Expense	143.00	143.00	143.00	143.00	143.00	143.00	143.00	143.00	143.00	143.00	143.00	143.00	1,716.00	0	0.50%
Purchases Services													0.00	0	0.00%
Legal & Accounting	166.00	166.00	166.00	166.00	166.00	166.00	166.00	166.00	166.00	166.00	166.00	166.00	1,992.00	0	0.58%
Dues & Subscriptions													0.00	0	0.00%
Taxes & Licenses													0.00	0	0.00%
Bank Charges	2.60	2.60	2.60	2.60	2.60	2.60	2.60	2.60	2.60	2.60	2.60	2.60	31.20	0	0.01%
Total Non-Medical Expenses	1,211.60	1,211.60	1,211.60	1,211.60	1,211.60	1,211.60	1,211.60	1,211.60	1,211.60	1,211.60	1,211.60	1,211.60	14,539.20	1	4.23%
Income (Loss) Before Other Revenue	4,860.40	5,004.40	5,088.40	5,184.40	5,310.40	5,442.40	5,616.40	5,844.40	5,982.40	6,198.40	6,282.40	6,378.40	67,192.80	5	19.54%
OTHER REVENUE															
Participation Fees														0	0.00%
Interest Revenue														0	0.00%
Other Revenue/Other Expense	100,000.00												100,000.00	7	29.07%
Total Other Revenue	100,000.00	0.00	0.00	0.00	0.00	0.00	0.00	0.00	0.00	0.00	0.00	0.00	100,000.00	7	29.07%
NET INCOME	104,860.40	5,004.40	5,088.40	5,184.40	5,310.40	5,442.40	5,616.40	5,844.40	5,982.40	6,198.40	6,282.40	6,378.40	167,192.80	12	48.61%

IPA
Balance Sheet – Healthy Families
January 1 – Decemeber 31, 2000

	Jan	Feb	Mar	Apr	May	Jun	Jul	Aug	Sep	Oct	Nov	Dec
CURRENT ASSETS												
Cash In Bank	15,000.00	15,000.00	15,000.00	15,000.00	15,000.00	15,000.00	15,000.00	15,000.00	15,000.00	15,000.00	15,000.00	15,000.00
Capitation Receivable	4,393.50	9,468.75	15,150.00	21,210.00	28,254.75	36,461.00	45,929.75	56,610.50	69,185.00	83,148.25	98,601.25	116,225.75
Maxicare Withhold												
UHP Withhold												
Risk Pool Receivable												
Total Current Assets	19,393.50	24,468.75	30,150.00	36,210.00	43,254.75	51,461.00	60,929.75	71,610.50	84,185.00	98,148.25	113,601.25	131,225.75
OTHER ASSETS												
Prepaid Expenses												
TOTAL OTHER ASSETS	0.00	0.00	0.00	0.00	0.00	0.00	0.00	0.00	0.00	0.00	0.00	0.00
TOTAL ASSETS	19,393.50	24,468.75	30,150.00	36,210.00	43,254.75	51,461.00	60,929.75	71,610.50	84,185.00	98,148.25	113,601.25	131,225.75
CURRENT LIABILITIES												
Accounts Payable	1,388.60	2,777.20	4,165.80	5,554.40	6,943.00	8,331.60	9,720.20	11,108.80	12,497.40	13,886.00	15,274.60	16,663.20
Accrued Expenses												
Accrued Expenses – IBNR	3,480.00	7,500.00	12,000.00	16,800.00	22,380.00	28,880.00	36,380.00	44,840.00	54,800.00	65,860.00	78,100.00	92,060.00
TOTAL CURRENT LIABILITIES	4,868.60	10,277.20	16,165.80	22,354.40	29,323.00	37,211.60	46,100.20	55,948.80	67,297.40	79,746.00	93,374.60	108,723.20
LONG-TERM LIABILITIES												
TOTAL LONG-TERM LIABILITIES	0.00	0.00	0.00	0.00	0.00	0.00	0.00	0.00	0.00	0.00	0.00	0.00
TOTAL LIABILITIES	4,868.60	10,277.20	16,165.80	22,354.40	29,323.00	37,211.60	46,100.20	55,948.80	67,297.40	79,746.00	93,374.60	108,723.20
EQUITY												
Paid In Capital	15,000.00	15,000.00	15,000.00	15,000.00	15,000.00	15,000.00	15,000.00	15,000.00	15,000.00	15,000.00	15,000.00	15,000.00
Retained Earnings – Prior												
Retained Earnings – Curr Yr	(475.10)	(808.45)	(1,015.80)	(1,144.40)	(1,068.25)	(750.60)	(170.45)	661.70	1,887.60	3,402.25	5,226.65	7,502.55
TOTAL EQUITY	14,524.90	14,191.55	13,984.20	13,855.60	13,931.75	14,249.40	14,829.55	15,661.70	16,887.60	18,402.25	20,226.65	22,502.55
TOTAL LIABILITIES & EQUITY	19,393.50	24,468.75	30,150.00	36,210.00	43,254.75	51,461.00	60,929.75	71,610.50	84,185.00	98,148.25	113,601.25	131,225.75
	0.00	0.00	0.00	0.00	0.00	0.00	0.00	0.00	0.00	0.00	0.00	0.00

SUMMARY

Healthy Families is a terrific health plan because it is ultimately underwritten by the state. The state of California is throwing money at us to conduct outreach and it has plenty of ready materials we can use for our outreach efforts. As previously stated, CMS's primary goal is to increase the number of members of Superior IPA by 81 percent. CMS can achieve this within the three-year time frame, because Superior IPA has a very large population of potentially eligible people in its service area. CMS will diligently inform the target market on the importance of health care for children, the value of the Healthy Families Program, and the exceptional service provided by Superior IPA.

BIBLIOGRAPHY

100% Campaign: Press Release. [Web Site] http://www.100percentcampaign.org/join.html [October 23–26, 1999].

Bernstein, S. (1999, September 12). News analysis; State reforms don't address problems of doctor groups. *The Los Angeles Times,* D4.

Edwards Cinema Corporate Office. [Interview].

Etzel, M. J., Walker, B. J., & Stanton, W. J. (1997) *Marketing,* 11th ed., Irwin McGraw-Hill.

Finger, A. L. (1999, April 12) *Could your IPA go under? Steer it to safety.* Medical Economics, Oradell, 76 (7), 205–214.

Gary Center, [Phone Interview]. (562) 691–3263.

Healthy Families Handbook. (1999) [Brochure]

Heath R. & Associates. (1999, September 13). *Healthy Families, Medi-Cal for Children, Information Update,* V. 5.

Lambert Printing Company. (1999, October 24). [Proposal] (562) 690–7372

La Opinion. [Phone Interview]

La Opinion, Para Ti Health Care Supplements. [Brochure] P. 2–3

La Opinion, Para Ti Health Care Supplements. [Brochure] P. 10–15

The MEDSTAT Group Inforum Consulting Services-Population Profile. (1999). p. 1 [Brochure]

The MEDSTAT Group Inforum Consulting Services-Population Profile. (1999). p. 2 [Brochure]

U.S. Post Office. [Interview].

Yahoo Yellow Pages, Yahoo [Web site]. www.yahoo.com

A2

MARKETING PLAN FOR PROFESSIONAL FITNESS

Developed by
IAIN MOZOOMBAR

Contents

EXECUTIVE SUMMARY

Professional Fitness will be an upscale health club located in the City of San Marino, California, and will be targeted at the over-40 age group. This club will offer state-of-the-art equipment and facilities. The aerobic room of Professional Fitness will be soundproofed to ensure that nonaerobic class participants can work out or relax with minimum discomfort. The club will be equipped with high-end weight resistance machines, exercise bicycles, stair climbers, treadmills, cross-country ski machines, satin-finished dumbbells and barbells, and a sauna in both the male and female locker rooms. The club will also provide child-care for members when they work out and will also house a health bar, pro shop, and an attractive members' lounge.

The decision to target the over-40 market was made so as to capitalize on the ongoing transition of the health club industry from an industry that primarily targeted the under-30 market, to one that focuses on the over-40, and family market. Currently, an increased emphasis is being placed on enhancing the quality of life for seniors through the use of specially designed weight training programs. Researchers have found these programs to be very effective in battling the physical and mental deterioration of the body as one moves into the "golden years."

The main differential advantage offered by Professional Fitness will be the unmatched level of personal service and pampering that will be extended to the clients. The aging of the American population, an increased health awareness, and the lack of another such upscale, over-40 facility in the primary trading area of the club will also contribute to the success of the club. The club is expected to have a potential market of 58,258 people. These potential clients will be geographically located from San Marino and the surrounding cities of Pasadena, South Pasadena, Arcadia, Alhambra, Monterey Park, Glendale, and La Canada Flintridge.

The start-up costs for the club are estimated to be $1,274,055. The club will charge an initiation fee of $675 and monthly dues of $75. This pricing strategy is conservatively expected to attract 1,200 clients in the first year, 1,800 in the second, and 2,300 by the end of the third year. The club will offer a limited membership of 2,500 people. The expected return on investment will be 15.1 percent in year one, 22.8 percent in year two, and 33.1 percent in year three. The club will break even with 1,096 members and is expected to achieve this within the first year. The estimated dollar gross sales figure for the first year is $1,371,040.31 and this is expected to increase to $2,570,343.27 by the end of the third year.

INTRODUCTION

Statement of Purpose

The purpose of this marketing plan is to document the credibility and feasibility of opening an upscale, health club in the City of San Marino, California—Professional Fitness. This upscale club will offer a soundproofed aerobic room, state-of-the-art weight stations, exercise bicycles, stair climbers, treadmills, cross-country ski exercisers, free weights, a sauna in both locker rooms, massage facilities, health bar, pro shop, an upscale member lounge, and a child-care center.

Background

Over the past decade, numerous varieties of health clubs have popped up all over America. Every major city has at least one major health club specializing in total body fitness. The booming movie industry in Southern California has played a major role in making California the most health-conscious state in the country. Southern California's climate and long summer days coupled with mild winters encourage an outdoor-oriented lifestyle. Be it trekking, sun tanning, biking, competitive sports, or just plain "loafing," Southern Californians want to look their best, hence the sprouting of fitness-oriented clubs all over the Southland.

The American Medical Association (AMA) has also placed a stronger emphasis on health and fitness for the aging population (40 and above) over the past five years. This factor has also played a great part in the health club boom. Other factors will be discussed in more detail in the environmental analysis sections.

Scope

This marketing plan will include an analysis of the situation, neutral, competitor, and company environments; the target market to be reached; opportunities and threats faced by Professional Fitness; marketing objectives, strategy, and tactics; financial implementation and control.

Limitations/Delimitations

A time constraint requiring the entire business plan to be completed within 10 weeks causes the content and detail of the business plan to be narrowed in focus.

Methods

This business plan consists of applied research since the strategies and tactics of this plan are going to be used by the owners and management of Professional Fitness to gain a competitive edge over its competitors. The data for the plan are collected mainly through secondary research and financial data are based on calculated estimates. Some of the results and conclusions used in the competitor analysis section were collected via a questionnaire instrument.

Assumptions

It is assumed that the economic environment of the primary trading area remains constant and also that the current low interest rate will prevail. It is also assumed that the current lifestyle trends of Southern Californians remain unchanged and that the viable fitness-oriented market segment continues to grow at the same rate.

Preview

SITUATIONAL ANALYSIS

The Situational Environment

The situational environment for Professional Fitness is to be analyzed using the following format:

1. Demand and demand trends
2. Social and cultural factors
3. Demographics
4. Economic and business conditions
5. State of technology for fitness equipment
6. Laws and regulations

Demand and Demand Trends. There are many factors that are affecting the demand for an upscale health club in San Marino. One of the most important factors is the life cycle of the health club industry. This industry grew at an increasing and phenomenal rate from the late 1970s to about 1989; since then, the industry is growing, however at a decreasing rate. On the product life-cycle chart, as illustrated in Figure A2-1, the industry would roughly be at point A.

According to *Club Industry,* a trade publication, from 1982 to 1987, the industry grew at the rate of up to 15 percent a year.[1] In 1987, there were an estimated 10,000 clubs around the country. Also, in 1987, an estimated 30 million Americans had memberships to at least one health club, up from 20 million in 1982.[2] These clubs ranged from aerobics-only to multipurpose facilities. In 1988, consumer spending on health clubs, massages, and the like, increased to a record high of 25 percent over 1987 and became the fastest growing category in personal care.[3]

In 1989, there were an estimated 30,000 clubs all over the country, thanks to a slew of company-owned fitness clubs. These company-owned clubs ranged from a basic

---

[1] Laura Loro, "Health Clubs Stretch Markets," *Advertising Age,* May 16, 1988: 38.

[2] Dennis Rodkin, "Health Clubs Sweat the Details in Ads," *Advertising Age,* Dec. 3, 1989: 39.

[3] Vivian Brownstein, "Consumers Will Help the Economy Stay in Shape Next Year," *Fortune,* Oct. 23, 1989: 32.

Figure A2-1   Life Cycle of the Health Club Industry

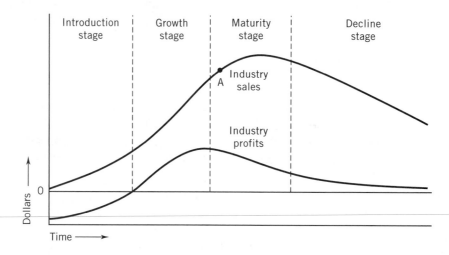

weight room with a few free weights and machines, where employees would work out during their lunch break, to comprehensive athletic facilities, like that of corporate giants AT&T, Saatchi & Saatchi Advertising, and Tenneco.[4]

In 1990, an industry estimate by *Club Industry,* showed that there were just under 33,000 clubs in the country, an increase of less than 10 percent.[5] Also, in 1990, Americans spent $5.3 billion on health club memberships and $1.73 billion on exercise equipment.[6]

The slight slowdown in the industry has been due in part to the recession which has been plaguing the United States since the middle of 1990. Investment and real estate loans have become increasingly difficult to obtain. The collapse of the savings and loan industry has also caused banks and investors to become more tightfisted.

Consumers of health club memberships are also becoming much more selective and educated in choosing a health club. This is due in part to the large number of clubs available, and also to the natural progression of any industry as it moves into the maturity stage of its life cycle. The industry has now become so competitive that a large number of clubs not emphasizing personal service and custom-tailored fitness programs have gone bankrupt. In fact, Mare Onigman, the editor of *Club Industry,* admitted that the battle is usually fought and won on the service side and that an increasing number of clubs are "servicing the daylights out of members" just to stay in business.[7]

Social and Cultural Factors.   Since the 1970s, health clubs have been a very popular way to meet people of the opposite sex and to make new friends. In fact, at one point in the mid-1970s, coed gyms began to take the place of singles bars! Over the past four years, health clubs that had initially focused only on the young adult market, and those that primarily marketed breathtaking physiques have seen their market shrink dramatically due to the aging of the baby boomers. According to the Census

---

[4] Brian O'Reily, "New Truths about Staying Healthy," *Fortune,* Sept. 25, 1989: 58.
[5] "Health Clubs Cool Down," *Club Industry,* March 1991: 17.
[6] Eleanor Branch, "Making Your Fitness Their Business," *Black Enterprise,* Sept. 1991: 83.
[7] Loro, p. 28.

Bureau, the number of people between the ages of 18 and 34 is projected to shrink by 11 percent during the 1990s.[8] The executive director of the Association of Quality Clubs (AQC), John McCarthy, stated that the industry was in a phase of major transition, from being one that focused primarily on the under-30 market, to an industry that focuses on the corporate market, families, and the 40-plus group.[9] This shift is not away from the aerobically toned baby boomers, but rather it is aimed toward improved health at all ages.

In a recent study of the 40-plus market, the AQC found that nearly 50 percent of those surveyed exercised at least three times a week, and nearly 75 percent of the respondents stated that they had become more concerned about their health. But, interestingly enough, only 10 percent of those surveyed belonged to a health club.[10]

In fact, advertisers are starting to recognize that ads featuring well-built, male Chippendale dancers and sexy, shapely, 22-year-old female models are scaring away millions of potential male and female customers who cannot expect to look that way. Thus, clubs like the Health & Tennis chain, are featuring an increasing number of older celebrities such as Cher, Victoria Principal, and Farrah Fawcett in their advertisements as they seem more credible to potential members.[11]

The new buzz word for health clubs is now wellness. Since the emphasis has now been shifted to the older age groups, many health clubs are evolving into comprehensive health centers, that are as concerned with the emotional and medical well-being of their members as they are with flabby thighs and love handles. This transformation has occurred as the consumer of the 1990s is, in general, demanding that clubs be concerned with the whole person.[12] Thus, most upscale clubs now offer seminars in stress management, nutrition, and smoking cessation. Some of these clubs are even affiliating with physicians, cardiologists, and plastic surgeons to provide medical services for their clients.

Over the past three years, an increasing number of executive women have started weight training. Women, who for years have dedicated themselves to slimmer thighs and flatter stomachs, have finally acknowledged the need for upper-body strength. For example, Darcy Troy, a Yale graduate and investment banker, said it was "the coolest thing … one minute, nothing. Next minute, muscles."[13] These women have found that upper-body strength improves posture, protects against backache and bone loss, and improves confidence.

This increase in the number of serious women weight trainers has given rise to a new kind of health club—women-only clubs. In addition to the normal aerobic floors and other amenities, these clubs usually have specially designed weight machines and poundages that are geared toward a woman's frame size and strength capabilities. This phenomenon, according to *Club Industry* magazine features editor, Dan Tobin, is because women who were in their early 20s during the heyday of the fitness boom in the early 1980s, are now in their early-to-mid-30s and are now less interested in joining a health club for social reasons.[14]

Finally, it seems to be currently chic to be able to remain fit, healthy, and physically strong during the "golden years," that is, ages 60 and beyond. A survey conducted by the

---

[8] Judith Waldrop, "Feeling Good," *American Demographics,* May 1990: 6.
[9] Rodkin, p. 38.
[10] "Health Clubs Look Beyond the Baby Boomers," *Changing Times,* Feb. 1990: 95.
[11] Loro, p. 28.
[12] Janice M. Horowitz, "From Workouts to Wellness," *Time,* July 30, 1990: 64.
[13] Dorothy Schefer, "The New Body Building," *Vogue,* May 1989: 368.
[14] Laura Broadwell, "Girls Just Wanna Work Out," *Women's Sports & Fitness,* Sept. 1990: 47.

Gallup Organization for the *American Health* magazine showed that the most rapidly growing segment of fitness enthusiasts is aged 50 or older. This segment increased by 46 percent from 1984 to 1986.[15]

A 43-question health survey was administered by *New Choices* magazine in June 1989 and one-half of the 5,600 subscribers who responded to the survey were aged 63 or older. Eighty percent of the respondents took at least one step to improve their health in 1989. The most popular methods included regular exercise and a good diet—low in fat, high in fiber, and plenty of fresh fruits and vegetables. Almost one-quarter (24 percent) of the respondents attend exercise regardless of their actual chronological age.[16] In general, the respondents were determined to take advantage of their capacity to live healthier and longer than ever before.

Demographics.   Selected demographics for San Marino and surrounding cities are shown in Tables A2-1 and A2-2. These demographics include population breakdown, size of the respective age groups, and the median age of the population. These statistics will be used later to help determine the target market for Professional Fitness.

Economic and Business Conditions.   As mentioned in the subsection on demand trends, the United States has been in a recession since the middle of 1990. This recession is unlike most other recessions in that it has hit white-collar workers as hard or harder than the blue-collar workers. Southern California has been hit especially hard

Table A2-1   Selected Population Breakdown

	Total Population	White	%	Black	%	Asian	%
San Marino	12,959	8,559	66.1	32	0.3	4,189	32.3
Pasadena	137,501	79,312	57.6	25,064	18.2	11,593	8.4
South Pasadena	23,936	16,711	69.8	745	3.1	5,086	21.3
Arcadia	48,277	34,512	71.5	374	0.8	11,321	23.5
Glendale	180,038	133,270	74.0	2,334	1.3	25,453	14.1
Alhambra	82,106	33,498	40.8	1,643	2.0	31,313	38.1
Monterey Park	60,738	16,245	26.7	374	0.6	34,898	57.5
La Canada Flintridge	19,378	16,645	85.9	81	0.4	2,397	12.4

Source: U.S. Census Bureau, 1990 Population and Housing Census.

Table A2-2   Age Groups and Median Age of Residents

	Aged 25–44	Aged 45–54	Aged 55–59	Aged 60–64	Median Age
San Marino	2,996	2,097	782	742	41.4
Pasadena	48,124	12,339	4,859	4,910	32.7
South Pasadena	9,157	2,764	1,046	959	35.0
Arcadia	12,793	9,848	4,865	4,217	38.9
Glendale	64,075	19,397	7,820	7,614	34.3
Alhambra	29,346	7,119	2,907	3,093	32.1
Monterey Park	18,982	5,870	3,007	3,113	33.9
La Canada Flintridge	4,837	3,110	1,161	982	40.8

Source: U.S. Census Bureau, 1990 Population and Housing Census.

[15] Waldrop, p. 6.
[16] Carin Rubenstein, "Here's to Your Health," *New Choices for the Best Years,* Jan. 1990: 37–38.

this time around due to the large reductions in defense and aerospace spending. Within the past two years, more than one million jobs have disappeared in California.

The business section of the *Los Angeles Times* recently reported that 220,000 jobs have been lost per month over the past six months. The level of the consumer confidence index has also decreased to a level of 46.3, its lowest level since December 1974.[17] This monthly index measures how consumers feel about the economy and its future prospects, and its low level indicates that the consumer may not be willing to spend enough to pull the economy out of its tailspin.

Although the index of consumer spending is not inspiring, economic data obtained from the months of January and February 1992 indicate that a national recovery is underway. These indicators show that consumers are not acting as depressed as they feel, the real estate segment is responding to lower financing costs, car sales have picked up slightly, and the industrial sectors seem to be gaining back a portion of their lost momentum.[18]

Despite the recession, the cities of San Marino and Pasadena are doing quite well. A comparison of the 1990 and 1991 *Survey of Buying Power* published annually by the *Sales and Marketing Management* magazine, shows that in Pasadena the percentage of households with an effective buying income (EBI) of $50,000 or greater increased from 25.9 percent in 1990 to 28.5 percent in 1991. The group with an EBI of $35,000 to $49,999 also increased from 14.7 percent to 15.5 percent during this period of time. This increase in the percentage of households with an EBI of $35,000 and over is also seen in Arcadia, Alhambra, Glendale, and Monterey Park. In all these cities, the percentage increase in households with an EBI of $50,000 and over is significantly greater than the percentage increase of the $35,000 to $49,999 group for 1990 to 1991. Thus, the business conditions for the primary trading area of Professional Fitness are very encouraging.

State of Technology.   The fitness equipment that is to be installed in Professional Fitness requires very little maintenance. Weight-resistance machines such as Cybex, Nautilus, David, and Flex require simple maintenance consisting of oiling and cleaning the cables and cams. Due to the low humidity in this area, rust would not be a worrisome factor. The spring-loaded mat that is to be used for aerobic classes would most likely require replacement every three to five years, depending on the level of usage. The saunas also require very little maintenance. The treated wood used in the construction of the saunas has to be inspected yearly and additional treatment or replacement of the panels might be needed.

Laws and Regulations.   For zoning purposes, the city of San Marino falls within the C-1 commercial zone. Health clubs are considered establishments that possess "characteristics of such unique and special form as to make impractical an advance classification of permitted or prohibited use in the C-1 zone."[19] Thus, each establishment has to apply for a conditional use permit on an individual basis. City Hall officials gave guaranteed assurance that the required permits and business licenses for an upscale health club could be easily obtained. The required permits also include a building and safety inspection permit and a fire and health safety permit. These licenses and permits would cost approximately $1,730.

---

[17] Michael Mandel, "Bummed-Out in America," *Business Week,* March 16, 1992: 34.

[18] James C. Cooper and Kathleen Madigan, "Cross Your Fingers, Knock Wood: That May Be a Recovery Out There," *Business Week,* March 16, 1992: 31.

[19] Los Angeles County City Ordinance, Article III—C-1 Commercial Zone, Sect. 23. 14 (C), p. 220.

A separate conditional use permit is also required for any renovations of the leased site in excess of 20 percent of its value, over the period of five years. Approval for the renovation or remodeling plans shall be granted within 30 days of the application. Landscaping the exterior of the building and screening of parking spaces need the approval of the Planning Commission. Parking spaces that use concrete surfacing or asphalt placed on soil treated with weed control require further approval by the city.

The Neutral Environment

The neutral environment is to be analyzed using the following four categories:

1. Financial environments
2. Government environments
3. Media environments
4. Special interest environments

Financial Environments.   Interest rates have currently dropped to their lowest levels in more than 15 years. The prime rate reported in the March 16, 1992, issue of *Business Week* index is 6.50 percent. Banks and other traditional lending institutions have vastly curtailed new business and other capital investment loans. Venture capitalists are currently also very careful about where they invest their money. However, good projects with minimal risks are still being funded, providing investors with competitive returns.

Funds needed to finance Professional Fitness can be obtained from either of three banks in the Pasadena area: Citizen's Bank, First Interstate Bank, or Bank of America. In general, these institutions quoted rates of 1 to 4 percent above prime for an unsecured, 8-year business loan amount of $375,000. The actual rate, be it prime-plus-one or prime-plus-four depends on the credit standings of the business lender. There is also a 1- to 2-point closing cost depending on the type of loan (secured or unsecured) and financial institution chosen. Funds from venture capitalists can also be sought at a competitive rate of 14 percent APR.

Government Environments.   Initially, in 1985, the Federal Trade Commission (FTC), the government "watchdog" for unscrupulous consumer trade practices, decided not to issue industry-wide rules that would have regulated health clubs. The FTC based their 1985 decision on the fact that the pervasiveness of fraud and abuse cases was not occurring nationwide. Thus, the FTC decided to act on a case-by-case basis.[20]

Since 1988, an increasing number of complaints lodged against numerous health clubs have also caused the FTC to step in and close down a large number of clubs. These complaints have ranged from "hard-sell" sales techniques and misleading contracts to deceptive advertisement. A large number of health clubs have been sued by patrons charging that serious injuries were caused by unskilled instructors and poor equipment maintenance.[21]

Many states including California have now legislated formal regulations concerning the operation of health clubs and spas.[22] In general, the regulations mandate the following:

---

[20] Margaret Engel, "Beware of Fitness Club Contracts," *Glamour,* Aug. 1987: 92.
[21] Walecia Konrad, "Health Clubs: Exercise Caution," *Business Week,* June 6, 1988: 142.
[22] "Is Your Health Club Healthy?" *Changing Times,* Sept. 1989: 116.

- A "cooling-off" period, during which a consumer can obtain a full refund of the paid membership fee. California law mandates this period to be 3 business days.

- A limit on the length of contract period. Some states forbid lifetime contracts.

- Cancellation rights for members, in the event that the club relocates or that the member becomes disabled.

- A surety bond amount ranging from as low as $50,000 in several states to as high as $200,000 in Maryland to cover losses in the event that the club folds. California legislates a bond amount of $100,000.

Media Environments. Over the past three years, there has been increasing coverage in such media as documentaries, magazines, and research journals on fitness for the older population; on the positive effects of weight-bearing exercises on bone density, and on the importance of good nutrition. This attention has resulted in positive publicity for the health club industry. The health club industry has received some bad publicity through lawsuits brought about by unsatisfied members and the closing of unscrupulous clubs by the FTC.

A widely publicized experiment performed by Tufts University researchers on nursing home participants aged between 86 and 96 yielded extremely positive and conclusive results. The participants, most of whom suffered from either arthritis, hypertension, or heart disease, were put on a weight-training program to strengthen their legs. After only two months on the program, all the participants either doubled, tripled, or even quadrupled their leg strength. Two of the participants had even gained enough leg strength to discard their canes![23]

Medical researchers have also found the best way to prevent the onset of osteoporosis in women is to develop maximum bone mass prior to bone loss. In the past, women have largely avoided strength training and have preferred to stick with aerobic toning only, because of a perceived social stigma attached to developing muscle mass. Researchers have found that strength training, especially in women, can have an extremely beneficial effect on bone strength and density, and are thus stressing the importance of a specially designed strength training program for women.[24]

In addition to regular physical activity, the importance of a diet low in saturated fat and high in fiber, fruit, and vegetables is also currently stressed in a variety of media.[25]

Special Interest Environments. Three influential special interest groups include the American College of Sports Medicine, the National Health Club Association of Quality Clubs, and the Institute for Aerobics Research.

In 1978, the *American College of Sports Medicine* (ACSM) equated fitness with aerobic exercise and recommended aerobic exercise three to five days weekly for 15 to 60 minutes for all healthy adults. Due to current proven research on the benefits of strength training, these 1978 guidelines were revised in 1990 to include a twice-weekly routine of 8 to 10 different weight-bearing exercises to strengthen the legs, back, and chest—in addition to the three to five weekly aerobic workouts.[26] The ACSM also certifies instructors in preventive and rehabilitative health and fitness. This revised recommendation of the ACSM serves as a great opportunity for the health club industry to expand its market.

The *National Health Club Association* (NHCA) is primarily a "trade union" for health clubs nationwide. It costs $180 in yearly dues. There are currently over 2,000 privately

---

[23] Vic Sussman, "Muscle Bound," *U.S. News and World Report,* May 20, 1991: 88.

[24] Kenneth H. Cooper, M.D., "Fighting Back Against Bone Loss," *The Saturday Evening Post,* March 1991: 32.

[25] Susan Zarrow, "The New Diet Priorities," *Prevention,* Sept. 1991: 36.

[26] Cooper, p. 32.

owned clubs in the NHCA. Some of the benefits include SBA loan assistance, health insurance plans for owners and staff, group liability insurance plans, sales training seminars, and management workshops.

The *Association of Quality Clubs* (AQC) assures that its member clubs adhere to a strict code of ethics. Affiliation with the AQC ensures club members that the club has attained a certain level of service and competence. Currently, there are approximately 1,550 clubs nationwide affiliated with the AQC. Most of these are upscale clubs that offer members seminars in weight reduction, stress management, and proper nutrition.

The *Institute of Aerobic Research* is the primary agency that certifies aerobic-class instructors. Certifications are available for physical fitness specialists and group exercise leaders.

The Competitor Environment

Professional Fitness has three main competitors. These health clubs are all located in the neighboring city of Pasadena. These clubs consist of the following:

1. Brignole Health and Fitness
2. Pasadena Athletic Club
3. World Gym, Pasadena

Brignole Health and Fitness. This health club is located on De Lacey Street in Pasadena. It has been in operation since 1985. This club will be the *primary competitor* of Professional Fitness. Brignole's offers a spring-loaded aerobic mat in the aerobics room; eight Lifecycles and Stairmasters; one tanning bed; a weight room consisting of Flex resistance machines and free weights, dumbbells ranging from 3 to 125 pounds; two squat cages, for intense thigh exercises (squats); a snack bar; and pro shop.

This club primarily targets the under 40, "yuppie" market and plans to merge with Sports Connection in the near future. This club is also going to be relocated to a larger facility, possibly in another neighboring city. Although the club is touted to be operated and owned by Mr. Doug Brignole, a top amateur bodybuilder from 1986 to 1988, this is not true. Brignole's is actually owned by a group of seven investors. These actual owners employ Mr. Brignole as the manager and pay him in addition to his salary, a small royalty to use his name for the club. Mr. Brignole has no formal marketing, management, or financial background and was once employed as a waiter in a Pasadena restaurant.

The annual membership fees have increased from $330 in 1987 to $550 presently with no initiation fee. The membership fee includes a personal training program and two free workouts with a trainer. The turnover at Brignole's is approximately 25 to 30 percent annually. Currently, the club boasts a membership of about 2,800 members.

Brignole's enjoys an enviable reputation with the members attending its aerobic classes and this can be considered as its greatest strength. Most aerobic instructors who teach at Brignole's are certified by the Institute of Aerobic Research and have won at least one award in nationwide or regional aerobic contests. Brignole Health and Fitness also offers child-care services (at no charge for the first hour) to its members.

Brignole's has three major weaknesses: untrained weight-lifting instructors, poor service attitudes, and poorly maintained weight-lifting equipment.

All of the instructors at Brignole's are male and none of them are certified by any reputable agency; most of them are not even certified. These instructors are able to spot a person during a lift, but have very little knowledge of the mechanics of proper form for the lift. The manager and the instructors also have a poor service attitude. They tend to give more personal service to female members who dress fashionably and are young, affluent, and attractive than to the average member, male or female. In other words, the level of personal service given to members is biased.

Finally, Brignole's has managed to turn away about half of its serious bodybuilders over the past five years, due to its poorly maintained and outdated equipment. In 1989 it promised its members that most of the weight-resistance machines would be given a complete overhaul and updated. This promise was never fulfilled through 1991.

Pasadena Athletic Club.   This club has been in operation for almost 20 years, opening in 1973; it is located on Walnut Street in Pasadena. This club would not be in direct competition with Professional Fitness because it concentrates on a different market segment. It offers purely aerobic-oriented amenities and does not have a weight-training room. The club offers 3 tennis courts, 6 racquetball courts, an Olympic-sized pool, an indoor basketball court, sauna and dry-steam rooms, and a Jacuzzi. It also offers aerobic classes throughout the day.

A nonrefundable, nontransferable, one-time initiation fee of $400 is charged for families and $300 for singles. The monthly membership dues for family membership is $65 and $43 for singles. This fee includes unlimited usage of the facilities that operate from 6 A.M. to 11 P.M. on weekdays and from 7 A.M. to 10 P.M. on weekends. There is presently a 13-month waiting period for membership at this club for new members. The total number of memberships is currently limited to 2,500.

Pasadena Athletic Club is primarily a family-oriented club as opposed to a singles club as are most health clubs. An informal survey at the club showed that members were very satisfied with the personal service that they received and the amenities available.

The strengths of Pasadena Athletic Club include personable service, a great variety of different amenities, and long operating hours, even on the weekends. Weaknesses include a lack of instructors and pool safety personnel, a long waiting period for membership, and the unavailability of child-care services.

World Gym, Pasadena.   This is a hard-core weight-lifting and bodybuilding gymnasium located on Altedena Drive in Pasadena. Although this club only opened on September 28, 1991, it already boasts a membership of about 1,200 members. Membership fees are $389 annually with no initiation fee. The club is open from 5:30 A.M. to 11 P.M. on weekdays and 7 A.M. to 7 P.M. on weekends.

World Gym has a land area of 10,000 square feet and does not have an aerobics room. The club offers state-of-the-art weight-lifting and bodybuilding equipment, including Cybex and Flex weight-resistance machines. It also has 10 Lifecycles, 8 Stairmasters, 2 treadmills, and an extensive variety of dumbbells, barbells, and weight racks. This club would not also be in direct competition with Professional Fitness as it targets primarily serious weight lifters and the under-40 market.

An effectiveness study was carried out on World Gym, Pasadena, in November 1991. A questionnaire (see Appendix) was used to gauge the level of satisfaction of its members with regard to the gym's offerings in terms of price, personnel, and equipment.[27] In general, the members were very satisfied with the level of service and equipment offered by the club. Almost one-third of the members were over 40 and three-quarters of the members lived within a six-mile radius of the club. There is also a three-to-one ratio of male to female members.

Strengths of World Gym include long operating hours, very personable owners and management, great equipment and training atmosphere. Its weaknesses include not hav-

---

[27] Iain Mozoomdar, "A Study to Determine the Effectiveness of World Gym, Pasadena" (unpublished), Nov. 1991.

ing a formal marketing plan, no planned specific target market of its members and also, a lack of a specific and directed promotion campaign.

The Company Environment

Professional Fitness is to be positioned as an upscale health club in the city of San Marino. It will offer state-of-the-art weight-resistance machines, exercise bicycles, stair climbers, treadmills, cross-country ski simulators, saunas, and aerobic area.

The club will also provide child-care facilities with no time limit as long as the member is working out on the premises. The club will also offer the services of a licensed, professional masseuse at a subsidized rate. The pro shop will carry fashionable workout gear targeted at the over-40 market. The snack bar will carry healthy food items, such as yogurt, low-fat cottage cheese, protein and fruit shakes, sandwiches and the like, that are low in fat, sugar, and cholesterol and generally abide by the guidelines put forth by the American Heart Association (AHA).

The club is to be managed by a certified physical fitness specialist. He or she would preferably have a degree in physical education from an accredited university and a minimum of two years' experience in managing an upscale health club. Marketing, management, and financial consultants will be used when necessary. All aerobic or weight instructors and personal trainers must be certified by a reputable certification agency such as the American College of Sports Medicine or the Institute of Aerobic Research. At least one staff, trained and certified by the American Red Cross in CPR, will be present at all times. The club will also periodically conduct seminars on stress reduction, nutrition, and time management, with emphasis on the over-40 population. Seminars in yoga and meditation will also be offered. The club will limit its membership to 2,500 people. Ideally, this figure will be obtained within the span of three years.

The club is to be financed by a limited partnership of six partners. The cost of each partnership unit is $150,000. Each partner is guaranteed a sum of $1,500 per month with additional income distributions based on yearly gross sales figures. Additional financing would come from either an unsecured, eight-year business loan from a traditional lending institution or from a group of venture capitalists with a guaranteed return of 14 percent APR.

The strengths of Professional Fitness include a superior service attitude; knowledgeable, trained, and dedicated staff; and a nonthreatening and comfortable training atmosphere.

The weaknesses of Professional Fitness include the lack of a management consultant and a financial consultant on the permanent staff, the nonavailability of an Olympic-sized pool and Jacuzzi, a possible waiting period needed for new members after three years, and the difficulty of finding land needed for expansion of the club in San Marino, if necessary.

THE TARGET MARKET

Professional Fitness is to be located in the city of San Marino, California. There are two main reasons for choosing this city for the location of Professional Fitness.

The city of San Marino has, for the past two decades, been perceived to be a rich, upper-class town. This perception of San Marino is perfect for the positioning of Professional Fitness. This is to be positioned as an upscale health club and should thus be located in an upper-class neighborhood. According to the latest census results available with per capita income statistics (1988), the per capita income for San Marino for the period of 1979 to 1987 increased 68.5 percent, from $21,485 to $36,196. The per capita income for Beverly Hills in 1987 was $36,690, only 1.4 percent higher than San Marino. These figures clearly confirm that the perceived wealth of San Marino residents is not without foundation. San Marino is chosen also because it is surrounded by affluent cities such as Pasadena, South Pasadena, and Arcadia.

Assuming that the per capita income increases at the rate of 8.5 percent a year, the per capita income in 1991 for San Marino residents should be around $46,233. This health club is thus going to target executives who earn at least $40,000 annually.

As mentioned in the section on competitor environment, a study on the effectiveness of World Gym, Pasadena, revealed that although one-half of their members were above 30 years old, surprisingly, about one-third of their members were over 40. This finding proves that there is a viable market segment of older consumers. This finding is also in agreement with a large amount of published literature as mentioned in Section I. Thus, Professional Fitness will target clients from the over-40 age groups.

The clientele of Professional Fitness will be targeted toward individual consumers and corporate consumers. This club will not, however, entice groups of executives from a particular firm using special group rate discounts. Group rate discounts will damage the image of Professional Fitness as being an upscale club.

Geographically, the clientele is to be targeted from the primary areas of San Marino, Pasadena, South Pasadena, and Arcadia. Secondary areas to be targeted include Alhambra and Monterey Park to the south, Glendale to the east, and La Canada Flintridge to the west. This geographic targeting is immensely important, because the previous study on World Gym showed that over 75 percent of their clientele lived within a six-mile radius of the gymnasium. Another study conducted by the American Service Finance company in 1989 also showed that 80 percent of a club's members come from within a 15-minute drive radius.[28]

The ethnic groups to be targeted include Caucasians, Asians, and blacks. The highest earning ethnic group are Asians. Historically, a large majority of executive health club patrons have been Caucasians. American-born Chinese and other Asians have assimilated the American fitness lifestyle and patronize executive health clubs with the same frequency as the Caucasians. Over the past decade, an increasing number of black executives are beginning to patronize upscale health clubs. This could be due to the fact that, as an ethnic group, their income has also been steadily increasing over the same period of time.

From the population and age breakdowns in Section 1, there are approximately 139,206 people aged 40 and over, and are either Caucasian, Asian, or black in the target market. From the percentages quoted by the 1991 Survey of Buying Power, there are on average 46.5 percent of the people with an effective buying income of $35,000 or over in San Marino and the surrounding seven cities. Thus the market potential for Professional Fitness consists of 64,731 people. According to the survey by the Association of Quality Clubs (Section I), only about 10 percent of them belong to a health-club-penetrated market. Thus, conservatively, Professional Fitness will have an *effective target market* of approximately 58,258 *people*. This is a conservative estimate, as people aged 65 and over were not included.

In summary, the typical customer profile of Professional Fitness shall include:

- Age group: 40 and over
- Income: $40,000 and over annually
- Sex: Male or female

---

[28] "American Service Finance Renewal Study (1989)," *National Health Club Association,* 1991 (reprinted with permission).

- Education: College graduates
- Occupation: White-collar workers—executives, or retirees
- Family life cycle: Full nest III, empty nest I, and empty nest II[29]
- VALS Scale: Achievers or Experientials[30]
- Benefits sought: Prestige, quality, and service
- Location: San Marino, Pasadena, South Pasadena, Arcadia, Alhambra, Monterey Park, Glendale, and La Canada Flintridge

OPPORTUNITIES AND THREATS

Opportunities

Professional Fitness is presented with the following opportunities:

- There are at present no upscale health clubs specializing in aerobic and weight training in San Marino.
- There are no clubs in the immediate vicinity that specialize in providing upscale exercise facilities for the over-40 segment.
- Current research by the AMA and the ACSM prove that weight training is beneficial for all ages, regardless of sex and physical condition.
- Only 10 percent of people over 40 belong to a health club.
- The current demographic shift of the American population is projected to cause the 18-to-34 age group to shrink 11 percent during the 1990s.

First, since there are presently no upscale health clubs in San Marino, Professional Fitness would be able to position itself easily in the market without facing stiff competition and entry barriers from other upscale club providers. The club would also be able to maintain an effective physical and psychological separation between itself and its three main competitors in Pasadena.

Second, there is no club in the primary trading area of Professional Fitness that specializes in clients aged 40 and over. This relatively untapped niche presents new and profitable market opportunities for the maturing health club industry. This segment also has special needs that can be adequately fulfilled by Professional Fitness. Some of the special requirements include the hiring of older instructors, specialized programs to serve the mature consumer, the "extra" personal service, or pampering expected by the older consumer, and so on.

Third, current medical research, as mentioned in Section I, also helps to educate and motivate the older consumer. This club presents the opportunity for older consumers in the primary trading area to enhance the quality of their life, and to enter the golden years armed with the necessary physical strength to combat painful and debilitating diseases such as arthritis and osteoporosis.

---

[29] Philip Kotler, *Marketing Management* (Englewood Cliffs, NJ: Prentice-Hall, 1991), 7th ed., p. 171.
[30] Ibid., p. 173.

Fourth, since a survey conducted by the Association of Quality Clubs showed that only 10 percent of people aged 40 and over belong to a health club, there is a viable and reachable market segment for the club.

Finally, the aging population also ensures that the over-40 market will expand in the 1990s and into the year 2000. Thus, the effective target market will increase beyond the estimated 58,258 people.

Threats

Threats faced by Professional Fitness include the following:

- Increased federal, state, or city regulations
- Lawsuits against the club
- Entry of new competitors
- Decline in the overall health club industry

First, increased regulations could potentially affect the profit motive of the club. The management of the club has to be alert for changes in the legal environment—environment scanning—and do their utmost to adapt to it.

Second, if lawsuits are brought against the club by members, the club will try to settle out of court to avoid excessive negative publicity. Ideally, this situation can be completely avoided through the use of qualified and trained personnel, and well-maintained equipment.

The last two threats—entry of new competitors and a decline in the industry—are inevitable. Professional Fitness will thus strive to maintain the goodwill of its customers through exceptional personal service and dedication. The club will also fiercely defend its position as an upscale club to enhance its prestigious appeal.

MARKETING OBJECTIVES AND GOALS

Mission Statement

Professional Fitness will provide an exceptional level of personal service and state-of-the-art equipment to our clients while maintaining a return of investment of 15 percent in the first year of operation. All of our clients and customers will be treated equally and with utmost respect regardless of race, sex, or religious preferences. Business operations will be conducted in a legal, ethical, and safe manner as described by federal laws, California state laws, and all applicable county and city ordinances.

Objectives of the Firm

- Establish a limited partnership under the laws of the state of California
- Achieve and maintain a return on investment of 20 percent by the end of year 2
- Break even within 18 months
- Achieve a minimum market share of 3.5 percent by year 3
- Achieve a minimum average sales volume of 100 memberships per month in year 1
- Achieve $1,300,000 in sales by the end of year 1
- Achieve $2,000,000 in sales by the end of year 2

MARKETING STRATEGY

As mentioned earlier, the health club industry's growth has slowed down from approximately 15 percent annually to just under 10 percent. Thus, although the industry is still growing, its sales are increasing at a decreasing rate, and it has thus reached the maturity stage of its life cycle. The industry has, until recently, been focusing primarily on the 18-to-34 age group.

Professional Fitness is to pursue a *market-nicher strategy.* It is also going to be positioned as a quality/price specialist—high-quality equipment and impeccable service, high-price end of the industry; and an end-user specialist—over-40 segment. This strategy is very attractive to Professional Fitness due to its relatively limited capital resources. Niche marketing has also proven to be successful for firms in mature industries. An ideal market niche has the following characteristics:

- Sufficient growth potential
- Sufficient size and buying power
- Negligible interest to major competitors

In addition, the "nicher" firm needs to have the capacity and resources available to serve the niche effectively, and be able to defend its position through built-up customer goodwill.[31]

As was explained in the previous sections, the over-40 segment has sufficient growth potential, size, and buying power. Also, the three competitors of Professional Fitness are currently not pursuing this segment. This club will be specifically designed to provide the manpower and resources needed to serve the segment and protect its position through built-up goodwill.

Since the industry is in its maturity phase, this club will be designed also to effectively serve the early majority and to compete in a monopolistic competition-based market structure. Thus, product differentiation is crucial for the long-term survival of the club and will be discussed in detail in the next section.

Professional Fitness will also try to increase its market penetration by encouraging the adoption of individual, tailor-made programs of weight training and aerobic classes that enhance the quality and preservation of life as the consumer ages, in place of other generic aerobic activities such as jogging, tennis, or golf. Hence, joining Professional Fitness will be a wiser and more educated choice than an upscale athletic or racket club, such as the Pasadena Athletic Club.

This strategy would most likely evoke a defensive response from Pasadena Athletic Club (PAC) and other such facilities. Due to its business experience, PAC might try to engage in price competition and attempt to use the superb-value strategy—offering high quality at a low price. While this strategy would be effective with a majority of products, health club consumers in Pasadena and its neighboring cities are typically upscale customers with relatively inelastic price sensitivities. Thus offering a lower price would most likely damage PAC's prestige factor and in effect, possibly lower its market share instead of increasing it.

Due to this customer profile and price inelasticity, Professional Fitness will not compete in price competition, rather it will defend its competitive position by enhancing the

---

[31] Ibid., pp. 395–396.

prestige and exclusiveness of the club; in short—"snob appeal." The level of personal service, ambience, and state-of-the-art technology will be emphasized.

MARKETING TACTICS

The market-nicher strategy of Professional Fitness is to be implemented using the four tactical variables of:

1. Product
2. Price
3. Promotion
4. Distribution

Product

The heart of Professional Fitness is its personable stuff and state-of-the-art equipment. This subsection is to be discussed using the following categories:

1. Equipment and facilities
2. Staff
3. Hours of operation

Equipment and Facilities. One of the objectives of this club is to promote "health club addiction." This can be achieved in part by the offering of state-of-the-art equipment and excellent facilities. Weight-resistance machines made by Cybex, David, Flex, and Nautilus will be offered. Satin-finished barbells and dumbbells will be purchased from Ironman Inc. The saunas will be made by an American leader in the field—Hex Equipment. Standard and recumbent type exercise bicycles will be offered, and purchased from Universal Inc. and Nautilus, respectively. The stair climbers will also be purchased from Universal Inc. Treadmills will be ordered from Quinton Fitness Equipment, known for its attractive state-of-the-art machines. Finally, cross-country ski exercisers that promote superior total-body aerobic workouts will be purchased from NordicTrack. Three massage tables will also be provided, along with the services of a professional masseuse at a special club rate for members.

Cybex weight machines come in an attractive white finish. The workmanship on these machines is superb, and they are designed according to stringent engineering standards. These machines offer a high degree of safety, reliability, and durability as well as a state-of-the-art appearance. In addition, Cybex machines offer an unparalleled degree of smoothness through their range of movement, and are ideal for people with joint stiffness or prior injuries. These machines are also angled correctly so as to lessen the chance of injury due to bad posture during a lift.

A unique feature of David weight machines is that, in addition to standard models, the company offers an extensive line of equipment designed primarily for women. These machines have lighter poundages and are designed for people that stand under 5 feet 7 inches. David machines are extensively used by women-only clubs all over the country. Professional Fitness will purchase some of these specially designed weight machines to cater to the needs of its female members and older members.

Flex and Nautilus machines are both attractively designed in blue or gray finishes. Both these companies offer state-of-the-art equipment that is functional, durable, and upscale. These companies also include a lifetime warranty on their machines and free scheduled maintenance by factory personnel for a period of two years. These machines also provide extremely smooth operation throughout their range of motion.

All the preceding machines use sealed ball bearings that help prolong the life of the machines by sealing out dirt and other environmental contaminants. These machines will also enhance the upscale appearance of the club.

The saunas made by Hex Equipment feature high-quality treated wood. Wood treatment is of utmost importance in the construction of the sauna, and the company prides itself in having the "best-treated wood in America." These saunas also feature individually adjustable heat controls located inside each sauna. This feature is also extremely useful in the prevention of heatstroke and dizziness. Most saunas are controlled externally and its occupants have no mechanical control over the interior temperature except to manually open the door when the heat becomes overbearing.

The standard and recumbent exercise bicycles made by Universal and Nautilus feature state-of-the-art technology and appearance. These machines are made for heavy commercial use. Recumbent bicycles are ideal for older members because they provide more comfortable seats that follow the natural curvature of the spine and thus offer better lower lumbar support. These machines also provide attractive computer controls and intensity level readouts.

Like its exercise bicycle, stair climbers offered by Universal also provide intensity readouts and a computer-controlled hydraulic stepping mechanism that is designed not to overly stress knees and ankles. NordicTrack's cross-country ski machines also provide smooth operation that reduces harmful stress on the joints. Finally, treadmills offered by Quinton Fitness are used in exclusive corporate clubs nationwide and also in NASA's astronaut training facility. They also feature a state-of-the-art appearance and technology.

The aerobic room will be partitioned off from the weight-training section of the club. A state-of-the-art sound system will be offered and a custom-made, spring-loaded mat will be ordered to lessen the intensity of impact on the knee joints. This room will be soundproofed to ensure maximum comfort for other members not attending aerobic classes. This would also enhance the prestigious appeal of the club.

Professional Fitness will also provide a child-care center staffed by certified child-care professionals. This center is to be used by members while they are working out. No time limits shall be imposed on the members.

A health bar serving foods low in fat, sugar, and cholesterol, and high in fiber will also be offered. This bar will serve low-fat yogurt, sherbet, protein shakes, and other such foods. Fresh juices and sandwiches will also be served.

A professional masseuse will also be available at a special club rate for members. Sixty-minute massages usually cost between $45 and $80. The club hopes to negotiate a price of $30 to $35 for its members.

The pro shop will feature the latest workout fashions targeted at the over-40 market. The member lounge will offer a large-screen television, laser disc player, videocassette recorder, and comfortable sofas for members. Members will be encouraged to use the lounge for informal business meetings and social purposes.

Staff. As mentioned in the subsection on company environment, Professional Fitness will only employ certified fitness personnel. The hired fitness personnel will be trained to provide exceptional personal service and formulate correct, custom-tailored exercise programs for the clientele. The club is to be managed by a physical fitness specialist. He or she must have a degree in physical fitness from an accredited university and at least two years' experience managing an upscale health club.

The manager will report to the board of directors, comprising the six partners. The manager will be given full authority to implement any training program for the fitness instructors employed by the club. Although the manager will also be given the autonomy to manage the club as he or she sees fit, the manager needs to report on the progress of any improvement plans or staff training schedule to the board of directors monthly. The board of directors will intervene only when it feels that the ongoing plans or training programs are contrary to the prestigious and sophisticated image and positioning of the club.

The manager will be paid an annual salary of $30,000 initially. A salary increase based on a good performance appraisal is possible after nine months. The manager will also receive additional monetary incentives if the club performs well financially after the first year of operation. The other employees will be started at a rate of $10 per hour based on a standard 40-hour week. This basic rate will be raised to $11 in the second year of the club's operations. Standard overtime pay will also be given. This rate will be one and one-half times hourly wage for weekdays and two times hourly wage for nonscheduled weekends. Employees will be required to work on some weekends.

Employees will be instructed in personal service, operating procedures, and personal hygiene. The club will also provide uniforms to the staff. Laundry and dry-cleaning expenses will be the responsibility of the employee.

Hours of Operation.   The club will be open seven days a week, from 5 A.M. to 11 P.M. on weekdays (Monday to Friday) and 7 A.M. to 10 P.M. on weekends. These hours are determined based on the research done on World Gym, Pasadena.

Price

Professional Fitness is to be priced as an upscale club. The use of a premium pricing strategy will be employed—high price and high quality. This strategy is very viable in the health club market in this geographic area due to the relatively inelastic price sensitivities of the upscale consumer.

As mentioned in the subsection on competitor environment, PAC is the only fitness club in the immediate area that charges an initiation fee. Their initiation fee is $300 and the monthly dues are $43 for single members, and $400 initiation and $65 monthly dues for families. This strategy has worked well for PAC as it has been pursuing good-value strategy—low price coupled with medium-quality product.

Professional Fitness will charge members a $675 initiation fee and monthly dues of $75. It will have a maximum membership of 2,500. This price range is justified because the club is to be positioned to promote and enhance a country club atmosphere and ambience. The club would not price itself out of the market with this price either, since exclusive clubs in Los Angeles charge as much as $2,000 in initiation fees.

The club expects to attract 1,200 members in its first year, 1,800 in the second, and 2,300 in the third year with this price. This is a conservative estimate, since World Gym, Pasadena boasts a membership of 1,200 members in just $5\frac{1}{2}$ months of operation.

Monthly expected cash flows, pro forma income statements, and balance sheets for a period of 36 months using this estimate will be shown in the next section, "Control and Implementation."

Various membership scenarios follow:

- Optimistic
  Year 1: 1,600 members
  Year 2: 2,100 members
  Year 3: 2,500 members

- Conservative
  Year 1: 1,200 members
  Year 2: 1,800 members
  Year 3: 2,300 members
- Pessimistic
  Year 1: 900 members
  Year 2: 1,500 members
  Year 3: 2,000 members

Promotion

The promotion campaign that is to be used to launch Professional Fitness will be divided into two segments:

1. Precommercialization phase including the Grand Opening
2. Regular promotional mix for the first two years of operation

Precommercialization Phase. The promotional campaign that is to be used in this phase is to last a period of 13 weeks. The Grand Opening, which is to last an entire week, occurs in the last week of this phase. The promotional budget for this entire phase is $100,000. The promotion mix that is to be used includes direct mail, print and radio media advertising, sales promotion, and publicity. The advertising platform will be designed to emphasize the high degree of personal service and the exclusive "country club" ambience of the club, the importance of improving the quality of life as one ages, and the benefits of feeling younger instead of looking younger. These issues will be the central theme for all the components of the promotion mix.

Direct mail will be used to reach corporate customers. This campaign will start at week 1 and continue through the grand opening. Color brochures will be sent out to selected businesses in all eight cities, especially in Glendale, Pasadena, and La Canada Flintridge, at the rate of 250 per week.

Print advertising and spot-radio advertising will be used. Advertisements will be placed in the *Los Angeles* magazine; the *Star News,* the Pasadena daily newspaper; and the Southern California Community newspapers for the cities of San Marino, Alhambra, Monterey Park, South Pasadena, and Arcadia. The *Los Angeles* magazine is chosen because it has readership of over 1 million upscale consumers, 70 percent of whom are over 35. This magazine also has the capability of offering a four-color display advertisement instead of black and white. The *Star News* has a readership of around 45,000 in the Pasadena, San Marino, and South Pasadena areas and about one-half of them are aged 40 and over. The Southern California Community Newspapers are weekly papers published every Thursday, and can be custom designed to reach the targeted cities previously mentioned. These papers have a readership of around 73,000, half of which are businesses.

Spot radio will also be used to target older audiences. KKGO 105.1 FM is the only classical music station in Los Angeles and has a listenership of 550,000 people spanning Ventura to San Bernardino counties. The station states that more than 80 percent of its audience are upscale consumers, aged 35 and over. Advertisements will also be placed on K-BIG 104.3 FM. This station boasts a listenership of more than 1 million weekly; about 40 percent of them are aged between 35 and 54.

Publicity releases will also be issued to various news stations. The publicity campaign will promote a cause-related marketing plan. A $25 donation will be given to either the Green Peace ecological movement or the Los Angeles Mission for every new member who joins Professional Fitness. The donation will be made quarterly. This campaign will also help the club's corporate social image and standing in the community.

The Grand Opening will take place on the last week of the phase—the thirteenth week. This event will be designed to last for an entire week. During the Grand Opening, the public relations personnel from the Los Angeles Mission and Green Peace will be invited to give promotional talks on their respective organizations. This event is also expected to attract fitness celebrities such as Arnold Schwarzenegger, Lou Ferrigno, and others. Snacks and entertainment will also be provided.

Sales promotion, in the form of a sweepstakes, will also be used during the Grand Opening. A five-day/four-night cruise for two to either Mexico or Hawaii will be offered daily throughout the seven days. The Grand Opening will last from Sunday to Saturday the following week.

The cost breakdown of this precommercial campaign and Grand Opening is shown in Table A2-3 and Figure A2-2. A Gnatt chart for the implementation of this campaign is shown in Table A2-4.

Regular Promotion Mix.   The cost of the promotion mix for the first three years of operation amounts to $108,000 yearly, or $9,000 per month. This mix is identical to that of the precommercialization phase, with the exception of times and frequency of advertising. For example, ads will be placed in the Los Angeles magazine every other month—six times per year. Sweepstakes will be offered only once a year, on the yearly anniversary of the club. The costs of this regular promotion mix are shown in Table A2-5 and Figure A2-3 and a Gnatt chart for its implementation is shown in Table A2-6.

Table A2-3   Promotion Campaign for Precommercialization Phase and Grand Opening

Direct Mail	
$4.00 per mailing × 3,250 mailings	$13,000.00
Print Advertising	
Newspapers	
Star News	
6 × 1/2-page ads @ $1,770.75	10,624.50
Southern California Community Newspapers (SCCN)	
6 × 1/2-page ads @ $1,315.20 (Thursdays)	7,891.20
Magazines	
Los Angeles	
3 × 4-color, 1/2-page ads @ $4,800 (monthly)	14,400.00
Radio Advertising	
KKGO 105.1 FM - Classical	
3 months × 48 spots/month @ $125 per 30-seconds	18,000.00
K-BIG 104.3 FM	
3 months × 48, 30-second spots/month @ $5,000	15,000.00
Sales Promotion	
7 × 5-day/4-night cruise for two to Mexico/Hawaii	
@ $1,000—awarded during Grand Opening	7,000.00
Grand Opening	
7 days × $500 per day	3,500.00
Subtotal	$ 89,415.70
Outside services—ad agency and miscellaneous	10,584.30
Total	$100,000.00

Figure A2-2   Precommercialization Promotion Mix Costs Allocation

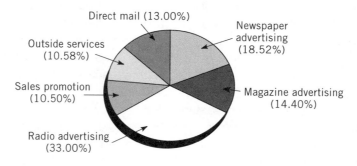

Direct mail (13.00%)
Newspaper advertising (18.52%)
Outside services (10.58%)
Sales promotion (10.50%)
Magazine advertising (14.40%)
Radio advertising (33.00%)

Table A2-4   Gnatt Chart for Precommercialization Promotion Mix

PROMOTION	WEEK												
	1	2	3	4	5	6	7	8	9	10	11	12	13
Direct Mail	▓	▓	▓	▓	▓	▓	▓	▓	▓	▓	▓	▓	▓
Star News			▓		▓		▓		▓		▓		▓
SCCN		▓		▓		▓		▓		▓		▓	
L.A. Magazine						▓					▓		
KKGO 105.1 FM	▓	▓	▓	▓	▓	▓	▓	▓	▓	▓	▓	▓	▓
K-BIG 104.3 FM		▓	▓	▓	▓	▓	▓	▓	▓	▓	▓	▓	▓
Sweepstakes													▓

Distribution

Professional Fitness is a direct service facility. Thus, to promote the upscale and sophisticated image that the club desires, the interior of the facility has to be decorated accordingly.

The interior of the club is to be designed using a subdued color scheme of a combination of pastel blue, pale green, pink, and ivory, since these colors tend to be preferred by educated people, and also seem to sell well throughout the country.[32]

The furniture and lighting fixtures will have an upscale appearance and complement the rest of the club's decor. The aim is to provide a facility that is conducive to upscale consumers. Furthermore, towels and other essential toiletries will be also provided for the clients.

---

[32] Marshall E. Reddick, *Entrepreneurship* (Los Angeles: California State University, Los Angeles, 1990), p. 143.

Table A2-5   Promotion Campaign for Year 1 to Year 3 of Professional Fitness

Direct Mail	
$4.00 per mailing × 1,200 mailings	$ I4,800.00
Print Advertising	
Newspapers	
Star News (2 times per month for 6 months)	
12 × ¹/₄-page ads @ $881.60	10,579.20
Southern California Community Newspapers (SCCN)	
26 × ¹/₄-page ads @ $621.30 (Thursdays)	16,153.80
Magazines	
Los Angeles	
6 months × 4-color, ¹/₂-page ads @ $4,515	27,090.00
Radio Advertising	
KKGO 105.1 FM-Classical	
6 months × 24 spots/month @ $125 per 30-seconds	18,000.00
K-BIG 104.3 FM	
6 months × 24, 30-second spots/month @ $2,500	15,000.00
Sales Promotion	
1 × 2-week cruise for two to Europe	
@ $4,500—awarded during Anniversary Party	4,500.00
Anniversary Party (AP)	
1 × $3,500 per event	3,500.00
Subtotal	$ 99,623.00
Outside services—ad agency and miscellaneous	8,377.00
Total	$108,000.00

Figure A2-3   Regular Promotion Mix Costs Allocation

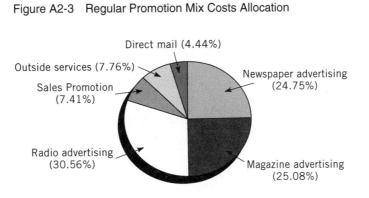

If this club is extremely profitable after three years, there is a possibility that the club might start an upscale health club franchise. This move will only take place after the Board of Directors incorporates the company, thus obtaining the rights to issue stock and sell bonds.

Table A2-6	Gnatt Chart for Promotion Mix of Year 1 to Year 3											
PROMOTION	MONTH											
	1	2	3	4	5	6	7	8	9	10	11	12
Direct Mail	■	■	■	■	■	■	■	■	■	■	■	■
Star News	■		■				■	■			■	
SCCN		■		■		■		■		■		
L.A. Magazine		■		■		■		■		■		■
KKGO 105.1 FM	■		■		■		■		■		■	
K-BIG 104.3 FM		■		■		■		■		■		■
Sweepstakes	■											

CONTROL AND IMPLEMENTATION

Start-Up Costs

The start-up cost for Professional Fitness is shown in Table A2-7. The total start-up cost is $1,274,055. Thus, a bank loan of $374,055 will be required. With the prevailing low interest rate, the assumption is that an unsecured, 8-year business loan is obtainable at a rate of prime plus two, that is, 8.5 percent. This assumed rate will be used in all future interest calculations.

The outlay required for the precommercialization promotional campaign and Grand Opening is calculated as part of start-up and fixed costs.

Break-Even Analysis

Since Professional Fitness makes a donation of $25 to charity for every new member who joins the club, the effective initiation fee is $650. The yearly dues for each member amount to $900 ($75 × 12). Thus, each new member pays an effective total of $1,550 for the first year of membership. Most of this fee represents fixed cost, the only variable amount being staff salaries. Out of each new member's $1,550 approximately 25 percent goes toward staff salaries. Thus:

Break-even volume = Fixed cost/Price − Variable cost
= $1,274,055/($1,550 − $387.50)
= 1,096 members

Table A2-7   Start-Up Costs

Remodeling and Equipment	
Equipment and furniture	$ 400,000
Remodeling and air-conditioning/heating system	675,000
Computer system	10,000
Inventory and supplies	15,000
Advertising	
Precommercialization promotion campaign	100,000
Deposits and Other Fees	
Lease of 12,000 square feet @ $1.20 per sq. ft.	
3 months prepaid lease + last month + 1 month security deposit	72,000
Utilities deposit	325
Legal fees	
Fire and health safety, city permits, and business license	1,730
Total Start-Up Costs	$1,274,055
Partners' equity	(900,000)
Loan Amount	$ 374,055

Pro Forma Monthly Cash Flows

Pro forma monthly cash flows have been computed for 36 months (Table A2-8a to A2- 8f). The health club industry in Southern California is relatively constant except for the months of January and May. There is usually an increase over normal membership numbers during these two months. In January, many people get very motivated about their New Year's resolutions to lose weight, and hence an increase in membership to health clubs. In May, people want to trim down before the summer months actually arrive so that they can fit into the previous year's swimsuits! For the rest of the year, the demand is relatively constant.

The following assumptions are made in the monthly cash-flow calculations:

- The club is to open on November 1, 199X. This is done so that the club gets two whole months to smooth out initial "kinks," before January arrives.

- The conservative membership assumption is used: 1,200 members in year 1; 1,800 in year 2: 2,300 in year 3.

- There is a constant level of memberships sold in year 1 for every month except for January and May. There will be 90 memberships sold every month for 10 months, and 150 memberships each month in January and May.

- Interest paid on the 8-year $374,055 loan amounts to $5,383.45 monthly at 8.5 percent APR. Monthly lease payments amount to $14,400. This lease payment starts on month 4, because there was three months' prepaid rent.

- In year 2, the club gets a 70 percent renewal rate and 30 percent of year 1's members drop out. An assumption made is that the club loses this 30 percent of year 1's members at a constant monthly rate. For example, by the end of year 2, the club will have 0.7 x 1,200 = 840 members who signed up in year 1. The 360 members who dropped out did so at a rate of 30 members a month. In order to have 1,800 members by end of year 2,960 new members must sign up in year 2. The new members joined the club at the constant rate of 75 per month for 10 months and 105 members each in January and

Table A2-8a Pro Forma Monthly Cash Flow for Professional Fitness for Month 1 to Month 6

	1	2	3	4	5	6
REVENUES						
Initiation Fees	$58,500.00	$58,500.00	$ 97,500.00	$58,500.00	$58,500.00	$ 58,500.00
Monthly Dues	6,750.00	13,500.00	20,250.00	31,500.00	38,250.00	45,000.00
Total Revenues	$65,250.00	$72,000.00	$117,750.00	$90,000.00	$96,750.00	$103,500.00
EXPENSES						
Salaries	$27,140.00	$27,140.00	$ 27,140.00	$37,700.00	$37,700.00	$ 37,700.00
Rent	0.00	0.00	0.00	14,400.00	14,400.00	14,400.00
Advertising	9,000.00	9,000.00	9,000.00	9,000.00	9,000.00	9,000.00
Maintenance	1,500.00	1,500.00	1,500.00	1,500.00	1,500.00	1,500.00
Administration	1,000.00	1,000.00	1,000.00	1,000.00	1,000.00	1,000.00
Supplies	1,000.00	1,000.00	1,000.00	1,000.00	1,000.00	1,000.00
Insurance	3,000.00	3,000.00	3,000.00	3,000.00	3,000.00	3,000.00
Utilities	2,500.00	2,500.00	2,500.00	2,750.00	2,750.00	2,750.00
Depreciation	6,833.33	6,833.33	6,833.33	6,833.33	6,833.33	6,833.33
Loan Interest	5,383.45	5,383.45	5,383.45	5,383.45	5,383.45	5,383.45
Outside Services	5,000.00	5,000.00	5,000.00	5,000.00	5,000.00	5,000.00
Total Expenses	$62,356.78	$62,356.78	$ 62,356.78	$87,566.78	$87,566.78	$ 87,566.78
NET PROFIT (LOSS)	**$ 2,893.22**	**$ 9,643.22**	**$ 55,393.22**	**$ 2,433.22**	**$ 9,183.22**	**$ 15,933.22**

Table A2-8b Pro Forma Monthly Cash Flow for Professional Fitness for Month 7 to Month 12

	7	8	9	10	11	12
REVENUES						
Initiation Fees	$ 97,500.00	$ 58,500.00	$ 58,500.00	$ 58,500.00	$ 58,500.00	$ 58,500.00
Monthly Dues	51,750.00	63,000.00	69,750.00	76,500.00	82,500.00	90,000.00
Total Revenues	$149,250.00	$121,500.00	$128,250.00	$135,000.00	$141,000.00	$148,500.00
EXPENSES						
Salaries	$ 37,700.00	$ 37,700.00	$ 37,700.00	$ 45,240.00	$ 45,240.00	$ 45,240.00
Rent	14,400.00	14,400.00	14,400.00	14,400.00	14,400.00	14,400.00
Advertising	9,000.00	9,000.00	9,000.00	9,000.00	9,000.00	9,000.00
Maintenance	1,500.00	1,500.00	1,500.00	1,500.00	1,500.00	1,500.00
Administration	1,500.00	1,500.00	1,500.00	1,500.00	1,500.00	1,500.00
Supplies	1,500.00	1,500.00	1,500.00	1,500.00	1,500.00	1,500.00
Insurance	3,000.00	3,000.00	3,000.00	3,000.00	3,000.00	3,000.00
Utilities	3,000.00	3,000.00	3,000.00	3,000.00	3,000.00	3,000.00
Depreciation	6,833.33	6,833.33	6,833.33	6,833.33	6,833.33	6,833.33
Loan Interest	5,383.45	5,383.45	5,383.45	5,383.45	5,383.45	5,383.45
Outside Services	5,000.00	5,000.00	5,000.00	5,000.00	5,000.00	5,000.00
Total Expenses	$ 88,816.78	$ 88,816.78	$ 88,816.78	$ 96,356.78	$ 96,356.78	$ 96,356.78
NET PROFIT (LOSS)	**$ 60,433.22**	**$ 32,683.22**	**$ 39,433.22**	**$ 38,643.22**	**$ 44,643.22**	**$ 52,143.22**

Table A2-8c Pro Forma Monthly Cash Flow for Professional Fitness for Month 13 to Month 18

	13	14	15	16	17	18
REVENUES						
Initiation Fees	$ 48,750.00	$ 48,750.00	$ 68,250.00	$ 48,750.00	$ 48,750.00	$ 48,750.00
Monthly Dues	93,375.00	96,750.00	102,375.00	105,750.00	109,125.00	112,500.00
Total Revenues	$142,125.00	$145,500.00	$170,625.00	$154,500.00	$157,875.00	$161,250.00
EXPENSES						
Salaries	$ 57,772.00	$ 57,772.00	$ 57,772.00	$ 63,580.00	$ 63,580.00	$ 63,580.00
Rent	14,400.00	14,400.00	14,400.00	14,400.00	14,400.00	14,400.00
Advertising	9,000.00	9,000.00	9,000.00	9,000.00	9,000.00	9,000.00
Maintenance	1,500.00	1,500.00	1,500.00	1,500.00	1,500.00	1,500.00
Administration	2,000.00	2,000.00	2,000.00	2,000.00	2,000.00	2,000.00
Supplies	2,000.00	2,000.00	2,000.00	2,000.00	2,000.00	2,000.00
Insurance	3,500.00	3,500.00	3,500.00	3,500.00	3,500.00	3,500.00
Utilities	3,250.00	3,250.00	3,250.00	3,250.00	3,250.00	3,250.00
Depreciation	6,833.33	6,833.33	6,833.33	6,833.33	6,833.33	6,833.33
Loan Interest	5,756.85	5,756.85	5,756.85	5,756.85	5,756.85	5,756.85
Outside Services	5,000.00	5,000.00	5,000.00	5,000.00	5,000.00	5,000.00
Total Expenses	$111,012.18	$111,012.18	$111,012.18	$116,820.18	$116,820.18	$116,820.18
NET PROFIT (LOSS)	$ 31,112.82	$ 34,487.82	$ 59,612.82	$ 37,679.82	$ 41,054.82	$ 44,429.82

Table A2-8d Pro Forma Monthly Cash Flow for Professional Fitness for Month 19 to Month 24

	19	20	21	22	23	24
REVENUES						
Initiation Fees	$ 68,250.00	$ 48,750.00	$ 48,750.00	$ 48,750.00	$ 48,750.00	$ 48,750.00
Monthly Dues	118,125.00	121,500.00	124,875.00	128,250.00	131,625.00	135,000.00
Total Revenues	$186,375.00	$170,250.00	$173,625.00	$177,000.00	$180,375.00	$183,750.00
EXPENSES						
Salaries	$ 69,388.00	$ 69,388.00	$ 69,388.00	$ 75,696.00	$ 75,696.00	$ 75,696.00
Rent	14,400.00	14,400.00	14,400.00	14,400.00	14,400.00	14,400.00
Advertising	9,000.00	9,000.00	9,000.00	9,000.00	9,000.00	9,000.00
Maintenance	1,500.00	1,500.00	1,500.00	1,500.00	1,500.00	1,500.00
Administration	2,250.00	2,250.00	2,250.00	2,250.00	2,250.00	2,250.00
Supplies	2,250.00	2,250.00	2,250.00	2,250.00	2,250.00	2,250.00
Insurance	3,500.00	3,500.00	3,500.00	3,500.00	3,500.00	3,500.00
Utilities	3,500.00	3,500.00	3,500.00	3,500.00	3,500.00	3,500.00
Depreciation	6,833.33	6,833.33	6,833.33	6,833.33	6,833.33	6,833.33
Loan Interest	5,756.85	5,756.85	5,756.85	5,756.85	5,756.85	5,756.85
Outside Services	6,000.00	6,000.00	6,000.00	6,000.00	6,000.00	6,000.00
Total Expenses	$124,378.18	$124,378.18	$124,378.18	$130,686.18	$130,686.18	$130,686.18
NET PROFIT (LOSS)	$ 61,996.82	$ 45,871.82	$ 49,246.82	$ 46,313.82	$ 49,688.82	$ 53,063.82

Table A2-8e Pro Forma Monthly Cash Flow for Professional Fitness for Month 25 to Month 30

	25	26	27	28	29	30
REVENUES						
Initiation Fees	$ 52,000.00	$ 52,000.00	$ 78,000.00	$ 52,000.00	$ 52,000.00	$ 52,000.00
Monthly Dues	137,625.00	140,250.00	145,875.00	148,500.00	151,125.00	153,750.00
Total Revenues	$189,625.00	$192,250.00	$223,875.00	$200,500.00	$203,125.00	$205,750.00
EXPENSES						
Salaries	$ 85,676.00	$ 85,676.00	$ 85,676.00	$ 85,676.00	$ 85,676.00	$ 85,676.00
Rent	14,400.00	14,400.00	14,400.00	14,400.00	14,400.00	14,400.00
Advertising	9,000.00	9,000.00	9,000.00	9,000.00	9,000.00	9,000.00
Maintenance	1,500.00	1,500.00	1,500.00	1,500.00	1,500.00	1,500.00
Administration	2,250.00	2,250.00	2,250.00	2,400.00	2,400.00	2,400.00
Supplies	2,250.00	2,250.00	2,250.00	2,400.00	2,400.00	2,400.00
Insurance	4,000.00	4,000.00	4,000.00	4,000.00	4,000.00	4,000.00
Utilities	3,750.00	3,750.00	3,750.00	3,750.00	3,750.00	3,750.00
Depreciation	6,833.33	6,833.33	6,833.33	6,833.33	6,833.33	6,833.33
Loan Interest	5,756.85	5,756.85	5,756.85	5,756.85	5,756.85	5,756.85
Outside Services	6,000.00	6,000.00	6,000.00	6,000.00	6,000.00	6,000.00
Total Expenses	$141,416.18	$141,416.18	$141,416.18	$141,716.18	$141,716.18	$141,716.18
NET PROFIT (LOSS)	$ 48,208.82	$ 50,833.82	$ 82,458.82	$ 58,783.82	$ 61,408.82	$ 64,033.82

Table A2-8f Pro Forma Monthly Cash Flow for Professional Fitness for Month 31 to Month 36

	31	32	33	34	35	36
REVENUES						
Initiation Fees	$ 78,000.00	$ 52,000.00	$ 52,000.00	$ 52,000.00	$ 52,000.00	$ 52,000.00
Monthly Dues	159,375.00	162,000.00	164,625.00	167,250.00	169,875.00	172,500.00
Total Revenues	$237,375.00	$214,000.00	$216,625.00	$219,250.00	$221,875.00	$224,500.00
EXPENSES						
Salaries	$ 95,356.00	$ 95,356.00	$ 95,356.00	$ 95,356.00	$ 95,356.00	$ 95,356.00
Rent	14,400.00	14,400.00	14,400.00	14,400.00	14,400.00	14,400.00
Advertising	9,000.00	9,000.00	9,000.00	9,000.00	9,000.00	9,000.00
Maintenance	1,500.00	1,500.00	1,500.00	1,500.00	1,500.00	1,500.00
Administration	2,400.00	2,400.00	2,400.00	2,400.00	2,400.00	2,400.00
Supplies	2,400.00	2,400.00	2,400.00	2,400.00	2,400.00	2,400.00
Insurance	4,000.00	4,000.00	4,000.00	4,000.00	4,000.00	4,000.00
Utilities	3,900.00	3,900.00	3,900.00	3,900.00	3,900.00	3,900.00
Depreciation	6,833.33	6,833.33	6,833.33	6,833.33	6,833.33	6,833.33
Loan Interest	5,756.85	5,756.85	5,756.85	5,756.85	5,756.85	5,756.85
Outside Services	6,000.00	6,000.00	6,000.00	6,000.00	6,000.00	6,000.00
Total Expenses	$151,546.18	$151,546.18	$151,546.18	$151,546.18	$151,546.18	$151,546.18
NET PROFIT (LOSS)	$ 85,828.82	$ 62,453.82	$ 65,078.82	$ 67,703.82	$ 70,328.82	$ 72,953.82

May. Thus, at the end of year 2, the club will have 840 members in their second year and 960 new members in their first year. This same 70 percent retention/30 percent loss is also used in year 3.

- A second manager is hired in year 2. The club is also assumed to maintain a staff-to-client ratio of 50 to 1. Thus, by the end of the second year, the club will employ 36 staff to service the expected 1,800 members.

Pro Forma Income Statements

Pro forma income statements have also been prepared for the period of three years (Tables A2-9, A2-10, and A2-11). The interest income reported on this statement is calculated based on two equal deposits into a 90-day money market fund paying an interest of 5 percent APR. The deposits are made in the beginning of the second period—month 4, and on day 1 of the fourth period of year 1—month 10. It is assumed that the interest income is paid on October 31 of each year.

In summary, the pro forma income statement shows a net income after taxes of:

- $192,848.97 for year 1
- $290,249.37 for year 2
- $421,829.95 for year 3

Table A2-9   Pro Forma Income Statement for Professional Fitness for Year 1 Ended October 31, 200X

REVENUES	
Initiation Fees	$ 780,000.00
Monthly Dues	588,750.00
Interest Income	2,290.31
Total Revenues	$1,371,040.31
EXPENSES	
Salaries	$ 443,340.00
Payroll Taxes (10%)	44,334.00
Rent	129,600.00
Advertising	108,000.00
Maintenance	18,000.00
Administration	15,000.00
Supplies	15,000.00
Insurance	36,000.00
Utilities	33,750.00
Depreciation	81,999.96
Loan Interest	64,601.40
Outside Services	60,000.00
Total Expenses	$1,049,625.36
Profit Before Taxes	$ 321,414.95
Taxes (40%)	128,565.98
NET INCOME	**$ 192,848.97**

Table A2-10   Pro Forma Income Statement for Professional
Fitness for Year 2 Ended October 31, 200X

REVENUES	
Initiation Fees	$ 624,000.00
Monthly Dues	1,379,250.00
Interest Income	9,119.91
Total Revenues	<u>$2,012,369.91</u>
EXPENSES	
Salaries	$ 799,308.00
Payroll Taxes (10%)	79,930.80
Rent	172,800.00
Advertising	108,000.00
Maintenance	18,000.00
Administration	25,500.00
Supplies	25,500.00
Insurance	42,000.00
Utilities	40,500.00
Depreciation	81,999.96
Loan Interest	69,082.20
Outside Services	66,000.00
Total Expenses	<u>$1,528,620.96</u>
Profit Before Taxes	$ 483,748.95
Taxes (40%)	193,499.58
NET INCOME	**<u>$ 290,249.37</u>**

Return on Investment (ROI)

The return on investment—ROI—can be calculated from the income statements. The fixed assets cost $1,274.055. Thus from the income statements, it can be seen that:

- ROI in year 1 = $192,848.97/$1,274,055 = 15.1%
- ROI in year 2 = $290,249.37/$1,274,055 = 22.8%
- ROI in year 3 = $421,829.95/$1,274,055 = 33.1%

Table A2-11　Pro Forma Income Statement for Professional Fitness for Year 3 Ended October 31, 200X

REVENUES	
Initiation Fees	$ 676,000.00
Monthly Dues	1,872,750.00
Interest Income	21,593.27
Total Revenues	$2,570,343.27
EXPENSES	
Salaries	$1,086,192.00
Payroll Taxes (10%)	108,619.20
Rent	172,800.00
Advertising	108,000.00
Maintenance	18,000.00
Administration	28,350.00
Supplies	28,350.00
Insurance	48,000.00
Utilities	45,900.00
Depreciation	81,999.96
Loan Interest	69,082.20
Outside Services	72,000.00
Total Expenses	$1,867,293.36
Profit Before Taxes	$ 703,049.91
Taxes (40%)	281,219.96
NET INCOME	**$ 421,829.95**

Pro Forma Balance Sheets

The pro forma balance sheets for Professional Fitness are shown in Tables A2-12, A2-13, and A2-14. The depreciation on fitness and office equipment was calculated using the straight-line method over a period of five years. The estimated total assets of the club during its first three years of operation are:

- Year 1: $1,015,474.78
- Year 2: $1,047,390.29
- Year 3: $1,159,708.53

Table A2-12   Pro Forma Balance Sheet for Professional Fitness for Year 1—October 31, 199X

ASSETS

CURRENT ASSETS
Cash		$ 15,000.00	
Short-term Investments		122,474.78	
Merchandise Inventory		5,000.00	
Office Supplies		5,000.00	
Total Current Assets			$ 147,474.78

BUILDING & EQUIPMENT
Building	$675,000.00		
Less Accumulated Depreciation	135,000.00	$540,000.00	
Fitness Equipment	$400,000.00		
Less Accumulated Depreciation	80,000.00	320,000.00	
Office Equipment	$ 10,000.00		
Less Accumulated Depreciation	2,000.00	8,000.00	
Total Building & Equipment			868,000.00
Total Assets			**$1,015,474.78**

LIABILITIES

CURRENT LIABILITIES
Salaries Payable	$ 45,240.00		
Account Payable	3,000.00		
Total Current Liabilities		48,240.00	
Total Liabilities			$ 48,240.00

PARTNER'S EQUITY

CONTRIBUTED CAPITAL
6 Partnership units at			
$150,000 per unit	$900,000.00		
Total Contributed Capital		$900,000.00	

RETAINED EARNINGS
		67,234.78	
Total Partners' Equity			967,234.78
Total Liabilities and Partners' Equity			**$1,015,474.78**

Table A2-13   Pro Forma Balance Sheet for Professional Fitness for Year 2—October 31, 199X

ASSETS

CURRENT ASSETS

Cash		$ 25,000.00	
Short-term Investments		361,390.29	
Merchandise Inventory		5,000.00	
Office Supplies		5,000.00	
Total Current Assets			$ 396,390.29

BUILDING & EQUIPMENT

Building	$675,000.00		
Less Accumulated Depreciation	270,000.00	$405,000.00	
Fitness Equipment	$400,000.00		
Less Accumulated Depreciation	160,000.00	240,000.00	
Office Equipment	$ 10,000.00		
Less Accumulated Depreciation	4,000.00	6,000.00	
Total Building & Equipment			651,000.00
Total Assets			**$1,047,390.29**

LIABILITIES

CURRENT LIABILITIES

Salaries Payable	$ 75,696.00		
Account Payable	3,500.00		
Total Current Liabilities		79,196.00	
Total Liabilities			$ 79,196.00

PARTNERS' EQUITY

CONTRIBUTED CAPITAL

6 Partnership units at			
$150,000 per unit	$900,000.00		
Total Contributed Capital		$900,000.00	

RETAINED EARNINGS

		68,194.29	
Total Partners' Equity			968,194.29
Total Liabilities and Partners' Equity			**$1,047,390.29**

Table A2-14   Pro Forma Balance Sheet for Professional Fitness for Year 3—October 31, 199X

ASSETS

CURRENT ASSETS

Cash		$ 35,000.00	
Short-term Investments		680,708.53	
Merchandise Inventory		5,000.00	
Office Supplies		5,000.00	
Total Current Assets			$ 725,708.53

BUILDING & EQUIPMENT

Building	$675,000.00		
Less Accumulated Depreciation	405,000.00	$270,000.00	
Fitness Equipment	$400,000.00		
Less Accumulated Depreciation	240,000.00	160,000.00	
Office Equipment	$ 10,000.00		
Less Accumulated Depreciation	6,000.00	4,000.00	
Total Building & Equipment			434,000.00
Total Assets			**$1,159,708.53**

LIABILITIES

CURRENT LIABILITIES

Salaries Payable		$ 95,356.00	
Account Payable		3,900.00	
Total Current Liabilities		99,256.00	
Total Liabilities			$ 99,256.00

PARTNERS' EQUITY

CONTRIBUTED CAPITAL

6 Partnership units at			
$150,000 per unit	$900,000.00		
Total Contributed Capital		$900,000.00	

RETAINED EARNINGS

		160,452.53	
Total Partners' Equity			1,060,452.53
Total Liabilities and Partners' Equity			**$1,159,708.53**

SUMMARY

Professional Fitness is to be located in the city of San Marino, California. It will be the first upscale weight training and aerobic facility in the city. The club will cater to the over-40 age group and will pride itself in offering an exceptional level of personal service to its members. This will be complemented by the offering of state-of-the-art fitness equipment. Equipment to be offered includes high-end weight resistance machines, exercise bicycles, stair climbers, treadmills, cross-country ski machines, a soundproofed aerobic room with a custom-designed, spring-loaded aerobic mat, satin-finished dumbbells and barbells, and a sauna in both the male and female locker rooms. The club will provide child-care facilities for members while they work out, and house a health bar, pro shop, and an upscale members' lounge.

The total start-up costs will be $1,274,055. Members will be charged an initiation fee of $675 and monthly dues of $75. At this price, the club will break even with 1,096 members. The club expects conservatively to attract 1,200 members in its first year, 1,800 in the second year, and 2,300 in the third year of operation. A 15.1 percent return on investment can be expected in the first year, 22.8 percent in the second, and 33.1 percent in the third. A positive monthly cash flow is obtained every month for the first three years of operation. Promotional expenses amount to $9,000 per month for the first three years of operation. This expense is to be viewed by the club as an investment for the future.

Professional Fitness will succeed due to the following differential advantages:

- None of the club's three major competitors are presently specifically targeting the over-40 market.
- There are currently no upscale weight training and aerobic clubs in San Marino.
- The level of service that will be offered by the club will be unmatched by any of its competitors.
- The aging of the American population will ensure that the potential market for Professional Fitness will increase in the future.
- Fees will be acceptable because of the relatively inelastic price sensitivities of upscale fitness consumers in the trading zone of the club.
- The increased emphasis on improving the quality of life for older people and the widely publicized benefits of weight-training programs for seniors will also ensure the success of the club.

BIBLIOGRAPHY

"American Service Finance Renewal Study (1989)," *National Health Club Association,* 1991 (reprinted with permission).

Branch, Eleanor. "Making Your Fitness Their Business," *Black Enterprise,* Sept. 1991:83–90.

Broadwell, Laura. "Girls Just Wanna Work Out," *Women's Sports & Fitness,* Sept. 1990:45–48.

Brownstein, Vivian. "Consumers Will Help the Economy Stay in Shape Next Year," *Fortune,* Oct. 23, 1989:31–32.

Cooper, James C., and Madigan, Kathleen. "Cross Your Fingers, Knock Wood: That May Be a Recovery Out There," *Business Week,* March 16, 1992:31.

Cooper, Kenneth H., M.D. "Fighting Back Against Bone Loss," *The Saturday Evening Post,* March 1991:32–36.

Engel, Margaret. "Beware of Fitness Club Contracts," *Glamour,* Aug. 1987:92.

"Health Clubs Cool Down," *Club Industry,* March 1991:17–18.

"Health Clubs Look Beyond the Baby Boomers," *Changing Times,* Feb. 1990:95.

Horowitz, Janice M. "From Workouts to Wellness," *Time,* July 30, 1990:64.

"Is Your Health Club Healthy?" *Changing Times,* Sept. 1989:116–118.

Konrad, Walecia. "Health Clubs: Exercise Caution," *Business Week,* June 6, 1988:142–143.

Kotler, Philip. *Marketing Management* (Englewood Cliffs, NJ: Prentice-Hall, 1991), 7th ed., pp. 171–173, 395–396.

Loro, Laura. "Health Clubs Stretch Markets," *Advertising Age,* May 16, 1988:28.

Los Angeles County City Ordinance, Article III—C-1 Commercial Zone, Sect. 23.14 (C), p. 220.

Mandel, Michael J. "Bummed-Out in America," *Business Week,* March 16, 1992:34–35.

Mozoomdar, Iain. "A Study to Determine the Effectiveness of World Gym, Pasadena" (unpublished), Nov. 1991.

O'Reily, Brian. "New Truths about Staying Healthy," *Fortune,* Sept. 25, 1989:57–66.

Reddick, Marshall E. *Entrepreneurship* (Los Angeles: California State University, Los Angeles, 1990), p. 143.

Rodkin, Dennis. "Health Clubs Sweat the Details in Ads," *Advertising Age,* Dec. 3, 1989:38–39.

Rubenstein, Carin. "Here's to Your Health," *New Choices for the Best Years,* Jan. 1990:35–39.

Schefer, Dorothy. "The New Body Building," *Vogue,* May 1989:368.

Sussman, Vic. "Muscle Bound," *U.S. News and World Report,* May 20, 1991:85–88.

Waldrop, Judith. "Feeling Good," *American Demographics,* May 1990:6.

Zarrow, Susan. "The New Diet Priorities," *Prevention,* Sept. 1991:33–36, 118–120.

APPENDIX A2-A

Questionnaire

A study is being conducted to help us run the gym more effectively. Please answer the questions honestly as we would like to know how you guys/gals *REALLY* feel! Thank you for your help.

1. Sex: _____ Male   _____ Female

2. Age: a. Under 21   b. 21–25   c. 26–30   d. 31–35   e. 36–40   f. Over 40 HANG IN THERE!

3. I have to travel _____ to get to the gym.

    a. 0–3 miles   b. 4–6 miles   c. 7–10 miles   d. 11–15 miles   e. 16–20 miles   f. Over 20 miles

4. I joined this gym because: (Check ALL that apply)

    a. the equipment is great!

    b. I want to get buffed! (or more attractive, for you gals/guys out there!)

    c. it is close to where I live or work.

    d. my friends joined and encouraged me to join too.

    e. of the abundance of attractive men/women! AT LEAST YOU WERE HONEST!

    f. the hours are very convenient.

    g. the training atmosphere is great!

    h. the membership fee was cheap/reasonable.

    i. Other: _____

5. I feel that the membership fee as compared to other similarly equipped gyms is:

    a. Cheap   b. A bargain!   c. Reasonable   d. Expensive   e. Exorbitant

6. I usually train (per week): a. 1–2X   b. 3X   c. 4X   d. 5X   e. 6–7X ANIMAL!!!

7. I usually train: a. Before 8 a.m.   b. 9–Noon   c. 1–3 p.m.   d. 4–7 p.m.   e. After 7 p.m.

8. I find the informational and teaching capabilities of the gym instructors to be:

    a. Excellent!   b. Good   c. Average   d. Poor   e. Ineffective   f. Never needed one!

9. I use the following equipment: (*Check # of times per week* for EACH equipment) THANKS!

	1X	2X	3X	4X	5–7X	Never (0X)
a. Bench presses (Flat or Incline)	____	____	____	____	____	____
b. Squat rack or leg press machine	____	____	____	____	____	____
c. Leg extension or curl machines	____	____	____	____	____	____
d. Weight stations/Assisted chin-up	____	____	____	____	____	____
e. Lower abs machine/Crunch board	____	____	____	____	____	____
f. Stairmaster	____	____	____	____	____	____
g. Lifecycle	____	____	____	____	____	____
h. Treadmill	____	____	____	____	____	____

10. For my purposes, the quantity and poundages of the free weights are:

    a. Sufficient   b. Insufficient   c. Don't use free weights so don't care!

11. I would like to see the following equipment added in the future:
    (Check *ALL* that apply! - Better more than less!)

    a. _____ Additional squat rack/free weights/benches/bars (any type) Specify:_____

    b. _____ Other machines   Specify:_____

    c. _____ There is NO NEED for more equipment. *Are you serious? Really?*

12. I feel that the shower facilities are:

    a. Excellent!   b. Above average   c. Average   d. Below average   e. Venice Beach is cleaner!!

A3

HONDA OF NORTH HOLLYWOOD

Developed by
AHMET MURAT MENDI
MISTY L. IWATSU
BARBARA PATTON

Contents

EXECUTIVE SUMMARY

Honda of North Hollywood is a dealership that sells Honda and BMW motorcycles and personal watercraft (PWC). Sea-Doo is the brand name of PWC currently sold at the dealership. Developing the personal watercraft side of the business is the focus of this marketing plan.

After identifying the product life cycle of PWC to be in the "mature" stage, and recognizing the high level of competition for profits that now exist, appropriate strategies have been set up.

To extend the product life cycle, it is important to differentiate new models and features of PWC. Local dealerships must become experts in promotion of the differentiation. Through excellent service centers, local dealers can take advantage of the service cycle's lag behind the product life cycle. That is, as sales decline, be prepared to give maximum service. Through segmentation, they can seek to identify new customers. Even with the superior knowledge of the Sea-Doo brand position that Honda of North Hollywood has, new avenues should be explored to continue an upward momentum in sales, and they should also consider adding a new brand to the product line.

There is an initial investment of $150,000 starting in October 1997 for facility expansion and suggested improvements in service and promotion. Also, $1 million will be spent to expand the product line to include another brand. Profit level is projected to substantially increase by the end of the third year.

Located in the center of the San Fernando Valley, Honda of North Hollywood has been in business for over 30 years. This longevity coupled with a talented and stable workforce, the high product knowledge of Sea-Doo, and the willingness to find new ways to service customers, give Honda of North Hollywood a competitive advantage in the Los Angeles area.

INTRODUCTION

The Personal Watercraft industry, or jet skis to the layman, have caused a great deal of upheaval in several bodies of water. "What is that noise?" beachfront property owners ask. "What in tarnation is all that ruckus?" fishermen ask. It's the newest in, on the water, in your face water toy. Anybody who is anybody is lining up to own one of these toys.

This is why motorcycle and boat dealerships have expanded their product lines to include these wondrous water toys

The first "Jet Ski" was introduced as a stand-up model in 1968 by Clayton Jacobson II. In 1975 Kawasaki launched the first wave of personal watercraft riding by producing a Jet Ski for the consumer market. Over the past two decades, other manufacturers from boat producers such as Mastercraft to snowmobile makers like Polaris and Bombardier have marketed their version of a personal watercraft (PWC). Each one is a little more technologically advanced than the previous. Current makes and models accommodate nearly every PWC enthusiast. They range from a stand-up style to a multi-person, sit-down runabout. What started out as one person's dream has now become a favorite pastime for many people.

In light of this new wonder toy and the very saturated competitive market that is out there, it's more important than ever for every dealership to have a solid marketing plan in which to work from. This helps the dealership to stay on track of goals and objectives to ensure that they are profitable.

William Robertson, Jr., owner of Honda of North Hollywood, contracted Misty Iwatsu, Ahmet Murat Mendi, and Barbara Patton to develop a marketing plan for the watercraft side of his dealership. The dealership is located in the heart of North Hollywood at the intersections of Burbank Blvd., Lankershim, and Tujunga Avenue at 5626 Tujunga Avenue, North Hollywood, CA.

The background of the dealership has a very impressive history. In 1940 Hollywood, William's grandfather opened a car body shop. In 1959, William's father, William Robertson, Sr., wanted to start racing motorcycles. William's grandfather, being the great father that he was, decided he would open a motorcycle dealership so they could get motorcycles at cost and his son would be able to race. They started their business with 5 motorcycles and were able to sell all 5 of them in their first year. In 1960, they sold 10 motorcycles and one Triumph. Then in 1961, William Robertson, Sr., and his father opened in its current location, which is now the hustle and bustle of North Hollywood. In 1969, they bought an automobile dealership and in 1990, Honda of North Hollywood expanded their product line by venturing into a new product, Sea-Doo personal watercraft. The corporation Bill Robertson and Sons, Inc. now employs 140 corporate employees and 26 to 32 of them work at the North Hollywood location.

In 1958, William Robertson, Sr.'s, wife gave birth to William Robertson, Jr. When little Billy was old enough to walk he went to work with his parents at the shop. During his school years he spent his summer vacations as a lot boy and eventually moved up into the parts department, then to the parts manager, then into sales, and sales management. After William graduated high school he went to the National Automobile Dealers Academy (NADA), which is an automobile college, and received his degree in automobile management. When he was 14, he started to race motorcycles and at 16 he became a professional motorcycle racer. In the last 10 years or so William Jr. became involved in off-road automobile racing, by racing in the big Baja off-road event called "the Baja 1000." He has raced several times and won quite a few of the races. The Baja 1000 is an off-road event in Baja California, Mexico, put on every year by S.C.O.R.E., the off-road racing sanctioning body. The course is at least 1,000 miles, and the first person to navigate the course and finish wins the race. During the last 2 years William has been involved in offshore watercraft racing. The dealership is currently sponsoring 8 motorcycle riders and 9 offshore personal watercraft riders. Two of these personal watercraft racers are the globally titled professional women's race team of Rage Racing, which consists of Misty Iwatsu and Taylor LeClaire. In 1996, Honda of North Hollywood just expanded their product line again with the addition of Sea-Doo jet boats and plans for the future may include carrying another brand of watercraft.

SITUATION ANALYSIS

Situation Environment

Although still popular, personal watercraft (PWC) sales are losing some speed as the industry matures and the laws get stricter. In 1995 sales of new PWC brought 42 percent growth over 1994, but sales in 1996 slowed due to a variety of factors: a late spring, market saturation, negative public opinion, and waterway closures.

PWC accounted for one-third of all new boat sales in 1996. However, PWC sales have leveled off at 200,000 units a year mainly because the "astonishing growth rate of PWC in the last five years could not continue," according to Jeff Napier, president of the National Marine Manufacturers Association.[1]

Neutral Environment

U.S. Coast Guard. The group is always on guard for any disturbances with the goal of keeping waterways safe and free. Not only do they police the waters, but also assist in water rescues.

Environmental Protection Agency. There are new EPA rules to try to cut pollution by watercraft. Engine prices will rise as blue smoke from inefficient outboards drop. Regular boats are mostly impacted but PWC oil or gasoline leakage may draw scrutiny.

Neighborhood. For millions of nature lovers, personal watercraft is an abomination, destroying tranquillity and endangering marine life. Most owners of waterfront property are hardly Jet Ski fans, and some states are considering letting local municipalities make their own rules. They are complaining not only about the danger created on the water due to irresponsible riding, but also about the noise.

Regulations about Using PWC. The following regulations may also have some negative effects on purchasing a PWC.[2]

- According to the U.S. Coast Guard, a "personal watercraft" is a Class A inboard boat—you are the captain legally in command of a powerboat and bound by the boating "rules of the road."
- One should know the watercraft, how it operates, the local boating laws, navigational marks and signs, and the rules of the road.
- Federal regulations require all personal watercraft to be registered and have an identification number on the PWC.

[1] Jeff Napier, "Napier Predicts Slight Sales Growth in 1997," *Boating Industry,* November 1996.
[2] Stewart R. L., "The Wonderful World of "Wet and Wild" Water-Sports," *Rough Notes* (May 1993), pp. 30–32.

- The required equipment includes personal flotation devices (PFDs) for each person on board, as well as a fire extinguisher. Eye protection, a wet-suit, footwear and gloves also are recommended.

- One must not operate a PWC while under the influence of alcohol or drugs.

- One must know and follow local ordinances, especially assigned operating areas and speed limits.

- All sailboats, commercial vessels, and fishing vessels have the right of way.

- One should stay to the right when approaching an oncoming craft. When about to cross paths with another boat, the craft on the right has the right of way.

- One should be mindful of proper etiquette, noise control, and ecologically sensitive areas.

State Regulatory Activity

California.   Senate Bill 1651, which would ban wake-jumping and other dangerous PWC maneuvers, is going back to committee for study. The bill also addresses the use of lanyards and self-circling devices. In its current form, the bill is consistent with the PWIA model law.

California Governor Pete Wilson's efforts to eliminate the state's Dept. of Boating and Waterways as part of a larger plan to streamline state government has apparently failed. After strong lobbying from boat owners in the state, members of the GOP-controlled Assembly decided not to eliminate funding for the agency. The agency operates boating safety programs, among other duties.

Other States.   Controversy continues to brew over the use of PWC's. More states and local governments are passing laws that restrict or ban the use of jet skis for safety, environmental and nuisance reasons. In 1996 a superior judge overturned a county ordinance banning the use of PWC on the Puget Sound in Washington State. The judge cited the Maritime's history of "freedom of the seas" to support his ruling. His opinion was that PWC users have the right to use public waters similar to those of powerboat users. The ruling follows several court rulings in Redding, CA, Batavia, IL, and West Marin County, CA.

Florida took the lead as 30 other states followed suit in passing legislation to regulate the use of PWC. The new rules include age limits and the use of helmets. Alabama has passed a licensing requirement not yet in force in California.

New Jersey has passed a mandatory education bill that requires all riders of PWC to attend a boating safety course. Industry executives believe that Florida took the lead as 30 other states followed suit in passing legislation to regulate the use of PWC. The new rules include age limits and the use of helmets. Alabama has passed a licensing requirement not yet in force in California.

Industry executives believe that education is better than mandatory licensing. Some manufacturers have even tied their warranties to boat safety training requirements. New environmental regulations will also affect popular waterway events such as racing. In some states, U.S. Coast Guard Event permits will now be required of larger events on or near waterways based on the negative environmental impact. Affected are all events that fall under 12 environmental impact sub-categories including events having more than 200 spectators, using hazardous materials, increasing noise levels, and involving waterway construction.

Local Level Regulations and Litigation

Monterey Bay, CA.   Special zones for PWC use are being created near Monterey, Santa Cruz, and Moss Landing. Sanctuary officials say the zones were instituted as a result of complaints from other water users about noise and the dangers of PWC. The PWIA was not successful with litigation to have the ban overturned. Area PWC owners are very upset with being segregated and forced to ride in 4-mile square areas.

Gulf of the Farrallones National Marine Sanctuary, CA.   An environmental group wants to ban PWC from this 948-square mile National Marine Sanctuary off the Marin County coastline. Environmentalists claim PWC are endangering wildlife, mammals, and birds.

Today 36 states have laws on the books that set minimum ages for personal watercraft operation, outlaw wake jumping, nighttime riding, and the "reckless operation" of these boats, and in many cases define no-wake zones.

Insurance. In recent years the industry as been under increasing attack by regulators. Nationally, only 5 percent of the boats on the water are personal watercraft, but they account for 30 to 40 percent of the accidents. Hence, the insurance premium increases as the risk of having an accident increases. McGraw Insurance Services is reputed to be the nation's largest writer of personal watercraft insurance. The California-based operation, according to spokesman Michael J. McGraw, offers insurance for individuals as well as a rental program. Insurance covering personal watercraft for individuals is underwritten by Northland Insurance Companies (rated A+ by A.M. Best Company).

According to McGraw, coverage is written through an admitted member company of Northland in every state except New Hampshire, Texas, Massachusetts, and New Jersey, where it is available on a nonadmitted basis.

"The basic package provides all risk physical damage for the personal watercraft, with a $250 deductible," says McGraw. "Liability coverage with limits of $15,000 is provided, but liability limits of up to $300,000 are available, as well as medical payments up to $2,500 and physical damage coverage for a trailer at a nominal additional charge."[3] The average premium for the basic package ranges somewhere between $200 and $300, depending upon the size of the personal watercraft, McGraw advises.

Competitor Environment

Since 1975 when Kawasaki, the company famous for its motorcycles, introduced the "Jet Ski" or "personal watercraft" to the consumer market, growth has continued. However, Kawasaki lost its role as market leader. Today's main competitors include Polaris, Sea-Doo, Tigershark, Yamaha, and WetJet. There are various types of models by which manufacturers compete for consumer dollars.

The original intent of personal watercraft was to give water skiers the opportunity to pilot their own vehicles and choose the direction they wanted to go. The most common watercraft was designed for a single rider who could sit or stand since the handlebar was adjustable. Then came the two-seater that required sitting with a fixed handlebar.

---

[3] Stewart R. L., "The Wonderful World of "Wet and Wild" Water-Sports," *Rough Notes* (May 1993), pp. 30–32.

The recent introduction of the three-seater has caused an explosion of interest and increased speculation as to the towing possibilities of PWC. This is the trend for 1997.

Different personal watercraft models have different engine sizes which determine the speed. These factors as well as model type determine the cost of owning a PWC, which can range from $4,500 to $8,000 each.

Although further growth is seen by PWC manufacturers, opening a dealership may not guarantee profits. There are many challenges to face. Factors that help to determine success are solid financial history, good credit, location, and attitude.

Direct Competitors. Local dealers that are also PWC dealerships within a 25-mile radius of Honda of North Hollywood:

Dealer	Location	Brands in Stock
Colby	22123 Ventura Blvd., Woodland Hills	Yamaha, Kawasaki
Berts Motorcycle Mall	900 West Foothill, Azusa	Sea-Doo, Yamaha, Kawasaki
Dick Allen	24601 Arch Street, Newhall	Sea-Doo, Yamaha
Simi Valley Honda	4346 Los Angeles Ave., Simi Valley	Sea-Doo
Honda of Hollywood*	6525 Santa Monica Blvd., Hollywood	Sea-Doo

* Also owned by William Robertson, Jr., who is the owner of Honda of North Hollywood.

William Robertson, Jr.'s, Sea-Doo dealership is centrally located in the San Fernando Valley. Besides selling Honda and BMW motorcycles and Sea-Doo watercraft, he operates a full-service technical operations center. Since he also owns Honda of Hollywood there is a friendly rivalry between his two dealerships.

Company Environment

The dealership has been in the same location in North Hollywood for more than 35 years. They have been carrying Sea-Doo brand PWC for seven years.

They have a decentralized management style and are working as a profit center independent from other stores. With 32 employees at this location, they achieved a strong teamwork environment in the dealership.

In addition to Sea-Doo PWC, they also carry Honda and BMW motorcycles. This enables them to differentiate their product line and avoid fluctuations in monthly sales figures due to the seasonality of PWC sales.

Finally, with close to $500,000 in profits for 1996, the dealership achieved an increase after several years of a stable profit level.

Competitive Advantages

They carry Sea-Doo brand PWC which has the largest market share (42 percent). The manufacturer of Sea-Doo, Bombardier Inc., has an extensive advertising campaign not only throughout the nation, but also heavily in the Greater Los Angeles area. The Bombardier Inc. corporation does all the marketing research necessary for the dealerships to help them identify their target market's characteristics, so local dealership does not have to put so much effort in improving the brand's promotion among target market.

Since the dealership sells only one brand of PWC, they know the product's features and benefits, and can sell and service it to the maximum.

The dealership has an established reputation in the area, having been there since 1961. They also have a low turnover rate of employees. Several have been there for numerous years with a solid knowledge base of the business.

They have a reliable service department, whose head has been there for more than three years. He is experienced in his business and knows how to select employees with necessary technical skills.

TARGET MARKET

The target market for this North Hollywood dealership are mainly sport enthusiasts who possess an interest in watercraft.

The following graphs and statistical data were collected from several different sources: the Southern California Bombardier Sea-Doo Dealers Association and research data from several personal watercraft magazines such as *Splash, Jet Sports, Personal Watercraft Illustrated,* and *Watercraft World.*

These graphs and data serve as a reference guide for the future goals and objectives of Honda of North Hollywood and will be useful to facilitate decision making should any problems arise and for the dealership to stay on track to their target audience.

The Media Marketing Research Institute (MRI) did a survey of the American consumer. They polled 40,000 nationally, 2,500 in Los Angeles County, and extracted this demographic breakdown of 890 Los Angeles men between the ages of 25–54 who earn a median income of $60,000 or more.

In a section entitled, "The Voice of the Consumer," MRI reported: "Today's consumer is speaking to us. They are telling us something about who they are and what they want. We can hear today's consumer speaking to us in their activities, the way they raise their children, and the purchases they make. If we listen carefully, we can hear the 'voice of the consumer.' It is only once we understand what they are saying, that we should begin to speak."[4]

The basic understanding of the MRI that needs to be kept in mind are:

Population: The specific group being studied.

Composition: Percentage of population given in a defined characteristic.

Index: The comparison of compositions; an index of 100 percent is equivalent.

Demographics

Demographic characteristics are those characteristics that make up the target audiences. This is the most fundamental profile.

The target audience for Sea-Doo is men 25–54 years of age. This age group is larger in Los Angeles than in the nation as a whole. The average annual household income in the Los Angeles area is above the national average. The primary target for Sea-Doo are those who earn $60,000 or more per year.

Chart 1   Age Distribution of Sea-Doo Customers   Chart 2   Income Distribution of Sea-Doo Customers

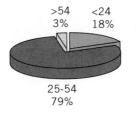

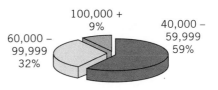

---

4 The Media Marketing Research Institute. 1997.

Chart 3   Marital Status of Target Customers   Chart 4   Education Level of the Target Market

Although there are fewer graduates in Los Angeles than nationwide, more than 80 percent of the primary target have attended college. The percentages of divorced and single men are higher in Los Angeles than the nation in the target market. However, the majority of the target market is married.

Geographic

Places where personal watercraft can be found include all of the following: lakes, rivers, oceans, and other waterways such as reservoirs or forebays. Most watercraft owners use all forms of water but the most popular ones are lakes and rivers. PWC owners spend 72 percent of their time on lakes and 35.5 percent on rivers. While some owners ride on the ocean and other waterways, they do not spend as much time there.

Chart 5   Ride Locations

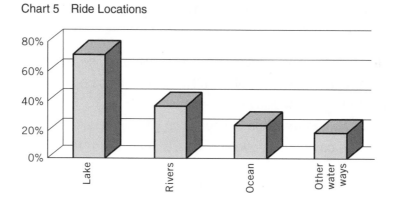

Most watercraft owners travel as far as 90 miles for riding; 60 percent of the owners drive up to 24 miles to go to their favorite riding spot, whereas, 40 percent travel more than 25 miles just to experience the thrill of riding PWC.

Chart 6   Distance to Ride Locations

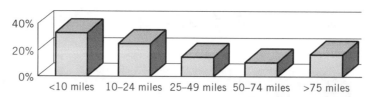

In Southern California, several opportunities arise in nearby lakes and oceans. Even though the majority of Los Angeles consumers spend their time on lakes, ocean riding is becoming more popular for the extreme sports enthusiast.

Psychographic

Average yearly use ranges from less than 60 days to more than 200 days per year, where 85 percent of the PWC owners ride up to 199 days per year. Most of the PWC owners have both watched PWC events on TV and attended PWC events within the last year.

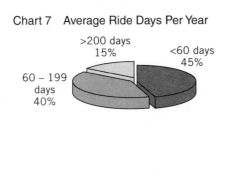

Chart 7   Average Ride Days Per Year

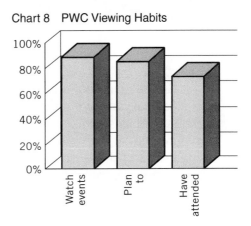

Chart 8   PWC Viewing Habits

Thirty-seven percent of those surveyed are planning to buy a new PWC for next season; what's more, 39 percent of people surveyed are undecided about whether to buy one, which indicates a great opportunity to enhance sales.

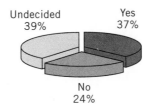

Chart 9   Plans to Puchase PWC for Next Season

Finally, the Los Angeles target market states that environmental concern is the most important issue in social concerns. Environmental concerns are consistent with the outdoor activities the target market enjoys in the Greater Los Angeles area. The popularity indexes for social concerns are given in the following table, where 100 indicates average popularity.

Table A3-1.   Social Concerns of Target Market

1. Environmental Cause	134
2. Recycling	118
3. Volunteer Work	85
4. Political Involvement	79
5. Contributed to PBS	79

Lifestyle

The target market (men, ages 25–54 years old, earning $60,000+) may buy the watercraft initially for themselves; however, statistics show that most members of the family also ride. In addition, the majority (67 percent) of the owners use their PWC for recreational riding; however, only 17 percent of the owners actually race and the rest (16 percent) belong to some type of PWC club or association.

Chart 10   Number of People in the Family
Who Ride PWC

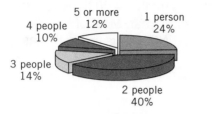

Chart 11   Life Style and Interests of PWC Owners

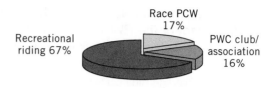

Sports activities in the Greater Los Angeles area tend to be more challenging, and are basically outdoor and fitness oriented. Though these sports are outdoor, they are individual and less competitive. More traditional sports like golf and softball are less popular among the target market. The popularity indexes for several kinds of sports are given in the following chart, where 100 indicates average popularity. Los Angeles is known for its weather and climate. This is consistent with target market that does not like to stay home but do different outdoor activities.

Chart 12   Popularity of Sports Activities

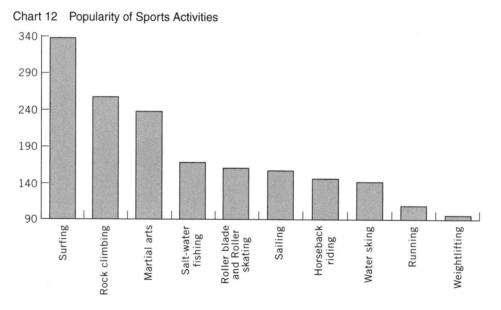

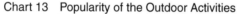

Chart 13   Popularity of the Outdoor Activities

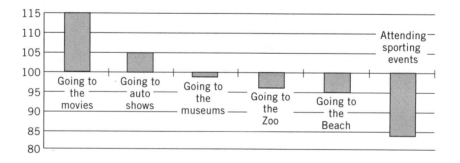

Media Market

Los Angeles is the second largest media market in the United States. There are 3,424,500 men in the Greater Los Angeles area which are defined as the target market of the dealership. This group consists of males who are between 25 and 54 years old. This is a large number in which to draw customers from. Los Angeles has the top affiliates and independent TV stations in the country, which is not surprising since Los Angeles is number one in the world's entertainment industry. The top television stations in the area are:

Table 2. Most Popular TV Stations in Los Angeles

Station	Network Affiliation	Channel
KABC	ABC	7
KCAL	Independent	9
KCBS	CBS	2
KCOP	Independent (UPN)	13
KNBC	NBC	4
KTLA	Independent (WB)	5
KTTV	FOX	11

The cable stations popular among the target market are:

Table 3. Most Popular Cable Televisions in Los Angeles

Station	% of Subscribers
Arts & Entertainment	26.8%
CNN-Cable News Network	47.8%
E!-Entertainment	11.9%
ESPN—Sport	47.7%
ESPN2—Sport	12.6%
Nick at Nite—Reruns of Old Shows	14.8%
TNT—Turner Broadcasting	20.0%
USA	20.3%

Attention should be focused on the sports-related channels and should be considered in future advertising.

The following table shows the target market's favorite radio stations that should be selected for radio advertisement:

Table 4. Most Popular Radio Stations in Los Angeles

Station	Format
KLOW-FM	AOR
KCBS-FM	Classic Rock
KRTH-FM	Oldies
KEI-AM	Talk
KTWV-FM	NAC
KLSX-FM	Entertainment/Talk
KROQ-FM	Alternative Rock
KOST-FM	Adult Contemporary
KBIG-FM	Adult Contemporary
KABC-AM	Talk
KYSR-FM	Adult Contemporary

The following table shows the target market's most widely read newspapers in Los Angeles, and their circulation figures for weekdays and Sundays.

Table 5.   Most Widely Read Newspapers in Los Angeles

Newspaper	Daily Circulation	Sunday Circulation
Los Angels Times	1,021,100	1,391,100
Los Angeles Daily News	204,200	217,700

The *LA Times* is the dominant paper in the market. Overall, newspaper readership among the target audience is below national average.

In addition, most of the watercraft owners read some type of watercraft magazine, mainly *Splash* (32 percent), to get the latest news and learn the latest developments about the new products as well as the parts necessary for maintenance.

Chart 14   PWC Magazines Read

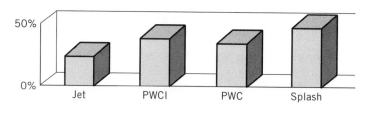

Finally the following table summarizes the advantages and disadvantages of major advertising media.

Table 6.   Advantages and Disadvantages of Major Media[5]

Medium	Advantages	Disadvantages
Television	Reaches extremely large audience; uses picture, print, sound, and motion for effect; can target specific audiences.	High cost to prepare and run ads; short exposure time and perishable message; difficult to convey complex information.
Radio	Low cost; can target specific audiences; ads can be placed quickly; can use sound, humor, and intimacy effectively.	No visual excitement; short exposure time and perishable message; difficult to convey complex information.
Magazines	Can target specific audiences; high-quality color; long life of ad; ads can be clipped and saved; can convey complex information.	Long time needed to place ad; limited control of ad position; relatively high cost; competes for attention with other magazine features.
Newspapers	Excellent coverage of local markets; ads can be placed and changed quickly; ads can be saved; quick customer response; low cost.	Ads compete for attention with other newspaper features; can't control ad position on page; short life-span; can't target specific audiences.
Direct Mail	Best for targeting specific audiences; very flexible (3-D pop-up ads); ad can be saved; measurable.	Relatively high cost; audience often sees it as "junk mail"; no competition with editorial matter.
Outdoor	Low cost; local market focus; high visibility; opportunity for repeat exposures.	Message must be short and simple; low selectivity of audience; criticized as a traffic hazard, eyesore.

[5] Sources: Courtland L. Bovee and William F. Arens, *Contemporary Advertising,* 4th ed. (Homewood, Ill.: Richard D. Irwin, 1992), pp. 437–44; and William G. Nickels, James M. McHugh, *Understanding Business,* 3rd ed. (Homewood, Ill.: Richard D. Irwin, 1993), p. 332.

Choosing between these alternative media should be based on careful analysis of the habits of the target audience, the product's attributes, and the cost of the medium. Moreover, correct scheduling must be made after the selection of the advertising medium. Taking the seasonality of the product into consideration, Flighting ("intermittent") schedule method seems to be the best alternative for scheduling.

NEED ANALYSIS

Current Needs of Target Market

As seen from the demographic profile, the target customers for Sea-Doo are male, ages 25–54 years old, with at least some college education, earning more then $60,000 per year. The Los Angeles market is young, affluent, and are trendsetters who are interested in more extreme sports that test individual abilities. These sports appeal to the adventurous spirit of people who are young at heart and like to live on the edge. Many of these outdoor activities take advantage of the local region's natural environment, especially the water. They do their own thing and are always on the go. They do not like to just sit at home and watch TV. They want the latest, the best in merchandise and sports equipment, and when they have questions or comments, they want to consult the experts either in person, by fax, or by e-mail. They also gather information from Web sites.

Current Products Meeting Needs

There are currently five major manufacturers of PWC. They are: (1) Sea-Doo, (2) Yamaha, (3) Kawasaki, (4) Polaris, and (5) Tigershark.

Chart 15   Popularity of Sports Activities

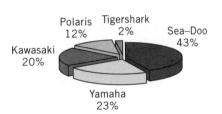

Even though Sea-Doo currently has 43 percent of the market share all the manufacturers have different products with many different characteristics. There is no one manufacturer that is better than the other and each product line has its strengths and weaknesses. PWC is measured on several different scales some of which are:

- Handling/Maneuverability
- Manufacturer's Reputation
- Fun Factor
- Stability
- Noise/Vibration
- Price/Value
- Comfort/Ergonomics
- Appearance/Styling

- Top Speed

All characteristics mentioned above are important factors for all customers. Each customer ranks each factor with different levels of importance, which is why the manufacturers have many different models.

How Well Competitors Are Meeting Needs

There are several dealerships in the Greater Los Angeles area. There is not any one dealership that stands out from the rest in satisfying all the needs of the consumer. Since dealerships do not carry all the manufacturers, and only carry one or two product lines, this has some advantage and disadvantages. If customers want a certain manufacturer, they have to go to different dealerships and comparison shopping is more difficult when they are ready to purchase. However, a dealership that has one or two product lines knows the strengths and weaknesses within the product lines they carry, and they are specialized in those products.

How Are the Needs of Target Market Expected to Change in the Near Future/Distant Future?

Since the number of product lines is increasing every year, the distinguishing points among the manufacturers will be the quality of their products as well as the quality of the after-purchase service that the dealers give. The target market will decide to buy a product not only because it has a powerful engine, but also has high-quality service and low maintenance costs. Even though the target market is in a high income group, the availability of different brands with different types of products will give the consumer the power of bargaining in purchasing PWC that they want. The profit margin for dealers is likely to diminish in the coming years. Since the market is getting closer to its maturity stage, maintenance of existing products will become as important as selling new ones for the dealers. Dealers should take customer satisfaction more seriously and develop new strategies to improve service quality.

Another factor important for the target market is virtual shopping through the Internet. The age group that is interested in PWC is also highly interested in the Internet. Having a Web page where consumers can not only reach to the dealers' products but also can order the products or parts online will become a very important factor in choosing a dealer.

On the other hand Web sites have disadvantages as well as advantages. The following table summarizes the disadvantages and advantages of a Web site. However, since the target market has great interference with the electronic media and Internet, it can be concluded that the advantages of having a Web page outweighs the disadvantages.

Table 7. Advantages and Disadvantages of Web Sites

Advantages	Disadvantages
Less expensive to put up large amount of information	Large images can take a long time to download
Quick to get up and running	Not everyone has Web access (yet)
Easy access (24 × 7, no human presence required)	Less control over page layout than in publishing systems
New and fun	Learning curve
Interactive	
Easy to update	
Feedback	

OPPORTUNITIES, PROBLEMS, AND COMPETITIVE DIFFERENTIAL ADVANTAGES

Through on site and extensive research, several problems and opportunities have been found. During the next 3 years a plan will be implemented to take advantage of the strengths and provide solutions to the problems found.

Opportunities

Low Turnover Ratio. Since many employees have been working for the dealership for a long time, they know how to work as a team. Moreover, the management is a very strong, cohesive group.

Team Atmosphere But Friendly Competition Among Departments. Teamwork among all departments is the key element in the success of this dealership. Further emphasis should be given to maintaining this atmosphere for the continuation of the success of the firm through job description and increasing communication among departments.

Some Employees Actually Use the Products. This tells the customers a lot. If the employees believe in the product enough to own one, it must be good. This also makes the employee more knowledgeable about the maintenance of that product.

Carries a Limited Product Line. This gives the dealership a competitive advantage. They become specialized in that brand so that they can handle any problem that may arise.

Service Department Is Well Trained and Specialized. Even though each technician can service any product that the dealership carries, they all have areas of specialization that they work in.

Problems

Square Footage Space Is Too Small. With the new acquisition of the property across the street, the service department can be moved and expanded so that the sales area in the original location can be reorganized to serve more customers in a more efficient environment. When customers come in, there is a perception of clutter especially with vehicles that need to be serviced. By implementing the move of the service department across the street, the customers will not see the extensive overlap of new products lines and products in need of service. By designing a waiting room in the main sales area of the shop, customers can peruse the new products while they are waiting. This also separates service from the rest of the departments which gives service a better environment for working without interrupting or disturbing the other departments.

Not Enough Parking. By expanding the sales department and moving the service department, the company will be able to get the products off the streets and onto the sales floor. This frees up street parking for customers. Customers with equipment to be serviced can park on the service side of the street, whereas prospective customers can park on the showroom side of the street.

Most Asked Question. "I just bought it, why did it break?" The service department can help to solve this problem. New customers who hear this question might think the dealership has a bad reputation and poor customer service or the product lines the dealership carries are not quality merchandise. The potential customer might decide either not to buy or purchase the product somewhere else. This question should be directed to the technicians not the parts or salespeople.

Salespeople Do Not Care About Jobs or Are Not Informed Enough. Developing job descriptions for each department will improve the efficiency since they will know exactly what is expected from them. All salespeople should be trained briefly in each department, so they are able to answer more general questions. By adhering to the job descriptions, salespeople will know what is expected of them.

Competitive Differential Advantage

A major area of concern will be the competition. Other dealers will not just sit by and let Honda of North Hollywood take the market share. The dealers will try several different promotions and pricing techniques to undercut the competition.

Honda of North Hollywood has several advantages. The first one is that it is located in the heart of North Hollywood and the San Fernando Valley. It has easy access to several freeways (i.e., 101, 134, 170, 405, and 5), all of which are only a few miles away. The pricing of the Sea-Doo product line will be very competitive and the customer service and friendly atmosphere will entice the customer to shop at Honda of North Hollywood. By using the newly constructed Web site, customers can check out the product line and ask questions about the parts and maintenance of PWC from their businesses or homes without wasting time sitting in traffic. Customers who are able to repair their own personal watercraft can order the necessary parts through the Web site by checking the parts list without taking the time of a salesperson.

North Hollywood has a very sophisticated inventory system which enables the dealership to keep the correct amount of necessary parts with minimum cost by keeping a 45-day inventory on hand at all times and automated reorder system.

MARKETING OBJECTIVES AND GOALS

- Enhance current customer base 20 percent by the end of the first year, 25 percent by the end of the second year and 30 percent by the end of the third year.

- Increase sales by 30 percent by the end of the third year. Due to the coming peak season, the renovations of the dealership will commence in October of 1997. The cost of this renovation will be financed through company resources.

- The redesign of the dealership to give better service to its customers should be started and completed before the peak season of 1998 starts.

- Add at least one new brand to its product portfolio to expand its customer base. During the first year, negotiations about adding a new product to dealership portfolio will be made with other manufacturing firms in the market. After selecting the manufacturer, additional sales and service personnel will be hired and trained to service that product. Current staff will go through new product training. The training should be completed and everyone related to that product should become experts before the peak season for 1998 starts.

- Improve the efficiency of staff to reduce costs. Throughout the first year management will develop job descriptions as well as write a policy and procedure manual. Management and employees will set employee goals and objectives and start annual performance evaluations. Maintain high level of employee expectations and be consistent in all areas of operation by following the company mission statement.

MARKETING STRATEGY

Differentiation

Each product has a life cycle that has four stages. After completing necessary research and studies in the areas of growth of the market segment, market pricing, governmental regulations, and profitability, it was apparent that the watercraft industry is in the maturity stage of the life cycle.

The maturity stage means that although there are many competitors in the industry, they are all competing for a smaller market share.

"Less efficient competitors go under or withdraw from the market. Buyers who have been purchasing the product exhibit repeat buying patterns, and although sales continue to increase during this stage, profits begin to fall."

"This stage encourages a strategy of entrenchment, yet a search for new markets is still possible."[6]

The industries strategy to maintain interest in PWC should be to introduce new models, improve features, and extend the product life cycle. From the one-seater in 1975 to the more recently introduced three-seater, manufacturers have sought ways to keep the customer dollars flowing in the direction of purchasing PWC, after-market parts, and other related products. Further differentiation will be helpful as the industry continues to mature through new products and accessory development, education, and information on new opportunities for the use of PWC.

By differentiating Honda of North Hollywood from other competitors at the dealership level, profits can increase through the servicing of PWC even as the product life cycle goes through the maturity and decline stages. Since the service cycle is as vital as the product life cycle, the dealer must know that parts inventory of new and dated PWC, appropriate pricing strategies, and good service technicians will be an important factor in maintaining customer satisfaction and for the continuation of a profitable business. This will also extend the life cycle of the PWC market. Even though Honda of North Hollywood sells only the Sea-Doo brand of PWC and it gives the dealer a competitive advantage of specialization in that product line, it is recommended, based upon extensive research, that the dealership should consider adding another brand to its product portfolio to enhance its customer base. Based upon its reputation, reliability, and also having the second largest market share in the industry with 23 percent, it is recommended that the Yamaha brand of PWC be added to the portfolio.

Some of the competitors already carry more than one brand line; however, Honda of North Hollywood will distinguish itself from the others by not only carrying two product lines with good reputations, but also by offering superior customer service. Combining a new Web site with technical support will allow this dealership to develop a superior image in customers' minds. Customers will think they are getting the best deal for the value of

---

6 William Cohen, *The Marketing Plan* 1995, 2nd ed. New York: John Wiley & Sons, Inc.

the dollar, which will be a step above any other dealership. As of now there is no other dealership that offers this superior service. This approach will help the dealership to become a leader in the high technological field that PWC is in.

Segmentation Strategies.   By defining the target market (males, ages 25–54, and earning a combined household income of $60,000 or more), the dealership can segment the market by taking only the greater Los Angeles area with a population of 10,831,000, males, ages 18 and up, and extrapolating men, ages 25–54, which leaves a target market population of 3,424,500 men. Further segmentation by region can be established by taking the San Fernando Valley and the Los Angeles areas, and by lifestyle of men who like outdoor activities and go on family outings.

Honda of North Hollywood can dominate the market by concentrating and fulfilling the needs and appealing to the segmented target market that no other dealership can meet though superior customer service and education. The dealership will use vertical penetration expansion by combining the marketing process while integrating all departments of the dealership (i.e., sales, service, and parts). This will make marketing and advertising easier and more effective by focusing on the dealership as a whole. There is also an advantage of economies of scale by combining the advertising budgets of all departments. This will help the whole dealership gain more profit.

Positioning Strategies

Bombardier Sea-Doo positioning refers to the position of the product in relation to competing products in the minds of the consumer. It is the responsibility of Bombardier Sea-Doo Corporation to position the product to the consumer at a national and international level.

Honda of North Hollywood currently promotes and sells only Sea-Doo PWC. It can maintain a strong position in the market because of the technical expertise provided to customers in the service and support areas. It can continue to promote Sea-Doo's speed and maneuverability over other brands by targeting buyers who value these features (i.e., PWC racers, and PWC enthusiasts). The knowledge about other brands that would appeal to families because of strong features of safety and stability should be considered in the product line, since research has shown that a high percentage of male purchasers are married.

To extend the PWC product life cycle, the industry must appeal to the next generation of buyers and the best way to do that is to excite and educate them early.

Competitors' Reaction

As the dealership becomes more successful, competitors will attempt to provide the same services or more, at the same prices. While anticipating the competition's reaction to the success of the dealership, the plan to use vertical expansion will be implemented by:

1. Increasing promotion incentives.
2. Expanding product lines based on consumer feedback and technological advancements.
3. Taking advantage of location and maximizing it.
4. Continuation of market research.

MARKETING TACTICS

The marketing tactics are the how-to's of the marketing strategies. It is a guide on how to implement and achieve the marketing strategy that has been developed and includes the necessary tasks and an implementation schedule. Tactics include promotion, place, price, and product.

Promotion

With the research on the target market, the most popular outdoor activity is going to the movies, one form of advertising that has not yet been exploited. Advertising in movie theaters is a great way to advertise to a captive audience while people are waiting for the movie to start. They will read the advertisements on the screen.

Every dealership must be able to generate excitement. This can be done by having videos displayed at all times in the sales area of the dealership. New product videos and race videos give the customers an idea on what PWC is all about.

PWC safety is a key area where much concern is voiced. Developing safety programs with the Department of Boating and Waterways along with the Coast Guard to certify each new PWC owner's knowledge about boating laws and regulations will give the dealership kudos from the industry. These classes should be offered once a month for customers and their families. Competing dealerships could be invited to participate and share the costs. Move the safety classes around to include all the dealerships for more visibility.

Promote beach and waterway cleanup twice a year. Environmentalists will start to think PWC owners are very concerned about the environment. It should be done once before the season starts and once after the season is over. The competition will probably use this same tactic, which will benefit the PWC industry. The competing dealerships could be invited to participate and turn this into a huge event for the area.

Family packs for owners and children's coloring books about PWC should be developed with the Honda of North Hollywood name and logo on it. This could include coupons for discounts of products and services, free samples, free PWC magazines, and an offer to join both the International Jet Sports Boating Association and any local PWC clubs. Information on local waterways, rules and regulations, and any other relevant information could also be included.

Make the dealership more visible to customers by new signage and a new paint scheme. Promote the dealership's location as being "the center of the San Fernando Valley."

Conduct demo ride days once a month for potential Sea-Doo buyers to be able to test ride the product before the purchase. Many of the competing dealerships already offer this service.

Honda of North Hollywood already has a Web site on the Internet. This Web site needs to be updated daily and kept fresh and exciting. Most current dealerships already have Web sites in construction or are already on the Internet. This trend in new media will keep the industry alive and the dealership in the minds of the customers when they shop for new products. This new form of media will also open up a door for catalog sales with a 1–800 number to be competitive. A catalog can be requested by any consumer either by phone, online, or in person, and can potentially increase sales in every department. This will increase the dealership's awareness across the nation.

Place

Expand the shop. Move the service department across the street. Expand the sales department.

Develop a waiting room area in the sales area for customers not only to be able to peruse the new product line but have a comfortable place to wait. Making distribution channels of product and service accessible and free from clutter is important in showcasing the product to the maximum.

Price

Since there is an industry standard on price, the prices of PWC at most dealerships are relatively stable and there is little room for manipulation. Honda of North Hollywood must promote the benefits of the dealership and provide excellent customer service to attract customers. There is little price variation between the competing dealerships in the area. This is especially true as the market becomes saturated.

Product

Add a new product line.

Assign one lot boy to each department.

Develop a policy and procedures manual.

Set up a performance schedule with goals and objectives for employees.

Develop job descriptions for each position.

These tactics will enhance and extend the product life cycle and success of the business. The development of employees' product knowledge and awareness of customer service requirements will help to ensure longevity of the dealership. Excellent customer service will add a competitive edge over other area dealerships.

ORGANIZATION, EVALUATION, CONTROL, AND IMPLEMENTATION

This section will cover the financial implementation and control aspects of the dealership as well as its organization and product development schedule, and will be separated into the following sections:

1. Organization Chart of the Company
2. Product Development Schedule
3. Break-even Analysis
4. Pro Forma Cash Flows (monthly)
5. Pro Forma Income Statements (quarterly)
6. Pro Forma Balance Sheet

Organization Chart of Company

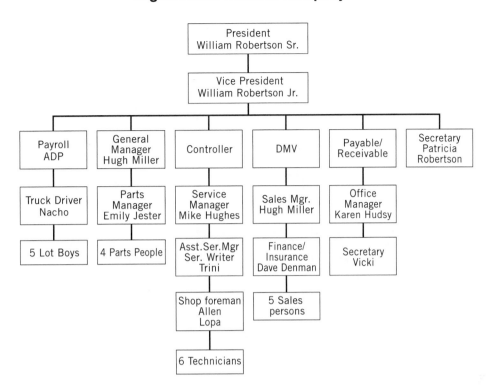

Project Development Schedule

The following product development schedule gives the projected monthly and cumulative yearly expenditures necessary to implement the plan for the next 30 months.

PDS for Fiscal Year 1

	Apr-97	May-97	Jun-97	Jul-97	Aug-97	Sep-97
Advertising	$ 15,000	25,000	25,000	25,000	25,000	25,000
Develop Policy & Procedure Manual	Implemented				Implemented	
Job Description					Implemented	
Employee Review Evaluations	$ 3,000					
Purchase Video Equipment	$ 750					
Special Events	$ 300	1,000	1,000	1,000	1,000	750
Safety Program	250	300	300	300	300	300
Beach Waterway Cleanup						250
Family Pack	$ 6,000					
Coloring Book	$ 1,000					
New Product Line						
Lot Boy						
Demo Rides	$ 750	750	750	750	750	
Catalog		10,000				10,000
Web Site Update	$ 100	100	100	100	100	100
Renovation of the Dealership						
Total Expenditures Per Month	**$ 27,150**	**37,150**	**27,150**	**27,150**	**27,150**	**36,400**
Cumulative Expenditures	**$ 27,150**	**64,300**	**91,450**	**118,600**	**145,750**	**182,150**

PDS for Fiscal Year 2

	Oct-97	Nov-97	Dec-97	Jan-98	Feb-98	Mar-98	Apr-98	May-98	Jun-98	Jul-98	Aug-98	Sep-98
Advertising	$10,000	10,000	10,000	10,000	10,000	15,000	15,000	25,000	25,000	25,000	25,000	25,000
Develop Policy & Procedure Manual			Review + Updated	Review + Updated								
Job Description			Review + Updated	Review + Updated								
Employee Review Evaluations	Review											
Purchase Video Equipment												
Special Events	$750	250	250	250	500	500	750	1,000	1,000	1,000	1,000	750
Safety Program	$300	300	300	300	300	300	300	300	300	300	300	300
Beach Waterway Cleanup							250					
Family Pack							6,000					
Coloring Book							1,000					
New Product Line	$500,000	100,000	100,000	100,000	100,000	100,000						
Lot Boy												
Demo Rides								750	750	750	750	750
Catalog		10,000						10,000				
Web Site Update	$100	100	100	100	100	100	100	100	100	100	100	100
Renovation of the Dealership	$50,000	50,000	25,000	25,000								
Total Expenditures Per Month	**$561,150**	**160,650**	**135,650**	**145,650**	**110,900**	**115,900**	**23,400**	**37,150**	**27,150**	**27,150**	**27,150**	**37,150**
Cumulative Expenditures	**$561,150**	**721,800**	**857,450**	**1,003,100**	**1,114,000**	**1,229,900**	**1,253,300**	**1,290,450**	**1,317,600**	**1,344,750**	**1,371,900**	**1,409,050**

PDS for Fiscal Year 3

	Oct-98	Nov-98	Dec-98	Jan-99	Feb-99	Mar-99	Apr-99	May-99	Jun-99	Jul-99	Aug-99	Sep-99
Advertising	$ 10,000	10,000	10,000	10,000	10,000	15,000	15,000	25,000	25,000	25,000	25,000	25,000
Develop Policy & Procedure Manual			**Review + Updated**									
Job Description			**Review + Updated**									
Employee Review Evaluations	Review											
Purchase Video Equipment												
Special Events	$ 750	250	250	250	500	500	750	1,000	1,000	1,000	1,000	750
Safety Program	$ 300	300	300	300	300	300	300	300	300	300	300	300
Beach Waterway Cleanup							250					250
Family Pack							6,000					
Coloring Book							1,000					
New Product Line												
Lot Boy												
Demo Rides								750	750	750	750	750
Catalog				10,000				10,000				10,000
Web Site Update	$ 100	100	100	100	100	100	100	100	100	100	100	100
Renovation of the Dealership												
Total Expenditures Per Month	**$ 11,150**	**10,650**	**10,650**	**20,650**	**10,900**	**15,900**	**23,400**	**37,150**	**27,150**	**27,150**	**27,150**	**37,150**
Cumulative Expenditures	**$ 11,150**	**21,800**	**32,450**	**53,100**	**64,000**	**79,900**	**103,300**	**140,450**	**167,600**	**194,750**	**221,900**	**259,050**

Break-Even Chart

The following table and chart show the break-even analysis. The break-even point is calculated by equation:

$$BE = \frac{FC}{P - VC}$$

Break-Even Analysis

Average Price per Unit	$ 6,245.64
Average Variable Cost per Unit	$ 5,636.16
Fixed Cost	$ 203,370
Break Even	334 units

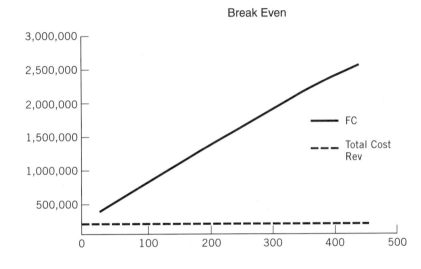

Cash Flow

Pro forma monthly cash flows have been computed for 30 months. PWC industry is a volatile business. The peak season is from April to September, so the number of PWC sold will increase in those months. Through the winter season the sales will decline and remain at a constant level.

- The start-up for the project is scheduled as April 1, 1997. This is done in order to increase the sales during the peak season starts.
- The construction is scheduled after the peak season ends for this year.
- Also, a new brand will be added to the product line in October 1997, and the dealership will be ready by all means to fully support the new brand before April 1998.
- All the expenses will be financed through company resources.

Cash Flow Analysis

	Apr-97	May-97	Jun-97	Jul-97	Aug-97	Sep-97
Beginning Balance Sources	0	(1,261)	26,017	63,295	92,833	130,111
Cash						
New Watercraft Sales	79,887	188,823	188,823	188,823	188,823	188,823
Used Watercraft Sales						
Service	5,929	14,014	14,014	14,014	14,014	14,014
Parts Sales	19,157	45,280	45,280	45,280	45,280	45,280
Other	2,947	6,965	6,965	6,965	6,965	6,965
Total	107,919	255,082	255,082	255,082	255,082	255,082
Uses						
Cost of Goods Sold	70,720	167,156	167,156	167,156	167,156	167,156
Construction Cost	–	–	–	–	–	–
Selling Expenses						
Comm. Sales Mngr	622	1,470	1,470	1,470	1,470	1,470
Comm. Sales People	1,413	3,341	3,341	3,341	3,341	3,341
Comm. F & I	495	1,171	1,171	1,171	1,171	1,171
Policy Expenses	7	18	18	18	18	18
Delivery Expense						
Demo and Other Expenses	12,150	12,150	2,150	2,150	2,150	11,400
Advertising	15,000	25,000	25,000	25,000	25,000	25,000
Advertising Credits	(125)	(296)	(296)	(296)	(296)	(296)
Personnel Expenses						
Comp. Owners	1,395	2,790	2,790	2,790	2,790	2,790
Comp. Supervisors	2,241	4,482	4,482	4,482	4,482	4,482
Comp. Clerical	923	1,845	1,845	1,845	1,845	1,845
Other Wages and Salaries	554	1,109	1,109	1,109	1,109	1,109
Payroll Taxes	594	1,189	1,189	1,189	1,189	1,189
Employee Benefits	231	463	463	463	463	463
Group Insurance						
Semi-Fixed Expenses						
Co Vehicle Expenses	83	166	166	166	166	166
Flr Plan Interest	706	1,411	1,411	1,411	1,411	1,411
Off Supp & Stat	39	77	77	77	77	77
Other Supp & Tools	377	753	753	753	753	753
Temp & Contract Serv.						
Contributions						
Outside Service	258	516	516	516	516	516
Travel & Entertainment	55	110	110	110	110	110
Laund & Uniforms	41	82	82	82	82	82
MBRSP, Dues Publ	10	20	20	20	20	20
Legal & Audit	89	178	178	178	178	178
Freight In/Out	43	86	86	86	86	86
Telephone	126	252	252	252	252	252
Postage	9	18	18	18	18	18
Training	13	26	26	26	26	26
Edp Services	139	278	278	278	278	278
Misc Exp	17	34	34	34	34	34
Fixed Expenses						
Rent	139	279	279	279	279	279
Amort Lshlds	34	69	69	69	69	69
Rprs & Maint	50	100	100	100	100	100
Dpr Bldgs & Imp						
Taxes Real Estate	36	72	72	72	72	72
Ins Bulds & Imp	15	29	29	29	29	29
Workers Comp	131	263	263	263	263	263
Utilities	139	279	279	279	279	279
Liability Ins	305	610	610	610	610	610
Taxes Other	56	112	112	112	112	112
DMV Variance	16	31	31	31	31	31
Depr Other	30	61	61	61	61	61
Equip & Rentals	2	4	4	4	4	4
Total Uses	109,180	227,804	217,804	217,804	217,804	227,054
Earnings Before Taxes	(1,261)	26,017	63,295	100,573	130,111	158,139
Less: Tax				7,740		
Cash Flow After Taxes	(1,261)	26,017	63,295	92,833	130,111	158,139
Add: Depreciation						2,000
Net Cash Flow	(1,261)	26,017	63,295	92,833	130,111	160,139

Cash Flow Analysis	Oct-97	Nov-97	Dec-97	Jan-98	Feb-98	Mar-98	Apr-98	May-98	Jun-98	Jul-98	Aug-98	Sep-98
Beginning Balance Sources	160,139	106,114	(24,348)	(129,810)	(245,272)	(325,984)	(411,696)	(299,163)	(200,380)	(91,597)	(91,324)	17,460
Company Resources	500,000											
New Watercraft Sales	90,780	90,780	90,780	90,780	90,780	90,780	408,512	408,512	408,512	408,512	408,512	408,512
Used Watercraft Sales												
Service	6,737	6,737	6,737	6,737	6,737	6,737	30,318	30,318	30,318	30,318	30,318	30,318
Parts Sales	21,769	21,769	21,769	21,769	21,769	21,769	97,962	97,962	97,962	97,962	97,962	97,962
Other	3,349	3,349	3,349	3,349	3,349	3,349	15,068	15,068	15,068	15,068	15,068	15,068
Total	622,636	122,636	122,636	122,636	122,636	122,636	551,861	551,861	551,861	551,861	551,861	551,861
Uses												
Cost of Goods Sold	80,363	80,363	80,363	80,363	80,363	80,363	361,635	361,635	361,635	361,635	361,635	361,635
Construction Cost	50,000	50,000	25,000	25,000								
Add New Brand	500,000	100,000	100,000	100,000	100,000	100,000						
Selling Expenses												
Comm. Sales Mngr	707	707	707	707	707	707	3,181	3,181	3,181	3,181	3,181	3,181
Comm. Sales People	1,606	1,606	1,606	1,606	1,606	1,606	7,227	7,227	7,227	7,227	7,227	7,227
Comm. F & I	563	563	563	563	563	563	2,533	2,533	2,533	2,533	2,533	2,533
Policy Expenses	8	8	8	8	8	8	38	38	38	38	38	38
Delivery Expense												
Demo and Other Expenses	1,150	650	650	10,650	900	900	8,400	12,150	2,150	2,150	2,150	12,150
Advertising	10,000	10,000	10,000	10,000	10,000	15,000	15,000	25,000	25,000	25,000	25,000	25,000
Advertising Credits	(142)	(142)	(142)	(142)	(142)	(142)	(427)	(427)	(427)	(427)	(427)	(427)
Personnel Expenses												
Comp. Owners	1,465	1,465	1,465	1,465	1,465	1,465	6,592	6,592	6,592	6,592	6,592	6,592
Comp. Supervisors	2,353	2,353	2,353	2,353	2,353	2,353	10,590	10,590	10,590	10,590	10,590	10,590
Comp. Clerical	969	969	969	969	969	969	4,359	4,359	4,359	4,359	4,359	4,359
Other Wages and Salaries	582	582	582	582	582	582	2,619	2,619	2,619	2,619	2,619	2,619
Payroll Taxes	624	624	624	624	624	624	2,809	2,809	2,809	2,809	2,809	2,809
Employee Benefits	243	243	243	243	243	243	1,094	1,094	1,094	1,094	1,094	1,094
Group Insurance												
Semi-Fixed Expenses												
Co Vehicle Expenses	87	87	87	87	87	87	393	393	393	393	393	393
Flr Plan Interest	741	741	741	741	741	741	3,334	3,334	3,334	3,334	3,334	3,334
Off Supp & Stat	41	41	41	41	41	41	183	183	183	183	183	183

(continued)

215

Cash Flow Analysis	Oct-97	Nov-97	Dec-97	Jan-98	Feb-98	Mar-98	Apr-98	May-98	Jun-98	Jul-98	Aug-98	Sep-98
Other Supp & Tools	395	395	395	395	395	395	1,780	1,780	1,780	1,780	1,780	1,780
Temp & Contract Serv.												
Contributions												
Outside Service	271	271	271	271	271	271	1,219	1,219	1,219	1,219	1,219	1,219
Travel & Entertainment	58	58	58	58	58	58	260	260	260	260	260	260
Laund & Uniforms	43	43	43	43	43	43	193	193	193	193	193	193
MBRSP, Dues Publ	11	11	11	11	11	11	47	47	47	47	47	47
Legal & Audit	93	93	93	93	93	93	420	420	420	420	420	420
Freight In/Out	45	45	45	45	45	45	204	204	204	204	204	204
Telephone	133	133	133	133	133	133	596	596	596	596	596	596
Postage	9	9	9	9	9	9	42	42	42	42	42	42
Training	13	13	13	13	13	13	60	60	60	60	60	60
Edp Services	146	146	146	146	146	146	656	656	656	656	656	656
Misc Exp	18	18	18	18	18	18	80	80	80	80	80	80
Fixed Expenses												
Rent	146	146	146	146	146	146	439	439	439	439	439	439
Amort Lshlds	36	36	36	36	36	36	163	163	163	163	163	163
Rprs & Maint	52	52	52	52	52	52	236	236	236	236	236	236
Dpr Bldgs & Imp												
Taxes Real Estate	38	38	38	38	38	38	114	114	114	114	114	114
Ins Bulds & Imp	15	15	15	15	15	15	69	69	69	69	69	69
Workers Comp	138	138	138	138	138	138	620	620	620	620	620	620
Utilities	146	146	146	146	146	146	658	658	658	658	658	658
Liability Ins	320	320	320	320	320	320	1,441	1,441	1,441	1,441	1,441	1,441
Taxes Other	59	59	59	59	59	59	265	265	265	265	265	265
DMV Variance	17	17	17	17	17	17	50	50	50	50	50	50
Depr Other	32	32	32	32	32	32	144	144	144	144	144	144
Equip & Rentals	2	2	2	2	2	2	10	10	10	10	10	10
Total Uses	653,598	253,098	228,098	238,098	203,348	208,348	439,327	453,077	443,077	443,077	443,077	453,077
Earnings Before Taxes	129,177	(24,348)	(129,810)	(245,272)	(325,984)	(411,696)	(299,163)	(200,380)	(91,597)	17,186	17,460	116,243
Less: Tax	23,063			—			—			108,510		
Cash Flow After Taxes	106,114	(24,348)	(129,810)	(245,272)	(325,984)	(411,696)	(299,163)	(200,380)	(91,597)	(91,324)	17,460	116,243
Add: Depreciation												2,000
Net Cash Flow	106,114	(24,348)	(129,810)	(245,272)	(325,984)	(411,696)	(299,163)	(200,380)	(91,597)	(91,324)	17,460	118,243

Cash Flow Analysis	Oct-98	Nov-98	Dec-98	Jan-99	Feb-99	Mar-99	Apr-99	May-99	Jun-99	Jul-99	Aug-99	Sep-99
Beginning Balance Sources	118,243	62,545	114,544	166,543	157,643	209,393	256,142	375,041	525,839	686,637	684,309	845,107
Cash												
New Watercraft Sales	188,823	188,823	188,823	188,823	188,823	188,823	566,470	566,470	566,470	566,470	566,470	566,470
Used Watercraft Sales												
Service	14,014	14,014	14,014	14,014	14,014	14,014	42,041	42,041	42,041	42,041	42,041	42,041
Parts Sales	45,280	45,280	45,280	45,280	45,280	45,280	135,840	135,840	135,840	135,840	135,840	135,840
Other	6,965	6,965	6,965	6,965	6,965	6,965	20,895	20,895	20,895	20,895	20,895	20,895
Total	255,082	255,082	255,082	255,082	255,082	255,082	765,247	765,247	765,247	765,247	765,247	765,247
Uses												
Cost of Goods Sold	167,156	167,156	167,156	167,156	167,156	167,156	501,468	501,468	501,468	501,468	501,468	501,468
Selling Expenses												
Comm. Sales Mngr	1,470	1,470	1,470	1,470	1,470	1,470	4,410	4,410	4,410	4,410	4,410	4,410
Comm. Sales People	3,341	3,341	3,341	3,341	3,341	3,341	10,022	10,022	10,022	10,022	10,022	10,022
Comm. F & I	1,171	1,171	1,171	1,171	1,171	1,171	3,513	3,513	3,513	3,513	3,513	3,513
Policy Expenses	18	18	18	18	18	18	53	53	53	53	53	53
Delivery Expense												
Demo and Other Expenses	1,150	650	650	10,650	900	900	8,400	12,150	2,150	2,150	2,150	12,150
Advertising	10,000	10,000	10,000	10,000	10,000	15,000	15,000	25,000	25,000	25,000	25,000	25,000
Advertising Credits	(148)	(148)	(148)	(148)	(148)	(148)	(444)	(444)	(444)	(444)	(444)	(444)
Personnel Expenses												
Comp. Owners	3,076	3,076	3,076	3,076	3,076	3,076	9,229	9,229	9,229	9,229	9,229	9,229
Comp. Supervisors	4,942	4,942	4,942	4,942	4,942	4,942	14,826	14,826	14,826	14,826	14,826	14,826
Comp. Clerical	2,034	2,034	2,034	2,034	2,034	2,034	6,103	6,103	6,103	6,103	6,103	6,103
Other Wages and Salaries	1,222	1,222	1,222	1,222	1,222	1,222	3,667	3,667	3,667	3,667	3,667	3,667
Payroll Taxes	1,311	1,311	1,311	1,311	1,311	1,311	3,932	3,932	3,932	3,932	3,932	3,932
Employee Benefits	510	510	510	510	510	510	1,531	1,531	1,531	1,531	1,531	1,531
Group Insurance												
Semi-Fixed Expenses												
Co Vehicle Expenses	183	183	183	183	183	183	550	550	550	550	550	550
Flr Plan Interest	1,556	1,556	1,556	1,556	1,556	1,556	4,667	4,667	4,667	4,667	4,667	4,667
Off Supp & Stat	85	85	85	85	85	85	256	256	256	256	256	256
Other Supp & Tools	831	831	831	831	831	831	2,492	2,492	2,492	2,492	2,492	2,492
Temp & Contract Serv.												

(continued)

Cash Flow Analysis	Oct-98	Nov-98	Dec-98	Jan-99	Feb-99	Mar-99	Apr-99	May-99	Jun-99	Jul-99	Aug-99	Sep-99
Contributions												
Outside Service	569	569	569	569	569	569	1,706	1,706	1,706	1,706	1,706	1,706
Travel & Entertainment	122	122	122	122	122	122	365	365	365	365	365	365
Laundry & Uniforms	90	90	90	90	90	90	271	271	271	271	271	271
MBRSP, Dues Publ	22	22	22	22	22	22	66	66	66	66	66	66
Legal & Audit	196	196	196	196	196	196	588	588	588	588	588	588
Freight In/Out	95	95	95	95	95	95	286	286	286	286	286	286
Telephone	278	278	278	278	278	278	835	835	835	835	835	835
Postage	20	20	20	20	20	20	59	59	59	59	59	59
Training	28	28	28	28	28	28	85	85	85	85	85	85
Edp Services	306	306	306	306	306	306	919	919	919	919	919	919
Misc Exp	37	37	37	37	37	37	112	112	112	112	112	112
Fixed Expenses												
Rent	154	154	154	154	154	154	461	461	461	461	461	461
Amort Lshlds	76	76	76	76	76	76	228	228	228	228	228	228
Rprs & Maint	110	110	110	110	110	110	330	330	330	330	330	330
Dpr Bldgs & Imp												
Taxes Real Estate	40	40	40	40	40	40	119	119	119	119	119	119
Ins Bulds & Imp	32	32	32	32	32	32	97	97	97	97	97	97
Workers Comp	289	289	289	289	289	289	868	868	868	868	868	868
Utilities	307	307	307	307	307	307	921	921	921	921	921	921
Liability Ins	673	673	673	673	673	673	2,018	2,018	2,018	2,018	2,018	2,018
Taxes Other	124	124	124	124	124	124	371	371	371	371	371	371
DMV Variance	35	35	35	35	35	35	104	104	104	104	104	104
Depr Other	67	67	67	67	67	67	201	201	201	201	201	201
Equip & Rentals	5	5	5	5	5	5	14	14	14	14	14	14
Total Uses	203,583	203,083	203,083	213,083	203,333	208,333	600,699	614,449	604,449	604,449	604,449	614,449
Earnings Before Taxes	169,742	114,544	166,543	208,543	209,393	256,142	420,690	525,839	686,637	847,434	845,107	995,905
Less: Tax	107,197			50,899			45,649			163,125		
Cash Flow After Taxes	62,545	114,544	166,543	157,643	209,393	256,142	375,041	525,839	686,637	684,309	845,107	995,905
Add: Depreciation												2,000
Net Cash Flow	62,545	114,544	166,543	157,643	209,393	256,142	375,041	525,839	686,637	684,309	845,107	997,905

Income Statement

Pro forma income statements have been prepared for the period of 30 months. They are prepared quarterly in order to calculate the tax that should be paid.

Income Statement 1997	Q-3	Q-4	Y-1		
Net Sales	618,084	765,247	1,383,330		
Less: Cost of Goods Sold	405,032	501,468	906,500		
Sell., Gen. and Adm. Exp.	149,757	161,195	310,951		
Operating Profit Before Depr.	63,295	102,584	165,879		
Less: Depreciation	500	500	1,000		
Earnings Before Interest and Tax	62,795	102,084	164,879		
Less: Interest	–	–	–		
Earnings Before Taxes	62,795	102,084	164,879		
Less: Tax	7,740	23,063	47,553		
Net Income After Taxes	55,055	79,021	134,076		

Income Statement 1998	Q-1	Q-2	Q-3	Q-4	Y-2
Net Sales	367,907	367,907	1,655,582	1,655,582	4,046,977
Less: Cost of Goods Sold	241,090	241,090	1,084,906	1,084,906	2,651,993
Sell., Gen. and Adm. Exp.	893,703	408,703	250,576	254,326	1,807,308
Operating Profit before Depr.	(766,886)	(281,886)	320,099	316,349	(412,324)
Less: Depreciation	500	500	500	500	2,000
Earnings Before Interest and Tax	(767,386)	(282,386)	319,599	315,849	(414,324)
Less: Interest	–	–	–	–	–
Earnings Before Taxes	(767,386)	(282,386)	319,599	315,849	(414,324)
Less: Tax			108,510	107,197	215,707
Net Income After Taxes	**(767,386)**	**(282,386)**	**211,089**	**208,652**	**(630,031)**

Income Statement 1999	Q-1	Q-2	Q-3	Q-4	Y-3
Net Sales	765,247	765,247	2,295,740	2,295,740	6,121,972
Less: Cost of Goods Sold	501,468	501,468	1,504,404	1,504,404	4,011,743
Sell., Gen. and Adm. Exp.	108,281	123,281	315,192	318,942	865,696
Operating Profit Before Depr.	155,498	140,498	476,144	472,394	1,244,533
Less: Depreciation	500	500	500	500	2,000
Earnings Before Interest and Tax	154,998	139,998	475,644	471,894	1,242,533
Less: Interest	–	–	–	–	–
Earnings Before Taxes	154,998	139,998	475,644	471,894	1,242,533
Less: Tax	50,899	45,649	163,125	161,813	421,487
Net Income After Taxes	**104,099**	**94,349**	**312,518**	**310,081**	**821,047**

Balance Sheets

Pro forma Balance Sheets have been prepared for a period of 30 months. The depreciation on fixed assets are calculated by using the straight-line depreciation method over a period of 3 years.

Balance Sheet	Year 1	Year 2	Year 3
Current Assets			
Cash and Equivalent	85,172	118,185	527,649
Receivables	255,082	551,861	765,247
Inventories	51,218	153,654	307,308
Total Current Assets	*391,472*	*823,699*	*1,600,204*
Fixed Assets	10,000	8,000	6,000
Depreciation	2,000	2,000	2,000
Total Assets	**399,472**	**829,699**	**1,604,204**
Current Liabilities			
Accounts Payable	209,472	662,452	545,012
Salaries Payable	17,860	41,004	57,286
Taxes Payable	23,063	107,197	161,813
Total Current Liabilities	*250,395*	*810,654*	*764,111*
Long-Term Debt			
Total Liabilities	**250,395**	**810,654**	**764,111**
Common Stock	15,000	15,000	15,000
Retained Earnings	134,076	4,045	825,092
Total Stockholders Equity	**149,076**	**19,045**	**840,092**
Total Liab. and Owners Equity	***399,472***	***829,699***	***1,604,204***

SUMMARY

Honda of North Hollywood is in a position to develop the personal watercraft side of their business by implementing strategies that will take advantage of the "mature" stage of the product life cycle.

Through differentiation, focus on the service cycle, segmentation, and brand positioning, the dealership will have competitive advantage in its 25-mile radius in the San Fernando Valley.

If Honda of North Hollywood makes the initial investment of $150,000 for renovation of the dealership as well as $1 million for adding a new brand, they can substantially improve their services and profit levels by the end of the third year.

BIBLIOGRAPHY

Alger, A. "Here They Come Again (Controversy Over the Use of the Jet Skis)," *Forbes* (June 3, 1996), p. 182.

Alger, A., Flanigan, W.G. "Snowmobiles of the Sea," *Forbes* (August 28, 1995), p. 304.

Argetsinger, A. "Deaths Rise as More People Ride the Waves," *Washington Post,* August 27, 1995.

Berkowitz, E., Kerin, N.R., Hartley, S., and Rudelius, W. *Marketing,* Irwin, 1994.

Cohen, William A. *The Marketing Plan,* Wiley, 1995.

Cohen, William A. *Model Business Plans for Service Businesses,* Wiley, 1995.

Fiataff, J. "Clearing the Pipeline," *Watercraft Business* (January 1997), p. 2.

Harris, J. C. *Personal Watercraft,* Crestwood House, 1988.

Henschen, D. "New Jersey Passes Mandatory Education: PWC Bill," *Boating Industry* (March 1996), p. 11.

Napier, J. "Napier Predicts Slight Sales Growth in 1997," *Boating Industry* (November 1996).

Paulsen, B. "Squeezing PWC: More States Are Finding Ways to Restrict Their Use," *Yachting* (May 1996), p. 32.

Steven, S. "Water Bikes Are Losing Some Speed," *Wall Street Journal,* September 17, 1996.

Stewart, R. L. "The Wonderful World of "Wet and Wild" Water-Sports," *Rough Notes* (May 1993), pp. 30–32.

Weeth, C. "Water Events Facing New Environmental Regulations," *Amusement Business,* February 20, 1995, p. 28.

"PWC: Many Challenges in Taking a Line," *Boating Industry* (June 1996), p. 50.

APPENDIX

Employee Questionnaire

1. What do you do?
2. Length of employment and why do you stay here?
3. What type of training do you get and how often?
4. Are you rewarded for initiative, innovation, and risk taking? How?
5. How are you compensated for sales?
6. Is it common for departments to work together?
7. Are there lots of rules and regulations?
8. Do you feel that you are part of the team?
9. Do you feel you are treated with respect?
10. How is the work environment?
11. What would you do to improve business?
12. What would make your job better and/or easier?
13. What expectations do you have of your boss? Are they met?
14. What is expected of you? Are you supported in your decisions?
15. Do you have a job description?
16. What expectations do you have of your employees?
17. Who do you ask questions of?
18. Are there incentives to improve?
19. Is your boss' style of management more coaching or dictative?
20. How could the business expand and become more profitable?

A4

MCM POWERSPORTS

Developed by
MISTY IWATSU
AHMET MURAT MENDI
CAROLINE YEUNG

EXECUTIVE SUMMARY

MCM Powersports will be a Los Angeles-based, privately held new service corporation promoting offshore endurance racing for the Personal Watercraft and Mini Jet boat industries. It will plan and coordinate a National Tour for the powersports racing industry in 9 states and 10 racing locations per year. The company's competitive advantage is that it will be the first and only sanctioned promoter in the market of PWC and Mini Jet boat endurance racing at a national level.

Each of the owners will invest $5,000 as capital for start-up costs and predicted cash shortages due to the cyclical nature of the business. MCM Powersports' main source of fund income will be from sponsorships through local and national corporations, ticket sales, and parking space fees and loans.

MCM Powersports has analyzed the PWC industry, and through secondary research, the findings are as follows: predicted sales are estimated to grow 12 percent annually through the year 2000. PWC will be the entry-level product purchase for most consumers rather than larger, more traditional watercrafts. An estimated amount of more than two million PWCs are currently being used in U.S. waters. This incredible rate of market growth also boosts the demand for PWC racing. Current promoters are far away from fulfilling the existing needs of the market, especially in endurance racing.

Start-up costs are estimated to be $124,440. The break-even dollar value for the corporation is $3,081,826. The firm expects to break even by 12 months. The return on investment is expected to be 61 percent and 72 percent in years 2 and 3 respectively, and a cash flow of $186,431 is projected by the first year of operation.

Contents

INTRODUCTION

Within the last decade, the number of Personal Watercraft (PWC) enthusiasts who demand an environment to test their skills and to compete with other PWC enthusiasts has increased dramatically. This created a great opportunity for an industry where promoters of the sport could conduct races all over the United States. MCM Powersports will be established as a Los Angeles-based offshore endurance promoter which conducts a National Tour for the PWC and Mini Jet Boat endurance racing industries. The races will be longer than closed course races since they measure the racer's endurance level rather than their speed. MCM Powersports will run both the Amateur and Pro divisions in PWC and Mini Jet Boats, as well as free-style competition. MCM Powersports will tour 9 states, 10 racing spots per year which are planned as follows: Northern California, Southern California, Colorado, Florida, Illinois, New Jersey, Ohio, Texas, Virginia, and Washington. MCM Powersports' objective is to foster and encourage competition as it will give riders and enthusiasts of all skill levels the opportunity to test themselves in regulated, safe environments.

MCM Powersports plans to contact local and national associations, manufacturers, dealerships as well as other companies that are leaders in their industry and are interested in sponsoring sport activities to sponsor part of the events' funding. In return, the sponsors will have the opportunity to display new products/services to approximately 40,000 people per event or 400,000 total at the booths that MCM Powersports will provide. The tour will be nationally televised and the sponsors will have numerous opportunities to advertise their name during all 10 events (see Appendix A).

SITUATIONAL ANALYSIS

Situation Environs

Business Conditions.   The first PWC was introduced as a stand-up model in 1968 by Clayton Jacobson II. Kawasaki, in 1975, launched the first mass produced stand-up model for the consumer market. Over the past three decades, several manufacturers have entered the market. The five biggest are Yamaha, Bombardier, Kawasaki, Polaris, and Tigershark.

PWC use has dramatically increased over the past few years. Today, there are more than two million watercraft registered in the United States. PWC sales, in dollar terms, is estimated to grow at a 12 percent annual rate through the year 2000 and will turn out to be the entry-level product for larger, more traditional craft like boats.

The value of PWC shipments, excluding mini jet boats, is forecast to almost double from $364 million in 1995 to $660 million in 2000. The total U.S. recreational boating market, including propulsion systems and accessories, will increase at approximately an 8 percent annual rate through the year 2005, from almost $9.5 billion in sales in 1995, to $13.6 billion in 2000 and $19.6 billion in 2005.

As the number of PWC enthusiasts proliferate, the number of people who want to test their PWCs as well as their skills will also increase. Under the current situation, the existing promoters are far from fulfilling the existing needs of the market, especially in endurance racing due to limitations such as finances, lack of knowledge, and lack of manpower.

State of Technology.   Last year, 47 new models of PWC were offered into the market. Models have evolved from two-seaters to three-seaters. In addition, the newer models are faster and safer, where the watercraft can move to speeds in excess of 70 mph and is equipped with a lanyard-type engine cutoff switch. This results in an increasing number of categories in which PWC enthusiasts can race.

Currently, none of the promoters in the industry utilize technology efficiently to improve their services, such as electronic scoring which is crucial in getting accurate race results to satisfy customer needs.

Demand Trends. Demand for-owning one or more PWC as well as using them as both racing and recreational purposes are much stronger than the demand trend for all other types of boats. Affordability (average price is approximately $5,700), high performance, and maneuverability have brought scores of new customers into the PWC market. Consumers want to enjoy using their PWC and demand new and improved products with better and more efficient features (top speed, predictable handling, and comfort).

Laws and Regulations. As the number of PWC on the water increase, public concerns about pollution and noise, accidents related to careless usage, speeding, and increasing number of fatal injuries, have come to the forefront in media and legislation. These factors forced a majority of the states to take restrictive actions against the use of PWC in the local waterways. The current trend of increasing regulations and bans on the usage of PWC may have a direct and indirect adverse effect on MCM Powersports.

PWC are subject to the same rules and requirements as any other powerboats plus additional requirements specific to PWC due to its maneuverability, speed, and limited protection which can be a dangerous combination for the racers as well as for other people using the same waterways. In addition to the general regulations in effect for motorboats, PWC racing promoters must also be aware that there are local laws and ordinances around the country that regulate racing conditions. There are many primary regulations that MCM Powersports as a race promoter will have to enforce and abide. A few provisions include: all racers must wear U.S. Coast Guard-approved personal flotation devices; a PWC can not be operated from one half hour after sunset to one half hour before sunrise; and a lanyard-type engine cutoff switch must be attached to the racer.[1] For a detailed list of other regulations that MCM Powersports will have to enforce, please refer to Appendix B.

Neutral Environs

There are many organizations that have concerns about the use of PWC. They include such groups as the Environmental Protection Agency, Personal Watercraft Industry Association (PWIA), environmental interest groups, and other organizations. Each has its own concerns and could help or hinder MCM Powersports.

Environmental Issues. The PWC racing industry has been attacked over many environmental issues, for example, toxic pollutants released into the environment by their use. As a result, MCM Powersports will have to force racers to refuel on land to reduce chances of gas spillage into the water, and to check and clean their engines well away from shorelines.

Another concern is turbidity. In shallow waters where PWCs can easily operate, the bottom becomes stirred up, suspending sediment that cuts down on light penetration and depletes oxygen. This can affect bird and fish feeding.

---

[1] International Jet Sports Boating Association, *1997 Official Competition Rule Book* (Santa Ana, CA, 1997), p. 10.

Vegetation is another concern for environmental issues. In coastal areas, MCM Powersports will be aware of low tide. Low water levels expose sea grass beds and other delicate vegetation. Disturbances can cause erosion and long-lasting damage.

A PWC near shore can also interrupt feeding and nesting wildlife, and cause animals to deviate from their normal behavior, which is illegal. Mammals such as otters, manatees, and whales can be injured by direct contact with a boat, and it is believed that the noise from watercraft can adversely influence breeding cycles and cause birth defects.

Personal Watercraft Industry Association (PWIA). The Personal Watercraft Industry Association (PWIA) was formed in 1987 as an affiliate of the National Marine Manufacturers Association. It was created to bring together companies that manufacture or distribute PWC in order to promote safe and responsible operation. The PWIA is actively involved in numerous consumer education and informational campaigns designed to raise awareness about proper operation of and regard for safety, and appropriate behavior. In addition, it monitors local issues; race promoters and its members strive to work proactively to minimize waterway-use conflicts. Therefore, it will closely monitor MCM Powersports' operations to ensure it is promoting proper operation in regard to safety, and appropriate behavior during the course of its race tours and competitive events.

U.S. Park Service. The U.S. National Park Service is under pressure from the National Parks and Conservation Association (NPCA) to regulate PWC. (NPCA is a private special interest group of park patrons.) As a result, the U.S. National Park Service is developing new rules to make it easier for PWC to be banned in National Parks. The agency has proposed a rule that would direct local park officials to determine the appropriateness of PWC use in each park and restrict or ban the boats if necessary. There has been a growing concern among many park superintendents about the impact of PWC on the tranquillity of parks. This will hinder MCM Powersports, since it will be prohibited from promoting racing events in parks.

Competitor and Company Environs

Company	Current Strategy	Strengths	Weaknesses	Competitive Advantage	Pricing
International Jet Sports Boating Association (IJSBA)	1. Looks for new ways to promote the sport 2. Increases exposure for sponsors and the participants 3. Provides an expansive media package for their sponsors and racers 4. Expands the scope and reach of their TV package for 1998 5. Continues cooperative relationships with regional event promoters	1. Well known in the industry for conducting national closed-course racing tours 2. As the international sanctioning organization, it promotes PWC racing	1. Lacks knowledge and experience of setting up endurance races as it solely sets up closed course races 2. There is a conflict of interest. IJSBA is the sanctioning organization as well as a race promoter. Its own interests can interfere with their neutrality toward governing PWC issues	1. As the international sanctioning organization, it promotes PWC racing	$20/day for spectator, $10/day for parking
Baja Promotions Racing (BP Racing)	1. Relies heavily on publicity and race coverage in featured magazines 2. Relies on radio and TV programs 3. Utilizes extensive and accurate computerized scoring programs	1. Well known in the industry 2. Has diverse business activities to help eliminate cash-flow shortages from the cyclical nature of the business 3. Had experience in holding endurance races	1. Has, other businesses aside, not concentrated solely on PWC race promoting 2. Does not have the ability or the expertise in setting up large events 3. Does not advertise; relies solely on publicity	1. First regional offshore endurance race promoter	No areas for spectator viewing
CT Sports	1. Relies on word of mouth 2. Publishes own newsletter once a month	1. Well known in the industry 2. Has a strong financial support 3. Experience in holding closed-course races	1. New at setting up endurance races. It is very expensive, and time consuming to organize 2. Does not have the ability or the expertise in setting up large events	1. In business over 10 years	No areas for spectator viewing

(continued)

Competitor and Company Environs (continued)

Company	Current Strategy	Strengths	Weaknesses	Competitive Advantage	Pricing
MCM Power-sports	1. New entrant into the industry 2. Corporate structure enables the transfer of ownership to a third party easily in case of financial difficulty. Hence, the exit strategy would be to transfer the ownership to another promoter in case of financial distress.	1. Advantages of being a corporation: limited liability, specialized management, easy to raise capital, unlimited life, ease of ownership transferability to avoid double taxation 2. Misty Iwatsu and Taylor LeClaire: years of racing and promoting experience 3. Implements the latest technology 4. Has strong image positioning	1. Organizing a corporation is complicated, costly, and time-consuming 2. Corporations are bombarded with more government rules and regulations than are the sole proprietorship or partnership	1. First into the national PWC endurance racing market 2. Will audit accounts once a year 3. Environmentally conscious company 4. High-quality event 5. Affordable prices 6. New products are shown at each event for purchase 7. Extensive TV coverage 8. Leader in technology 9. Misty Iwatsu and Taylor LeClaire: years of racing and promoting experience 10. Has strong image positioning	<u>1998</u> 1 Day: Ticket—$7 Parking—$5 Two Day: Ticket—$10 Parking—$8 <u>1999</u> One Day: Ticket—$8 Parking—$5 Two-Day: Ticket—$12 Parking—$8 <u>2000</u> Two-Day: Ticket—$9 Parking—$5 Two-day: Ticket—$15 Parking—$8

TARGET MARKET

Demographics

The target audience for MCM Powersports is single men between the ages of 21–39 years old, with an average annual household income of $60,000 and over.[2]

Psychographics

The majority of PWC owners use their PWC for recreational riding; 9 percent of the PWC owners race and 16 percent of all PWC owners belong to some type of PWC club or association. In addition, MCM Powersports will provide a Web site as a part of its customer service, since two-thirds of the target market have computers and 78 percent use modems.[3]

Geographics

MCM Powersports will tour 9 states, 10 racing spots per year which are planned as follows: San Francisco, California; Orange County, California; Boulder, Colorado; Orlando, Florida; Chicago, Illinois; Seaside Heights, New Jersey; Cincinnati, Ohio; Dallas, Texas; Virginia Beach, Virginia; and Richland, Washington. MCM Powersports will use the IJSBA Regional Breakdown list and provide at least one event in each region.

Product Usage

There are more than 2.4 million watercraft registered in the United States. There are potentially 2 million owners. The target market may initially buy PWC for themselves; however, statistics show that 32 percent[4] of watercraft owners share their PWC with family and friends. MCM Powersports will have a potential market of 2.6 million people.

PROBLEMS, THREATS, AND OPPORTUNITIES

Problems

Problems that may be encountered in the Mini Jet Boat and the PWC industries are:

- Upcoming regulations of PWC and mini jet boats
  Since there are 2.4 million PWC operated annually, and the Mini Jet Boat has just surfaced in the market, laws and regulations will be more stringent. This is due to organizations wanting to ban PWC in lakes, oceans, and waterways. To help stop the bans, MCM Powersports will provide an opportunity for watercraft enthusiasts to be heard by placing a booth where people can write to their legislator. They will also be able to sign petitions to stop bans on their favorite lake or waterway.

---

[2] "PWC: Many Challenges in Taking a Line." *Boating Industry* (June 1996), p. 50.
[3] Media Kit, *Splash Magazine* (1997).
[4] Department of Boating & Waterways. *PWC News* (Sacramento. CA, 1997), p. 7.

- High injury rate for the PWC and mini jet boats

  The injury rate has gone down during the last year. However, the negligent use of PWC by uneducated users has provided a serious concern for the sport of watercraft riding. MCM Powersports will help the PWC industry by offering water safety certificate courses free of charge. Each person attending the program will receive a certificate stating that they completed the water safety course provided by the U.S. Coast Guard.

  There are many environmental issues that may become problems for MCM Powersports. They are the following:

- A concern is turbidity

  To avoid this, MCM Powersports will encourage its racers to operate their PWC in deeper water. If racers do have to traverse shallow water, they should run at idle speed.

- PWC can interrupt feeding and nesting wildlife, as well as disturb water fowl and other marine animals, which causes animals to deviate from their normal behavior, and is illegal

  MCM Powersports will abide by state enacted noise ordinances/legislation and help to reduce the noise pollution that could cause harmful results to various marine life.

Threats

- Inclement weather may become a threat for MCM Powersports

  People may not be willing to attend an open-air event if it is raining. To handle this threat, it may be necessary to keep extra tarps and canopies available for distribution to vendors and to put on the stands for spectators.

- New promoters trying to capitalize on the events

  To handle this threat, MCM Powersports will invite local promoters to participate in the event. MCM Powersports will gain valuable experience from other promoters and promote a positive presence to the industry.

- MCM Powersports will be vulnerable to inflation or depression

  If the discretionary income becomes tighter, MCM Powersports will streamline costs to be even more cost-effective. During depressionary or inflationary conditions, the first thing people cut from their spending is the expensive leisure activities. MCM Powersports will try to overcome this problem by implementing an affordable ticket policy. (See Appendix C.)

- There may also be other major trade shows, such as car shows, in the area operating at the same time as an MCM Powersports event

  MCM Powersports will provide space for its sponsors as well as other PWC manufacturers and local dealers to display their new product offerings from PWC to Mini Jet Boats, and its accessories. This allows sponsors to reach their consumers without extra cost.

Opportunities

- The need in the market for a national endurance race tour is not currently being met

  Several regional promoters are holding local offshore endurance races, but they do not have the technical knowledge or support to put on an event of this magnitude. MCM Powersports is a premier promoter, so it will be able to support and advance the sport of offshore endurance racing to the national level.

- The media is a powerful force that can influence society as a whole

    In order to use the power of media, contributing reporters will write stories for all the PWC magazines and newspapers across the country. Press releases will be implemented to provide maximum coverage for the event. This will enable free publicity for the company as well as PWC endurance racing.

- The staff has firsthand knowledge in the PWC industry, racing, and promotion

    Several members of MCM Powersports have been in the PWC industry for several years and are well known in the industry. Through networking and other race events several members of MCM Powersports have been mentioned in magazines and newspapers. This can enable MCM Powersports to find sponsors and raise capital to support its activities easier than expected.

- MCM Powersports will provide the latest technology through the integrated technology systems that will be developed

    MCM Powersports will be able to capture all of the PWC enthusiasts who come to the events for further development of mailing lists and to segment the target population by advertising to them directly. With the use of laptops, the site event crew can maintain contact with the home office via e-mail. MCM Powersports will use the latest technology in scoring the races. A Web page will also be set up where PWC enthusiasts can not only find the latest news about events and activities, but also find the latest developments in laws and regulations, technology, and product offerings of major manufacturers. MCM Powersports will also provide an e-mail address for people to make comments, suggestions, or ask questions which MCM Powersports will answer.

- MCM Powersports can easily adapt to change

    Being a relatively small company, MCM Powersports does not have a large bureaucracy nor will it allow itself to be set in its ways. MCM Powersports wants to provide premier watercraft racing at a low cost for the whole family. In order to be able to do this, it must be able to adapt to the needs of the target market.

- MCM Powersports will just specialize in promoting endurance race nationally, which will enhance specialization

MARKETING OBJECTIVE AND GOALS

Mission Statement

To market and grow as the only existing national offshore racing promotions company in the United States while continuously improving consumer attractiveness and profitability.

Objectives
- To establish a premier national offshore endurance race series
- Be the number-one premier promoter in the United States and bring promoting to a new level of competition
- Achieve maximum return of investment by keeping costs low and promoting heavily
- Achieve high audience participation
- Provide cost-effective entertainment for the whole family
- Promote and function as an environmentally conscious company

- Provide a commodity for sponsors and investors by hiring an independent auditing firm to report to them
- Break-even by the end of the first year
- Create a healthy organizational structure with an effective, loyal sponsorship, and establish necessary networking connections for the future success of the firm
- Expand the tour to 12 events from 10 by the end of the third year

Goals

- Achieve break-even at – $3,081,826 by the end of the first year
- MCM Powersports' staff expects to gain experience, discover and remedy any unforeseen problems with operations, marketing, and sales
- MCM Powersports will have a goal of 40,000 spectators with 5,000 cars per event
- MCM Powersports expects to have 80 racers per event
- Achieve the following returns on investment per year, which is calculated by the ratio of net income to average total assets:

Year 1:	Year 2:	Year 3:
ROA – 3%	ROA – 61%	ROA – 72%
Profits – $1,958	Profits – $156,306	Profits – $435,380

- Its long-term goals are to create a strong financial structure and to create a strong image/position among the industry and among PWC enthusiasts by increasing its total assets to $866,432
- Improve the negative images of PWC through incorporating safety classes and community involvement. This will bring awareness to safe PWC operations
- Help watercraft enthusiasts ages 16 and over at all skill levels compete in a safe racing environment
- Promote the sport of PWC racing as a fun event for everyone to enjoy

MARKETING STRATEGY

- MCM Powersports will be first in the market. Spectators and businesses will see and test out these events for further participation and support
- The niche market for MCM Powersports will also be the target market. There are currently over 2.6 million people in this market to advertise to
- MCM Powersports can capitalize on the unique expertise of the management team. Misty Iwatsu and Taylor LeClaire have been able to make many contacts in the PWC industry and have numerous years of racing experience
- MCM Powersports will have the financial resources of a corporation. By being a corporation, it will provide numerous benefits and compete at a level no other promoter can match
- MCM Powersports will position itself as affordable family entertainment with spectator participation for the general public and a premier race promoter to the race participants and sponsors by offering low prices and high-quality entertainment

MARKET TACTICS

Product

The following classes have been set for amateurs: Open, 785, Sport, Ski, Women, Veterans, free-style, Mini Jet Boat 1 engine, and Mini Jet Boat 2 engines. The following program for Pros is as follows: Open, 785, Sport, Ski, Women's, Veterans, Free-style, Mini Jet Boats 1 engine, and Mini Jet Boats 2 engine.

For spectator entertainment, the course will be set up as an extended closed course (see Appendix D). It will be approximately a two-mile track. There will be two options set up for the amateurs, which consist of option 1: fewer buoy turns but longer distance, and option 2: more buoy turns but shorter distance. In the Pro course setup there will be four options: options 1 and 2 are same as above, and option 3 is going a longer distance around buoys, or option 4, which is jumping a ramp. (See Appendix E.)

For audience participation, MCM Powersports will select 5 volunteers to judge the free-style competition each day. MCM Powersports will provide a 20-minute training program on the difficulty ratings of each maneuver performed. In return for their participation, MCM Powersports will offer them free gifts. The compound will be set up for ease of traffic flow and high visibility of the race course.

MCM Powersports will be the leader in technological advances since it will utilize magnetic stripe cards for its race and audience participants. Each person will be able to swipe their card to enter raffles, to vote for their favorite racer, and to visit booths. As each person swipes his/her card, pertinent and crucial information such as name, telephone number, address, and identification number (if applicable), as well as psychographic and behavioral data will be recorded on a database system for organizing better events in the future. This database will also create an opportunity to rent the names to mailing-list companies, major PWC manufacturers, and local dealers for additional income.

Place

Because a service is intangible, unlike physical products, it needs personal contact with its customers. Therefore, MCM Powersports will implement a direct channel of distribution to reach its target market.

MCM Powersports will be conducting its racing across the United States in 10 different locations. Each location will consist of a two-day event. The first day will be amateur racing and the second day will be Pro racing.

In order to meet the demands of the different segments of its target market and to challenge the participants, MCM Powersports will conduct its races in several kinds of waterways. In choosing the waterways, MCM Powersports will give the maximum importance to protecting nature and the environment.

Promotion

Being an environmentally sound company, MCM Powersports will organize two beach clean-ups to promote the clean environment—one before the event starts, to have a fresh startup, and one after the event is over, to clean up the mess we caused. To help implement this, MCM Powersports plans to contact local colleges and universities for volunteers to help make these events a success.

MCM Powersports will emphasize keeping the waterways safe, hence, host water-safety courses offered by the U.S. Coast Guard. The course teaches people safe boating habits and will be offered several times during the weekend. Each person completing the course will receive a certificate of completion. This will enable the watercraft community to create a positive image to the public in addition to providing a public service for the industry. The goal for the first year will be to award 100 certificates, 150 and 200 certificates for the second and third years, respectively.

MCM Powersports plans to contact local dealerships, Chamber of Commerce, local businesses, and local promoters to help assist in the events, to give them a new outlet for advertising, and offer them 40,000 potential new contacts for their business.

As part of the added promotion benefits, MCM Powersports plans on having a meet and greet event for the racers and manufacturers. At each event there will be a different Pro racer and Manufacturer for a question-and-answer period to answer questions about themselves and the products they sell. The registration for Pro's will be kept to a minimum during the first year with 100 percent Pro payback purse for the first-place winners. This is to entice professional riders to attend the events and attract more spectators.

Taking the seasonality of the product into consideration, 10 months a year the company is planning to advertise heavily in PWC magazines such as *Splash, Personal Watercraft Illustrated, Watercraft World,* and *Jet Sports,* on local radio stations, and on local cable TV stations such as ESPN, ESPN2, FoxSports, and Sports Network prior to and during the events as well as conducting live interviews.

MCM Powersports will also use direct mail campaigns from lists provided by the IJSBA and DMV Boater registration to inform potential consumers of the events and Web site where they can receive the latest up-to-date information on each event.

MCM Powersports will hire an independent firm to audit the financial accounts once a year. In addition, an annual report will be issued for its sponsors to explain the activities done and where the money was spent.

Price

MCM Powersports learned from competitors' mistakes of pricing too high. MCM Powersports will be able to reduce risk by entering at a low price. In addition, being first in the market will discourage competition. See Appendix C for ticket and booth prices.

ORGANIZATION, EVALUATION, CONTROL, AND IMPLEMENTATION

Organization

The company will have four managing partners:

Misty L. Iwatsu – President	A. Murat Mendi – VP of Finance
Taylor LeClaire – VP of Operations	Caroline Yeung – VP of Marketing

Detailed organizational chart and product development schedule can be found in the Appendix (see Appendixes F and G).

Break-Even Analysis

The following assumptions are used to calculate the break-even point: In calculating the unit price, the money from sponsors, accessory sales, and video cassette sales was deducted from total revenues. The revenue used to calculate unit price is found as $3,779,600. Since the assumptions are that the total number of participants will be 400,000 and cars coming will be 50,000, and other items will have 1,109, it is assumed that total units involved will be 451,109. Therefore, the unit income will be: $\dfrac{\$3,779,600}{451,109} = \$8.38$

MCM Powersports has found that variable cost will be $631,342. This figure was divided into total units involved. Therefore, the unit variable cost will be: $\dfrac{\$631,342}{451,109} = \$1.40$

After calculating the unit revenue, unit cost, and fixed cost the break-even point was found out by using the following formula: $BE = \dfrac{FC}{P - VC}$ Then, percentages of each item such as ticket sales revenues, and parking fee revenues in total revenues are used to break down this figure. The following table summarizes the results.

Break-Even Analysis		Break Down of Break-Even Figure	
Average price per unit	$8.38	# of tickets sold	39,156 (88.67%)
Average variable cost per unit	$1.40	# of parking spaces sold	4,894 (11.08%)
Fixed Cost	$3,081,826	# of racers registered	59 (0.13%)
Break-Even Point	44,159	# of booths rented	49 (0.11%)
		# of mailing lists rented	1 (0.00%)

Cash Flow

Pro forma cash flows have been calculated for 36 months. The following figures are found as year-end cash flows for three years (see Appendix H).

Year 1:	Year 2:	Year 3:
$186,431	$618,122	$1,459,702

Profit-and-Loss Statement

Pro forma Income (Profit-and-Loss) statements have been prepared to figure out the net income for each year. Findings are summarized below (see Appendix I).

$1,958 **(year 1)** $156,306 **(year 2)** $435,380 **(year 3)**

Balance Sheets

Pro forma balance sheets are prepared for three years. The depreciation of the fixed assets is calculated using the straight-line method over a period of three years. Total assets of the company will be (see Appendix I):

$147,640 **(year 1)** $378,002 **(year 2)** $866,432 **(year 3)**

SUMMARY

MCM Powersports will be a premier promoter in the United States and expects to be successful in the business by promoting and implementing the strategies that will take advantage of the expertise found in all of the partners.

Through the mission statement, MCM Powersports hopes to have a competitive advantage over other promoters in the United States.

By making the initial investment, MCM Powersports hopes to attract sponsors and venture capitalists to invest in the organization. Each partner will invest $5,000 in order to cover part of the start-up costs. Net income for each year would be:

- $1,958 (year 1)
- $156,306 (year 2)
- $435,380 (year 3)

MCM Powersports' competitive advantage is that it will tap into the PWC endurance racing market, which other competitors have not done. In addition, MCM Powersports will be the only IJSBA-sanctioned national offshore endurance race promoter. The company will be able to gain in this market and cater to PWC enthusiasts who seek the thrill and competitive edge of endurance races.

BIBLIOGRAPHY

Alger, A., "Here They Come Again (Controversy Over the Use of the Jet Skis)." *Forbes* (June 3, 1996), p. 182.

Alger, A., Flanigan, W. G. "Snowmobiles of the Sea," *Forbes* (August 28, 1995), p. 304.

Argetsinger, A. "Deaths Rise as More People Ride the Waves," *Washington Post,* August 27, 1995.

Berkowitz, E. N., Kerin, R., Hartley, S., and Rudelius, W. *Marketing.* Irwin, 1994.

Cohen, William A. *The Marketing Plan.* Wiley, 1995.

Cohen, William A. *Model Business Plans for Service Businesses.* Wiley, 1995.

Department of Boating & Waterways, *PWC News* (Sacramento, CA, 1997), p. 7.

Fiataff, J. "Clearing the Pipeline," *Watercraft Business,* (January 1997), p. 2.

Harris, J. C. *Personal Watercraft.* Crestwood House, 1988.

Henschen, D., "New Jersey Passes Mandatory Education: PWC Bill," *Boating Industry* (March 1996), p. 11.

International Jet Sports Boating Association. *1997 Official Competition Rule Book* (Santa Ana, CA, 1997), p. 10.

Media Kit, *Splash Magazine* (1997).

Napier, J. "Napier Predicts Slight Sales Growth in 1997," *Boating Industry* (November 1996).

Paulsen, B., "Squeezing PWC: More States Are Finding Ways to Restrict Their Use," *Yachting* (May 1996), p. 32.

Steven, S. "Water Bikes Are Losing Some Speed." *Wall Street Journal,* September 17, 1996.

Stewart, R. L. "The Wonderful World of "Wet and Wild" Water-Sports," *Rough Notes* (May 1993), pp. 30–32.

Weeth, C. "Water Events Facing New Environmental Regulations," *Amusement Business* (February 20, 1995), p. 28.

"PWC: Many Challenges in Taking a Line," *Boating Industry* (June 1996), p. 50.

APPENDIX A

$1,000,000 for Title Sponsorship.   This is for the title of the tour. This will be one sponsor with no other competing companies. This sponsor will receive the title of the event in their name as well other perks. For example they will have free booth space, free advertising on all of the materials distributed, and the Web site will feature their name and logo. They will have unlimited access to the VIP booth at all events as well as all event access, and free ad space on the TV monitors that will be stationed around the event compound. MCM Powersports will showcase them at all events, and be available for promotional need if necessary. Banners with the sponsor name will be prominently displayed throughout the event and in addition the buoys at the start/finish line will feature their name. There will be a hospitality suite available for their use at each of the events. All mass media advertising will prominently display the name of the title sponsor. There will also be numerous other benefits than just the ones stated here.

$500,000 for Exclusive Sponsorship.   These will be non-competitive companies. The benefits for this sponsor are as follows: they will receive free booth space, free advertising on all promotional materials distributed, the Web site will list them as sponsors, will have access to the VIP booth at all events as well as all event access and free ad space on the TV monitors that will be stationed around the event compound. MCM Powersports will showcase them at all events, and be available for promotional need if necessary. Banners with the sponsor name will be prominently displayed throughout the event and, in addition, some of the buoys will feature their name. There will be a hospitality suite for their use at each of the events. All mass media advertising will display the names of the sponsors. There will also be numerous other benefits than just the ones stated here.

$250,000 for Official Sponsorship.   These will be non-competitive companies. The benefits for this sponsor are as follows: they will receive free booth space, free advertising on all promotional materials distributed, the Web site will list them as sponsors, have access to the VIP booth at all events as well as all event access and several free ad space spots on the TV monitors that will be stationed around the event compound. MCM Powersports will announce them at all events. Banners with the sponsor name will be prominently displayed throughout the event, and some buoys will feature their name. There will be a hospitality suite available for their use at each event. All mass media advertising will display the names of the sponsors. There will also be numerous other benefits than just the ones stated here.

$100,000 for Associate Sponsorship.   The benefits for this sponsor are as follows: they will receive free booth space, free advertising on all promotional materials distributed, the Web site will list them as sponsors, have limited access to the VIP booth at all events as well as limited all event access and access to ad space on the TV monitors that will be stationed around the event compound. MCM Powersports will announce them at all events. Banners with the sponsor name will be displayed throughout the event as well as on some of the buoys that will feature their name. There will be hospitality suite available for their use at each event.

APPENDIX B

Laws and Regulations

Regulations for Race Promoters. The following are the primary regulations that MCM Powersports as a race promoter will have to enforce and abide by:[5]

- PWC racers must wear U.S. Coast Guard-approved personal flotation devices
- PWC racers are prohibited to operate a PWC between the hours from one half-hour after sunset to one half-hour before sunrise
- A lanyard-type engine cutoff switch must be attached to the racer in case the racer is displaced from the craft or if the craft is not upright
- No PWC shall exceed a noise level of 90 decibels when subjected to a stationary, on-site sound level test, or 75 decibels when subjected to a shoreline test
- All PWC racers have to abide by "no negligent operation" statutes

The following IJSBA criteria/regulations are required for PWC and Mini Jet boat race promoters:

Body of Water
- Predictable water level or favorable tidal fluctuation
- Must secure event area from boat traffic
- Race course water depth minimum of 4 feet—maximum 50 feet

Land Area
- 1400 feet long × 150 feet wide (pits 1,000 feet, spectator area 400)
- Authority to charge admission and install security fencing
- No signage restrictions

Parking
- Safe and secure participant parking area located adjacent to race site. Able to accommodate at least 1,000 vehicles, including fifth-wheel trailers with separate parking for VIP's
- Parking for ambulance and staff equipment trucks near race site

Regulations for Pre-Event Planning

Pre-event planning is essential to conducting a successful event. Therefore, the following regulations set up by the IJSBA are required for PWC race promoters.[6]

Red Cross Courses
The Race Director, Course Marshals and safety boat personnel must take the American Red Cross Standard First Aid course and Basic Water Safety course.

Event Site
The following event site criteria must be followed:
- The location must be large enough to safely accommodate all types of events (e.g., endurance race and freestyle)

---

[5] International Jet Sports Boating Association. *1997 Official Competition Rule Book* (Santa Ana, CA, 1997), 10.
[6] Ibid., p. 13

- Beach and adjacent land areas for pit locations, launching facilities, spectator viewing; rider and spectator parking and overall access to the water for both spectators and riders should be considered

Coast Guard/Coast Guard Auxiliary

- The promoter must contact the Coast Guard or Coast Guard Auxiliary several months prior to the event to investigate their regulations and complete a marine event application.

Fire Department

Contact Fire Marshal for criteria requirements prior to and during the event because they have the authority to cancel an event at any time. Criteria include such things as posting no smoking signs, keeping fire lanes open, tents which exceed a certain limit may be required to have a certificate of fire retardation.

Office of the City Clerk

Contact the Office of the City Clerk in the city where the event will be held several months in advance. The promoter may be required to purchase a city business license and complete an application for special event or temporary use permit.

State Department of Revenue

Contact the Department of Revenue in the state where the event will be held. The promoter may have to complete a tax application and pay an application fee. After the event, the promoter may have to pay a tax based on ticket sales, exhibitor booth sales, and any other revenue specified by the Department of Revenue.

Parks and Recreation Department

Contact the Parks and Recreation Department; they may require a land use fee.

Fish and Game

Contact the Fish and Game; they may have a list of regulations regarding the use of the facility.

Emergency Response Vehicle

The race promoter must supply an emergency response, rescue and transport vehicle(s) (e.g., ambulance) that meets the requirements of the authorizing local jurisdiction as stated in the IJSBA sanction agreement.

One vehicle must be present at all times during the entire event. The event must stop if the vehicle leaves the event site. Racing may resume once the vehicle or a replacement returns.

Emergency response vehicle personnel must consist of one driver and one medical attendant capable of providing care at the basic life support level.

Exhibit Sales

The race promoter must check with the Facility Manager for approval to sell exhibit space. Some facilities may not allow the promoter to sell exhibit space due to existing concession contracts.

Insurance Coverage

Promoters will purchase insurance coverage for personal injuries. The insurance costs $630 for the first day, $380 for the second day and it covers two-day setup before the event (Thursday, Friday), the weekend, and one day tear-down after the event (Monday). The coverage includes:

- $200,000 participant (racer or pit crew)
- $7,500 in excess medical benefits

- $7,500 in accidental death or dismemberment
- $1,000,000 single limit liability per occurrence

Regulations for Racing

The following regulations are required for those who are interested in PWC racing:

- Using an approved PWC by the International Jet Sports Boating Association (IJSBA)
- A competition level membership in the IJSBA
- A U.S. properly fitting wetsuit and full-coverage helmet with chin, eye, feet, and mouth protection
- Knowledge of the IJSBA competition rules and regulations

APPENDIX C

The following table summarizes the pricing for tickets and parking fees.

MCM Powersports	1998		1999		2000	
Event	1 day	2 days	1 day	2 days	1 day	2 days
Ticket Sales	$7	$10	$8	$12	$9	$15
Parking	$5	$8	$5	$8	$5	$8

The following table summarizes the booth rental prices for each event.

MCM Powersports	10 by 10	10 by 20
Regular	$200	$300
IJSBA Affiliated	$175	$275
All 10 Events	$100	$150

APPENDIX E – A SAMPLE EVENT SCHEDULE DAY AT THE RACES FOR AMATEURS

6:00–8:00 A.M. – Sign-up/Registration/Tech Inspection

This is when the amateur racers go to the sign-up area to register for the day's events. The amateur racers will fill out the entry form, present their IJSBA membership card, and pay their entry fees. The IJSBA provides many benefits to its members, especially the right to race (all racers must be members of the IJSBA). This can be done at the registration booth during sign-up. Registration closes at 8:00 A.M. All PWC must then proceed to the tech inspection area to have their PWC checked out for any infractions to the rules and regulations of the IJSBA boat specifications.

Note: All events will allow Pre-Registration either the Saturday before the race or weeks in advance. Check out MCM Powersports' Pre-Registration Information Page that can be accessed from our Web page. Since the space is limited pre-registration is highly recommended.

8:00 A.M. – Riders Meeting

All amateur racers will be called to a designated area by the race director to go over information such as the course layout, starting procedures, course officials, caution flags, and what to do if you have a question or complaint. The practice and race order will also be posted at this time.

8:30 A.M. – Practice

All amateur racers will be given a chance to learn the course and become comfortable with it. A course official will lead a group of amateur racers around the course for one lap; it is up to the amateur racers to know the course.

9:00 A.M. – Morning Session Racing Begins

Three out of seven classes will race in the morning. These are: 785, and Sport/Ski (combined). The first of 3 classes will be called to the starting line by 9:00 A.M. While the first sets of racers are on the line, the next group of racers will already be making their way toward the starting line. This early preparation is to ensure races flow smoothly without having to wait for racers to make their way to the starting line. Each race will be 90 minutes long; 2 races are scheduled for the morning session. Before the afternoon session starts the free-style competition will take place.

12:30 P.M. – Afternoon Session Racing Begins

The rest of the classes will race at this session. These are: Open, Women/Vets, Mini Jet Boats 1 engine/2 engines. Open, and Women/Vets will go first in the first part of the afternoon session. There will be a half-hour break at 3:30 P.M. for resetting the course for Mini Jet Boat races. The races are scheduled to end at 5:30 P.M.

8:00 P.M. – Award Ceremony

Top five finishers in each class will be awarded. Raffle prizes for racers from sponsors will also be given at that time.

APPENDIX F

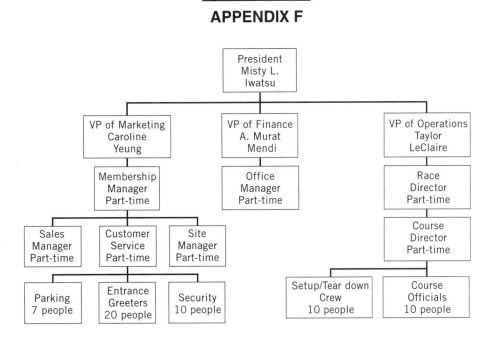

APPENDIX G

Product Development Schedule Year 1

Task	January				February				March				April				May				June				July				August				September				October				November				December			
Week	1	8	15	22	29	5	12	19	26	5	12	19	26	2	9	16	23	30	7	14	21	28	4	11	18	25	2	9	16	23	30	6	13	20	27	3	10	17	24	1	8	15	22	29	5	12	19	26	3	10	17	24
Setting up the firm																																																					
Development of Policy and Procedures Manual																																																					
Sponsor connections																																																					
Sponsor follow-up																																																					
Place reservations																																																					
Site logistics																																																					
Race course logistics																																																					
Purchase Equipment																																																					
Inviting Pros																																																					
Plan Advertising Cmp.																																																					
Advertising																																																					
Safety Program Guidelines																																																					
Web site setup																																																					
Prepare event 1																																																					
Setup event 1																																																					
Event 1																																																					
Prepare event 2																																																					
Setup event 2																																																					
Event 2																																																					
Prepare event 3																																																					
Setup event 3																																																					
Event 3																																																					
Prepare event 4																																																					
Setup event 4																																																					
Event 4																																																					
Prepare event 5																																																					
Setup event 5																																																					
Event 5																																																					
Prepare event 6																																																					
Setup event 6																																																					
Event 6																																																					
Prepare event 7																																																					
Setup event 7																																																					
Event 7																																																					
Prepare event 8																																																					
Setup event 8																																																					
Event 8																																																					
Prepare event 9																																																					
Setup event 9																																																					
Event 9																																																					
Prepare event 10																																																					
Setup event 10																																																					
Event 10																																																					

Product Development Schedule Year 2

Month	January				February				March				April				May				June				July				August				September				October				November				December			
Task \ Week	1	8	15	22	29	5	12	19	26	5	12	19	26	2	9	16	23	30	7	14	21	28	4	11	18	25	2	9	16	23	30	6	13	20	27	3	10	17	24	1	8	15	22	29	5	12	19	26	3	10	17	24
Sponsor follow-up																																																				
Place reservations																																																				
Site logistics																																																				
Race course logistics																																																				
Purchase Equipment																																																				
Inviting Pros																																																				
Plan Advertising Cmp.																																																				
Advertising																																																				
Safety Program Guidelines																																																				
Web site setup																																																				
Prepare event 1																																																				
Setup event 1																																																				
Event 1																																																				
Prepare event 2																																																				
Setup event 2																																																				
Event 2																																																				
Prepare event 3																																																				
Setup event 3																																																				
Event 3																																																				
Prepare event 4																																																				
Setup event 4																																																				
Event 4																																																				
Prepare event 5																																																				
Setup event 5																																																				
Event 5																																																				
Prepare event 6																																																				
Setup event 6																																																				
Event 6																																																				
Prepare event 7																																																				
Setup event 7																																																				
Event 7																																																				
Prepare event 8																																																				
Setup event 8																																																				
Event 8																																																				
Prepare event 9																																																				
Setup event 9																																																				
Event 9																																																				
Prepare event 10																																																				
Setup event 10																																																				
Event 10																																																				

Product Development Schedule Year 3

Task	Month / Week
	January 1, 8, 15, 22, 29 — **February** 5, 12, 19, 26 — **March** 5, 12, 19, 26 — **April** 2, 9, 16, 23, 30 — **May** 7, 14, 21, 28 — **June** 4, 11, 18, 25 — **July** 2, 9, 16, 23, 30 — **August** 6, 13, 20, 27 — **September** 3, 10, 17, 24 — **October** 1, 8, 15, 22, 29 — **November** 5, 12, 19, 26 — **December** 3, 10, 17, 24
Sponsor follow-up	
Place reservations	
Site logistics	
Race course logistics	
Purchase Equipment	
Inviting Pros	
Plan Advertising Cmp.	
Advertising	
Safety Program Guideines	
Web site setup	
Prepare event 1	
Setup event 1	
Event 1	
Prepare event 2	
Setup event 2	
Event 2	
Prepare event 3	
Setup event 3	
Event 3	
Prepare event 4	
Setup event 4	
Event 4	
Prepare event 5	
Setup event 5	
Event 5	
Prepare event 6	
Setup event 6	
Event 6	
Prepare event 7	
Setup event 7	
Event 7	
Prepare event 8	
Setup event 8	
Event 8	
Prepare event 9	
Setup event 9	
Event 9	
Prepare event 10	
Setup event 10	
Event 10	

Management Team

Misty Iwatsu is the president of MCM Powersports. She has more than 13 years of retail management experience. She has been a Personal Watercraft Endurance racer for more than 7 years. She has also assisted promoters in organizing watercraft events. She has been a team manager for several race teams and was responsible for gaining sponsorship and media recognition. She has earned several national titles in the Personal Watercraft endurance racing field. She is achieving her B.S. degree at California State University, Los Angeles, in marketing, management, with a minor in Economics. She attended the Fashion Institute of Design and Merchandising and received her A.A. degree in marketing, management.

Ahmet Murat Mendi is the vice president of finance. He has more than 4 years of experience in the finance field. He received his B.A. degree in management at Bogazici University and will achieve his master degree at California State University, Los Angeles. He has also done extensive research in the economic and risk management fields.

Caroline Yeung is the vice president of marketing. She has more than 3 years of experience in the marketing field. She has earned her B.S. degree in marketing, management at California State University, Los Angeles. She has done numerous marketing plans and advertising campaigns for highly visible companies.

Taylor LeClaire is the vice president of marketing. She has more than 10 years in the retail management field. She has been in the Personal Watercraft industry for more than 3 years. She has assisted promoters in staffing events and has earned a national title in Personal Watercraft endurance racing.

APPENDIX H

Cash Flow Analysis	Month 1	Month 2	Month 3	Month 4	Month 5	Month 6	Month 7	Month 8	Month 9	Month 10	Month 11	Month 12
Beginning Balance	$ 20,000	$ 112,700	$ 1,245,560	$ 975,933	$ 773,057	$ 639,976	$ 506,894	$ 373,813	$ 218,232	$ 262,440	$ 237,104	$ 211,768
Loan	$ 100,000											
Sources of Funds												
Sponsorship		$ 1,150,000		$ 690,000	$ 690,000	$ 690,000	$ 690,000	$ 690,000				
Ticket sales				$ 620,000	$ 620,000	$ 620,000	$ 620,000	$ 620,000				
Parking				$ 57,500	$ 57,500	$ 57,500	$ 57,500	$ 57,500				
Racer registration			$ 1,000	$ 7,000	$ 7,000	$ 7,000	$ 7,000	$ 6,000				
Booth rental			$ 21,500	$ 21,500	$ 21,500	$ 21,500	$ 21,500					
Mailing list					$ 49,920	$ 49,920	$ 49,920	$ 49,920	$ 49,920			
Accessory sales				$ 18,750	$ 37,500	$ 37,500	$ 37,500	$ 37,500	$ 18,750			
Video cassette					$ 1,125	$ 1,125	$ 1,125	$ 1,125	$ 1,125			
Total Sources	$ –	$ 1,150,000	$ 22,500	$ 1,414,750	$ 1,484,545	$ 1,484,545	$ 1,484,545	$ 1,462,045	$69,795	$ –	$ –	$ –
Uses of Funds												
Startup costs												
New promoter fee	$ 300											
Establishing firm	$ 5,000											
Salary												
Full time		$ 8,000	$ 8,000	$ 8,000	$ 8,000	$ 8,000	$ 8,000	$ 8,000	$ 8,000	$ 8,000	$ 8,000	$ 8,000
Part time			$ 2,240	$ 2,240	$ 2,240	$ 2,240	$ 2,240	$ 2,240	$ 2,240	$ 2,240	$ 2,240	$ 2,240
Temporary hires				$ 11,400	$ 11,400	$ 11,400	$ 11,400	$ 11,400				
Insurance												
Equipment		$ 2,500	$ 2,500	$ 2,500	$ 2,500	$ 2,500	$ 2,500	$ 2,500	$ 2,500	$ 2,500	$ 2,500	$ 2,500
Event				$ 2,060	$ 2,060	$ 2,060	$ 2,060	$ 2,060				
Permit fees		$ 2,000										
Interest paid		$ 873	$ 873	$ 873	$ 873	$ 873	$ 873	$ 873	$ 873	$ 873	$ 873	$ 873
Computer equipment												
Computers		$ 1,852	$ 1,852	$ 1,852	$ 1,852	$ 1,852	$ 1,852	$ 1,852	$ 1,852	$ 1,852	$ 1,852	$ 1,852
Software for magnetic cards			$ 5,000									
Magnetic card readers			$ 61,000									
Magnetic cards				$ 18,000	$ 18,000	$ 18,000	$ 18,000	$ 18,000				
Other office equipment		$ 1,944										
Office supplies		$ 500	$ 500	$ 500	$ 500	$ 500	$ 500	$ 500	$ 500	$ 500	$ 500	$ 500

TV cameras				$1,500,000	$1,500,000	$1,500,000	$1,500,000	$1,500,000				
AT & T Business 1 Rate for 1–888 numbers		$222	$222	$222	$222	$222	$222	$222	$222	$222	$222	$222
Advertising												
Prepare TV commercial			$75,000									
Air the TV commercial			$5,000	$5,000	$5,000	$5,000	$5,000	$5,000				
Designing magazine Ad			$1,500									
Print ad space			$7,900	$7,900	$7,900	$7,900	$7,900	$7,900	$7,900	$7,900	$7,900	$7,900
Record radio commercial			$500									
Air the radio commercial			$4,500	$4,500	$4,500	$4,500	$4,500	$4,500				
Equipment												
Personal Watercraft			$120,000									
Course equipment			$9,440									
PWC maintenance			$3,000	$3,000	$3,000	$3,000	$3,000	$3,000				
Transportation												
Setup and tear down			$20,000	$20,000	$20,000	$20,000	$20,000	$20,000				
Travel			$11,780	$11,780	$11,780	$11,780	$11,780	$11,780				
Hotel			$2,100	$2,100	$2,100	$2,100	$2,100	$2,100				
Plaques, gifts, prizes			$3,700	$3,700	$3,700	$3,700	$3,700	$3,700				
Rent tents			$10,000	$10,000	$10,000	$10,000	$10,000	$10,000				
Utilities	$250	$500	$500	$1,000	$1,000	$1,000	$1,000	$1,000	$500	$250	$250	$250
Miscellaneous	$1,000	$1,000	$1,000	$1,000	$1,000	$1,000	$1,000	$1,000	$1,000	$1,000	$1,000	$1,000
Lawyer fees	$1,000		$1,000									
Total Uses	**$7,300**	**$17,140**	**$292,126**	**$1,617,626**	**$1,617,626**	**$1,617,626**	**$1,617,626**	**$1,617,626**	**$25,586**	**$25,336**	**$25,336**	**$25,336**
Earnings Before Taxes	**$(7,300)**	**$1,132,860**	**$(269,626)**	**$(202,876)**	**$(133,081)**	**$(133,081)**	**$(133,081)**	**$(155,581)**	**$44,209**	**$(25,336)**	**$(25,336)**	**$(25,336)**
Less: Tax	$(7,300)	$—	$—	$—	$—	$—	$—	$—	$—	$—	$—	$—
Earnings After Taxes	**$(7,300)**	**$1,132,860**	**$(269,626)**	**$(202,876)**	**$(133,081)**	**$(133,081)**	**$(133,081)**	**$(155,581)**	**$44,209**	**$(25,336)**	**$(25,336)**	**$(25,336)**
Net Cash Flow	**$112,700**	**$1,245,560**	**$975,933**	**$773,057**	**$639,976**	**$506,894**	**$373,813**	**$218,232**	**$262,440**	**$237,104**	**$211,768**	**$186,431**

Cash Flow Analysis	Month 1	Month 2	Month 3	Month 4	Month 5	Month 6	Month 7	Month 8	Month 9	Month 10	Month 11	Month 12
Beginning Balance	$186,431	$160,750	$1,283,486	$1,195,509	$1,014,520	$925,407	$836,293	$747,180	$635,566	$699,914	$672,650	$645,386
Sources of Funds												
Sponsorship		$1,150,000		$690,000	$690,000	$690,000	$690,000	$690,000				
Ticket sales				$720,000	$720,000	$720,000	$720,000	$720,000				
Parking				$57,500	$57,500	$57,500	$57,500	$57,500				
Racer registration				$11,000	$11,000	$11,000	$11,000	$10,000				
Booth rental			$1,000	$21,500	$21,500	$21,500	$21,500					
Mailing list			$21,500		$72,000	$72,000	$72,000	$72,000	$72,000			
Accessory sales				$18,750	$37,500	$37,500	$37,500	$37,500	$18,750			
Video cassette					$1,125	$1,125	$1,125	$1,125	$1,125			
Total Sources	$ –	$1,150,000	$22,500	$1,518,750	$1,610,625	$1,610,625	$1,610,625	$1,588,125	$91,875	$ –	$ –	$ –
Uses of Funds												
Salary												
Full time	$8,000	$8,800	$8,800	$8,800	$8,800	$8,800	$8,800	$8,800	$8,800	$8,800	$8,800	$8,800
Part time	$2,240	$2,464	$2,464	$2,464	$2,464	$2,464	$2,464	$2,464	$2,464	$2,464	$2,464	$2,464
Temporary hires				$12,540	$12,540	$12,540	$12,540	$12,540				
Insurance												
Equipment	$2,500	$2,625	$2,625	$2,625	$2,625	$2,625	$2,625	$2,625	$2,625	$2,625	$2,625	$2,625
Event			$2,100	$2,163	$2,163	$2,163	$2,163	$2,163				
Permit fees	$873	$873	$873	$873	$873	$873	$873	$873	$873	$873	$873	$873
Interest paid												
Computer equipment												
Computers	$1,852	$2,037	$2,037	$2,037	$2,037	$2,037	$2,037	$2,037	$2,037	$2,037	$2,037	$2,037
Magnetic cards				$18,900	$18,900	$18,900	$18,900	$18,900				
Office supplies	$500	$625	$625	$625	$625	$625	$625	$625	$625	$625	$625	$625
TV cameras				$1,575,000	$1,575,000	$1,575,000	$1,575,000	$1,575,000				
AT & T Business 1 Rate for 1–888 numbers	$222	$233	$233	$233	$233	$233	$233	$233	$233	$233	$233	$233
Advertising												
Prepare TV commercial			$78,750									
Air the TV commercial				$5,250	$5,250	$5,250	$5,250	$5,250				
Designing magazine ad			$1,575									
Print ad space	$7,900	$8,295	$8,295	$8,295	$8,295	$8,295	$8,295	$8,295	$8,295	$8,295	$8,295	$8,295
$ 8,295												
Record radio commercial												
Air the radio commercial			$525	$4,725	$4,725	$4,725	$4,725	$4,725				
Equipment												
PWC maintenance				$3,150	$3,150	$3,150	$3,150	$3,150				
Transportation												
Setup and tear down				$21,000	$21,000	$21,000	$21,000	$21,000				
Travel				$12,369	$12,369	$12,369	$12,369	$12,369				
Hotel				$2,205	$2,205	$2,205	$2,205	$2,205				
Plaques, gifts, prizes				$3,885	$3,885	$3,885	$3,885	$3,885				
Rent tents				$10,500	$10,500	$10,500	$10,500	$10,500				
Utilities	$250	$263	$525	$1,050	$1,050	$1,050	$1,050	$1,050	$525	$263	$263	$263
Miscellaneous	$1,000	$1,050	$1,050	$1,050	$1,050	$1,050	$1,050	$1,050	$1,050	$1,050	$1,050	$1,050
Auditing fees	$50,000											
Lawyer fees	$25,000											
Total Uses	$25,336	$27,264	$110,477	$1,699,739	$1,699,739	$1,699,739	$1,699,739	$1,699,739	$27,527	$27,264	$27,264	$27,264
Earnings Before Taxes	$(25,336)	$1,122,736	$(87,977)	$(180,989)	$(89,114)	$(89,114)	$(89,114)	$(111,614)	$64,348	$(27,264)	$(27,264)	$(27,264)
Less: Tax	$346		$ –		$ –	$ –			$ –			$ –
Earnings after taxes	$(25,682)	$1,122,736	$(87,977)	$(180,989)	$(89,114)	$(89,114)	$(89,114)	$(111,614)	$64,348	$(27,264)	$(27,264)	$(27,264)
Net Cash Flow	$160,750	$1,283,486	$1,195,509	$1,014,520	$925,407	$836,293	$747,180	$635,566	$699,914	$672,650	$645,386	$618,122

Cash Flow Analysis	Month 1	Month 2	Month 3	Month 4	Month 5	Month 6	Month 7	Month 8	Month 9	Month 10	Month 11	Month 12
Beginning Balance	$618,122	$506,259	$1,627,758	$1,534,384	$1,447,908	$1,477,307	$1,506,705	$1,536,104	$1,558,107	$1,645,205	$1,616,704	$1,588,203
Sources of Funds												
Sponsorship		$1,150,000		$690,000	$690,000	$690,000	$690,000	$690,000				
Ticket Sales				$900,000	$900,000	$900,000	$900,000	$900,000				
Parking				$57,500	$57,500	$57,500	$57,500	$57,500				
Racer registration			$1,000	$11,000	$11,000	$11,000	$11,000	$10,000				
Booth Rental			$21,500	$21,500	$21,500	$21,500	$21,500					
Mailing list					$96,000	$96,000	$96,000	$96,000	$96,000			
Accessory sales				$18,750	$37,500	$37,500	$37,500	$37,500	$18,750			
Video Cassette					$1,125	$1,125	$1,125	$1,125	$1,125			
Total Sources	$ –	$1,150,000	$22,500	$1,698,750	$1,814,625	$1,814,625	$1,814,625	$1,792,125	$115,875	$ –	$ –	$ –
Uses of Funds												
Salary												
Full time	$8,800	$9,680	$9,680	$9,680	$9,680	$9,680	$9,680	$9,680	$9,680	$9,680	$9,680	$9,680
Part time	$2,464	$2,710	$2,710	$2,710	$2,710	$2,710	$2,710	$2,710	$2,710	$2,710	$2,710	$2,710
Temporary hires				$13,794	$13,794	$13,794	$13,794	$13,794				
Insurance												
Equipment	$2,625	$2,756	$2,756	$2,756	$2,756	$2,756	$2,756	$2,756	$2,756	$2,756	$2,756	$2,756
Event			$2,205	$2,271	$2,271	$2,271	$2,271	$2,271				
Permit fees												
Computer Equipment												
Computers	$2,037	$2,241	$2,241	$2,241	$2,241	$2,241	$2,241	$2,241	$2,241	$2,241	$2,241	$2,241
Magnetic Cards				$19,845	$19,845	$19,845	$19,845	$19,845				
Office Supplies	$625	$781	$781	$781	$781	$781	$781	$781	$781	$781	$781	$781
TV Cameras				$1,653,750	$1,653,750	$1,653,750	$1,653,750	$1,653,750				
AT & T Business 1 Rate for 1–888 numbers	$233	$245	$245	$245	$245	$245	$245	$245	$245	$245	$245	$245
Advertising												
Prepare TV Commercial			$82,688									
Air the TV commercial			$1,654	$5,513	$5,513	$5,513	$5,513	$5,513				
Designing Magazine Ad	$8,295	$8,710	$8,710	$8,710	$8,710	$8,710	$8,710	$8,710	$8,710	$8,710	$8,710	$8,710
Print ad space			$551	$4,961	$4,961	$4,961	$4,961	$4,961				
Record Radio Commercial												
Air the radio commercial												
Equipment												
PWC Maintenance				$3,308	$3,308	$3,308	$3,308	$3,308				
Transportation												
Setup and tear down				$22,050	$22,050	$22,050	$22,050	$22,050				
Travel				$12,987	$12,987	$12,987	$12,987	$12,987				
Hotel				$2,315	$2,315	$2,315	$2,315	$2,315				
Plaques, Gifts, Prizes				$4,079	$4,079	$4,079	$4,079					
Rent tents				$11,025	$11,025	$11,025	$11,025					
Utilities	$263	$276	$551	$1,103	$1,103	$1,103	$1,103	$1,103	$551	$276	$276	$276
Miscellaneous	$1,050	$1,103	$1,103	$1,103	$1,103	$1,103	$1,103	$1,103	$1,103	$1,103	$1,103	$1,103
Auditing fees	$50,000											
Lawyer Fees	$25,000											
Repay Loan												$100,000
Total Uses	$101,391	$28,501	$115,874	$1,785,226	$1,785,226	$1,785,226	$1,785,226	$1,770,122	$28,777	$28,501	$28,501	$128,501
Earnings Before Taxes	$(101,391)	$1,121,499	$(93,374)	$(86,476)	$29,399	$29,399	$29,399	$22,003	$87,098	$(28,501)	$(28,501)	$(128,501)
Less: Tax	$10,471		$ –			$ –			$ –			$ –
Cash Flow After taxes	$(111,863)	$1,121,499	$(93,374)	$(86,476)	$29,399	$29,399	$29,399	$22,003	$87,098	$(28,501)	$(28,501)	$(128,501)
Net Cash Flow	$506,259	$1,627,758	$1,534,384	$1,447,908	$1,477,307	$1,506,705	$1,536,104	$1,558,107	$1,645,205	$1,616,704	$1,588,203	$1,459,702

APPENDIX I

Income Statement	Year 1	Year 2	Year 3
Net Income	$ 8,572,725	$ 9,203,125	$ 10,223,125
Less: Cost of Goods Sold	$ 8,298,495	$ 8,536,248	$ 8,938,698
Sell., Gen. and Adm. Exp.	$ 198,200	$ 299,369	$ 421,905
Operating Profit Before Depr.	***$ 76,030***	***$ 367,508***	***$ 862,522***
Less: Depreciation	$ 64,128	$ 128,256	$ 192,384
Earnings Before Interest and Taxes	***$ 11,902***	***$ 239,252***	***$ 670,138***
Less: Interest	$ 9,599	$ 10,471	$ 10,471
Earnings Before Taxes	***$ 2,303***	***$ 228,780***	***$ 659,667***
Less: Tax Paid	$ 346	$ 72,474	$ 224,287
Net Income after taxes	***$ 1,958***	***$ 156,306***	***$ 435,380***

Balance Sheet	Year 1	Year 2	Year 3
Current Assets			
Cash and Equivalent	18,889	313,321	865,810
Account Receivable	–	–	–
Inventories	495	553	622
Total Current Assets	*19,384*	*313,874*	*866,432*
Fixed Assets	192,384	192,384	192,384
Depreciation	64,128	128,256	192,384
Total Assets	***147,640***	***378,002***	***866,432***
Current Liabilities			
Accounts Payable	15,096	16,000	16,111
Salaries Payable	10,240	11,264	12,390
Taxes Payable	346	72,474	224,287
Total Current Liabilities	*25,682*	*99,738*	*252,788*
Long-Term Debt	100,000	100,000	–

A5

BIRRALEE PRIMARY SCHOOL (AUSTRALIA)

Developed by
QUAH SUAT HONG
WELLY TEHUNAN
VANESSA YAU

Used with permission of the authors and Professor Ken Grant, Monash University, Victoria, Australia

Contents

EXECUTIVE SUMMARY

This plan analyzes the industry environment of the Victoria Primary School sector, in particular, Birralee Primary School. Others factors that aid in the analysis of the industry, include the changing trends in the environment, industry life cycle, industry attractiveness and structure, and competition. These helped to formulate and develop the corporate and marketing objectives, strategies, and tactics for Birralee Primary School.

The corporate objectives of Birralee Primary School are *to increase the school's market share, in terms of student number from 5.46 percent in 1998 to 6 percent by January 2002* and *to improve the school reputation among all the primary schools in the same region from a current rating of 2.73 to a rating of 3.5 by the end of 2002.* To achieve this, Birralee has to pursue a corporate strategy by horizontal growth. Tactics such as targeting the promotional activities to new area of coverage, foster good relationship with external organizations (local businesses and kindergartens), and increasing the range of teaching programs are used to enforce the corporate strategy.

In the marketing plan, more specific objectives, strategies, and tactics are developed, with an aim of aiding the school in achieving their corporate objectives. *The marketing objectives of Birralee Primary School are to increase the number of student enrollment from 185 in 1999 to 205 by the end of 2001,* and *to improve the school reputation among all the primary schools in the same region from a current rating of 2.73 to a rating of 3.5 by the end of 2001.* Several marketing strategies are used to obtain these objectives. They include promotional strategy of fund raising, sponsorship from local business and developing good relationship with local kindergartens, product strategy of introducing Asian language program, and place strategy of exploring new medium for information distribution. The tactics in achieving the strategies are carrying out two major fund-raising events per year (during March 2000 and 2001, and October 2000 and 2001), instead of several ones, drafting a proposal to seek sponsorship from local businesses, a visiting team formed to organize shared activities between Birralee and the kindergartens, applying for local subsidies from Community Development Grant Program through the Manningham City Council, and developing a Web site with general information of the school.

Once the marketing tactics and strategies are implemented in the year 2000 and 2001, they are expected to generate about $15,000 in projected income (mainly from the fund-raising events) and $11,800 in expenses, thus creating a surplus of $38,700 from the available fund of $35,500. Also, once the student enrollment increases, there is a possibility of an increase in the government funding of an unspecified amount.

1.0 STRATEGIC PLAN

1.1 Mission Statement

Birralee Primary School is committed to providing a quality education with a supportive, friendly, caring environment to enhance the students with a range of learning experiences and to develop their self-esteem, confidence, and independence.

1.2 Corporate Objectives

- To increase the school's market share (in terms of student number) from 5.46 percent (see Appendix 1) in 1998 to 6 percent by January 2002 (6 percent market share is a revised objective—refer to the gap analysis).

- To improve the school reputation among all the primary schools in the same region from a current rating of 2.73 to a rating of 3.5 by the end of 2002 (see Appendix 2—survey of the people in the area).

1.3 Situation Analysis

1.3.1 Market Size.   There were 1,694 primary schools in Victoria at February 1998, 24 fewer than in 1997. Most of the change in school numbers occurred in the government sector.[1]

Table 1   Number of Schools by School Type and Sector, Feb 1997–1998.

School Type	Government		Catholic		Independent		All schools	
	1997	1998	1997	1998	1997	1998	1997	1998
Primary Schools	1270	1253	386	384	62	57	1718	1694

1.3.2 Industry Segmentation.   Primary education offers students general information and prepares them for further education, and a valued role in society. The providers of primary school services include state and territory governments, Catholic dioceses, and other non-government schools (refer to Appendix 3).

---

[1] *Summary Statistics—Victoria School Feb. 1998,* Department of Education Victoria, 1998, p.5

1.3.3 *Industry Life Cycle*

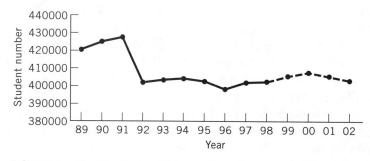

FIGURE 1   The Life Cycle of Primary School Industry in Victoria[2]

Primary education industry in Victoria is in mature phase (shown in Figure 1), for the following reasons:

- Number of primary school students is stable at a lower rate from 1992 to 1999 when compared to the trend from 1989 to 1991 (Figure 1).

- Average rate of the real growth in industry gross product for the whole Australia (2.1 percent in 1997–1998) (see Appendix 4), is below that of real growth in the general economy (the rate of growth in GDP is 4.7 percent in 1997–98).[3] It is assumed that this trend will be reflected in Victoria for a number of periods.

- The number of primary schools being established has been in a phase of decline. Over the five years to 1998, the number of primary schools in Victoria decreased by 1.17 percent on average (see Appendix 5).

- The population's demographics (a decline in the primary school-age students), combined with compulsory nature of the primary level education, impose a natural market limit.

1.3.4 Industry Attractiveness

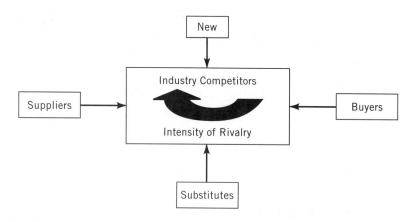

FIGURE 2   Porter's Five Forces Model

---

[2] *Summary Statistics—Victoria School Feb, 1998,* loc. cit. p. 12.
[3] *Australian Economic Indicators,* Australian Bureau of Statistics, July 1999, p. 22

Summary of industry attractiveness (refer to Appendix 6)

- The industry is not attractive due to the high intensity of competition.

- The government plays a central role in the industry.

- Despite the medium level of bargaining power by suppliers and buyers, the mature state of the industry, future availability of teaching staff, and low growth of the primary school students will affect the industry's well-being in the long run.

1.3.5 Driving Forces and Trends

- There is an increasing usage of technology-based teaching in the schools as more schools are using computers in the classrooms, as well as facilitating the work in the office.

- The movements in the level of mean gross weekly income (increase from $596 in 1994–95 to $625 in 1996–97)[4] affects parents' selection of non-government schools.

- Community perception of the quality and desirability of government, private, or church-associated education affects the parents' schools of choice.

- The number of primary schools enters into a decline phase due to government budgeting pressures, and consequent relationship of the education system. Over the five years to 1993, the number of government primary schools decreases by 1.6 percent overall.[5]

- The government's commitment to improve literacy and numeracy standards is set for a boost with the development of a new Curriculum and Standards Framework for Victorian schools, thus forcing primary schools to improve their teaching quality.

- Students moving to private schools because of the increased concern about perceived falling standards of government schools. The attendance rate in government primary schools is 70 percent in 1998.[6]

1.3.6 Critical Success Factors

- Location of the schools. Primary-aged children normally attend schools in close proximity to their homes. Therefore, schools need to be located in a geographical location within close proximity to large number of primary school-age children.

- Status and reputation of the schools. Schools with good reputation improve parents' perception and thus they are more likely to consider the schools as one of their choices. Status and reputation are directly related to the school's tradition, quality and level of teaching staff, facilities of the schools, educational programs, and other equipment.

- Adequate public relations and marketing skills. This is important to increase public awareness, attract students, and maintain a positive image of the schools.

- Number of students. There are economies of scale available to schools with larger student numbers. In Victoria, government schools with low student numbers need to be closed due to the limited government educational budget.

1.3.7 Main Customers of the Industry

- Mainly households with young children studying in kindergarten and reaching the age of primary education.

- The student population for primary schools is classified according to the age, level of schooling, religion, and genders.

---

[4] *Household Income,* www.abs.gov.au, 1998
[5] *IBIS Industry Report 1997–98, Small Business Victoria,* 1998, p.5
[6] Ibid.

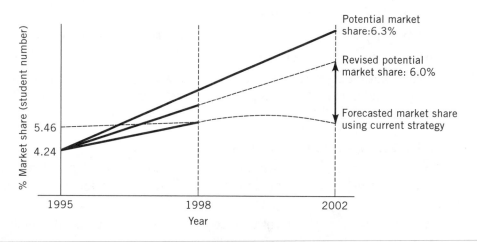

FIGURE 3   Gap Analysis for Birralee Primary School

1.3.8 Gap Analysis.   The gap analysis identified the gap between the revised potential market share and Birralee's projected market share (in terms of student number). The revised market share is obtained after conducting situation analysis of the school. The gap indicates huge opportunities for Birralee to grow and gain market share. Birralee has a desire to grow and increase their market share. However, due to the limited resources and captivity, which the organization has, Birralee needs to develop new strategies to attract more students.

1.3.9 Ansoff Matrix.   As for the old format, the school is adopting an existing product within the existing market strategy, which is dependent on the children reaching primary school age living within 500m of the Birralee School. The school currently wants to extend into the new market (area within 1 km of the school and with the increased Asian families in the region) and continuously attract children in the existing area to enroll in the school. Therefore, Birralee needs to develop the growth strategy in order to achieve this aim.

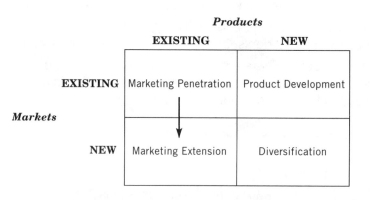

FIGURE 4   Ansoff Matrix Model for Birralee Primary School

1.3.10 Corporate strategy and tactics

Strategy

Birralee corporate strategy is to achieve the horizontal growth by expanding the school's market into a wider coverage area, as well as improved promotional activities to increase awareness and improve the school's reputation.

Tactics

- Target the promotional activities to new area of coverage (refer to Appendix 2).
- Foster good relationship with external organizations (local businesses and kinder-gartens) to increase awareness and reputation.
- Increase the range of teaching programs to attract more students.

1.3.11 Assumptions

- Children reaching the primary school age will go to primary schools in Victoria and not in other states. Therefore, it is assumed that the primary school industry in this marketing plan is Victorian industry.
- The plan considers only nine primary schools, which are considered to be direct competitors of Birralee.
- The latest ABS census data (1996) is assumed to be relevant in aiding our analysis and strategy formulation.

2.0 MARKETING PLAN

2.1 School Profile

The following table provides the general information for the Birralee Primary School:

Table 2 Birralee Primary School Profile

Birralee Primary School Profile	*Details*
Year of Establishment	• Established in 1971
Current Enrollment No.	• Currently has 185 students and will have a confirmed enrollment number of 190 students in the 1st semester of 2000
District	• Manningham district
Location	• Doncaster
Market Coverage Area	• Doncaster, Box Hill North and Balwyn North
Staff No.	• Currently has 15 teachers and administration staff
Facilities	• Playground, canteen, library, Art/Craft room, 2 computers with Internet access per classroom, sick bay, multi-purpose hall
Teaching Programs	• 8 major curriculum—English, Maths, Science, Technology, Health and Physical Education, Arts, Study of societies and environment, LOTE (Italian)
Other Programs' Activities	• Prep A program operates as a specialized program for young school-age children (from kindergarten to prep) who may not be mature enough to join the prep class
	• Art & craft lessons held for one hour per week for every grade. The areas of painting, drawing, printing, modeling, constructions, textiles, collage and art appreciation are covered in a developmental progression.

(continued)

Table 2   *(continued)*

Birralee Primary School Profile	*Details*
Other Programs' Activities (continued)	• Out-of-hours childcare is held at school from 7:15 A.M. to 8:45 A.M. and from 3:30 P.M. until 6:00 P.M. every weekday. Snacks and drinks are provided for children under the child-care services. • At least one exclusion is held per term. Other camping and exclusion programs may take place depending on circumstances. • Perceptual Motor program (PMP) is held for all children from Prep A to grade 2, with an aim to give children an opportunity to learn and develop confidence in the fundamental skills. • Swimming lessons are conducted at the Aquarena in either term 3 or 4 of each school year. • Tennis skills program is held for each grade once per fortnight within the school grounds. • Pastoral care services • Religious education • Annual school concert

2.2   Birralee Life Cycle

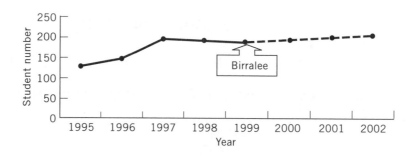

FIGURE 5   Birralee Primary School Life Cycle

An organisation is said to be in competitive turbulence stage if the sale is slowing down and profit per unit is declining. In the case of Birralee Primary School, our analysis shows that it is in this stage because (refer to Table 3):

• The growth rate from 1997 to 1998 is –1.56% as compared to the previous years (16.54 percent and 29.73 percent in 95–96 and 96–97, respectively).

• The 1999 and 2000 enrollment number is 185 and 190 students respectively (growth rate of –2.12 percent in 98–99 and 2.7 percent in 99–00), resulting in low growth rate compared to the previous years and the average growth rate.

2.3   Competitor Analysis

The schools listed below have been identified as the main competitors of Birralee Primary School.

Table 3   Analysis of School Enrolment

Name/Year	1995	1996	1997	1998	% change 95–96	% change 96–97	% change 97–98	Average growth rate (%)
Birralee Primary School	127	148	192	189	16.54	29.73	−1.56	14.9
Doncaster Garden Primary School	300	307	316	305	2.33	2.93	−3.48	0.59
Doncaster Primary School	303	342	410	480	12.87	19.88	17.07	16.61
Greythorn Primary School	498	502	486	519	0.80	−3.19	6.79	1.47
Templestowe Valley Primary School	189	181	165	191	−4.23	−8.84	15.76	0.89
Manningham Park Primary School	165	145	191	173	−12.12	31.72	−9.42	3.39
Anderson's Greek Primary School	352	354	377	409	0.57	6.50	8.49	5.18
Mont Albert Primary School	572	580	582	580	1.40	0.34	−0.34	0.47
Boroondara Park Primary School	290	306	373	400	5.52	21.90	7.24	11.55
Box Hill North Primary School	197	212	216	213	7.61	1.89	−1.39	2.70

Summary of data analysis from the table above:

- Birralee Primary School held a market share of 4.24 percent, 4.81 percent, 5.80 percent, and 5.46 percent in 1995, 1996, 1997, and 1998 respectively.

- Most of the schools experienced an increase in their enrollment number. A few schools experienced a slight decrease, including Birralee Primary School.

- In terms of average growth rate from 1995 to 1998, most schools experienced little growth in their level of enrollment. However, a few schools like Birralee have an average growth rate of 14.9 percent, which is second highest among the group.

For general information of the competitors, please refer to Appendix 7.

2.4   Birralee Customer Profile

- Households with low to medium income level, with young children aged 5+.[7]
- Living within the school suburb of approximately 10 minutes' drive.[8]

2.5   SWOT Analysis

Strength

- The children were taught in small classes, which allow individual students to receive more attention. Moreover, the smaller classes encourage better class interaction and reduce incidents of bullying and lack of attention from teachers.

- The school is located in a quiet neighborhood, which is conducive for learning.

Weaknesses

- The location of Birralee Primary School is isolated and not really accessible by public transport.

---

[7] *Interview with Sue Rathbone (Principal of Birralee Primary School),* on September 17, 1999.
[8] Ibid.

- The school lacks of sufficient facilities (such as computer laboratory and separate music room) to be perceived by potential parents as a high-quality school for their children.

Opportunities

- There is an increase in the number of Asian families who live in the area of Doncaster (about 7.1 percent of the residents in the Manningham district are of Asian origin) (see Appendix 8). They can be regarded as an untapped market for Birralee Primary School.

Threats

- There is a decreasing number of Italian families[9] (which is Birralee's "traditional customers") living in the area of Doncaster, thus affecting the enrollment number.
- The increase of elderly people living in the area of Doncaster (about 30 percent of the residents in the Manningham district are 50 years old and above, whereas the percentage of people under the age of 18 is only 23 percent) (see Appendix 8) means less primary-school-age students in the area.
- The trend for smaller families means fewer children for primary schools.
- Smaller family size and the increase in general level of disposable income means that more parents can afford to send their children to private schools instead of government schools like Birralee.

2.6 Financial Position

Table 4   Summary of Financial Position in Accordance to 1999 School Global Budget (see Appendix 9 for Full Details)

Annual Budget Expenses	*Amount ($$$)*	*%*
Leadership and Teaching	464,000	59.9
Teaching Support	69,000	8.9
Premises	39,000	5.0
On Costs	78,000	10.1
Disability and Impairment	63,000	8.1
English as Second Language	11,000	1.4
Priority Programs	51,000	6.6
Total School Global Budget	**775,000**	**100**

The budget shown is partially funded by the government. The school has to raise the remaining amount themselves, via voluntary donation in the form of school fee ($135 per student), local sponsorship, and various fund-raising activities (such as sausage sizzle and chocolate drive). The school generally spends about $500 per year on promotional activities, including brochures and advertisement in local newspapers.

---

[9] *Interview with Sue Rathbone, Kathy Sweeny and Rhonda Zerbi,* on September 17, 1999, September 24, 1999, and September 27, 1999, respectively.

2.7 GE Screening Grid

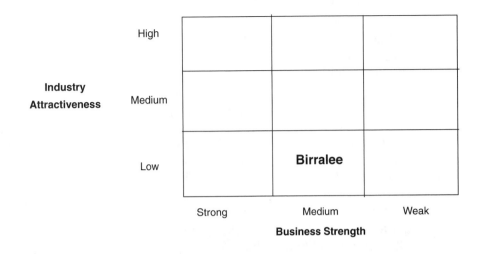

FIGURE 6   GE Screening Grid for Birralee Primary School

According to the analysis, industry attractiveness is low because:

- Unfavorable growth rate (see Appendix 5)
- High competitive intensity
- Extensive control by the government in terms of schools budgets and teaching curriculum.

Business strength is medium because:

- Small relative market share of 0.33 (see Appendix 1)
- High average growth rate (refer to Table 4)
- Strong customer loyalty from parents[10]

2.8   Marketing Objectives

- To increase the number of student enrollment from 185 in 1999 to 205 by the end of 2001.
- To improve the school reputation among all the primary schools in the same region from a current rating of 2.73 to a rating of 3.5 by the end of 2001 (see Appendix 2).

The marketing objectives are similar to the corporate objectives due to the small size of the organisation.

2.9   Marketing Strategy

Promotional strategy: to increase the school's public exposure (eventually its enrollment) via fund raising, sponsorship from local business and developing good relationship with local kindergartens.

---

[10] *Interview with Kathy Sweeny and Rhonda Zerbi,* on September 24, 1999 and September 27, 1999, respectively.

Product strategy: to introduce an Asian language program to attract students from an increasing number of Asian families living in the area as specified in the strategic plan.

Place strategy: to improve the distribution of information using new medium in order to disseminate information about the school quickly and effectively to existing and potential parents.

2.10   Marketing Program and Tactics

Fund Raising.   A fund-raising committee will be formed to organise two major fund-raising events per year (during March 2000 and 2001, and October 2000 and 2001). The nature of these events will be such that they involve greater participation from the public other than the school's population. Each event will incorporate different activities, which may include the existing ones, such as the Chocolate Drive, food stalls, and second-hand book sale. Kathy Sweeny will be in charge of the team, which is comprised of the new principal, Mr. Graham Gordon, members of Parents Committee, and all teachers. For each event, the estimated costs will be $5,000, and the projected income will be $7,500.

Sponsorship from Local Business.   A proposal should be drafted to seek sponsorship from local businesses. The project will involve all parents who will seek new contacts in exchange for "intangible rewards" from the school, such as publishing their names in the school's newsletter. Parents will be informed of the details in a "special" parents meeting, which will take place on November 1, 1999 at 7.30 P.M. (subject to change). Mr. Graham Gordon and Rhonda will be in charge of who will supervise the progress of the program. The details of the proposal should be finalised by October 25, 1999. Should the project succeed, the school will continue this with similar details in the year 2001.

Create a Good Relationship with the Local Kindergartens.   A number of local kindergartens are contacted to explore the opportunities of working together. A "visiting team" is formed to organise activities such as Buddy system between kindergarten students and students from Birralee Primary Schools, teachers promoting the school in the local kindergartens, and other shared activities. The team consists of teachers, and will be closely supervised by the school principal and Rhonda, especially in terms of objectives and details of this program. This program will take place several times during the year, starting from the beginning of the study term in 2000. The program will initially incur the cost of $300 including transport and promotional activities such as brochures. Any additional expenses will be revised in the near future.

Offer Asian Language Program.   The school applies for local subsidies from Community Development Grant Program 2000/2001 by the Manningham City Council (see Appendix 10 for the copy of the application form). The application is to be submitted by September 17, 2000 (subject to change by the Manningham City Council)

Prior to the approval of the applications, the members of the school board and the principal will meet and discuss plans to be conducted after the approval from Manningham City Council has been given. If this is the case, the language program will be introduced as early as the beginning of 2001.

Explore Other Mediums of Promotions.   The school develops a Web site with general information about the school and is updated regularly for any current events and policy changes. Any staff in the schools or parents who have the knowledge of creating a Web site and are willing to do the job voluntarily will be in charge of it. The Web site will be completed by the end of 1999. Brochures emphasizing the benefits of small school environment will be distributed to the households living in the school targeted area. Mr. Graham Gordon will prepare all the printing and distribution of the brochure before the start of study period in 2000. All distribution and printing costs will amount to $200.

For a summary of the marketing tactics and program, please refer to Appendix 11.

2.11 Budgeting

The financial budget for 2000/2001 is shown as follows:

		Year	
	2000	*2001*	*Total*
Available Fund			
Funds from: School Council Reserve	$5,000	$5,000	$10,000
Fund Raising	$4,000	$4,000	$8,000
Printing	$1,000	$1,500	$2,500
Advertising	$500	$500	$1,000
Telephone	$4,500	$4,500	$9,000
Copy Paper	$2,500	$2,500	$5,000
Total fund			**$35,500**
Projected Income			
Fund Raising	$7,500	$7,500	$15,000
Projected Expenditure			
Fund Raising	$5,000	$5,000	$10,000
Meeting Expenses (refer to section 2.10 – Sponsorship)	$100	$100	$200
Transportation and Promotional Kits (refer to Section 2.10 – Kindergarten)	$300	$300	$600
Promotion and Advertising	$500	$500	$1,000
Total Costs			**$11,800**
Surplus			**$38,700**

These budgets are subject to change according to the financial adjustments from the school.

2.12 Contingency Plan

If the current planning environment changes substantially during the life of this marketing plan, the following contingency plans will be considered.

- To pursue the stabilize strategy. Birralee can choose to maintain its operation, with the small number of student enrollment, and continue to serve the people within the school's distance.
- To pursue the harvest strategy. Birralee primary school should cease its operations due to the lack of competitive advantage and the poor fit with the future direction of the school.

2.13 Implementation

This marketing plan is to be presented by the planners (Welly Tehunan, Quah Suat Hong, and Vanessa Yau) to Ken Grant (acting as marketing advisor to Birralee Primary School) and the representatives of Birralee Primary School on October 18, 1999. The presentation will take place at Monash University, between 7 and 9 P.M.

Having heard the presentation, the school's representatives are to present the plan to the school board at the designated time and venue. The school board will further assess the plan on criteria such as availability of resources required to carry out the plan.

Assuming that the plan is approved, the school board will arrange a special meeting (a week after the school board meeting) with representatives from local kindergartens and small businesses, parents, and members of the Parents Committee. The aim is to communicate the plan to the participants and to obtain their feedback to be used for further improvement on the plan.

The planners can be contacted to assist the schools in any stage of the plan, especially in terms of answering questions and presenting the plan to the school board during the special meeting. We can be contacted at 03-95760182 and 0412182806.

2.14 Evaluation, Monitoring, and Control

Evaluation of the marketing plan will provide a feedback loop to the next marketing plan. This evaluation is the start and the end of the marketing plan. The evaluation can be used to find new opportunities and threats, keep performance in line with expectations, and also to solve specific problems that may occur.

A marketing audit will be conducted yearly to evaluate whether the plan still offers the best tactics. This will be conducted by the Program manager (the person in charge of each proposed strategy) in conjunction with the other staff members.

To ensure the marketing plan was implemented properly, it is to be monitored every six months. The monitoring process should take place in June 2000 and December 2000. The plan will be monitored by analysing the number of student enrollment received to study in the school. The enrollment number will be monitored every half yearly to ensure that it is increasing. A survey of parents and the people living within close proximity to the school is to be conducted to measure the effectiveness of the strategy (such as fund raising) and any change in the reputation of the school.

In addition, the school should conduct external analysis on the annual basis to detect any changes in the external environment (such as competitors and population demography).

BIBLIOGRAPHY

- Summary Statistics—Victoria School Feb. 1998, Department of Education Victoria, 1998
- Australian Economic Indicators, Australian Bureau of Statistics July 1999
- IBIS Industry Report 1997–98, Small Business Victoria, 1998

Internet Access
- Household Income, www.abs.gov.au, 1998

Personal Interview
- Interview with Sue Rathbone (Principal of Birralee Primary School), on September 17, 1999.
- Interview with Kathy Sweeny (President of the Community Relations Committee), September 24, 1999.
- Interview with Rhonda Zerbi (Vice President of the School Council), on September 27, 1999.

APPENDIXES

APPENDIX 1

Analysis of School Enrollment and Their Market Share

Name/Year	1998	% of Market Share	Relative Market Share
Birralee Primary School	189	5.46	0.33
Doncaster Garden Primary School	305	8.81	0.53
Doncaster Primary School	480	13.88	0.83
Greythorn Primary School	519	15	0.89
Templestowe Valley Primary School	191	5.52	0.33
Manningham Park Primary School	173	5	0.30
Anderson's Greek Primary School	409	11.82	0.71
Mont Albert Primary School	580	16.77	3.07
Boroondara Park Primary School	400	11.56	0.69
Box Hill North Primary School	213	6.16	0.37
Total	3459	100	———

Calculation of market share in percent:
   (Number of students in a particular school/Total number of students) $\times$ 100

Calculation of relative market share:
   (Number of students in a particular school/The number of students in the largest competitor's school)

APPENDIX 2

Summary of Survey

Likert scale:	**1**	**2**	**3**	**4**	**5**
	very poor	poor	average	good	very good

- 25 adults in the nearby area (see Appendix 11—the area within the orange line) were interviewed on September 20–21, 1999.

- 65 percent (17 people) of the interviewees are aware of the existence of large primary schools listed in Appendix 6 (those schools with more than 300 students). These schools tend to be more heavily advertised than smaller primary schools.

- When measured against the Likert scale, Birralee Primary School scored an average of 2.73 in terms of its general reputation.

- When asked about the things that determine good primary schools, the interviewees frequently mentioned three things: facilities of the schools, location of the school, and teaching standard. Birralee Primary School was ranked quite low in the first two because of its small size and the fact that the school is quite isolated.

- While the survey is not conclusive, it serves as an indication as to where the school currently stands in the public's perception.

APPENDIX 3

Segmentation of Primary School

(*Source: IBIS Industry Report 1997–1998. Small Business Victoria,* 1998)

a. Government Schools

These primary schools are established on the basis of population criteria, whose students' composition is determined by the local community profile. Ideally, this profile is the establishment of appropriate curriculum emphasis, and the budget allocation to different programs within the schools such as literacy and English as second language.

b. Catholic Schools

The Catholic education system is managed and run by National Catholic Education Commission, its state subsidiaries, and local Catholic dioceses. Most teachers in Catholic schools are now laypeople and many have no affiliation to Catholic faith.

c. *Other Non-Government Schools*

These schools may have religious affiliations, particularly Anglican, or be independent non-denominational schools. The larger other non-government schools tend to be old, well-established schools with excellent reputations and strong tradition.

APPENDIX 4

Real Growth for the Primary Education Industry in Australia (in $ term)

	'95–'96 (%)	'96–'97 (%)	'97–'98 (%)
Industry Turnover	3.4	2.5	2.1
Industry Gross Product	3.4	2.5	2.1
Employment	1.0	0.8	0.4
No. of Establishments	−0.3	−0.3	−0.4
Domestic Demand	3.4	2.5	2.1
Total Wages	3.4	2.5	2.1

Source: IBIS Industry Report 1997–98, Small Business Victoria, 1998.

APPENDIX 5

Estimation of Average Percent Change of Victoria Primary Schools Over the Past Five Years

School Type	Year				
	1994	1995	1996	1997	1998
Primary (All Primary Schools)	1776	1750	1741	1718	1694
Percent Change	N/A	−1.46	−0.51%	−1.32	−1.40

Source: Summary Statistics Victoria Schools 1994–1998, Department of Education.

- According to the table above, the average percent change of the number of primary schools in Victoria is calculated as follows:

$$-(1.46\% + 0.51\% + 1.32\% + 1.40\%)/4 = -1.1725\%$$

APPENDIX 6

Porter's Five Forces

Threat of New Entrants: Low

- The cost of facilities and equipment is high.
- Each school must attract sufficient number of students to achieve economic viability.
- Each school must have high-quality teaching and other staff to attract students' enrollment.
- The tradition and reputation of existing schools are already established and long lasting.
- The government restricts the establishments of new primary schools, and thus more difficult to obtain government funding.

Bargaining Power of Suppliers: Medium to High

- The government plays an important role in the industry, since it provides the guidelines for teaching and administration. This is even the case with the government schools, since the government allocates funds for each school.
- For each type of suppliers (see Appendix 13), primary schools are able to choose the services from a number of services. Thus, the switching cost is low.

Bargaining Power of Buyers: Medium

- Parents are able to choose from a number of primary schools within a particular area. For example: there are 16 primary schools within the Manningham District in Victoria to choose from (see Appendix 12).
- The switching cost is high due to the time, money, and effort involved in getting a new school for students.

Availability of Substitutes: Low

- There is almost no substitute for primary educating due to its compulsory nature.

Intensity of Rivalry: High

- A large number of schools are competing within the same region. As mentioned earlier, 16 primary schools are competing with each other within the Manningham District
- Exit barrier is high since it involves large investment in the schools, as well as its reputation and tradition.

Other Factors to Consider

- Primary education industry is in a mature stage, with the number of schools established decreasing (growth rate of −0.3% in 1995–1996, to −0.4% in 1997–1998), as well as the domestic demand for primary school (growth rate of 3.4 percent in 1995–1996, to 2.1 percent in 1997–1998). (See Appendix 4.)
- There is a possibility that the growth prospects of the industry may be hampered by the availability of teaching staff. A study conducted for university deans of education predicts that there will be a shortage of 4,700 primary and secondary teachers nationally by the year of 2000.
- The rate of growth in the population of primary school students in Australia is low (an average rate of 0.55 percent per year) compared to the growth in the overall percent population (1.3 percent per year), due mainly to a declining female fertility rate, an aging population, and high elder immigration to Australia.[1]

---

[1] *IBIS Industry Report, Small Business Victoria,* 1997–1998.

APPENDIX 7

Major Competitors Profile

- Nine schools are identified as the major competitors to the Birralee Primary School. All these schools are located in three different districts, namely Boroondara District, Manningham District, and Whitehorse District.

School in Boroondara District

Name (Primary School)	Boroondara Park Primary School	Greythorn Primary School
Year of Establishment	1989	1953
Current Enrollment No.	400	519
Location	North Balwyn	North Balwyn
Facilities	• Extensive playing fields	• School hall
	• 2 large ovals	• Computerised library
	• Performance/Arts department	• Well-equipped gym
	• Air-conditioned and portable classroom	• Uniform and swap shop
	• Computer room	
	• Computerised library	• French room
	• Recreation hall/gymnasium	• Extensive outdoor play areas
	• Art room	• Art room
	• Open, airy classroom	• Canteen
	• Canteen	
Teaching Programs	• 8 major curriculum	• 8 major curriculum
		• LOTE (French)
Other Activities	• Educational enhancement	• Christian religious education
	• Cultural and artistic programs	• After-school care program
	• Sporting and leisure programs	• Camp and exclusion
	• Leadership and decision-making programs	• House system
	• Pastoral care and concealing programs	
	• Religious activities and services	
	• Camps and exclusion	

Schools in Whitehorse District

Name (Primary School)	Box Hill North Primary School	Mont Albert Primary School
Year of Establishment	N/A	1917
Current Enrollment No.	213	580
Location	Box Hill North	Mont Albert
Facilities	• Library	• Library
	• Canteen	• Art room
	• Playground	• Performing art centre
	• Computer lab	• Canteen
		• Computer centre
		• Hall
Teaching Programs	• 8 major curriculum	• 8 major curriculum
		• LOTE (Italian)
Other Activities	• After-school care program	• After-school care program
	• Religious education program	• Reading recovery program
		• Art/craft studies
		• Music/drama studies
		• Swimming program
		• Camping and touring program
		• Gifted and talented student program
		• Teacher-student relationship meeting

Schools in Manningham District

Name (Primary School)	Andersons Creek Primary School	Doncaster Gardens Primary School	Doncaster Primary School	Manningham Park Primary School	Templestowe Valley Primary School
Year of Establishment	N/A	N/A	1860	N/A	N/A
Current Enrollment No.	409	305	480	173	191
Location	Warrandyte	Doncaster East	Doncaster	Lower Templestow	Lower Templestow
Facilities	• Full-size breakfast stadium • Computer labs • Computerised library • Playground • Canteen	• Computer labs • Computerised library • Playground • Canteen • Library	• 100-seat theatre • Full-size gymnasium • Basketball courts • Music room • Art/craft Centre • Extensive playground • Full-size oval • Computer lab • Canteen	• Video conferencing facilities • Art room • Fully computerised library • 300-seat hall • General purpose room • Canteen	• Computer lab • Library • Canteen • Language room • Playground
Teaching Programs	• 8 major curriculum • LOTE (Italian)	• 8 major curriculum	• 8 major curriculum • LOTE (Chinese)	• 8 major curriculum • LOTE (Japanese/Italian)	• 8 major curriculum
Other Activities	• After-school child care program • Early years literacy intervention program • Reading recovery program • Buddy system	• After-school care program • Dancing class • Singing class • Drama and musical performance • Buddy system	• After-school care program • Visual Arts studies • Student welfare and discipline program • Reading recovery program • Media Studies • Drama class • Instrumental music program • Instrumental music program • Cultural Awareness program • Study enrichment programs • Swimming program • Religious Education program	• After-school care program • Individualised Special needs program • Parents and friends club • Perceptual motor program	• Big Friends/Little Friends program • After-school care program • Camping program • House system

APPENDIX 8

Statistics of Population and Housing in Manningham District

According to the Australian Bureau of Statistics Census of Population and Housing 1996 the estimate percentage of Asian residents in Manningham District is calculated as follows:

$$2\% \text{ (China)} + 2.8\% \text{ (Hong Kong)} + 2\% \text{ (Malaysia)}$$
$$+ 0.3\% \text{ (Vietnam)} = 7.1\%$$

The percentage of elder people is calculated as follows:

$$14.7\% \text{ (Age 50–59)} + 8.5\% \text{ (Age 60–69)}$$
$$+ 5.6\% \text{ (Age 70–84)} + 1.2\% \text{ (Age 85+)} = 30\%$$

The percentage of people under 17 years old is calculated as follows:

$$5.2\% \text{ (Age 0–4)} + 17.8\% \text{ (Age 5–17)} = 23\%$$

- The chart below shows the trend of the 9 primary schools' enrollment numbers from 1995–98

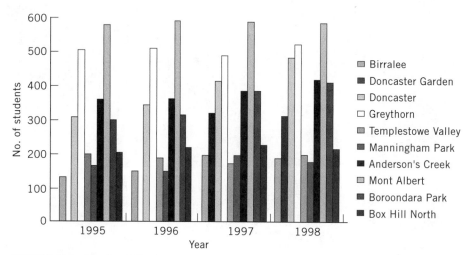

FIGURE A8.1   Enrolment Number
Source: Summary Statistics Victoria Schools 1995–98

APPENDIX 9

1999 School Global Budget

MEMORANDUM

TO: Principals and Head Teachers
General Managers (Schools)

FROM: B J Beaumont, General Manager
School Personnel and Resources

SUBJECT: **CONFIRMED 1999 SCHOOL GLOBAL BUDGETS**

DATE: 8 April 1999

Please find enclosed the confirmed 1999 School Global Budget (SGB) for your school. The Principal Classification Budget and principal class entitlements for 1999 are also included.

As usual, the confirmed SGB is based on enrolments as per the February census. Revisions resulting from new information, such as enrolment audits, will be issued periodically to affected schools.

An updated *Guide to the 1999 School Global Budget* is being issued separately to all schools. The Guide outlines the major changes reflected in the confirmed SGB. The changes have also been highlighted in the covering memo to the Guide.

In addition, allocations are included in the confirmed SGB for the Victorian Early Years Literacy Program for all Primary schools which completed an Early Literacy plan.

CASES reports will reflect the confirmed SGB from pay 9822.

Contact telephone numbers for enquiries are included in the *Guide to the School Global Budget.*

for B J BEAUMONT
General Manager
School Personnel and Resources

DEPARTMENT OF EDUCATION
SCHOOL GLOBAL BUDGET
1999 CONFIRMED-SUMMARY

Budget Version: 2   **Version Date: 09/04/1999**

                                         Version Time: 16:28:42

Host School: 4991   **Birralee Primary School**   **Total Enrollment:**   186.0

Region: 33   School Type: Primary

Enrolment P-2:   95.0   Enrolment 3–6:   91.0   Primary Ungraded: 0.0   **Total Primary:**   186.0

Enrolment 7–10   0.0   Enrolment 11–12   0.0   Secondary Ungraded: 0.0   **Total Secondary:**   0.0

Summary

Total Core	$650,633.35
Total Disability and Impairment	$63,478.00
Total English as a Second Language	$10,882.00
Total Priority Programs	$51,079.80
TOTAL SCHOOL GLOBAL BUDGET	**$776,073.15**
Notional Cash Allocation	$87,847.10
Notional Credit Allocation	$688,226.05

PRINCIPAL CLASSIFICATION BUDGET

TOTAL SCHOOL GLOBAL BUDGET	776,073.15
WorkCover:	−462.25
Superannuation Charge:	−44,955.00
Principal Class Salary Variation	13,168.08
Principal Classification Budget	743,823.98

PRINCIPAL CLASSIFICATION ENTITLEMENT

Range   645,750.00–819,000.00   Principal Class IIB   Assistant Principal Class IA   Asst Prin Entitlement   100

The 1999 Principal Classification Budget is calculated by adjusting the School Global Budget to exclude workcover and superannuation

A further adjustment, the Principal Class Salary Variation, represents two factors:

The increase or decrease in principal class salary entitlements that would result in the event of these positions being vacated where the encumbent position differs from the new entitlement

A correction factor, which enables principal class positions in schools which have a total PCB near the top of a PCB range to be automatically classified according to the next highest range

DEPARTMENT OF EDUCATION
SCHOOL GLOBAL BUDGET
1999 CONFIRMED-SUMMARY

Budget Version: 2

Version Date: 09/04/1999

Version Time: 16:28:42

Host School: 4991   **Birralee Primary School**   **Total Enrollment:** 186.0

Region: 33   School Type: Primary

| Enrolment P-2: | 95.0 | Enrolment 3–6: | 91.0 | Primary Ungraded: | 0.0 | **Total Primary:** | 186.0 |
| Enrolment 7–10 | 0.0 | Enrolment 11–12 | 0.0 | Secondary Ungraded: | 0.0 | **Total Secondary:** | 0.0 |

School: 4991   Birralee Primary School   TYPE: Primary

Particulars	Type	EFT/SQ.M STUDENT	RATE	AMOUNT $
SLN-Index: 0.569	Location_Index: 0:00	Expenses Code		
Core				
Leadership and Teaching				
Principal Class I	Credit	1.00	$57,925.00	$57,925.00
Assistant Principal Class IA	Credit	1.00	$57,925.00	$57,925.00
Leading Teachers – Level 2	Credit	1.00	$51,731.00	$51,731.00
Level 1 Teachers	Credit	6.00	$45,400.00	$272,400.00
Performance Incentives & Special Payments	Credit	0.00	$0.00	$11,544.00
Core – Primary Relief Teacher	Cash	9.00	$1,430.90	$12,878.10
				$464403.10
Teaching Support				
Teaching Support – Credit	Credit	0.00	$0.00	$35,992.86
Teaching Support – Cash	Cash	0.00	$0.00	$29,572.51
Literacy Allocation	Cash	186.00	$20.00	$3,720.00
				$6928.37
Premises				
Contract Cleaning – Normal Use (sq.m)	Cash	897.00	$16.70	$14,979.90
Contract Cleaning – Low Use (sq.m)	Cash	504.00	$3.45	$1,738.80
Grounds Allowance (sq.m)	Cash	19,576.00	$0.16	$3,132.16
Utilities	Cash	0.00	$0.00	$10,340.96
Maintenance and Minor Works Funding	Cash	0.00	$0.00	$8,915.87
				$39,107.69
On Costs				
WorkCover Premium	Credit	0.00	$0.00	$462.25
Revised/New Scheme Superannuation Charge	Credit	9.00	$4,995.00	$44,955 00
Core – Payroll Tax (%)	Credit	487,517.86	$6.65	$32.419 94
				$77,837.19
Total Core				$650,633.35

(continued)

DEPARTMENT OF EDUCATION
SCHOOL GLOBAL BUDGET
1999 CONFIRMED-SUMMARY

Budget Version: 2

Version Date: 09/04/1999

Version Time: 16:28:42

Host School: 4991
Region: 33

Birralee Primary School
School Type: Primary

Total Enrollment: 186.0

Enrolment P-2:	95.0	Enrolment 3–6:	91.0	Primary Ungraded:	0.0	**Total Primary:** 186.0
Enrolment 7–10	0.0	Enrolment 11–12	0.0	Secondary Ungraded:	0.0	**Total Secondary:** 0.0

School: 4991   Birralee Primary School   TYPE: Primary

Particulars	Type	EFT/SQ.M STUDENT	RATE	AMOUNT $
SLN-Index: 0.569	Location_Index: 0:00	Expenses Code		
Disability and Impairment				
New Integration Students – Level 2	Credit	0.00	$0.00	$8,530.00
New Integration Students – Level 4	Credit	0.00	$0.00	$54,948.00
Total Disability and Impairment				63.478.00
English as a Second Language				
ESL – Level 1	Credit	28.00	$264.00	$7,392.00
ESL – Level 2	Credit	5.00	$340.00	$1,700.00
ESL – Level 3	Credit	3.00	$422.00	$1,266.00
ESL – Level 4	Credit	1.00	$524.00	$524.00
Total English as a Second Language				$10,882.00
Priority Programs				
LOTE Allocation	Credit	0.00	$0.00	$13,950.00
Literacy Coordination	Credit	0.00	$0.00	$16,758.00
Reading Recovery	Credit	0.00	$0.00	$17,803.00
Teacher Professional Development	Cash	0.00	$0.00	$2,568.80
Total Priority Programs				$51,079.80
School Total				$776,073.15

APPENDIX 10

Copy of Community Development Grant Program

MANNINGHAM
BALANCE OF CITY AND COUNTRY

COMMUNITY DEVELOPMENT GRANT PROGRAM 1999/00
Application Form

Please read the *Community Development Grant Program Guidelines* prior to applying for funding. Applicants are required to complete each section. Please attach additional information if required. Typed applications are preferred. Faxed and late applications *will not* be accepted.

An information session will be held 6.30pm – 7.30pm on
Thursday 26 August, 1999
"THE FUNCTION ROOM"
MANNINGHAM CITY COUNCIL
699 Doncaster Road
Doncaster Vic 3108

Closing date for applications is 5.00pm Friday 17 September, 1999

SECTION 1 – ORGANIZATION DETAILS

1.1　Organization Name . . . .

1.2　Contact Person . . . .

1.3　Address . . . .

　　　Postcode . . . .

1.4　Telephone Number. . . . . Facsimile Number . . . .

1.5　Names and Positions of Principal Office Bearers . . . .

　　　. . . . .

　　　. . . . .

　　　. . . . .

1.6　Is the organization incorporated? Yes/No　　　Registration Number . . . .

1.7　If the organization is **not** Incorporated, which organization will auspice your organization? . . . . .

　　　. . . . .

　　　Registration Number . . . .

1.8   Purpose of your organization

SECTION 2 – APPLICATION SUMMARY

2.1   Name of Project/Program . . . .

2.2   Total Amount of Funding Requested $ . . . .

SECTION 3 – PROJECT/PROGRAM INFORMATION

3.1   Description of Project/Program.
In this section please provide the following information about the project/program:
- Description.
- Commencement and completion dates.
- Location.
- Target Group/s.
- Expected number of participants.
- Other organization/groups who will be involved in your activity *(explain how they will be involved)*.

3.2   Objectives of the Project/Program.

3.3   List three expected outcomes of the project/program *(the outcomes need to be specific, achievable and measurable).*

SECTION 4 – FINANCIAL INFORMATION

Supplied

4.1   Please supply a copy of your organizations last audited financial statement.   **Yes/No**

4.2   Has other financial assistance been sought for this project/program?   **Yes/No**
If yes, please give details. This may include sponsorship or government funding.

4.3   Have you received funding from Council in the last three years?   **Yes/No**
If yes, please give details.

4.4   Program/Project Budget:

(A)   Income – list all sources and amounts of income (including anticipated income) for example: donations, fees, charges, grants, organization contributions. [Income (A) and Expenditure (B) must balance]

Source	**Amount**
....	$ ....
....	$ ....
....	$ ....
....	$ ....
....	$ ....
....	$ ....
....	$ ....
....	$ ....
....	$ ....
.... Total Income	$ ....

(B)   Expenditure – list all costs of the program/project. [Income (A) and Expenditure (B) must balance]

Item of Expenditure	**Amount**
....	$ ....
....	$ ....
....	$ ....
....	$ ....
....	$ ....
....	$ ....
....	$ ....
....	$ ....
....	$ ....
.... Total Income	$ ....

Total Amount of funding requested from Council $ ....

4.5   **Organizations Contribution**
Applicants must demonstrate their contribution to the project. Please list all non-financial contributions, for example: volunteer hours, facilities or equipment. (Financial contributions should be included in 4.4 (A)).

....

....

....

....

....

4.5   I hereby apply for funding through the *Community Development Grant Program* on behalf of:

Organization:...

Signed:..

Position: ....

Date: ....

CLOSING DATE FOR APPLICATIONS IS 5.00PM FRIDAY 17 SEPTEMBER 1999

Send applications to:

Customer Service Officer
Cultural and Leisure Services Unit
MANNINGHAM CITY COUNCIL
PO Box 1
DONCASTER VIC 3108

MANNINGHAM
BALANCE OF CITY AND COUNTRY

If you have any queries please contact:
Customer Service Officer
Telephone: 9840 9393

Manningham City Council
COMMUNITY DEVELOPMENT GRANT PROGRAM
FUNDING GUIDELINES 1999/00

Introduction

The *Community Development Grant Program* is conducted annually by Council in recognition of the importance and value of community development in the City of Manningham. This is reflected in the *Corporate Plan 1998–2001,* which states:

- *Culture and Leisure.* Promote, facilitate and provide a diverse range of quality cultural and leisure facilities, programs and services, based on community development principles, to residents of and visitors to the City of Manningham which enhance cultural heritage, quality of life, community development and healthy lifestyles.

- *Social and Community Services.* Facilitate the equitable distribution of a range of diverse, quality social and community services to all sections of the community by maximising the use of available resources and encouraging community activity based on community principles.

- *Health and Well-Being.* Promote and support the optimum physical, psychological and emotional health and well-being of the community.

Council has allocated **$68,525** for the 1999/00 *Community Development Grant Program.* Grants are offered **once** a year.

Information about other Council grant programs is available on request.

Purpose

The purpose of the *Community Development Grant Program* is to facilitate and support non-profit community organisations in the City of Manningham to develop projects and programs which benefit and meet the needs of the community.

Objectives

The objectives of the Community Development Grant Program are to:

- Strengthen community identity, promote Manningham and Manningham City Council through a diverse range of projects and programs.

- Facilitate opportunities to participate in a broad range of activities which promote community development, for example in the areas of:
  - community service
  - leisure and recreation
  - arts, culture and heritage
  - welfare
  - information
  - health
  - education
  - environmental education and interpretation
  - natural heritage

- Support community projects and programs that address demonstrated needs in specific areas, for example: people with disabilities, people of non English speaking backgrounds (NESB) and from specific ethnic populations, and Aboriginal and Torres Strait Islanders.

- Promote and integrate environmentally sustainable practices.

- Encourage the innovative and effective use of community resources.

- Reflect and promote the cultural richness and diversity of the City of Manningham, including the heritage and environmental qualities.

- Support and encourage community organisations to develop partnerships and networks with fellow agencies, businesses, schools and local government, thereby enhancing the sense of community and effective use of resources.

- Provide opportunities for the development of a range of skills through the management and participation in projects and programs.

Eligibility

- Applicants must make and demonstrate their financial and non financial contribution to the project or program, for example: staff resources, volunteer hours, funds, facilities, equipment, sponsorship or donations.

- The project or program must be located within the City of Manningham.

- Preference will be given to applications from organisations located within the City of Manningham.
- Priority will be given to cooperative ventures between two or more community organisations.
- Organisations must be non profit and incorporated. If the organisation is not incorporated it must be auspiced by another organisation that is incorporated (this arrangement must be confirmed by written agreement).
- Preference will be given to applications that demonstrate effective planning (including financial planning and sustainable practices), clear objectives and evaluation processes.
- Funds will only be allocated for direct program or project costs, for example:
  - materials
  - workers costs (not ongoing salaries)
  - advertising & promotion
  - venue rental
  - equipment/equipment hire
  - transport

Eligibility Exclusions

The following will **not** be considered eligible:

- Capital works.
- Ongoing costs eg. staff salaries, administration, maintenance.
- Applicants who have not met the requirements of previous grants from Council, for example: have not completed the evaluation forms or acknowledged Council support in publicity and promotion.
- Organisations who request funding for a program or project that is the responsibility of other levels of government.
- Community organisations who already receive Council funds to undertake a specific activity for which funding is being sought.
- Programs or projects that are seen as a duplication of existing programs or projects in the municipality.

Assessment

- An independent Assessment Panel consisting of: a Councilor, representatives from relevant Council Advisory Committees and appropriately skilled community representatives, will assess applications and allocate funds. The Assessment Panel will consist of a maximum of six people.
- Council Officer/s will provide advice to the Assessment Panel.
- Assessment Panel members must declare any pecuniary interest.

- The Assessment Panel reserves the right to recommend the transfer of an application to a more appropriate grant program.

Conditions of Grant

Grants are allocated to community organisations from the *Community Development Grant Program* according to the following conditions:

- Programs and projects will not be funded retrospectively.
- Funds will be allocated **once** a year.
- Only one application per community organisation/project will be considered in any year. Therefore any organisations jointly applying for funds should submit only one application.
- Acknowledge Manningham City Council in all promotional material including: media, programs, flyers, advertisement, billboards and banners etc. The Council logo must be reproduced according to the corporate style guide, which is available from the Marketing Unit.
- Utilise funding only for the stated purpose.
- Allocation of funds to a community organisation for any purpose, in any funding round, must not be taken as a commitment of subsequent funding.
- The recipients of the *Community Development Grant Program* shall take out, and keep current a liability insurance policy in a form approved by Council, in the joint names of the Manningham City Council and the recipient for a minimum sum of $5 million (or more), insuring Council and the recipient against all actions, costs, claims, charges, expenses, and damages whatsoever which may be brought or made or claimed against them arising out of, or in relation to, the said activity. The policy shall also contain a cross liability clause.
- Programs and projects must be completed within twelve months of funding, unless an alternative written agreement has been reached with the Cultural Development Officer.
- Within two months of completing the program or project an evaluation report must be submitted on the supplied form, incorporating a financial statement of income and expenditure of the total project or program.
- Grant recipients are required to sign a proforma agreeing to the above *Conditions of Grant* prior to receiving the grant.
- Grants will be paid by cheque.
- If funding is not utilized for the stated purpose, the organisation receiving the funding must guarantee repayment in full, plus interest earned.
- Funding must be deposited and maintained in a Bank approved by Council and not invested outside

that Bank without written approval. (List supplied with *Conditions of Grant.*)

- Grant recipients must be willing (on request) to supply a complete copy of the program/project, accounts/books for examination by the Council auditor.

Applications

- An information session for intending applicants will be held:

**THURSDAY
26 August 1999
6.30–7.30 pm
in the Function Room
Municipal Offices
699 Doncaster Road,
Doncaster 3108**

It is recommended that all potential applicants, particularly first time applicants, attend this session.

- *Community Development Grant Program* Application Forms are available from the Cultural and Leisure Services Unit or the Social and Community Services Unit, Manningham City Council.

- If you require an application package, further information or assistance in completing your application please contact:

**Cultural and Leisure Services Unit
or
Social and Community Services Unit
MANNINGHAM CITY COUNCIL
699 Doncaster Road
DONCASTER VIC 3108
9840-9393
9840-9269
9840-9426
9840-9257**

- Application packages are available by Email on request.
- Upon request Funding Guidelines will be available in community languages.

**Applications close
at 5.00pm**

FRIDAY 17 SEPTEMBER 1999

Applications will not be accepted after this date.

All applications must be on the designated application form.

Faxed applications will not be accepted.

Schedule

- Advertise the availability of the grants week beginning 16 August 1999.
- Information session conducted 6.30–7.30pm, Thursday 26 August 1999.
- Applications close 5.00pm Friday 17 September 1999.
- Applications will be assessed and funds allocated by mid November 1999.
- Applicants advised of the outcome of their applications at the end of November 1999.
- Signing of agreements to grant conditions and distributions of grants during December 1999.
- *The schedule may be affected by the number of applications and vary accordingly.*

G:\QADOCS\COMSERV\CLSERV\CAL1070
Thursday, August 12, 1999

APPENDIX 11

Summary of the Strategy and Tactics

Strategy	Aim	Action Plan	Person-In-Charge	Time	Cost
Conduct fund-raising activities	• To raise public awareness of the school • To increase fund to finance additional school activities and improve existing facilities	• Fund-raising committee will be formed to organise 2 major fund-raising events per year, instead of several ones. The nature of these events will be such that they involve greater participation from the public other than the school's population. • Each event will incorporate different activities which may include the existing ones, such as the Chocolate Drive, food stalls, and second books selling, etc.	• Kathy Sweeny will be in charge of the team. • The fund-raising committee will consist of the principal, Mr. Graham Gordon, members of Parents Committee and all teachers.	• The fund-raising events will occur twice a year: during March 2000 and 2001, and October 2000 and 2001.	• For each event, the estimated costs will be $5,000, and the projected income will be $7,500.
Sponsorship from local businesses	• To increase fund to finance additional school activities and improve existing facilities • To raise public awareness of the school	• A proposal should be drafted to seek sponsorship from local businesses. • All parents will be involved to seek new contacts in exchange of "intangible rewards," such as publishing their names in the school's newsletter. • Parents will be informed of the details in "special" parents' meeting.	• Mr. Graham Gordon and Rhonda will be in charge. • Mr. Gordon and Rhonda, with the help of parents' committee member, will be following up on the developments of each participating parent.	• The details of the proposal should be finalised by October 25, 1999. • The parents meeting will take place on November 1, 1999 at 7.30 P.M. (subject to change). • Should the project succeed, the school will continue this with similar details in 2001.	• Beverages (tea and coffee) and stationaries for the meeting: $60.

Create good relationship with the local kindergartens	• Create a good working relationship with the local kindergartens. • To increase awareness of the school among the "potential students."	• A number of local kindergartens are contacted to explore the opportunities of working together. • A "visiting team" is formed to organise activities such as Buddy system between kindergarten students and students from Birralee Primary Schools, teachers promoting the school in the local kindergartens, and other shared activities.	• The school principal and Rhonda will be supervising this activity in terms of objectives and details of this program. • The "visiting team' will consist of teachers.	• This program will occur several times during the year, starting from the start of study term, and right throughout the year 2001.	• $300 including transport, promotional
Offer Asian language program	• To attract potential students from the Asian families living in the area. • To improve the prestige of the school.	• The school applies for local subsidies from Community Development Grant Program 2000/2001 by the Manningham City Council (see **Appendix 10**). • The discussed plan will be adjusted accordingly once the subsidy is granted.	• The details of the program will be discussed among the members of the school board and the principal.	• The application should be submitted by 17 September, 2000 (subject to change by the Manningham City Council) • If successful, the language program will be introduced as early as the beginning of 2001.	• No projected costs at this point of time.
Explore other mediums of promotions	• To increase the awareness of the school • To improve the perception (technology advanced) of the schools from the community.	• Develop a Web site with general information about the school, and update regularly for any currently events and policy changes. • Brochures emphasising the benefits of small school environment are distributed to local household's letterbox. • Publication in the local newspaper should be maintained and continued.	• Any staff in the school who has the knowledge to develop the Web site will be in charge of it. If not, ask for the help from parents who have the knowledge and volunteer to do it. • Mr. Graham Gordon will be in charge of all the printing and distribution of the brochure, and of the publication in the local newspaper.	• The Web site should be competed by the end of 1999. • Distribution of brochures and publication in local newspaper will be carried out before the start of the study period in 2000 and will continue throughout the whole year.	• No obvious fee for setting up a Web site. There is considerable free Web hosting in the Internet. • $200 including printing, distribution costs, etc.

APPENDIX 12

Schools in Manningham District of Victoria
(Source: Victorian Government Schools, *www.softweb.vic.edu.au schools melbdist.htm,* 1998)

- Andersons Creek Primary School
- Beverley Hills Primary School
- Birralee Primary School
- Bulleen Heights Schools
- Donburn Primary School
- Doncaster Garden Primary School
- Doncaster Primary School
- Doncaster Secondary College
- Manningham Park Primary School
- Milgate Primary School
- Park Orchards Primary School
- Serpell Primary School
- Templestowe College
- Templestowe Heights Primary School
- Templestowe Park Primary School
- Warrandyte High School
- Warrandyte Primary School
- Wonga Park Primary School

APPENDIX 13

Suppliers for the Primary Schools
(Source: *IBIS Industry Report 1997–98. Small Business Victoria,* 1998)

Preschool education
- Suppliers of potential students for primary schools

Government administration
- Provides guidelines, budgets, and teaching curriculum

Electronic equipment manufacturing
- Provide schools with the necessary laptops, computers, and photocopier to aid the teaching of the students

Newspaper, books and stationery retailers
- Provide publicity, the necessary textbooks, teaching materials, and office equipment

Non-residential building constructions
- Provide building construction for the schools

Childcare services
- Provide child care for busy parents whose children are left in the schools

---

APPENDIX 14

Criteria for Choosing Primary Schools
(Source: *IBIS Industry Report 1997–98, Small Business Victoria,* 1998)

Each parent has a different set of criteria for making a decision in their choice of their children's primary schools. Below are the common factors that affect their decisions.

- Convenience of the location of primary schools.
- The quality of teaching staffs and programs.
- The quality of facilities and equipment in the schools.
- The proximity of the primary schools to the desired secondary schools. Some primary schools may compete with combined primary and secondary schools which can provide continuity of education.
- The reputation, tradition, and status of the schools.
- The cost of education, which is influenced by the level of government funding to non-government schools, and the extent of extra facilities and opportunities provided by the schools. Catholic-affiliated schools tend to receive higher government grants, and charge significantly lower fees than other non-government primary schools.
- The schools' religious affiliation.
- The degree of promotional activities being conducted to increase parents' awareness of the schools' existence.

A6

RESOLVE OF GREATER LOS ANGELES

Developed by
CATHERINE HOUWEN
DOUGLAS JERIC
OLUFEMI TALBOTT
ANTHONY TIRONA

Contents

EXECUTIVE SUMMARY

Infertility can be a devastating experience. It could change every aspect of a couple's life. The need for compassionate support and information for couples who are exploring family planning options due to infertility is very real. Yet, most of the attention is focused on the physical aspects of infertility. The emotional aspects often go unnoticed and are untreated. Because fertility is a private and personal issue, many couples do not share this experience openly with friends and family. Consequently, they may experience and suffer intensely while feeling uncertain about their options.

Resolve of Greater Los Angeles fills this need by offering compassionate support and providing information to help cope with this dilemma. Couples and single people are able to face their fears and find a way to resolve their issues through usage of the services offered by Resolve.

In the Greater Los Angeles area, the population is very dense and diversified. At this time, Resolve has attracted the upper middle-class white population to use their services. The interest of the chapter is to expand into the other market segments within the county. Before this can be realized, Resolve of Greater Los Angeles needs to first stabilize their volunteer forces, then, look for new pools of potential volunteers and/or members. Some restructuring of their operations will help in efficiency. In this marketing plan, there are steps provided on how to market existing activities and ideas on how to expand the resources to adopt new activities.

Consistency in delivering loving care to couples on the emotional roller coaster of infertility is the goal of Resolve's service business.

INTRODUCTION

What Is Resolve's Purpose?

Resolve is a national, nonprofit consumer organization with this mission: "To provide timely, compassionate support and information to people who are experiencing infertility and to increase awareness of infertility issues through advocacy and public education."[1]

Their goals are to provide compassionate support and information about infertility to couples who are experiencing infertility. This occurs from the onset of infertility, throughout the process of potential family building to resolution. Nationally and locally, Resolve would like to be the advocate for people with infertility by increasing public awareness about infertility issues and their organization. They also support research in the field of infertility.

The Los Angeles Chapter of Resolve would like to expand its membership by (1) retaining more members, (2) recruiting new members, and (3) recruiting constituent groups.

Who Are Their Customers?

As America's population ages, a void is felt in many American homes whose journey to parenthood ended up in infertility. Resolve, an organization run by a volunteer board consisting of individuals who have experienced medical concerns regarding infertility or who have adopted children, support individuals or couples with similar experiences. The majority of users of their services are white, upper-middle-class couples. One of Resolve's goals is to expand to other ethnic populations and economic groups.

What Do Their Customers Value?

Infertile couples value the right to build their families through a variety of methods. Resolve is there to ensure these individuals make informed choices in order for them to recognize the long-term implications of their decision in their lives and in the lives of others. Resolve, however, does not get involved in decisions concerning medical methodology. Those decisions are left with the individuals and their physicians. By specializing in the narrow segment of the infertility market (i.e., emotional support, counseling, education, and referrals in the short term), we believe Resolve has a strong impact on their customer needs.

What Is Our Hypothesis for a Strategic Direction?

There is a consensus among demographers that the percentage of women experiencing infertility since the 1980s is stable. However, the absolute numbers of women reporting infertility increased dramatically in the 1980s. During this time, more women were over 35 years or were delaying childbearing to later years. Advances in reproductive assisted technology with changes in management of medicine will affect the mix of infertility service utilization. What will be important to Resolve to note is not necessarily the percentage of infertile women but the percentage of infertile women who seek medical services. It is crucial for service providers to continue to have a good understanding of the demographic factors for the potential patient base as it changes over the next 25 years.

We believe that the infertility market has very few services. Resolve is and may continue to be successful because it penetrates the market as a flexible, customer-focused organization. The major challenge is to stabilize and expand the volunteer base by recruit-

---

[1] Resolve Chapter Operations Manual.

ing and retaining more members and constituent groups. Right now, Resolve's market is expanding while their volunteer base is shrinking.

SITUATIONAL ANALYSIS

Situational Environment

Demand and Demand Trends.   Looking at the projections stated in the strategic hypothesis above, demographers foresee a potential decline in numbers of infertile women in the United States while the baby boomers pass the childbearing age. Their projections, indeed, did show a slight decline in the numbers of infertile women in 2010 and 2015 in the United States.[2]

The estimates of infertility for 1995 from the paper by Stephen et al. in the journal *Fertility and Sterility,* are taken from Cycle 5 of the National Survey of Family Growth (conducted by the National Center for Health Statistics). In this data, stable rates of infertility were observed in 1982 and 1988 cycles of the National Survey of Family Growth. In 1995, the overall percentage of infertile women increased from 8.4 percent in 1982 and 1988 to 10.2 percent in 1995. In absolute numbers this means in the United States, the number of infertile women rose from 4.5 million in 1982 to 4.9 million in 1988 and 6.2 million in 1995. The 1995 figures include the large number of baby boomers in their later reproductive years.

A series of projections indicated that in the year 2000, between 5 and 6.3 million women could be infertile. This number will increase to 5.4 to 7.7 million in 2025. There will be stability or a decline in the numbers of infertile women according to their projections in the years 2005 to 2020. In the year 2020, the numbers will be on the rise again. What really influences this data is the population age structure.

Advances in reproductive assisted technology with changes in management of medicine will change the mix of infertility service utilization. Women who seek services are a select group. They are likely to be older, married, white, and wealthier than the overall infertile population.

What is important for service providers like Resolve to note is the percentage of infertile women who seek medical services. For example, according to the Stephen paper, of the 6.2 million women with impaired fecundity, only 44 percent sought medical help for infertility. This number is identical to the 1988 percentage.

Better public awareness of infertility and the increase in infertility service providers have affected a portion of the increase in infertility rates. It is very crucial for service providers to continue to have a good understanding of the demographic factors for the potential patient base as it changes over the next 25 years.

Neutral Environment

Financial Environment.   The Los Angeles Chapter of Resolve creates its funds for its operations through:

- Its educational events such as their annual symposium
- Monthly meetings with lecturers
- Sale of educational materials such as pamphlets
- The "hot-line"

---

[2] Stephen, Elizabeth & Chandra, A; Updated projections of infertility in the United States: *1995–2025, Fertility and Sterility,* vol. 70, no. 1, July 1998, pp. 30–34.

- Advertisement space in their newsletter
- Membership dues

Financially, Resolve of Greater Los Angeles is stable. More information on their financial status and our forecasts will be discussed later.

Government Environment

Resolve is very active in the political issues surrounding their services. They are active in lobbying Washington to create more accessible options in building families for infertile couples. The costs for adoption or treatments for combating infertility are very high, even if done through the state of California. There are legal matters surrounding adoption that make this option difficult. A lot of work is needed in these areas. Resolve National is dedicated to this cause.

For the Los Angeles Chapter of Resolve, California laws are important. Below is the California Law pertaining to infertility:

The California law requires certain insurers to offer coverage for infertility diagnosis and treatment. That means group health insurers covering hospital, medical, or surgical expenses must let employers know infertility coverage is available. However, the law does not require those insurers to provide the coverage; nor does it force employers to include it in their employee insurance plans.

The law defines infertility as:

- The presence of a demonstrated condition recognized by a licensed physician and surgeon as a cause of infertility; or
- The inability to conceive a pregnancy or carry a pregnancy to a live birth after a year or more of sexual relations without contraception.

The law defines treatment as including, but not limited to:

- Diagnosis and diagnostic tests;
- Medication;
- Surgery; and
- Gamete Intra-fallopian Transfer, also known as GIFT.

The law specifically exempts insurers from providing invitro-fertilization coverage. In addition, the law does not require employers that are religious organizations to offer coverage for treatment that conflicts with the organization's religious and ethical purposes (California Health and Safety Code, Section 1374.55).

Insurance is required to cover infertility treatment with the exception of invitro fertilization.

Competitor Environment

Although there appears to be no direct competitors for Resolve of Los Angeles, there are indirect competitors. Internal medicine or Obstetric/Gynecology Specialists are reluctant to send their patients to Resolve because of concern that they will lose their patient to infertility specialists. In the very heavy HMO environment, it is more difficult for physicians to make ends meet because they are not reimbursed fully for the services they provide. If the patient population they have leaves, they lose the revenue gained from the patient. This is a real problem, not just a perception. The climate for these physicians has changed dramatically to be able to accept the referrals of their patients easily.

The major competitor for Resolve is the Internet. People can find information easily and conveniently on the Internet and remain anonymous. Resolve needs to "link" up with these Web sites to gain access to the market available.

Other Infertility Organizations (on the Web):

- *American Society for Reproductive Medicine*
- *American Society of Andrology*
- *Association of Reproductive Health Professionals*
- *Conceiving Concepts*
- *The Endocrine Society*
- *European Society for Human Reproduction and Embryology*
- *Ferre Institute*
- *Fertility Weekly*
- *Hannah's Prayer: Christian Infer & Preg/Infant Loss Support*
- *Infertility Internet chatsite*
- *Infertility Online @ Univ. of North Carolina*
- *International Council on Infertility Information Dissemination*
- *Journal of Reproductive Medicine*
- *Ladies in Waiting (Christian support group*
- *North American Menopause Society*
- *Organization of Parents Through Surrogacy*
- *Oxford Fertility*
- *Pacific Coast Fertility Society*
- *Perspectives Press (infertility book publisher)*
- *Polycystic Ovarian Syndrome Association*
- *Society for the Study of Reproductive Medicine*
- *Society for the Study of Fertility*
- *RESOLVE*
- *Yale Reproductive and Placental Research Unit*
- *Women's Health Interactive*

A new support group is developing in the Los Angeles area. They are called, "In Search of an Angel" and have received excellent media coverage in a local Pasadena newspaper, *The Pasadena Star News*. Resolve may be able to dissolve this group into their organization. One support group, Hannah's Prayer, has international chapters, an excellent Web site, a chat room on Thursdays, and no membership fees. At this time, they do not have a chapter in the greater Los Angeles area. Resolve needs to keep monitoring their activities. The one major problem Hannah's Prayer has is it is too diversified. They support a variety of problems, from Pregnancy loss to Early infant death. Donations are the major income source. This group only targets women.

A majority of support groups in the United States is focusing on loss of children.

RESOLVE	INCIID	IN SEARCH OF AN ANGEL
National Organization • Influential • Lobbying Power • Well recognized for law-making abilities • Reputation—recognized by infertility clinics as good source for their patients	*National Organization* • Entire focus on medical & psychological aspects of infertility treatments • No local chapters	*Local Organization* • Informal setting for group discussions • Linked with Center for Reproductive Health & Gynecology
Quality • Hot-line with trained volunteers • Face-to-face contact • Interaction with professionals/access to professional help • Experienced, empathetic volunteers	• Free literature on Internet • 90 percent of resources—online	• Face-to-face contact • Some interaction with professionals • Small groups of empathetic couples • Hot-line poorly manned
Accessibility • Local-advantage over Internet • Web site (potential advantage) • Few direct competitors • Literature for a fee	• On-line support mechanisms • E-mail groups • Free literature	• Local • Web site poorly set up • Newsletter • Just starting
Phone: Information: (818) 547-9942 Hot-line 310-326-2630 Web site: www. Resolve.org stin712@AOL.com	Hot-line Web site: ww.iniid.org	Hot-line 805-222-4595 Web site

Two types of potential competitors affect the Los Angeles area. An example of the first type of competitor is a company called INCIID. Their services are all done on-line. This will attract the population that prefers to have privacy in their personal needs. Literature is free as well as all their services. INCIID is heavily sponsored by the pharmaceutical industry.

"In Search of an Angel" is an example of a locally formed organization. A group of people who meet once a week at potluck dinners, discuss their experiences on family planning. They have no professionals to guide them. It is just a few people with a common problem supporting one another. Resolve may want to offer their services to aid in their goals. These two organizations are not as dominant as Resolve.

Company Environment

Resolve is a National Not-for Profit Consumer organization run by a volunteer board consisting of individuals who have experienced medical concerns regarding infertility or who have adopted children. Their focus is to support individuals or couples with the same experiences. The National Corporation (see Figure below for organization chart) is comprised of Members of the Corporation who are elected by the Board of Directors to serve a 5-year term. They do not have full voting rights but elect the Board of Directors and vote on changes in the by-laws. Resolve is governed by the Board of Directors. Their role is to determine policy and set goals for the organization. They have full voting rights and number among 7 to 30 members. Board members' duration in office

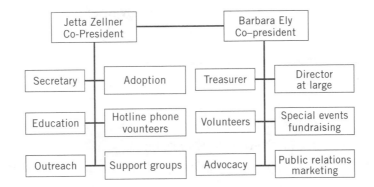

Organizational Structure of Resolve

is for 2 years with a limit of 8 years. Meetings are held twice a year. The executive committee consists of officers elected by the Board from members of the Board of Directors. They carry the offices of Chair, Secretary, Treasurer, and Vice-Chair or Co-Chair. Committees and time-limited task forces are selected from the general membership, members of the corporation and members of the board of directors. The different committees they form include:

Finance and Operations	Reviews the financial status, set budgets and long-range plans.
Nominating and Board Development Committee	Recruits new members of the corporation and directors. Works closely with the Executive Director. Recommends number of board positions to be filled each year. Administers the election of officers.
Fund-Raising and Development Committee	Supports board members in fulfilling their fund-raising responsibilities. Makes presentations about Resolve to potential donors such as foundations, corporations, and individuals.
Policy Committee	Examines policy issues—develops recommendations to the board.

This national organization has 50 chapters nationwide. In California, there are 4 chapters: one in northern California; one in the greater LA area, which includes cities as far west as Upland; the Orange County chapter, which includes the San Bernardino/Riverside areas; and the San Diego chapter.

The nucleus of the Los Angeles chapter consists of 20 people. The rest are a volunteer force controlled by this group. The two founding members of this group are from medical backgrounds: MA's.

Support from the National Organization consists of advice, bylaws, literature, guidelines for the support groups (i.e., how long support groups should last), telephone support, and legal support (i.e., lawsuits on employers who do not carry insurance for covering infertility).

Resolve volunteers have experienced the "emotional roller-coaster" of infertility. They create the bulk of the people who provide education and support on the issues of family building. Currently, volunteers are targeted to tasks that match their talents.

Competitive Advantage

Determination of Competitive Advantage

1. *National Organization*
   A. Influential
   B. Lobbying Power
   C. Well recognized for lawmaking abilities
   D. Reputation—recognized by infertility clinics as good source for their patients
   E. Help with finding speakers
2. *Quality*
   A. Hot-line—trained volunteers who work it
   B. Face-to-face contact
   C. Interaction with professionals/access to professional help
   D. Experienced, empathetic volunteers
3. *Accessibility*
   A. Local—advantage over Internet
   B. Web site (potential advantage)
4. Few direct competitors

Target Market

Los Angeles Chapter of Resolve is interested in stabilizing their current market and then expanding into different segments of the demographic mix in the Los Angeles area. The following are the main markets Resolve of Greater Los Angeles is and is potentially targeting.

	Members	*Volunteers*
Primary	White, upper-middle class, females aged 25–44	Ex-members
Secondary	Hispanics	College people
	Asian African American	New members
	Male segment	Doctors
	Couples	Gay community
	Gay community	

Demographics, Lifestyles, and Psychographics

Based on current research, the demographics of people with infertility are outlined as follows. About 1 percent of women 18–44 years of age (500,000) were currently seeking to adopt a child at the time of their interview in 1995. Only 0.2 percent (100,000) had applied to an adoption agency.

The following information divides women by infertility status. The "infertile" category is determined by the standard medical definition of infertility, which is: a married couple is classified as "infertile" if they have not used contraception and not become pregnant for 12 months or more. About 7.1 percent of married couples, or 2.1 million, were infertile in 1995 compared with 2.3 million in 1988 and 2.4 million in 1982. In each of these years, about 1.0 million were childless and infertile. The total number of infertile couples is declining. Hispanic infertile married women make up 11 percent (222 M), Black is 10 percent (217 M), White is 70 percent (1,477 M), and Other is 9 percent (183 M).[3]

Infertile married women between ages 35–44 years make up 56 percent (1,170 M) of the total infertile married women.

Demographics, Social, and Cultural Factors in the Los Angeles Area[4]

- Los Angeles County has about 3.1 million Catholics.

- Los Angeles County has about 3 million Hispanics, two-thirds of whom are Catholic. This demographic is important when targeting members. The religious beliefs of patients strongly influence the service sought. For the Catholic population, adoption is a viable option, although not the only one to be offered.

- The overall infertility rate has fallen since 1976, although the number of affected woman increased in some age groups.

- According to a 1990 Gallup poll, 84 percent of childless adults under the age of 40 would like to have children; 60 percent of childless adults aged 40 or older wish they had had children.

- In 1995, 11 percent of all married couples with a wife aged 15–44 (3.1 million) had problems conceiving or carrying a pregnancy to term.

- The total number of childless couples with a wife aged 35–44 experiencing difficulties has increased 37 percent. The number of people seeking help has risen also.

- Infertility problems originate in the male in about 40 percent of cases, women 50 percent, and it is a joint problem about 10 percent of the time.

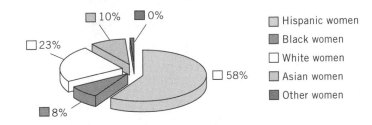

Los Angeles County: Total Women Between Ages 20–49 Percent

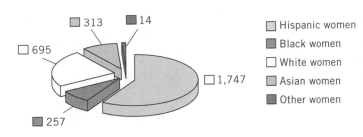

Los Angeles County: Total Women Between Ages 20–49 (In Thousands)

---

[3] 1995 National Survey of Family Growth.
[4] 1997 Revised U.S. Census.

- A woman's age is a significant factor in impairment rates. Among childless couples, 36 percent with a wife aged 35–44 had impairment, compared with 8 percent with a wife aged 15–24 and 20 percent with a wife aged 25–30.

- 85 percent to 90 percent of infertile couples seeking treatment could benefit from low-tech remedies such as surgery and drugs, but 10–15 percent may not respond to conventional methods.

- The number of U.S. infertility clinics performing high-tech procedures increased from 84 in 1985 to 270 in 1992.

- The bulk of the procedures are done on people under age 35.

- According to NCHA nearly one in four women, aged 15 to 44 (or their current partner) has been sterilized; 10 percent of women regretted their decision; 1 percent tried to have it reversed.

- High-tech infertility treatments cost $7,000 to $11,000 per try. Procedures involving donor eggs can be even more expensive.

- 38 percent of larger business offer some type of infertility coverage for their workers, an increase of 50 percent since 1989.

- People who seek IVF or other high-tech treatments tend to be affluent.

- Carrying a pregnancy to term is also difficult for infertile couples. In 1988, 13 percent of confirmed pregnancies ended in miscarriage.

Los Angeles County 1997 (est)

	Total Women Between Ages (Thousands)						
	20–49	*20–24*	*25–29*	*30–34*	*35–39*	*40–44*	*45–49*
Hispanic women	1,747	325	331	351	311	250	180
Black women	257	36	41	49	50	44	37
White women	695	80	105	122	135	131	122
Asian women	313	41	57	57	56	55	47
Other women	14	2	3	3	3	2	2
Total women	3,027	484	537	582	554	482	388

	Total Women Between Ages Percent						
	20–49	*20–24*	*25–29*	*30–34*	*35–39*	*40–44*	*45–49*
Hispanic women	58%	67%	62%	60%	56%	52%	46%
Black women	8%	7%	8%	8%	9%	9%	10%
White women	23%	16%	20%	21%	24%	27%	31%
Asian women	10%	9%	11%	10%	10%	11%	12%
Other women	0%	0%	0%	0%	0%	0%	0%
Total women	100%	100%	100%	100%	100%	100%	100%

Infertility Services.   The NSFG is one of the few reliable sources of nationally representative data on the use of infertility services. Data from this source states: Of the 60.2 million women of reproductive age in 1995, 15 percent (9.3 million) have used some kind of infertility service—medical advice, tests, drugs, surgery, or other treatments—compared with 12 percent (6.8 million) (Appendix 2). Infertility services include medical help to get pregnant and services (beyond routine prenatal care) to prevent miscarriage. Among childless women 35–44, 21 percent had received infertility services. The most common infertility services were medical advice, tests on the woman or man, and the use of ovulation drugs. Surgery or treatment for blocked tubes and assisted reproductive technologies were less common. About 2 percent of women of reproductive age (about 1.2 million women) had an infertility visit in the past year and 13 percent had no visits in the past year, although they had received infertility services at some time in their lives. Having recent infertility services was most common among married childless women—8 percent of whom had an infertility visit in the last year (Appendix 3); 84 percent of women under age 40 would like to have children. This amounts to more than 9,652 million women of which 14.7 percent (1,421 million) are infertile.

There are 157 physicians in the Los Angeles Metropolitan area who are members of the American Society for Reproductive Medicine (ASRM). (Appendix 12).

There are at least 11 reproductive medical centers located in the LA area:

• West Coast Infertility and Reproductive Associates	Beverly Hills
• The Fertility Institute	Tarzana
• California Fertility Associates IVF Program	Santa Monica
• Center for Advanced Reproductive Care	Redondo Beach
• Huntington Reproductive Center	Pasadena
• University of Southern California IVF Program	Los Angeles
• UCLA Fertility Center IVF Program	Los Angeles
• Tyler Medical Clinic	Los Angeles
• Century City Hospital Center for Reproductive Medicine	Los Angeles
• University Infertility Associates	Long Beach
• Center for Male Reproductive Medicine	Los Angeles
• Growing Generations	Los Angeles
• Northridge Center for Reproductive Medicine	Northridge
• Pacific Fertility Medical Centers	Los Angeles

State of Technology. Assisted Reproductive Technology (ART) process: In 1995, most of the ART cycles (76 percent) did not produce a clinical pregnancy; 24 percent resulted in a clinical pregnancy. Of this 24 percent, 19 percent had successful births of which 12 percent were single births and 7 percent were multiple births. A woman's age is the most important factor affecting the chances of a live birth when using the woman's own eggs. Rates are relatively constant for age 34 years and younger, but decline with age after 34. Success rates are zero among women aged 47 years and older. However, the success rate for cycles using donor embryos is constant (around 30 percent) for all age groups from 22 to 50.

Many factors contribute to the success of an ART procedure. Some of these factors are related to the patients themselves, such as their age and the cause of their infertility. Others are related to the training and experience of the ART clinic and laboratory professionals and the quality of services they offer.

Problems, Threats, and Opportunities

Strengths	Weaknesses
Reputation	High Volunteer Turnover
Influential	Web Site
Lobbying Power	Hot-Line
Hot-Line	No Permanent Meeting Place
Face-to-Face Contact	
Accessibility—Local, Web Site	
Few Direct Competitors	

Opportunities	Threats
Better Forecasting	Internet
Expand to New Market Segments	Competitors
Internet	e.g., INCIID
Financial	Hannah's Prayer
	In Search of an Angel

The service provided by the Los Angeles chapter of Resolve is facing the perception that medical professionals such as the Obstetricians and Gynecologists partner with Resolve to gain access to patients.

Another problem facing Resolve's LA chapter is the fact that there is a high turnover of volunteers within a short period. Based on marketing research, it is much easier to retain present customers/users than to develop new users.

From our research, Web site chat rooms seem to be the most direct competition of Resolve LA chapter in terms of geographic location. Many people see infertility as a personal problem and hence they are not prepared to talk about it in the open where their identities can be known. The Internet is also a potential opportunity for Resolve. Recent surveys reveal positive trends in Internet use which will benefit Resolve through the use of their Web site (see Appendix 11).

At present, the target market for the LA chapter of Resolve is the upper middle-class of the community for its volunteer base as well as its funding. This situation could be a problem in the long run because the market is limited. Expansion to the lower economic groups as well as other ethnic groups such as the large Hispanic population is a great opportunity.

Los Angeles County has a larger population than that of 42 states in the nation. The geographic area targeted is densely populated with over 9.6 million people. Forty percent of California's population resides here, allowing ease of coverage of the target market as well as recruiting of volunteers. The LA chapter of Resolve can reach a wider target audience by a strong marketing plan. Resolve can meet its objective of providing timely, compassionate support and information to people who are experiencing infertility and increase the awareness of infertility through advocacy and public opinion. This can also aid in prompting people to volunteer for the chapter.

Promotion is an area where the LA chapter of Resolve has failed to capitalize. The newsletter is an example of a tool to promote within. Publicity campaigns will increase brand recognition and improve awareness of their services.

MARKETING OBJECTIVES AND GOALS

Objective: To remain stable

Goal #1: To increase volunteers 100 percent within one year

- Retain current volunteers
- Reactivate old volunteers
- Recruit new volunteers
  - current members
  - students
  - doctors
  - retirees
  - second-hand experience
  - gay couples

Goal #2: To increase membership by 100 percent within two years

- Public education
- Improvement of symposium
- Improvement of meetings
- Improvement of communication
  - Hot-line
  - Web site
  - Newsletter
  - Membership drive program
  - Monthly meeting to general public
  - Radio
  - Press release
- Advertising
  - Flyers
  - Waiting rooms

MARKETING STRATEGY

Considering the narrow focus and niche competition necessary for this business to sustain a competitive advantage and the fact that they are the dominant player in this field, a marketing strategy that builds on this strength is critical for success. The market for Resolve's services is expanding, while the number of volunteers within the organization is shrinking. Forming strong relationships with the volunteers, both past and present, is perhaps one of the most critical aspects for this business' marketing success. By combining the needs of the clientele outside the organization with the needs of the volunteers within the organization as a major focus, the organization will not only build relationships to create new members and volunteers, but also create strong loyalty with existing volunteers within the organization. A business process that tracks individual customer and volunteer needs will need to be created and implemented. For example, sending a birthday card to a volunteer satisfies the special need to be recognized.

In an attempt to build and foster brand equity in a manner consistent with its values, Resolve should attempt to align itself with opinion leaders who champion the cause of support for infertile couples. By remaining active in such organizations as ASRM and assisting in the efforts of educating the public, this organization should foster additional recognition and brand equity among people who are closely associated with the care of infertile couples while simultaneously helping to accomplish its mission of strengthening America's families through the caring during the difficulties of infertility.

Human Resources Strategies and Tactics

Volunteerism. Resolve of Greater Los Angeles demonstrates the following needs related to volunteers:

1. Recruiting more people.
2. Motivating people to do their job.
3. Retaining volunteers—What needs to be done to motivate members? Are there other "pools" of people from which to recruit?

Resolve of Greater Los Angeles has 700 members and 30 core volunteers. There is one volunteer coordinator. The main recruitment for membership is from patients who first come to Resolve for counseling. This creates a pool of people who are there only temporarily until family building is successful. Therefore, there is great turnover in the volunteer force. This creates the barriers in the ability to cement teamwork since it takes a while for people to work well together.

Resolve of Greater Los Angeles needs to explore other sources for volunteers. Using the membership they have, there could be a membership drive for friends or acquaintances from the general membership. Outside the membership, there are many ways to create new volunteers for an organization. Resolve could have a counselor present at one of these clinics to recruit. A pool that could build a consistent volunteer force is the high school or college students. They will be willing to learn, retain the knowledge and apply it. Some institutions to draw upon include:

- USC (213)740-2311
- Claremont Colleges (909)621-8114
- Pepperdine (310)456-4000
- Whittier College (562)907-4200
- University of La Verne (909)593-3511
- UCLA (310)825-7068

The Cal State systems offer their students credit while participating in community service (see Appendix 20). Some sororities have a requirement that the members must work a certain number of hours per month. If anyone in the organization is a member of a sorority, they could network with them to recruit volunteers. In any of these pools, we have a mutually beneficial situation. Youth volunteers and Resolve members will gain better knowledge with which to manage and plan their future in family planning. Los Angeles youth will become productive after school and on weekends instead of being idle and getting into mischief. The Gay Community in the Los Angeles area could potentially be a great resource of volunteers and new members.

Past members who lose touch need to be kept informed. Resolve must maintain contact through examples listed. The chapter should send birthday cards to their children, newsletters, and an annual letter discussing their ideas for the future and asking for responses. This would be viewed as a symbol of warmth and care from the point of view of the ex-patients. The LA chapter of Resolve can also have retreats with past patients, current patients, spouses, and loved ones. This event could bring joy and allow the past and present members to forget the pains of family building options. Even if these members do not respond, Resolve is trying to keep their interest. Once their children are old enough, the past members may come back. Resolve LA chapter can also have an award ceremony where volunteers will be recognized for the efforts and part that they have played in the success of the chapter.

To retain the volunteers in the organization, Resolve could retrain old members as counselors. This will give the volunteers a sense of responsibility that could be a driving force for some of the group. One way to use them is to offer satellite meetings in clinics and churches in the outlying communities. The volunteers would organize these meetings themselves with the aid of the volunteer coordinator overseeing the volunteer pool. By training volunteers at a bi-monthly meeting or even at a monthly meeting, old members become the new counselors. Here is an opportunity to invite back old members to become counselors, moderators, or speakers on their experiences.

For the recruitment process, the volunteer coordinator should discuss the post for which you wish to recruit a volunteer with the board and membership.

Areas to discuss include:

- Preferred qualifications and work experience of volunteer
- Proposed objectives for the volunteer replacement.
- Key activities/work duties for the volunteer.
- Targets against which the volunteer's work can be assessed.
- Means by which the volunteer can share skills with other volunteers.
- Where the volunteer will work in the structure of the organization and the resources available.

One way to find out if an individual within Resolve is interested in a certain position is to send interest cards to the membership at a meeting and ask if they are interested in the job or simply pose the question, "What are your interests?"

To maintain productive volunteers:

The volunteer must have accurate expectations of the work she/he is asked to do. The importance of guidance, support, and feedback from fellow volunteers and friends is important for them to remain motivated. Volunteers may ask a lot of questions or even question existing practices. Often they have new ideas that may help improve the existing techniques and practices. (See Appendixes 4 to 7.)

Professional Partnering Strategies and Tactics

A better understanding in the approach toward the medical profession will help Resolve of Greater Los Angeles gain their support and use of their services.

Offering internships at the permanent offices of Resolve for professional people with skills in biology, medicine or related medical fields can increase the interest level of

Resolve. The potential is the opportunity to recruit a volunteer pool of professionals such as resident physicians who are innovative and represent the future of the medical profession.

Professional support: A better liaison with professionals such as doctors, lawyers, adoption agencies, and industry supporters of annual symposia, in organizing the use of their services. Creating physician awareness and willingness to refer patients to their services, Resolve needs an advisory board to create the network of liaisons to different professionals and adoption agencies. Demographics show:

A. Leaders/Influential people are needed to prompt and stimulate support.
B. People do not support unless they feel a personal connection.
C. Middle-aged college-educated, white-collar workers are most likely to volunteer.
  • Advertising directed should include Web site and toll-free number.

One way to partner is by working directly with the adoption agencies or infertility clinics. By doing this, Resolve could indirectly gain support through physicians' offices. The adoption agency or infertility clinic could refer the patient to Resolve. The patient, in turn, will discuss their emotional support groups (Resolve) with the physicians. Another approach is to use the industry supporters of the annual symposia. They have an interest in physicians referring patients to Resolve. As a sponsor, the industry supporter wants a good return on his/her investment. The more people who come to the symposium or use Resolve's services, the more products the industry supporter will sell.

Resolve has had almost no problems in getting professionals to speak at their meetings or symposia because the professional gets a good return in potential patients. When the professional speaks at the meeting, it is a great time to ask if he/she would like to become a professional member. Word-of-mouth in the medical community goes a long way.

Family practitioners are a very large market that should not be overlooked. They see many couples with family planning problems. Sometimes, nothing is done due to the lack of patient and physician awareness of the alternatives available for family planning for infertile couples. Flyers and outreach packages delivered to the family practice offices could tap into a new enormous market for Resolve.

Resolve needs a way to get specialists such as obstetric/gynecology physicians (ob/gyn) involved in the organization. The perceived concern is ob/gyn physicians see the patients early in the diagnosis. They are afraid of losing their patients to the infertility specialists if they use Resolve as a support group. Educating the ob/gyn physicians on the services offered by Resolve through brochures, flyers, and so on will do much to overcome this problem.

By linking electronically or professionally with the various agencies for adoption as well as the infertility clinics, Resolve should strengthen their position with the market. Some of the agencies and clinics that Resolve can collaborate with are listed below.

Adoption Agencies

California Association of Adoption Agencies.   This organization is very active in supporting and lobbying bills related to adoption that were or are before the legislature. They have a Web site that is continually updated with the newest amendments. It states in the Web site that it may "take up to a couple of days for the newest amendments to be on line." On this Web site, there is a synopsis on the different bills in process.

Member agencies provide:

- identified/designated adoption
- open adoptions between adoptive parents and birth parents, facilitated by licensed agencies
- non-identified adoption
- special needs adoption
- inter-country adoption
- counseling and education services
- post adoptive services

CAAA. This organization believes that a uniform standard of adoption practices is necessary to ensure that the best interests, needs and rights of children and other parties to the adoption process are met. They support the present California system of state-supervised nonprofit adoption agencies. The organization opposes efforts that permit unregulated and unlicensed for-profit groups or individuals from performing agency functions. CAAA receives funding from state government. (See Appendix 14.)

Adoption Assistance Program (AAP). CAAA believes AAP is an essential proactive service to ensure all children who need permanent homes can be adopted. Their services include children with "special" needs and foster children. This program has experienced a rapid increase in usage. This may be a way for people to adopt without dealing with the initial costs.

Sierra Adoption Services (SAS). This organization is an accredited member of California Association of Services for Children and the North American Council on Adoptable Children.

Resolve would benefit by making their presence known or more pronounced in the Infertility Clinics. Some Infertility Clinics in the Los Angeles Basin are:

Birth Plus
Cedars-Sinai UCLA Center for Reproductive Medicine
Center for Human Reproduction (Tarzana)
Center for Male Reproductive Medicine (Los Angeles)
Center for Surrogate Parenting (Beverly Hills)
The Fertility Institutes (Tarzana) (Beverly Hills) (others)
The Institute for Male Urology, Inc. (Encino)
Laguna Niguel Fertility Center
Loma Linda University Center for Fertility and Invitro-fertilization
Pacific Fertility Medical Centers (Los Angeles) (San Francisco)
Surrogate Parenting Services (Laguna Niguel)
Werlin-Zarutskie Fertility Centers (Irvine) (Laguna Niguel)
West Coast Infertility and Reproductive Associates (Beverly Hills)
West Coast Fertility Centers (Fullerton) (Fountain Valley) (Anaheim)
Woman to Woman Fertility Center

MARKETING TACTICS

Marketing Mix

Product

- Service

Price

- $45 annual membership
- $125 professional membership fee
- Hot-line
- Sessions
- Resolve will not turn anyone away on the basis of ability to pay

Place

- Web site
- Central meeting location
- Newsletter
- Doctors' offices/Clinics

Promotion

- Online services
- Symposium
- Radio
- Newspapers
- Seminar
- Press releases
- TV
- Meeting to general public
- Hot-line

Additional Comments

Product

Resolve provides services such as compassionate support and information about infertility to couples from its onset throughout the process of potential family building to resolution. Nationally and locally, Resolve serves to be the advocate for infertile people by increasing public awareness about infertility issues and their organization. They also support research in the field of ART.

Place

Public Awareness and Stability Tactics. Before they can achieve stability, Resolve needs to find a permanent office location. By having a main meeting place or office, coordination of promotion of Resolve and coordination of volunteers would be easier. There would be a place to store their literature, records, and other important administrative items, as well as a location where volunteers could come to work on ongoing projects. Resolve could also contact the city council real estate planning division about sites to be donated for their use. Other places to contact for the donated office space are the Los Angeles City Hall real estate planning office (phone: [213]-847-6440). This could also provide a good opportunity for Resolve to work within a hospital.

Communication. The main source of communication with the membership is through the newsletter. This is an important way to keep in contact with the past members. One place the newsletter can have a major impact is on the Web site of the Los Angeles chapter. People who are browsing the Web will read the articles and may call the hot-line for other services that are advertised in the newsletter. This may also cut expenses for Resolve.

Online Services. Resolve's Web site needs to be continually updated. Since the main competitor for Resolve is the Internet, it would be advantageous to be linked to as many sites as possible. It is through these links that people will discover the services of Resolve.

Suggested links:

- Demographics
- Infertility Support Groups
- National and local health organizations
- Adoption—support groups, churches, or agencies
- International organizations

There are people who prefer using the Internet as opposed to interacting with a live person. This could create competition for Resolve. To offset any competition, Resolve could have a chat room. If they cannot get volunteers to man the chat room continuously, they could have certain times of the day where live people are available to moderate discussions in the chat room.

To properly set up a Web site, we recommend having it done by someone who has experience in doing this type of work. One source the Los Angeles chapter could try is Dean S. Tripodes at Information Technology Management. His E-mail address is *webmaster@baywalk.com.* His fees are $1,000 for setting up the site. After 10 hours, the fee is $85.00 per hour. For maintenance of the Web site, terms are negotiable. If he is unable to meet Resolve's expectations, other contacts are available. (See Appendix 24.) Appendix 8 contains a list of questions to ask yourselves before working with someone so you are better prepared.

Hot-Line. People out there still need to communicate with a live person. The hot-line is very important for this reason. It is very informative on the upcoming meetings and activities for the chapter. The major problem with the hot-line information service is that the person on the recording talks too fast for an individual whose second language is English. A Spanish version of the message would help retain the Latino leads.

Resolve Should Provide a 1-800 Number. Twenty-five percent of donors (monetary) say their relationship with an organization would be greatly improved by the availability of an 800 number they could call with questions about the organization.

A. Have recording advertising their services (to reduce hang-ups)
  • Include Web address, specific meeting times
B. Need to ascertain how many calls/hang-ups per day the center receives.
C. Does this justify a full-time person to answer the telephone?
D. Request sponsor to pay for the 800 line in exchange for a 10-second promo.

Promotion

In order for Resolve to improve their brand recognition:

• Media Services are mandated to give some free air-time for not-for-profit organizations. Advertising agencies such as Satchi & Satchi, Shiat Day, and Western International Media (see Appendix 24) provide assistance to nonprofits in organizing their advertising and marketing campaigns. The campaign would include details such as how, when, and where to advertise, as well as how much money would be spent. Airtime could be during Sunday afternoon or evening, during daytime television, and on stations such as Discovery channel.

• Free advertising could also be obtained through the following Internet companies:
  • Ad Council—this is free and includes TV, radio, and the Internet; the contact person is Akiko Yabuki e-mail: media_materials@adcouncil.org
  • Web Hotel—provides free space on its site for nonprofit advertising e-mail: *jimt@ouroffice.com;* phone: 1-800-651-8788

• Promotion can also be obtained by appearing on daytime talk shows such as Leeza, who can be contacted by email: *Leeza@nbc.com.*

• The Women's Referral Service

• Resolve's public service announcement (PSA) (obtained through the Hawaii chapter) could be viewed in waiting rooms of infertility clinics, obstetrics/gynecology offices or family practice offices. Healthlink Services have set up televisions in many clinics throughout Southern California for videos that play all day.

• The chapter can advertise on the community service program of various radio stations and television stations, as well as in health sections of newspaper. (See Appendixes 15 to 19.)

• Brochures could be distributed to the targeted clinics with educational materials for patients. There also could be another brochure with educational information for professionals. If Resolve could link up with a university, hospital, or Medical Group with CME accreditation, income could be made by offering CME brochures on infertility and adoption. Have the university underwrite the costs for the CME credits in exchange for recognition on the brochure. This could be an avenue to gain more membership as well.

• Resolve could offer Lamaze classes as a means of support for the past members and volunteers. This would be a great avenue to find more patients and/or members because Family Planning Clinics that offer Lamaze classes also see the patients with infertility.

• The Women's Referral Service provides direct exposure to more than 4,000 women's businesses. Membership includes networking at any or all of the 17 chapters and ongoing support from a personal marketing consultant. Additionally, the Women's Yellow Pages targets specifically to women and has a circulation of over 90,000. This is a great way to promote the Resolve name and reputation. Contact Lynn Hall at (818) 995-6646.

- Set up booths in malls as advertising (contact the Chamber of Commerce in the individual cities to accomplish this). In some malls, there are kiosks with advertising signs. In areas where Resolve wants to expand, such as the Hispanic communities, this would be very effective.
- Flyers are effective and inexpensive ways of advertising services. Volunteers for delivery of these flyers could be obtained through the court systems.
- Promote the moniker, "Family Building Options."

IMPLEMENTATION AND CONTROL

Financial Strategy

Fund raising not only builds up the revenues within the organization, but also promotes membership, increases public awareness, provides opportunities to build a supportive network, and enhances the credibility of the chapter. Funding for the chapters of Resolve is evenly split between the chapter and national. The main source of revenue for yearly operational costs is from the annual symposium. The main goal for the symposium is the educational aspect. However, for monetary gain the goal should be to raise the maximum amount of money with the minimum amount of administrative cost.

If the symposium is the major source of revenue for the chapter, Resolve needs a better way to allocate funds, improve fund raising, and expand the budget.

Ideas to Market the Annual Symposium

Symposia and meetings have sporadic attendance. Their meetings are on Saturdays from 10 to noon. Demographics have shown:[5]

A. Sundays are the most popular days for *volunteering*
   - 7 hours per adult is available for leisure time on Sundays.
B. *Socializing* is best on Mondays and Tuesdays
   - Friday is next
   - Need to change meeting times from Sunday.

Consider not having meetings on Monday nights in the fall due to Monday night football.

The symposia may need a change in format or new topics such as parenting after the family is created. This may bring back the patients who were initially in the program before they achieved conception. This may be a great drawing card to keep these "former" members in the loop. As their children reach a stage where the new parents have more time, these former members would be a valuable asset to encourage other people in the program and to get new membership and/or volunteers.

Before setting up a symposium, a committee with clearly delegated responsibilities is recommended. Areas of responsibility are: program coordination, recruiting speakers, scheduling, publicity, site location and logistics, literature table that can be used for the membership drive, registration, invitations and program, audiovisual needs, food planning.

---

[5] American Demographics, "Seven Days of Play," March 1993.

Program Coordination and Speaker Recruitment. The program coordination needs to be started at least 6 months before the event. Contacts within the organization as well as through previous speakers are a good place to start. There are some clinics or hospitals that have known speakers who would be willing to talk since it is a "win-win" situation for the speaker, patients, and Resolve. Adoption agencies may be able to give you a lead on people who are great speakers. One source where the Los Angeles chapter could gain assistance in finding speakers as well as assist in costs and coordination is Serono.

Site Location and Logistics.   The committee involved in the site could be wearing several hats. Setting up the symposium site requires a site visit to ensure all the needs are fulfilled and that the logistics of the meeting are satisfied. If there are going to be exhibitors, Resolve will make sure they get good exposure because they are supporting the meeting and would like a good return on their investment of time and money. If they are satisfied, they will return next year.

The chapter will meet with the convention center personnel to discuss your needs and what the center can deliver. Set up the terms of the contract and have them send it to you or have the option to take it with you to reread. Try to get a good rate from them because Resolve is a nonprofit organization. Determine if they have audiovisual equipment. What are the costs involved? Inquire about meals. Ask about the menus, costs, and discounts if any. Once you have a site, get the floor plan for the whole area you are going to use. See how you will be setting up the lecture room while you are there. Then look again at the floor plan while you visualize the room. Is there anything you overlooked? The exhibit hall floor plan is very important for setting up industry. A sample letter (see Appendix 22) addresses the issue of where the exhibitor goes when they arrive at the hall. Any dispute will be handled before the meeting. Sending a copy of the hall floor plan is very helpful.

Exhibitors.   The exhibitor recruitment should begin a year before the meeting. Time-line is extremely important for successful representation. Since the meeting is in October, Resolve must contact the various companies the previous December. Most companies would have already allocated their funds to activities for the current fiscal year, therefore, the letters and telephone calls for exhibitors should begin in December of the previous year. Remember to thank them for their participation. (For sample letter, see Appendix 23.)

Special Events

Before beginning any fund-raising event, plan what new programs Resolve would like to start and the programs already in progress. Look at the costs of setting up the fund raiser and how the organization will maintain or increase funding sources. Then once clarity on what you plan to do is established, make a clear presentation to potential donors as to the purpose for which their contributions will be used. This is how to begin underwriting many fund-raising events. Resolve is a 501©(3) charitable organization. Donations are tax deductible, an important reminder to give to potential donors. While one or more persons are working on underwriting, create a time-line and define tasks for the various coordinators. The coordinators are responsible for making sure the volunteers are clear on who is responsible for each phase of the tasks and that they are coordinated. This could be an activity to accomplish as a team.

Fund-Raising Activities

- For underwriting, investigate companies that will match funding or that will contribute as volunteers.

- Find underwriting through baby-related products.

- Get a printing company to donate the printing costs for the program, tickets, or any other printed materials. (See Appendix 24 for suggested printing companies and graphic artists.)

- As a fund raiser, have an Internet auction of a celebrity's memorabilia. Use the influence of the celebrity as a drawing card for the symposium. Use his/her resources for advertising. Perhaps his/her fame could be useful for a sponsorship Gala.

- Have a silent auction event for members, volunteers, and their families.

- Start a donation drive through a mailing to existing and past members. In the donation letter, state that many companies offer a matching donation. (Appendix 21 lists more than 1,100 companies that match funds.)

- An individual direct mailing program is recommended each November to correspond with the Christmas season and year-end tax planning. Also, include past members, current members, and any individuals presently or previously involved with Resolve.

Another option for Resolve is grants. Grant writers write grants for revenue from local companies such as insurance companies or health insurance companies, medical or fertility clinics, and health care systems. Grant writers may ask for a percentage of the money granted. This is small fee for money one would not have otherwise. Even more cost effective would be to train a volunteer in grant writing. Revisions Grant Services is a good source for training. They can be contacted at (248) 443-9625, email: *info@revisions-grants.com* or access their Web site at *http://www.revisions-grants.com*. Relationships with associated clinics and agencies that are requesting a grant to help themselves and, thereby helping Resolve, are a positive way to promote a strong bond and partnership with the clinic. Resolve will gain more membership, publicity, and money. The clinic will have a service to send their patients for strong support.

The time line in asking for financial aid is very important. For example, asking for underwriting for the symposium should be done before December of the year before the event. This way, the donators can include the expense in the fiscal year. Also, begin a semiannual letter campaign requesting donations; suggested months are April and November. Furthermore, the newsletter must request that donations be mailed to Resolve.

One way to obtain additional funding is through underwriting. For the flyers that are distributed to the physicians' offices, the printing company making the flyers could underwrite the costs. In return, Resolve could put an advertisement in the flyer for the printing company. Resolve could have advertisements included in the flyers of local related businesses for a fee. Some ideas for small fund-raisers are listed in detail in Appendix 3.

The services of an executive director are a viable option for the Los Angeles chapter. The remuneration for the person considered would be from the proceeds obtained from their promotional activities for the symposium. An example would be money from the exhibitors the promoter would bring into the meeting. Our recommendation for the short term is not to do this until annual revenues reach a point that will sustain a director. The executive director would be too expensive for the amount of funds raised at the symposium.

Financial Information

Resolve has operated profitably for the last three fiscal years, with total revenue consistent the last two years (Financial Highlights Chart below). The primary revenue generators for each of the last two years are the annual symposium and the sponsorships. The major expenses for each year are the annual symposium and the chapter newsletter.

The chart also illustrates the inconsistent revenues and expenses for each of the last 3 years. For example, the revenue generated by the symposium and the expenses for the symposium are opposite of each other going from year to year. This inconsistency makes the future project planning more difficult and less predictable. Overall, the Symposium and Sponsorships have been the greatest revenue generators for Resolve and will continue upon Plan implementation, although other categories will contribute more revenue for Resolve.

Financial Forecast Chart

Summary of Financial Data	1999	2000	2001
Revenue			
Book	$ 2,700	$ 3,225	$ 3,800
Membership Revenue	9,500	13,927	19,990
Symposium	25,000	25,000	27,500
Donations	1,225	3,600	5,175
Advertisements	3,000	4,250	5,500
Sponsorships	32,200	34,800	38,580
Other	3,300	5,800	5,900
Total Revenues	$ 76,925	$ 90,602	$ 106,445
% Increase	22%	18%	17%
Expenses			
Advertising	–	–	–
Book	2,025	2,419	2,850
Newsletter	7,485	8,667	9,353
Public Education	800	1,000	1,200
Public Relations	5,000	5,000	5,000
Symposium	26,000	27,000	28,000
National Meeting	1,800	1,800	1,800
Travel	2,000	2,000	2,000
Office	5,117	2,931	3,422
Other	9,190	11,581	14,936
Total Expenses	$ 59,418	$ 62,398	$ 68,561
Net Income	$ 17,507	$ 28,204	$ 37,884

Below are detailed monthly income statements through December 31, 2001. In summary, the Plan projects revenues to increase to $106M for the year ending 2001, up from $63M for 1998 (Financial Forecast Chart). Key areas that the Plan will take advantage of are: newsletter advertisement income, individual and corporate donations, and further increases in sponsorships. For example, currently donations are under $500/year and within 3 years the Plan projects donations to increase to over $5,500 per year. Of course, with the increase in members, the revenue of other areas such as membership revenue and book sales revenue will increase also. Conversely, expenses are also projected to increase but the revenues will outpace the expenses and net income increases each year. While the net income will increase each year, this additional income has not been assigned to additional programs since it is earmarked for contingencies and future programs (i.e., to provide Resolve with financial stability).

Although these Projections are aggressive, these projections are attainable with implementation of the Plan. The total membership is projected to increase to 1,750 by January 2002 from the current base membership of 700.

Financial Highlights Chart

Summary of Financial Data	1996	1997	1998
Revenue			
Book	$ 2,766	$ 351	$ 2,660
Membership Revenue	223	–	3,685
Symposium	23,464	31,401	18,530
Donations	388	323	397
Advertisements	980	650	2,930
Sponsorships	–	30,000	31,025
Other	15,445	5,248	3,851
Total Revenues	$ 43,266	$ 67,973	$ 63,078
Expenses			
Advertising	–	5,095	–
Book	2,367	1,785	–
Newsletter	9,597	6,209	3,272
Public Education	2,479	4,203	709
Public Relations	86	5,224	555
Symposium	13,616	16,757	25,321
National Meeting	1,531	4,358	1,957
Travel	–	1,194	1,947
Office	5,093	7,301	1,962
Other	2,346	2,515	4,346
Total Expenses	$ 37,115	$ 54,641	$ 40,068
Net Income	$ 6,151	$ 13,332	$ 23,010

Below is a summary of the Plan's major programs and associated expenses and revenues.

During FY99 major additional programs and expenses include:

- PR Firm $ 5,000
- Volunteer Recruitment Mailing Campaign $1,325
- Donation Letter Mailing $ 315
- Volunteer Appreciation Recognition/Awards $ 300
- Database Management Software $ 995
- Web Site Revision $1,100
- Convention Kiosks $2,175

These FY99 expenses are offset by additional revenue generated:

- Donations/Corporate Matching Funds $1,225
- Increase in Newsletter Advertising Rates & Income $1,500
- Increased Membership Revenue $4,500
- Increase in Sponsorships $2,200
- Increased Symposium $7,000

12/31/99 Membership Total—900

FY00 major program and expenses include:

• PR Firm	$5,000
• Volunteer Recruitment Mailing Campaign	$1,256
• Donation Letter Mailing	$1,380
• Volunteer Appreciation Recognition/Awards	$2,800
• Web Site Maintenance	$ 360
• Convention Kiosks	$2,175

These FY00 expenses are offset by additional revenue generated:

• Donations/Corporate Matching Funds	$3,600
• Fund Raising	$2,500
• Incremental Increase in Advertising Rates & Income	$1,500
• Incremental Increased Membership Revenue	$3,700
• Incremental Increase in Sponsorships	$3,800

12/31/00 Membership Total—1,325

FY01 major program and expenses include:

• PR Firm	$5,000
• Volunteer Recruitment Mailing Campaign	$1,256
• Donation Letter Mailing	$1,380
• Volunteer Appreciation Recognition/Awards	$2,500
• Web Site Maintenance	$ 360
• Convention Kiosks	$2,175

These FY01 expenses are offset by additional revenue generated:

• Donations/Corporate Matching Funds	$3,600
• Fundraising	$2,500
• Incremental Increase in Advertising Rates & Income	$1,500
• Increased Membership Revenue	$5,000
• Increase in Sponsorships	$3,780

12/31/01 Membership Total—1,750

Project Development Schedule

There are a lot of activities to fine-tune and examine in order to stabilize and expand the volunteer base as well as enter new markets in the Greater Los Angeles area. Maintaining the old while establishing the new requires implementation of this plan in a stepwise fashion. Following is a chart showing the time line we recommend. It is important to set up the new projects in a stepwise fashion; otherwise, the team will be overwhelmed. For instance, one recommended activity mentioned earlier is to hand deliver the flyers and printed materials to the physicians' offices. In order to do this a stable volunteer base needs to be established. Once the volunteers have been recruited, set up a pilot territory with a few offices to be targeted. Once the logistics of the program are worked out, expand the number of offices. Once milestones are hit, go to the next project.

Implementation

Volunteers and Memberships

- Go to colleges to recruit volunteers. Letter campaigns, flyers, and posters should be done at the beginning of each semester: May, September, and January.

- Sororities and fraternities have volunteer programs mandated as an activity the members must participate.

- June—letter campaign for new members. Send letters to all members requesting their help and any friends interested.

- July—letters to old members.

    1. Ask them to rejoin/become volunteers/and/or donate money.

    2. Contact the Los Angeles Chambers of Commerce—register for volunteerism.

    3. Ask if old members would like to discuss their experiences with Resolve during their time of need. See if there is interest in organizing satellite meetings where they look after the logistics of the meetings. The volunteer coordinator aids in the training of the old membership and oversees the smooth operation of the satellite meetings.

- June/July—include the recruitment letters in the same mailing as the information for the symposium.

- November—recruitment letter in the newsletter, symposium, on the Web site.

- March—Have an annual Awards Recognition Banquet. The awards could be certificates, ribbons, and trophies (if you get them underwritten). Volunteers can be recognized for activities such as numbers of hours spent volunteering a year.

- Community boards in malls or pamphlets left at bookstores such as Barnes and Noble are ways to create brand recognition as well as drive in potential members and volunteers.

- Three to four years from the time of implementation of this plan, start letter campaigns to ask for money from matching corporate funds. Also, ask companies to promote volunteerism within their companies. The pharmaceutical companies that promote infertility products would be a good place to begin.

- Many companies, including IBM and Romac Corporate Services, encourage their employees to participate in community services. The Romac Corporate Offices can be reached at 120 W. Hyde Park Place, Tampa FL 33606.

- A fashion show can be put on for the members. The logistics and set up of this event is simple. Just call Nordstrom's Marketing Department and ask to speak to the fund-raising department. There is a breakfast, a nice stage, models, clothes, set-up and takedown, music; lights all organized by Nordstrom. The fashion show is held one to two hours before store opening. Your obligation is to get 250 to 300 guests at the fashion show. Tickets to this event could be sold for revenues. No costs are involved except the time for selling tickets.

Interest in cultural diversity is important to Resolve. The main membership is the upper middle-class segment. Resolve would like to expand to the lower economic groups. To build up the clientele in the Hispanic and Asian population, place public service announcements on Hispanic and Asian radio and television stations (see Appendix 15 to 18). Kiosks in the malls with a Spanish advertisement on Resolve would reach the Hispanic population.

RESOLVE
Greater Los Angeles
Family Building Options

	5–99	6–99	7–99	8–99	9–99	10–99	11–99	12–99	1–00	2–00	3–00	4–00	5–00
VOLUNTEER													
Recruitment Letter							×						
New Members		×											
Old Members			×										
Collegiate	×				×						×		×
Awards/Recognition Brunch											×		
LA County Volunteer			×										
LA County Chambers of Commerce Registration			×										
MEMBERSHIP													
Recruitment Letter							×						
New Members		×						×					
Old Members			×							×			
Professional Members Q&A Sessions (Open To Public)													
ASRM/Infertility Clinics							×	×	×	×	×	×	×
Adoption Specialists										×	×	×	×
Fertility Clinic Info/Updates													×
Literature Dissemination (Personal Delivery)				×	×	×	×	×	×	×	×	×	×
Flyers				×	×	×	×	×	×	×	×	×	×
Expand Office Base for Delivery of Literature													
Adoption Specialists											×		
Balance of ASRM and OBGYN													
Kiosk-LA Women's Show (Annual)		×											
Kiosk-Worldwide Marriage Encounter (Annual)				×									
Kiosk-Latino Family Fest (Annual)				×									
Kiosk-Women's HIV (Annual)						×							
Kiosk – Black Business Expo (Annual)													
SYMPOSIUM						×							
Letters to Exhibitors							×						
Follow up Phone Call to Exhibitors										×			
Final Follow Up Letter			×										
Letters and Phone Calls for '99 Symposium	×	×	×										×
Book Site Location (for the Following Year)						×							
Media Blitz (Community Calendar for TV)				×	×								
Letters to Members				×	×								
Send Reminder Letters						×							
Letter to Non-Members Gained from All Info Booths and Web Site				×	×								
WEB SITE													
Webmaster	×												
Registration of Web Site		×											
Software Implementation (Database Software)	×	×											
Update Web Site Daily	×	×	×	×	×	×	×	×	×	×	×	×	×
Update Database MGT. Software													
DONATION													
Letters							×	×					
Buy/Rent Database Names for Donors						×							
BRAND RECOGNITION/Education													
PSA Tapes		×											
LA Country Chambers of Commerce Registration				×									
Newspaper Press Release					×								
HOTLINE													
Add Spanish Speaking Recording										×			
(Wo)Manned Phone Lines											×		
Get Sponsorship to Pay for Hotline (Local 800)													
NEWSLETTER	×			×			×			×			×
Upgrade Newsletter (Request Volunteers on Front Page)				×			×			×			×
Update Chapter Current Events				×			×			×			×
Request Donations							×						

–00	7–00	8–00	9–00	10–00	11–00	12–00	1–01	2–01	3–01	4–01	5–01	6–01	7–01	8–01	9–01	10–01	11–01	12–01	1–02	2–02	3–02	4–02	5–02
					×												×						
												×											
	×												×										
			×				×				×				×					×			×
									×												×		
						×						×					×						
	×						×						×						×				
	×	×	×	×	×	×	×	×	×	×	×	×	×	×	×	×	×	×	×	×	×	×
	×		×		×		×		×			×	×		×		×		×		×	×	
			×				×					×			×				×				×
	×	×	×	×	×	×	×	×	×	×	×	×	×	×	×	×	×	×	×	×	×	×
	×	×	×	×	×	×	×	×	×	×	×	×	×	×	×	×	×	×	×	×	×	×
	×				×			×					×				×				×		
	×						×						×						×				
												×											
		×											×										
		×											×										
			×													×							
		×																					
			×													×							
					×												×						
									×											×			
	×											×											
	×										×	×	×										×
			×													×							
		×	×												×	×							
	×	×										×	×										
			×												×								
	×	×										×	×										
	×	×	×	×	×	×	×	×	×	×	×	×	×	×	×	×	×	×	×	×	×	×
							×																
					×	×											×	×					
			×														×						
			×													×							
										×													
		×			×			×				×			×		×			×			×
		×			×			×				×			×		×			×			×
		×			×			×				×			×		×			×			×
					×												×						

Professional Memberships. The key to succeeding in collaborating with the medical community is to get the health care professionals involved with the organization. In return, the medical community would reciprocate the exposure.

- Starting in August, begin personal delivery of literature and flyer dissemination.
- There are a number of conventions at the Los Angeles Convention Center to gain access to potential new members and professional members. Setting up a kiosk at these conventions will expose Resolve to a large audience. For example, if a kiosk is set up at the Latino Family Festival, there are potentially 20,000 attendees who may stop at your kiosk. If only 10 percent come, that is 2,000 people. (Assume 10 percent of the people at the convention have infertility problems.) If only 1 percent actually become members, that is 20 more members/volunteers than before. The financial budget accounts for participating in four of these conventions annually. The following table lists a few conventions that may be of interest.

Date	Event Name	Type	Estimated Attendance
June 11–13	1999 L.A. Women's Show	Public Show	42,000
July 29–Aug 2	Worldwide Marriage Encounter	Convention	N/A
July 25	Festival of Brides	Public Show	3,000
Aug. 28–29	Latino Family Festival '99	Public Show	20,000
Sept.10–12	L.A. Black Business Expo'99	Public Show	22,000

- Involvement of professionals as guest lecturers at the public education meetings or question-and-answer sessions encourages loyalty within the medical community. One idea to gain a win-win situation is to invite health care professionals to the meetings for a fee of $100. Resolve guarantees a certain number of attendees. If the number is not reached, the speaker is reimbursed the $100 fee. Our time line is set in such a way as to minimize confusion. Initially, have the infertility clinics or ASRM physicians give lectures on a monthly or biweekly basis. After three months, start adding lectures from adoption specialists. Lawyers are included in this group. It is good for couples to understand the legal process involved in adoption.
- Two to three years from the beginning of this plan, consider public education meetings in Spanish or Asian languages.
- Brand recognition is extremely important for the general public to identify the service Resolve offers.
- Immediately order videotapes from the Hawaii chapter of Resolve. To cover the Los Angeles area, contact Adlink at 310-477-3994. The company is a cable consolidator. The video will be sent to all the cable companies to be played as a public service announcement. By doing this, there is no cost to Resolve and only one telephone call.
- The logo or symbol of Resolve should be on everything.
- In September, have press releases in the newsletter. Include press releases on the Web site.
- Beginning in September, contact the local newspapers to feature infertility in the health section. Be sure the newspaper includes information on the services offered by Resolve.
- To effectively reach the Hispanic, Asian, and African populations, have press releases or feature articles in the local newspapers. Literature and flyers as well as tear-off pads containing information about Resolve and how to join, should be strategically placed in the health care workers' offices.

- Volunteer and member recruitment can be done effectively through kiosks in the community malls. This is one way to reach the Hispanic populations in Los Angeles. At the kiosk, educational materials could be sold.

Communication

- Maintain the newsletter. This is a very important link with the membership and volunteers, new and old.
- Quarterly updates of February, May, August, and November will keep members well informed.
- May—On the front page request volunteers and write an article on their importance. An article could discuss how best to recruit or motivate volunteers.
- August—Request donations and volunteers on the front page. Upgrade with the addition of chapter current events. Ask the general membership to spread the word about the services of Resolve. Ask friends to join and ask if their employers match donations or have volunteer programs in their organizations—a great way to tap into new potential membership pools.
- In the newsletters going to the current members, insert a special leaflet to discuss what the organization is doing. Give recognition to the volunteers by beginning "Volunteer of the Month." The newsletter article could be a discussion on how the volunteers got the job done efficiently or how they took the next step forward to go beyond the call of duty. Have the volunteers involved in the vote to build camaraderie.
- Solicit advertisements from various sources such as medical groups, clinics, and attorneys' offices for a fee. This will aid in underwriting the costs of the newsletter.
- On-line subscriptions of the newsletter will save costs on mailings.

On-Line

- May—Consult a Web master to improve or create a Web site that is easy for the membership to update the information. Access to this capability needs to be controlled.
- The current web site is not linked to National Resolve. In June, we recommend modifying the Web site. Link to the national Web site. Register with the search engine under Los Angeles. This will cost $50 annually. Continually update the Web site.
- Resolve needs to link to other Web sites such as

Demographics	Adoption-support, churches, agencies
Infertility Support Groups	International Organizations
National & Local Health Organizations	Women's Search Engine

A chat room is very useful for feedback, counseling, and many other purposes.

Software Implementation

- Currently there is no membership database software, only a paper list of members. A database management software system will organize and report information for members, donors, volunteers, professionals, and potentials. There are many software programs written specifically for nonprofits (see Appendix 9 and 10); however, the best software for the price and features is Omnium Gatherum, a membership management and fund-raising software. The price for this software is less than $1,000. Additionally, Omnium Gatherum allows volunteer activity tracking and project tracking.

- GuideStar has a program that unites all 501(c) (3) nonprofit groups with a very large network.
- To build an effective Web site, look at the best practices within the National Infrastructure. Perhaps an "on-line subscription" of the newsletter will increase "hits" on the Web site. If this is not feasible, the chapter could include two-month-old issues on-line to encourage people to subscribe or become members.

Hot-Line

- The information line is very important for people seeking information for alternatives. People who have English as a second language find communication on telephones to be difficult. Therefore, information needs to be disseminated at a slower speaking pace.
- January 2000, we recommend adding a Spanish-speaking recording and have Spanish-speaking counselors.
- April 2000—Set aside allotted times to have volunteers answer the hot-line immediately.
- June—Advertise on the Web site that the hot-line is personalized, manned, or automated. Statistics have shown if a hot-line is personalized, hang-ups drop by 25 percent. When people are on hold, have 15-second advertisements instead of music.
- April 2000—Get sponsorships to pay for the hot-line or even a local 800 number. One market to attract sponsors is the ARSM members. While people are being transferred to another line, have a 15-second commercial stating: "This message is sponsored by..."

Symposium

The most important step in organizing any symposium is remaining in a structured time-line every year. This will decrease the fluctuations of expenses from one year to the next. For 1999, it is very important to contact the exhibitors and potential underwriters immediately. Send letters during the first week of May. On the day letters are posted, call the potential sponsors and discuss the information in the letter. During the telephone call try to get some sort of commitment. After receiving the telephone call, potential sponsors will be expecting the letter.

The following recommendations in the time line will be for the 2000 symposium.

- November 1999: Right after the symposium: Thank-you letters to this year's supporters. Send letters to exhibitors for next year.
- October 1999: Book site for next year's symposium.
  Begin contacting businesses, the medical community, and the legal community to underwrite the next symposium.
- January 2000: Start recruiting speakers for this year. This activity should be completed at least 9 months before the symposium.
- February 2000: Follow-up phone call.
- July 2000: Final follow-up letter.
- June–July 2000: Send letters to membership by mail, E-mail or newsletter.
  Public Service Announcements on radio, TV, and newspapers.
- September 2000: Reminder letters to membership.
- Late August–early September: Logistics of meeting completed.

Grant Services   There are a number of companies on-line that offer services in grant writing. Some companies offer to write grants for a percentage of the awarded moneys. The best people to consult are those who guarantee their work. There is also the option of training an internal volunteer in grant writing.

SUMMARY

Resolve is an organization committed to providing emotional support and education for people experiencing family-building issues. Although Resolve is under heavy competition from the Internet due to the amount of information available on the Web, Resolve's competitive advantage is the personal and face-to-face contact.

Capitalizing on this advantage and implementing the activities in the Plan, Resolve will double its membership to 1,400 members within two years and to 1,750 members in three years. In addition, the volunteer base will increase 100 percent with revenues increasing to $106,000 from $63,000 in this three-year period.

This Plan provides the outline for continued success for the Los Angeles chapter and provides the outline for diversification into other demographic markets.

BIBLIOGRAPHY

Marmot, M.G. and Fuhrer, R. et al. "Contribution of Psychosocial Factors to Socioeconomic Differences," in Health Milbank Q 1998; 76(3):403–48, 305.

Keefe, David L. "Reproductive Aging Is an Evolutionarily Programmed Strategy that No Longer Provides Adaptive Value," *Fertility and Sterility,* vol. 70, no. 2 (August 1998), 204–206.

Haupt and Kane. *Population Handbook,* 4th ed. (Washington, DC: Population Reference Bureau, 1998).

Stephen, Elizabeth & Chandra, Anjani. "Updated Projections of Infertility in the United States: 1995–2025" *(Fertility and Sterility),* vol. 70, no. 1 (July 1998), p. 30–34.

Velde, E.R. and Cohlen, B.J. "The Management of Infertility," *The New England Journal of Medicine,* vol. 340, no. 3, p. 224–225.

Resolve Chapter Operations Manual.

1995 Assisted Reproductive Technology Success Rates National Summary and Fertility Clinic Reports Vol. 3—Western United States CDC, December 1997.

On-Line References:

www.sierraadoption.org

www.california-adoption.org/member

www.resolve.org

www.ihr.com/infertility/newsgrp

www.ipl.org/ref/AON

APPENDICES*

*Note: Because appendices to this plan are extensive, most have not been included.

APPENDIX 1: DEMOGRAPHICS 15–44 YEAR WOMEN

Table 51. Number of currently married women 15–44 years of age and percent distribution by infertility status, according to selected characteristics: United States, 1995

Characteristic	Number in Thousands	Total	Surgically Sterile	Infertile	Fecund	Number Infertile	% Infertile
			Percent Distribution				
All women	29,673	100	41.0	7.1	52.0	2,107	
Age at interview							
15–24 years	2,805	100	6.2	4.4	89.4	123	6%
25–34 years	12,242	100	27.3	6.6	66.1	808	38%
35–44 years	14,625	100	59.1	8.0	32.9	1,170	56%
Parity 0 (without child)							
15–44 years	5,685	100	13.1	17.1	69.8	972	
15–24 years	1,157	100	2.5	6.0	91.6	69	
25–34 years	2,810	100	6.5	13.5	80.0	379	
35–44 years	1,718	100	31.1	30.3	38.6	521	
Parity 1 or more (with at least one child)							
15–44 years	23,988	100	47.6	4.7	47.7	1,127	
15–24 years	1,649	100	8.8	3.3	87.8	54	
25–34 years	9,432	100	33.5	4.5	62.0	424	
35–44 years	12,907	100	62.9	5.0	32.2	645	
Education at interview 1							
No high school diploma or GED 2	2,807	100	51.8	8.5	39.7	239	
High school diploma or GED	11,534	100	50.3	8.1	41.5	934	
Some college, no bachelor's degree	7,163	100	41.1	6.6	52.3	473	
Bachelor's degree or higher	7,162	100	27.1	5.6	67.2	401	
Race and Hispanic origin							
Hispanic	3,178	100	36.4	7.0	56.7	222	11%
Non-Hispanic white	23,077	100	41.8	6.4	51.8	1,477	70%
Non-Hispanic black	2,069	100	46.6	10.5	42.9	217	10%
Non-Hispanic other	1,349	100	28.9	13.6	57.5	183	9%

1. Limited to women 22–44 years of age at time of interview.
2. GED is general equivalency diploma.
Note: Percents may not add to 100 due to rounding.

APPENDIX 2: DEMOGRAPHICS: 15–44 YEAR WOMEN RECEIVING INFERTILITY SERVICES.

Table 55.   Number of women 15–44 years of age, percent who have ever received an infertility services, and percent who have ever received the specified infertility services, by selected characteristics: United States, 1995

Characteristic	Number in Thousands	Any Services	Advice	Tests on Woman or Man	Ovulation Drugs	Surgery or Treatment for Blocked tubes	Assisted Reproductive Technology
		Percent Distribution					
All women	60,201	15.4	6.4	4.2	3.0	1.5	1.0
Age at interview							
15–24 years	18,002	4.4	1.1	0.2	0.3	0.1	—
25–34 years	20,758	17.1	6.3	3.7	3.1	1.2	0.8
35–44 years	21,440	22.9	10.9	8.1	5.2	2.9	2.1
Parity, age, and marital status							
No births	25,242	6.4	4.6	3.7	2.2	1.1	1.2
15–24	14,113	1.2	0.5	0.2	0.2	0.1	0.1
25–34	7,139	8.7	6.5	4.6	3.0	1.0	1.1
35–44	3,991	20.7	15.5	14.5	8.0	4.8	5.3
Married	5,685	20.9	16.0	13.6	8.3	4.1	4.7
Unmarried	19,558	2.2	1.2	0.8	0.4	0.2	0.1
1 or more births	34,958	21.8	7.7	4.6	3.6	1.8	0.9
15–24	3,889	16.1	3.3	0.3	0.6	0.5	—
25–34	13,620	21.5	6.2	3.1	3.1	1.3	0.6
35–44	17,449	23.4	9.8	6.7	4.6	2.4	1.4
Married	23,988	24.1	9.2	6.0	4.6	2.1	1.1
Unmarried	10,970	16.8	4.3	1.6	1.3	0.9	0.5
Education at interview							
No	5,424	14.9	3.3	2.0	1.2	0.7	0.2
High	18,169	20.0	7.8	4.9	3.9	2.0	1.1
Some	12,399	19.4	7.8	5.6	3.3	2.0	1.2
Bachelor's	11,748	18.0	10.3	7.1	5.3	1.9	2.2
Poverty level income at interview							
0–149	10,072	16.6	4.8	2.1	1.5	0.9	0.2
0–99	5,992	14.2	4.0	1.7	0.9	0.5	0.1
150–299	14,932	17.9	6.3	3.9	3.1	1.4	0.6
300 percent or higher	22,736	20.3	10.3	7.6	5.3	2.5	2.2
Race and Hispanic origin							
Hispanic	6,702	13.4	4.9	2.4	1.7	0.9	0.6
Nonhispanic	42,522	16.3	7.2	4.9	3.5	1.6	1.2
Nonhispanic	8,210	13.0	3.8	2.2	1.4	0.9	0.3
Nonhispanic	2,767	12.3	5.0	3.9	2.9	1.9	1.4

APPENDIX 3: DEMOGRAPHICS: 15–44 YEAR WOMEN VISITS TO GET PREGNANT OR PREVENT MISCARRIAGE

Table 56. Number of women 15–44 years of age and percent distribution by the number of visits for medical help to get pregnant or to prevent miscarriage (made by her or her husband or cohabiting partner) in the 12 months prior to interview, according to selected characteristics: United States, 1995

Characteristic	Number in Thousands	Total	Never Had an Infertility Visit	Number of Visits in Last Year				
				None	Total	1 or More		
						1	2	3
					Percent Distribution			
All women 1	60,201	100	85.4	12.6	2.0	1.0	0.2	0.8
Age at interview								
15–24 years	18,002	100	96.2	2.5	1.4	0.8	0.1	0.5
25–34 years	20,758	100	83.7	13.1	3.3	1.8	0.3	1.2
35–44 years	21,440	100	77.8	20.8	1.4	0.4	0.2	0.8
Parity, age, and marital status								
0 births	25,242	100	93.7	4.1	2.2	1.0	0.3	0.9
15–24 years	14,113	100	98.9	0.3	1.9	0.5	–	1.4
25–34 years	7,139	100	91.4	4.5	5.1	2.2	0.6	2.3
35–44 years	3,991	100	79.5	16.9	3.6	0.7	0.6	2.3
Married	5,685	100	79.3	12.7	8.0	3.2	1.1	3.7
Unmarried	19,558	100	97.9	1.6	0.5	0.4	–	0.1
1 or more births	34,958	100	79.2	18.9	2.0	1.0	0.2	0.8
15–24 years	3,889	100	86.0	10.4	3.7	1.6	0.5	1.6
25–34 years	13,620	100	79.6	17.7	2.7	1.6	0.1	1.0
35–44 years	17,449	100	77.5	21.7	0.8	0.3	0.1	0.4
Married	23,988	100	76.9	20.9	2.2	1.1	0.2	0.9
Unmarried	10,970	100	84.3	14.6	1.1	0.5	0.2	0.4
Education at interview 2								
No high school diploma or GED 3	5,424	100	86.4	12.1	1.6	1.1	0.1	0.4
High school diploma or GED	18,169	100	81.0	16.7	2.3	1.2	0.3	0.8
Some college, no bachelor's degree	12,399	100	81.2	16.9	2.0	0.9	0.2	0.9
Bachelor's degree or higher	11,748	100	82.5	14.5	3.1	1.3	0.3	1.5
Poverty level income at interview 2								
0–149 percent	10,072	100	84.7	13.9	1.4	0.7	0.3	0.4
0–99 percent	5,992	100	86.7	11.6	1.8	0.9	0.2	0.7
150–299 percent	14,932	100	83.2	15.2	1.7	1.1	0.1	0.5
300 percent or higher	22,736	100	80.2	16.8	2.9	0.3	1.4	1.2
Race and Hispanic origin								
Hispanic	6,702	100	87.4	10.2	2.4	1.2	0.4	0.8
Nonhispanic white	42,522	100	84.3	13.6	2.1	1.0	0.2	0.9
Nonhispanic black	8,210	100	88.2	10.3	1.6	0.9	0.2	0.5
Nonhispanic other	2,767	100	88.0	10.8	1.1	0.2	0.2	0.7

A7

SNEAK PEEK: A STUDENT'S GUIDE TO UNIVERSITY COURSES

Developed by
DAVID GRAJEDA
TONETTE DOVE
ANTHONY B. LUJAN
DONNA TOM
HUEI MING TSAI
CAROLINE WANG

Contents

EXECUTIVE SUMMARY

This marketing plan was developed to study the economic feasibility of distributing a campus publication. *Sneak Peek: A Student's Guide* serves as a detailed brochure for students about courses offered at the California State University at Los Angeles (CSULA) campus. Preliminary research indicates there exists a strong demand for this product and a stable target market. As of fall 1989 the student population of CSULA was 20,804 and has remained fairly constant at the 20,000–21,000 range for the past four years (see Appendix A7-A). Primary research data have established that 70 percent of the target market would be willing to purchase this product at a price range of under $10 (Appendix A7-B). Of this market, 50 percent will be captured the first year (i.e., 35 percent of the total market) and sales are expected to increase by at least 50 percent per year thereafter. Further appeal is that the brochure has very low overhead, minimal competition, and benefits both students and the quality of CSULA's education.

This venture would require an initial capital investment of $18,000 (6 shares at $3,000 each). This initial capital investment will be paid back the first year. Furthermore, a first-year return on investment of 44 percent is expected. The sales projection for the initial year is $128,055.53. Of the first year's revenue, 12.8 percent will be from local business advertising sales. Throughout the five-year projection sales are projected to grow tremendously.

INTRODUCTION

The objective of this marketing plan is to study the feasibility of publishing a student's inside guide to courses and instructors at CSULA. Based upon a preliminary survey of 450 currently enrolled CSULA students, an 88 percent favorable response rate for this product and a 70 percent buy rate from students who wished to purchase this product was established. This survey represents a cross-section of all students currently attending CSULA. Surveys were purposely done at random times during the day and evenings throughout campus. This gave a representative mix of undergraduate and graduate students as well as dormitory and commuter students (see Appendix A7-C).

Demand for the product will be strong because CSULA has a high percentage of commuter students (97 percent) with limited access to "word-of-mouth" recommendations on class and instructor information. Primary research data on 450 randomly selected CSULA students indicate only 62 percent had access to "word-of-mouth" recommendations from friends for classes they were planning to take the next quarter. This information gap is further compounded by the fact that many CSULA students have less time for social interactions than traditional college students. Many CSULA students are trying to balance full-time jobs and family responsibilities in conjunction with school demands (see Appendix A7-A). This guidebook will provide a reasonable alternative to traditional "word-of-mouth" recommendations college students of the past utilized when they had the time and opportunity to develop a social network with fellow dorm residents and classmates.

Promotion and advertising of this publication will be directed along CSULA's mass communication channels (CSULA *University Times* ads, quarterly *Schedule of Classes* ads, campus flyers, and advertising/sales booths during new student orientation days). Students will be offered discount coupons for the publication or free advertising of their used books on a selected basis. This will be a means of generating increased awareness and interest in the guidebook.

Printing and advertising costs will constitute the major expense. To maintain production costs at a minimum and keep the final product at a reasonable price to cost-conscious students, the guidebook will be limited to 160 pages for the initial printing. The guidebook will consist of five sections:

1. Information on courses and instructors.
2. Business advertising space (encourage free or discount coupon offers).
3. Invitation for students to participate in the next publication as a respondent.
4. Invitation to advertise in the recycler section for free.
5. Recycler section (will need to limit this section since it is being used as a promotion technique—i.e., loss leader).

One method that will be employed to offset publishing costs is to entice local businesses (fast-food, laundry, printing or photocopying establishments, bookstores, apartment managers, or other student-oriented services) to advertise in the guidebook for a fee. This additional advertising revenue will make it feasible to keep the price charged for the publication under $10. This should aid greatly in overcoming student price resistance.

Based on the results of a random survey of 450 CSULA students, sales and market share projections will be forecasted for the initial year. This will be followed by a complete analysis of capital expenses, promotion and distribution costs, start-up costs, and a quarter-to-quarter cash-flow projection for a five-year period.

SITUATIONAL ANALYSIS

In this section various factors that affect the marketability of the product will be discussed. Customer profile, relevant social and cultural factors, prevailing economic and business conditions, legal and political aspects, and other environmental factors impacting the product will be examined.

Customer Profile

Sneak Peek's target market is comprised of CSULA's student body. Of the total quarterly 20,000 plus enrollment, the specific target marketing will be directed toward the freshman, sophomore, and junior class levels. It is this 45.2 percent of total students, who enroll in the general and lower division courses, that have been selected for the student guide's first edition. Currently totaling 12,407, this undergraduate segment population will be the primary focus, but not to the exclusion of the 54.8 percent senior class level. It is believed the intended target market will actively seek this product. *Sneak Peek* enhances the opportunity to effectively choose classes which otherwise would require informational networking that may not be easily accessible.

Location Profile

Realistically, the two most visible and therefore most ideal sites to sell the product would be the University Square Bookstore and the Student Book Mart located at 1689 N. Eastern Avenue. These two locations have established themselves as CSULA student-oriented outlets and generate tremendous student traffic. Secondary methods of generating sales would be to employ direct marketing techniques to solicit sales through advertising in the CSULA quarterly *Schedule of Classes,* the CSULA *University Times,* and flyers distributed throughout campus. Another ideal site location would be to set up a booth during new student orientation days and distribute sales information on the guidebook.

The fact that this venture does not require a permanent storefront as a prerequisite to doing business is a definite advantage. By avoiding this major fixed overhead expense this business can be initiated on a shoestring budget.

Sales Projections

The average student at CSULA spends approximately $40 to $50 on textbooks per course. The guidebook will be priced at under $10.

Most students would perceive this as a bargain. Insights obtained from the publication are valuable if they allow one to avoid the ordeal of registration's drop-and-add. Also, there is the added "hook" of the recycler section to aid in increasing sales. Students will have the opportunity to contact other students and purchase used books at a savings. Thus, all or a significant portion of the cost of the guidebook can be recouped. Another positive selling feature of the guidebook is the discount or free coupons offered by local merchants in the business advertising section.

Based on the CSULA student survey a conservative sell rate of 35 percent of the 20,804 total student population is anticipated. This represents 50 percent of the students who said they would buy based upon a selling price of less than $10. Therefore, the first-year sales projection on guidebooks is approximately $111,602 based upon an introductory direct mail price of $5 and a wholesale price of $4 for the publication. The calculation used was a 70 percent buy response × 50 percent sales rate × total CSULA student population × selling price of guidebook × 4 issues per year (with the added stipulation that direct mailing will account for 20 percent of total sales for the first year). Sales are targeted to increase by 50 percent per year since 88 percent of the respondents saw a need for the publication, but only 70 percent said they would actually buy. Through "word-of-mouth" customer recommendations and additional product features, the remaining market population will be captured within a three-year period.

Additional revenue will be attained through advertising sales to local businesses: $175 per quarter, $330 for two quarters, $435 for three quarters, and $540 for four quarters for a $1/4$-page advertisement in the guidebook. This represents 50 percent less than rates charged by the CSULA *Schedule of Classes* publication. Revenues generated from this source will add a minimum of $10,000 to $15,000 in yearly profits using a conservative target of 20 advertisers per issue. Therefore, total sales projections for the first year from sales of guidebooks and sales of advertising space is $128,055.53.

Additionally, if the option to charge $2 per used book ad is utilized in the Recycler Section, profits will increase once again.

Competition

As with any business, competition is always a critical factor. Currently, CSULA does not have a publication similar to the guidebook available for its students. Thus, one significant advantage to be enjoyed at the introduction of this publication is a monopoly on the market. To capitalize on this advantage, the first year will be used to refine the publication through soliciting suggestions for improvement in the product's format from customers, and revising to meet these new standards as quickly as possible. Thus, competition strategy will be to keep the publication price low and the product quality high in order to discourage competitors from entering the marketplace. estimate will be made at the time of each payment. Other than the risk of a libel suit and payment of taxes, there are no other basic regulations at the federal level that must be complied with.

At the state level, according to Jamie Green of the State Board of Equalizations, quarterly periodicals are not subject to state taxes. Therefore, the price charged for the guidebook is the price that must be charged to retail customers. State sales tax will not be collected at the wholesale or the retail level. By registering *Sneak Peek* at the office of the State Board of Equalization, a resale number can be obtained through which sales can be made to vendors. No business license is required at the state level. This type of licensing is done only at the municipal level.

Obtaining a normal business license to fulfill city level requirements involves filing and paying license fees at the county clerk's office. Two licenses are required: the Consumer Retail Sales License (CRS) and the Wholesale Sale License (WSL). The CRS has an initial cost of $100.78, and the WSL has a first-time cost of $107.50. Every January thereafter, the CRS requires a payment of $1.25 per $1,000 worth of units sold. Similarly, every subsequent January the WSL requires a payment of $1.25 per $1,000 worth of units sold. Once these two licenses are obtained, it is legal to operate this business in the city.

However, this does not mean that *Sneak Peek* automatically receives the approval of the California State University at Los Angeles. According to Ruth Goldway, Director of Public Affairs–CSULA, the first step in getting the school to approve this project is through the Office of Student Life, Student Union 425. Vera Perez, Office of Student Life, stated that printing the guidebook could be approved by the university. However, final approval must be obtained from Central Reservations, Student Union 410. Any item that is circulated throughout the university must have a university stamp of approval.

Once *Sneak Peek* has this stamp, total freedom is allowed in marketing it to students. Setting up a table in front of the Student Union would cost $25 per day and promote high visibility of the product. On the other hand, selling this guidebook through the University Book Store would require the approval of Catherine Rembol, CSULA Book Store Manager. Ms. Rembol claims that the retail cost to students for each guidebook would be the product's wholesale price plus a 25 percent markup.

PROBLEMS AND OPPORTUNITIES

A primary survey of 450 CSULA students yielded encouraging statistics. Seldom does a company have the opportunity to market a new product to a target group where 88 percent of the market believes there is a need for that product, 63 percent of the target market is willing to participate in the production of that product, and 70 percent of the market is also willing to buy the finished product when it becomes available (see Appendix A7-C, Table 2). It was interesting to note that 97 percent of the freshman class (the best indicator of future sales) believes there is a need for this product and 76 percent are willing to buy the guide if it is priced at less than $10. Once again, this reinforces the belief that even with access to "word-of-mouth" recommendations (52 percent for freshmen), students are still eager to find out more about classes and instructors, especially from a reasonably priced source.

It is expected that the demand for this product will continue to grow until the full market share of 70 percent is attained and then remain constant because customers will be encouraged to repeat buy each quarter. Some students may choose to photocopy sections of the guide rather than purchase it, but this will be a relatively low number due to the low price ($5) of the product. To encourage repeat buyers, the courses selected for the guide will vary slightly each quarter to correspond to courses offered by the university. Additionally, emphasis will be placed on obtaining business advertisers that will offer discount coupons on goods and services in their advertisement through the guidebook. Finally, the possible savings on purchasing used books through the guide's Recycler Section will spur sales and encourage repeat buyers.

Perhaps the primary obstacle to the success of this venture will be compiling the required data quickly enough to update the publication every quarter. This requires being totally dependent upon the input of students responding to invitations to be part of the student panel. Therefore, the incentives offered (discount coupon or free advertising space) must be compelling enough to entice students to participate. Based on the students surveyed, 63 percent of the respondents said they were willing to participate for these incentives. Of this group, 60 percent preferred receiving the discount coupon, 25 percent the free advertising, and 15 percent had no preference (see Appendix A7-C, Table 3). It is anticipated that one person using the telephone to collect all required information should be able to update the publication each quarter.

Due to the quarterly publication of the product, inventory levels must be monitored very carefully. With experience, the ability to accurately judge demand for the product will be gained. Strict inventory control will increase profits by reducing the amount of outdated merchandise created by the quarterly turnover of this product. To address this problem, the "Just-in-Time" method of inventory control will be utilized.

FINANCIAL ANALYSIS

In order to determine start-up and operational costs the following financial analysis was compiled:

1. *Initial Investment.* The initial investment for the proposed business is for capital equipment (typewriter, telephone, answering machine) and miscellaneous expenses (stationery, phone line, optional P.O. box). This business is designed to be run out of one's

home. As stated earlier, the major expense will be printing and postage costs for the respondents.

2. *First-Year Operations.* From the target sales of $111,602 for the first year, the net income of $38,320 is derived after deducting cost of sales and all other operating expenses. (See Appendix A7-N, Table 2, Projected Profit and Loss Statement—Year 1.) This represents a return of 30 percent on sales and 44 percent on investment. A positive cash flow of $33,450 is projected at the end of the first year of which $30,000 is available for distribution to the partners ($5,000 per partner). The break-even sales for the first year are based on a total fixed cost of $6,934.28.

3. *Five-Year Projection.* In the five-year projection, sales are estimated to grow at 50 percent for year 2, 75 percent for year 3, 40 percent for year 4, 25 percent for year 5. This growth objective is realistic based upon the sales strategy not only of the guide-book but of increasing sales from local business advertising and student used-books advertising in subsequent years.

OPERATIONAL ASPECTS

This section will describe the actual product to be published and the process utilized to gather and coordinate course/instructor information from fellow students.

Product

The publication will consist of six sections:

1. Course/instructor information
2. Local business advertising
3. Invitation to be a student respondent
4. Invitation to advertise in Recycler Section for free
5. Recycler Section
6. Invitation to place an advance order

The largest section of the guidebook (70–90 pages) will be the information on course requirements and instructors. The criteria for segmenting courses were based on identifying those courses needed by students to fulfill their undergraduate degree requirements. General Education courses form the foundation for every undergraduate student. Selecting these courses will result in the greatest demand for this guidebook and promote active sales. For the first edition of the guidebook, General Education courses that attract the most enrollment will be selected. Essentially, courses offering more than two choices of instructors will be included in the guidebook. This translates into surveying approximately 128 classes for course requirements and instructor information to be published in the first edition of the guidebook.

Future issues will utilize the same basic strategy as above. Each quarter, courses will be analyzed and those with the highest enrollment selected for publication. Future expansion and marketing strategy would call for plans to produce a separate guidebook for graduate students and select majors with high enrollment. For example, analyzing the core requirements of Business and Economics majors would yield a marketable product as well as examining Child Development and Nursing coursework (see Appendix A7-A).

Once the courses for inclusion into the publication are selected, responses from students who wish to participate in the publication (Appendix A7-F) will be culled to select those who are currently taking the courses to be evaluated. These students will be contacted by phone and the appropriate information collected (see Appendix A7-I). A minimum of three to five students will be polled for each course in order to gain a representative overview of students' opinions on course and instructor requirements (see Appendix A7-I and Appendix A7-D). This information will be compiled, collated, and organized for final publication. By updating course requirements each quarter, any recent changes in course requirements will be noted. This action does not obviate the necessity of including a disclaimer stating in effect that up-to-date information on courses and instructors has been compiled, but there is no guarantee that future courses taught by this instructor will follow the described format. Although course requirements may vary slightly from quarter to quarter, the information presented on instructors' teaching and grading methods is still applicable and will be valuable to customers.

The final product is envisioned to be approximately 160 pages and will be printed by Art's Press, 4727 E. Olympic Blvd., Los Angeles, CA 90020, (213) 262-0431. The guidebook will consist of 40 pages of 11×17 inch standard stock white paper saddle-stitched down the middle (160 total pages of $8^1/_2 \times 11$ inch paper printed on both sides) with a goldenrod cover of slightly heavier stock paper and done in one-color print. Total printing time for 2,000 copies is seven days, plus an additional seven days to typeset the first edition. Total printing cost for the first batch of 2,000 copies is $2,500, including typesetting. Additional runs of 2,000 copies will take 7 days' printing time and cost $1,900 per batch as quoted by Paul Go, owner of Art's Press.

The Just-In-Time method of inventory control will be utilized and the appropriate number of copies reordered when available stock drops below 500 copies. Since this publication is updated quarterly, outdated merchandise from overestimating demand is a concern. It is anticipated that after the first two quarters of publication, data on product demand will become accurate.

MARKETING STRATEGY

Basically, the guidebook will consist of the six sections mentioned previously. Each section will play a distinct role in the marketing of the product.

PRODUCT STRATEGY

Overall product strategy was to develop a product that was of universal appeal to CSULA students. A guidebook on course and instructor information seemed the most logical product to market to students. To separate this publication from the CSULA General Catalogue, which also gives course information, the guidebook will include information on grading methods and student insights. Also, a more free-flowing, entertaining style of writing will be employed to make the publication enjoyable to read. Therefore, initial product strategy was threefold:

1. Offer course information from a student's perspective with student tips on how to do well.
2. Keep the price of the publication low to fit students' tight budgets.

3. Offer free services or discounts on merchandise to create the feeling that the buyer was getting his money's worth.

To accomplish these objectives, six sections to the guidebook were devised.

Section 1: Course/Instructor Information (70–90 pages). This section will contain a brief description of course content to lend substance and credibility to the product. This description will be kept short so as to not cover the same information presented in the CSULA *General Catalogue.* Students' insights on how to prepare for tests and helpful hints will be included. Student comments on instructors will be carefully reviewed to ascertain if they are appropriate for inclusion in the guidebook. There is no wish to threaten or antagonize instructors by becoming too personal or subjective in instructor evaluations. Each course will receive a half-page write-up in the guidebook.

Section 2: Local Business Advertising (10–20 pages maximum). This section was designed as a means of offering free or discount goods to students from local merchants while serving as an important source of revenue for the guidebook through paid advertising fees. Local merchants will be strongly encouraged to offer student discounts when placing their advertisements.

Section 3: Invitation to Be a Student Respondent (2 pages). This will save the cost of advertising in other publications to recruit student participants (see Appendix A7-F). A copy of the student Participant Questionnaire (see Appendix A7-I) will be included in the guidebook so interested students will know what information will be needed in evaluating courses for the guidebook. The invitation will include a postcard size prepaid reply card for interested students to mail in to the guidebook's P.O. box.

Section 5: Recycler Section (40–50 pages). This section contains brief ads for used books (see Appendix A7-H). Students will call each other based on information contained in the ad. The staff of the guidebook will not be involved with these used-book sales. Depending on student response, there are plans to turn the recycler into a third avenue of income in the future through sale of used-book advertising.

Section 6: Order Form for Advance Book Sale (1 page). This form will allow students to order the next issue of the guidebook in advance (see Appendix A7-J). By selling at a retail price ($5/copy) instead of a wholesale price ($4/copy), an additional $1/copy of sales revenue is obtained at the expense of $0.35/copy in mailing costs. More important, advance sales will help in maintaining adequate inventory levels.

It is projected that direct mail sales will constitute 20 percent of total sales the first year and increase slightly each year as students become familiar with the content and quality of the product.

PRICE STRATEGY

Marketing strategy dictates setting the price of this publication below $10 per copy. In fact the price for the first edition is only $5 by direct mail (postage and handling included), or $5 through the university bookstore or the Student Book Mart. This will allow the publication to be perceived as a bargain. It offers students a range of desirable features as well as the opportunity to recoup their investment through the recycler section and merchant discount coupons. This low price will lend an initial price advantage over future competitors and hopefully discourage them from entering the market. It will also make it easier to repeat sell the publication each quarter to the same clientele.

As a means of keeping production costs low and therefore product price low, local businesses will be actively solicited to advertise in the publication and offer free services or goods. Advertisements in *Sneak Peek* can be done on a quarterly or yearly basis for fees far lower than conventional advertising rates. The CSULA *Schedule of Classes* is published quarterly and charges for a quarter-page ad: $350 for 1 quarter, $660 for 2 quarters, $870 for 3 quarters, and $1,080 for 4 quarters. Businesses in the CSULA local area will be approached to solicit advertisements at a rate 50 percent lower than those charged by the publishers of the CSULA quarterly *Schedule of Classes.* This additional revenue will be used to keep the price charged for the guidebook low. It is anticipated that 10 to 20 business ads will be placed in the guidebook each quarter the first year. Business advertising revenue is targeted to increase by 50 percent each year.

PROMOTION STRATEGY

The promotion for this product will concentrate on mass advertising through campus publications and activities. Direct mail solicitation through the CSULA *Schedule of Classes,* the CSULA *University Times,* and flyer distribution throughout campus will be utilized. Also, information and sales booths will be set up on campus during new student orientation days.

Advertising costs for the above mentioned publications are as follows: CSULA *University Times* has a flat fee of $337 per year for an advertisement that is placed in the classified section of the campus newspaper in a two-column, 3-inch deep, boxed enclosure. It will run for 30 consecutive issues. The *University Times* is printed three days a week, Monday, Wednesday, and Thursday, with a circulation of 8,000 copies each quarter; 6,000 copies are printed each Monday and Thursday; and 12,000 copies are printed for registration, welcome back, and special issues. The *University Times* has a daily readership over 23,500 of which 20,000 are students, 1,500 are faculty, and 2,000 are campus employees (see Appendix A7-J). The *University Times* is distributed free on campus from circulation boxes located at high traffic points and also at the student housing complexes.

The CSULA *Schedule of Classes* is issued on a quarterly basis. The advertising fee for a quarter-page ad depends upon the frequency: $350 for 1 quarter, $660 for 2 quarters, $870 for 3 quarters, $1,080 for 4 quarters. The University Square Bookstore orders 23,000 to 25,000 *Schedule of Classes* per quarter according to Katherine Rembold, general manager of the bookstore.

Posters will also be utilized on campus to inform potential customers of this publication. The posters will be placed in high traffic points, such as the Student Union, the cafeterias, in and around the library, kiosks, and housing complexes. The size of the poster mentioned will be 11 × 17 inches.

Flyer distribution promoting the features of the publication and how to obtain a copy will be hand placed on car windshields during the period of class registration. The size of the flyers mentioned will be $8^{1}/_{2} \times 11$ inches.

DISTRIBUTION STRATEGY

This product will be available for in-person sales through the University Square Bookstore and the Student Book Mart. Rates these establishments charge for their services are as follows: the University Square Bookstore will mark up the wholesale price charged them by 25 percent to obtain the retail price. The Student Book Mart will discount the retail selling price of the University Square Bookstore by 10 to 15 percent to obtain their selling price.

Alternatively, the publication can be purchased at the booth set up during new student orientation days provided this does not conflict with sales at the University Square Bookstore. Permission to operate a booth outside the Student Union can be obtained through the Student Union management.

Another source for obtaining the publication will be through the direct mail ads run in the *Schedule of Classes* and the *University Times.* Purchases can be made by calling the listed telephone number to request an order form or by sending in an order form and a check to a P.O. box or dropping it off at a campus mailbox. Approval from the university as a legitimate business is required before a campus mailbox can be obtained from the Associated Student Office, Student Union 424. One of the incentives for students to use direct mail purchase is the opportunity to order the publication in advance to obtain the guidebook before it is released through the bookstores. Advance sales give students first opportunity to purchase the used books offered. In terms of product distribution, advance sales are beneficial in maintaining adequate product inventory levels. It decreases demand peaks and reduces unplanned shortages due to insufficient supply.

Statistics will be followed for each of the above mentioned distribution methods to determine which avenues generate the most sales. Future advertising budget and distribution efforts will be concentrated on the most effective mediums.

IMPLEMENTATION SCHEDULE

The advertising period of *Sneak Peek* will extend throughout CSULA's school year. Advertising will be heavy beginning the fifth week of spring 1990. This is *Sneak Peek's* introduction period. Promotion continues through the summer quarter with emphasis on the third through eighth week coinciding with student registration. Special emphasis will be placed on promotion for new student orientation and the fall 1990 quarter.

1. *Immediate.* Collecting data will begin the first week of the spring 1990 quarter. Class schedule data will be continuously accumulated throughout the school year. Information such as the instructors' curriculum data and students' input will be gathered until the second week of the fall 1990 quarter.

2. *Spring 1990 Quarter.* During this period, *Sneak Peek's* advertising and promotion begins as follows:

   University Times ads: Submit ad for year-round circulation.
   Flyers and posters: Print up and distribute. Announce arriving campus product.
   Schedule of Classes: Submit ad to directory of classes for each upcoming quarter scheduled publication.

   In this quarter, students will be invited to participate in a survey in exchange for free advertising of a used book or for a $2 discount coupon off the purchase price of the publication.

3. *Summer 1990 Quarter.* All scheduled objectives, except product distribution, implemented. Advertising, data collection, editing, and promotion will continue through the

span of this quarter. Accumulated data are edited and revised. Organization of collected information is prepared for the fall 1990 quarter's second week.

4. ***Fall 1990 Quarter.*** Advertising, promotion, printing, and distribution are the main emphasis of this scheduled section. By the end of week 1, all required editing will be completed and the finished draft sent to the printer. The final product will be made available by the fourth week. This is the optimum time for release of this publication since it coincides with peak demand for the product.

Distribution (direct mailing and bookstore circulation) will begin the fifth week. This will correspond with CSULA's winter 1991 *Schedule of Classes* and winter registration period. Promotional activities will be carried through as indicated under the Promotion heading of the Implementation Schedule (Appendix A7-M).

FINANCIAL DATA

The initial investment is a relatively low amount of $3,000 for each person with a total of $18,000. The reason for this low initial investment is the low cost of expenses. For example, a retail outlet is not needed, personnel is limited, and the distribution is solely through the bookstores or through mail order. These advantages greatly reduce costs. The initial fiscal year will start from fall 1990. The financial data used are in a conservative form so all projections of expenses and costs will not be less than actual cost. Also, the expected sales will not be less than the actual sales. Sales of $128,055.53 are expected for the first year from both guidebook and advertising sales. Total sales will grow by 50 percent for year 2, 75 percent for year 3, 40 percent for year 4, and 25 percent for year 5. Total sales of $588,255.07 are expected by year 5. The best selling season is the fall quarter (see Appendix A7-N, Profit and Loss Statement). The seasonal factors used were: fall 1.35, winter 1.1, spring 0.9, and summer 0.65. These factors are based on the enrollment of students each quarter on campus. For example, the fall quarter is the highest selling quarter because it has the largest enrollment, and summer will be our lowest quarter in sales because it has the smallest enrollment. *Sneak Peek* is so profitable that the return on investment is 44 percent, which is 10 percent more than normal in the industry. This is due to high student demand for this item. Each investor will receive a $5,000 distribution for the first year. This will increase by 15 percent for year 2, 50 percent for year 3, 75 percent for year 4, 50 percent for year 5. The distribution for each investor will increase fivefold by the end of year 5.

CONCLUSION

In conclusion, this marketing plan has clearly outlined why this product will be successful. High student demand for this product (88 percent), as exhibited by willingness of students to participate in the production of the guidebook (63 percent) and in their desire to purchase the finished product (70 percent), has conclusively been established. Thus, the first caveat of marketing has been accomplished, namely, "Produce or obtain a product that sells itself." Another positive feature is the variety of ways this publication generates revenue: through direct mail sales, wholesale sales, business advertising sales, and student advertising sales. Besides being highly profitable with a 44 percent first return on investment and first-year sales of $128,055.53, required initial start-up capital is minimal ($18,000) due to low overhead and very low product costs. This, coupled with the flexibility of being able to quickly adapt the publication to respond to student needs or to branch off into more specialized guidebooks for specific degree majors, ensures both the present and future viability of this product.

Bibliography

Cohen, William, *Building a Mail Order Business.* John Wiley & Sons, New York, 1982.

Office of Public Affairs and Analytical Studies, *Facts #2: Fall 1989 Enrollment Information.* California State University at Los Angeles, January 1990, p. 2.

Office of Public Affairs and Analytical Studies, *Facts #1: Fall 1988 Enrollment Information,* California State University at Los Angeles, January 1989, p. 2.

Office of Public Affairs and Analytical Studies, *Facts Sheet: Fall 1987, Enrollment Information,* California State University at Los Angeles, January 1988, p. 1.

References

Ruth Goldway, Public Affairs Director (213) 343–3050.

Katherine F. Rembold, General Manager of Student Bookstore (213) 343–2500.

Terrance Timmins, J. D., Coordinator, Legal Information CSULA (213) 343–3110 or (213) 343–3414; State Board of Equalization, County Clerk's Office.

Appendix A7-A

CALIFORNIA STATE UNIVERSITY, LOS ANGELES TARGET POPULATION STATISTICS

Apportioned by class level, part-time, and full-time status
Years 1987, 1988, and 1989

	Fall 1987		Fall 1988		Fall 1989	
Total	21,189	100.00%	21,150	100.00%	20,804	100.00%
Freshmen	2,903	13.70	3,363	15.90	3,375	16.22
Sophomores	2,373	11.20	1,967	9.30	2,144	10.31
Juniors	4,047	19.10	3,997	18.90	3,888	18.69
Seniors	5,827	27.50	5,901	27.90	5,976	28.73
Grad-PB	6,039	29.50	5,922	28.00	5,421	26.05
Part-time	10,806	51.00%	10,617	50.00%	10,358	49.80%
Full-time	10,383	49.00	10,300	49.00	10,446	50.20
Comprehensive exams			233	1.00		

Fall 1989 Population Statistics		
Commuter students	20,217	97.18%
Campus residents	587	2.82

Sources:
Office of Public Affairs and Analytical Studies, *Facts Sheet: Fall 1987 Enrollment Information,* California State University, Los Angeles, January 1988, p. 1.
Office of Public Affairs and Analytical Studies, *Facts #2: Fall 1988 Enrollment Information,* California State University, Los Angeles, January 1990, p. 2.
Office of Public Affairs and Analytical Studies, *Facts #3: Fall 1989 Enrollment Information,* California State University, Los Angeles, January 1990, p. 2.

Appendix A7-B

GUIDE TO CLASSES AND INSTRUCTORS OF CSULA SURVEY

1. Male _____ Female _____

2. Freshman _____ Sophomore _____ Junior _____ Senior _____

   Graduate student _____ Instructor _____

3. Do you think there is a need for a student guide to classes and instructors of CSULA?

   Yes _____ No _____

4. Do you think students have a right to know each instructor's course requirements and grading personality habits before signing up for their course?

   Yes _____ No _____

5. Do you have access to word-of-mouth recommendations from friends for the classes you intend to take next quarter?

   Yes _____ No _____

6. Would you be willing to participate anonymously as one of the students we polled to gain information on courses and instructors in exchange for a $2.00 discount coupon on our publication or an opportunity for free advertising of a used book you wish to sell?

   Yes _____ No _____

   I prefer: Discount coupon _____ Free advertising _____

7. Would you be willing to pay less than $10.00/copy for this publication?

   Yes _____ No _____   Thank you for your participation in this survey.

Appendix A7-C

STATISTICAL ANALYSIS OF CSULA COURSE/INSTRUCTOR GUIDE SURVEY

Table 1: CSULA Student Sample Population Breakdown by Class Levels

	Freshman	Sophomore	Junior	Senior	Grad.	Total
No. of students	64	92	119	132	40	450
% of total	14	21	27	29	9	100

Table 2: Percentage of "Yes" Response to Survey Questions*

	Freshman	Sophomore	Junior	Senior	Grad.	Total
Need for guide	97	85	86	92	79	88
Right to know	96	83	88	91	83	88
Access to word-of-mouth recommendations	52	65	60	73	40	62
Willingness to participate	67	71	60	59	43	63
Will buy guide	76	76	73	66	54	70

*Also polled 1 instructor who voted "yes" on "Need for Guide" and "Right of Students to Know" course and instructor information before signing up for a class.

Table 3: Analysis of Incentive Offering for Student Participation (in %)

	Freshman	Sophomore	Junior	Senior	Grad.	Total
Willingness to participate	67	71	60	59	43	63
Discount coupon	58	72	56	54	47	60
Free ad	33	20	20	29	29	25
Either	9	8	24	17	24	15

Appendix A7-D

SAMPLE FORMAT OF COURSE/INSTRUCTOR INFORMATION

Course number/section:

Instructor:

Course requirements: Tests (number of tests)
                            (Comprehensive or non-comprehensive final exam)
                            (Multiple choice, essay, true/false format)
                            (covers lectures only, textbook only, or both)
                            Papers
                            Projects
                            Presentations
                            (What percentage do each of the above contribute to the final grade)?

Course Information: (Obtained from students who have taken this course previously)

1. Plan to spend _____hours outside of school studying for this course each week.

2. On a scale of 1 to 5, to what degree does this class give you practical knowledge you could apply immediately to improve your job or personal life? (Use: Not at all = 1. A great deal = 5)

This course received a _____ rating

3. Students felt that this class (_____did _____did not _____not sure) offer them more than they originally expected when they enrolled for the class.

4. Students (_____would _____would not) recommend this course to their friends.

5. Students felt it (_____was _____was not) necessary to do well in prerequisite requirements to handle the class load of this course.

6. Students gave this class an average difficulty rating of _____(using a scale of 1 to 5 with Easy = 1, Average = 3, Extremely difficult = 5)

Additional student comments:_____

_____

_____

APPENDIX A7-E

SAMPLE FORMAT OF LOCAL BUSINESS ADVERTISING

CHOICES

Located next to Eagles' Landing

Choices has an all-you-can-eat buffet and salad bar with courteous waiters to serve you. So why not keep those lunch dates on campus and let us serve you in a quiet relaxing atmosphere.

Mon. - Fri. 11:30 a.m. - 1:45 p.m.   (Fri. soup & salad bar only)

PJ's

Located next to King Hall, for those people who have to eat on the run. We have a nice selection of grab-and-go-items

Mon. - Thurs. 7:30 a.m. - 8:00 p.m.

CAMPUS

THE PUB

Second Floor Student Union
J.Newbauer's has a large menu to choose from including a variety of hot sandwiches, Itza-pizza, beer and wine.

45" GIANT screen TV

Mon. - Thurs. 11:00 a.m. - 8:30 p.m.
So come by and check us out

Pumperknikles
deli FIRST FLOOR STUDENT UNION

Pumperknikles offers a wide variety of fresh sandwiches and salads.
Fast friendly courteous service. Custom line of non-dairy frozen yogurt.

Mon. - Thurs.   10:30 a.m. - 8:00 p.m.
Fri. & Sat.   10:00 a.m. - 1:30 p.m.

Eagles' Landing Cafe

Eagles' Landing offers a large selection of food for all tastes

Including Mexican cuisine, deli, Itza-pizza, grille, and a large selection of hot entrees. Try our garden fresh salad bar.

Mon. - Thurs.   7:00 a.m. - 6:30 p.m.
Friday   7:00 a.m. - 1:30 p.m.

EAGLE EXPRESS

Our modular food service trailer located in Lot C
Beverages, Sadwiches, Snacks and other grab & go items
Open Mon. - Thurs. 9:00 a.m. - 8:30 p.m.

THE SPOT

Our Convenience Store Located in Housing Phase I

From self-serve drinks and snacks to microwavable dinners. Also, most of your household items to stock up the apartment.
Open Sun. - Fri. 5:00 p.m. - 10:30 p.m.

Appendix A7-F

SAMPLE FORMAT OF INVITATION TO BE A STUDENT RESPONDENT

Join the Crowd!

Be a participant in our next issue. Fill in the application below and we'll send you a $2.00 discount coupon good for our next issue if you're selected to be a student participant.

Name:_____

Phone: (   ) _____ Best time to call me is _____ A.M. _____12–6 P.M. _____ P.M.

Classes I'm taking Fall quarter 1990:

  Course No.   Section   Instructor   Time

_____

_____

_____

_____

_____

Mail to: Sneak Peek
      P.O. Box 109
      Monterey Park, CA 91754

Appendix A7-G

SAMPLE FORMAT OF INVITATION TO ADVERTISE IN RECYCLER

Do You Have a Used Book You'd Like to Sell?

Put an ad in our recycler section. **It's Free!**

Hurry, though—we only have a limited number of ads we can run.

Name of book: _____

Course/Instructor: _____

Your first name: _____

Phone number: _____

Best time for buyer to call you is: _____ A.M. _____ Afternoons _____ P.M.

Selling Price: _____ (Optional)

Mail to: Sneak Peek
      P.O. Box 109
      Monterey Park, CA 91754

Appendix A7-H

SAMPLE FORMAT OF RECYCLER SECTION FOR USED-BOOK ADVERTISING

USED BOOKS FOR SALE . . . . . BUY NOW!

Principles of Accounting
Accounting 200A
Prof. M. Davidson
$18.00
Contact: Tim
(818) 388-9276
Leave message on machine

Fundamentals of Astronomy
ASTR 151
Prof. R. Carpenter
$22.00
Contact: Jonathan Riley
(213) 728-3535
Call anytime between 2 P.M. and 5 P.M.

Basic Spanish
SPAN 100A
Prof. G. McCurdy
$20.00
Contact: Juli McNamara
(213) 555-3667
Call between 3:30 P.M. and 4:30 P.M.

Extemporaneous Speaking
SPCH 150
Prof. Robert Powell
$26.00
Contact: Ann Markell
(818) 377-8799
Call between 10 A.M. and Noon

Modern Man
ANTH 250
Prof. E. Oring
$27.00
Contact: Reanna
(213) 377-5988
Leave message on machine

Principles of Biology
BIOL 101
Prof. Wayne P. Alley
$32.00
Contact: Anthony
(213) 666-5667
Leave Message

Principles of Biology
BIOL 101
Prof. Wayne P. Alley
$32.00
Contact: Donna
(818) 322-2633
Call between 10 A.M. and 2 P.M.

The World of Plants
BIOL 155
Prof. B. Capon
$34.00
Contact: Caroline
(213) 585-2356
Leave message on machine

Appendix A7-I

SAMPLE FORMAT OF STUDENT TELEPHONE SURVEY

Instructions: Please call in all information to our telephone answering machine operating 24 hours a day. Start at the top of the page with your *name, ID number, phone,* and *address.* Then proceed to the questions and give your responses in order using complete sentences (Example: Say "Question 1: I spend 5 to 10 hours outside of school studying per week," etc.). You must call in your responses before the following date _____. We will send your $2.00 discount coupon to your address as soon as your telephone survey is received. Thank you for your participation in this survey.

Name _____ Phone _____

Address _____ Zip Code _____

Student respondent number _____(Stamped in right upper corner of this form)
(Students, please be completely honest in answering all questions. Remember, other students will be relying on your answers for the selection of their classes. Furthermore, feel free to make additional comments at the end of this questionnaire.)

1. How many hours outside of school did you have to study per week?

    _____ 0–5 _____ 6–10 _____ 11–20 _____ more than 20 hours.

2. To what degree did your class give you knowledge you could apply immediately to improve your job or personal life?

    On a scale of 1 to 5, I would rate this class a _____.

    (Use Not at all = 1, Average = 3, and Helped a great deal = 5)

3. Do you feel that the class offered more than you originally expected?

    _____ Yes _____ No _____ Not sure

4. Would you recommend this course to your friends? _____ Yes _____ No

5. Does doing well in the prerequisites for this course come in handy for handling the class load?

    _____ Yes _____ No

6. How do you rate the difficulty of this course on a scale of 1 to 5? _____

    (Use Easy = 1, Average = 3, and Extremely difficult = 5)

Any additional comments concerning course or instructors are welcome. If you have suggestions on questions to ask in the future issue please let us know. This publication is for your benefit, so let us help you get the information you need to pick your classes!

Appendix A7-J

SAMPLE FORMAT OF INVITATION TO PLACE ADVANCE ORDER
(to be run in the *University Times* 4 weeks prior to release of our guide)

Order Your Next Issue of Sneak Peek in Advance!

Be the first to buy your books through our recycler section.
Give yourself the time to plan your classes next quarter.
Get the inside scoop on courses and instructors with Sneak Peek as your guide.

Send a check or money order for $5.00 (includes tax, postage, and handling charge) to:
  Sneak Peek
  P.O. Box 109
  Monterey Park, CA 91754
(If you have a discount coupon, take $2.00 off above price and mail in check and coupon.)
Yes, I'd like to order the Winter quarter of Sneak Peek now.

Send to: Name _____

        Address _____

Appendix A7-K

CSULA UNIVERSITY TIMES ADVERTISING RATES

OUR READERS

- Cal State L.A. has the most culturally rich and distinctly varied student body of any university in the nation.

- Located in the heart of the San Gabriel Valley, it is within 5 miles of most major communities.

- The average student is 28 years old, financially independent and active in the purchasing process.

- The *University Times* has a captive audience of more than 20,000 students, 1,500 faculty and 2,000 additional campus employees. Our daily readership is over 23,500.

DISTRIBUTION

The *University Times* is distributed free on campus from circulation boxes located at high traffic points, at the Student Housing complexes and local businesses.

CIRCULATION

8000—Monday, Wednesday and Thursday—Fall, Winter and Spring quarters
6000—Monday and Thursday—Summer quarter
12,000—Registration, Welcome back and Special issues

DISPLAY ADVERTISING RATE

LOCAL OPEN RATE—$6.60 per column inch. Pickup rate—$6.30 (Same ad must appear without changes twice in a week).

BUSINESS RATE—$5.60
(On-campus businesses)

CAMPUS RATE—$4.60

ASSOCIATED STUDENTS RATE—$4.30
(CSLA recognized student organizations)

FREQUENCY DISCOUNT

3x to 6x per month $5.94
7x to 10x per month. $5.61
11x more per month $5.28

Frequency discounts DO NOT apply to Annual Contracts.

ANNUAL BULK CONTRACT RATES

75″ to 100″. $5.60
100″ to 300″. $5.30
301″ to 500″. $5.00
501″ to 700″. $4.60

Terms

All local rates are NET. Any commissions or charges by representing agencies are additional.

Annual bulk space must be contracted in advance of insertions and publication date. If total inches do not run as contracted, the next higher rate will be charged retroactively. Frequency ads should be the same ad with minimal or no copy changes and must run regularly throughout the quarter. If frequency of insertions is not maintained as contracted, the next higher frequency rate will be retroactively charged.

COLOR CHARGES

Spot color ROP. $100.00
Color specified $130.00

Four color process ask Advertising Manager

Appendix A7-K. Continued

INSERTS
$55 /M single sheet
$75 /M multiple sheet

All prices are net. Advertising Manager must receive sample copy one week prior to insertion for review. Inserts must be delivered to printer one week prior to publication. 8,000 minimum or complete run.

Commissionable $11.00

Representatives
American Passage Media Corp.   (800) 426-5537
CASS Communications, Inc.   (800) 888-4044
College Media Placement Service, Ltd.   (818) 848-8799

CLASSIFIED RATES
15 words or less 10 cents for each additional word. Quarterly contact rates available.

1–3 consecutive insertions $4.00/day
4–6 consecutive insertions $3.75/day
7–9 consecutive insertions $3.50/day
10–12 consecutive insertions $3.25/day

CLASSIFIED DISPLAY

Local classified display rate . . . . $6.60 pc (2 inch minimum)

Classified ads are payable in advance. A check must accompany all mailed ads. For billing information contact Business Manager.

COPY DEADLINES
Monday . . . . Noon previous Wednesday
Wednesday . . . . Noon previous Friday
Thursday . . . . Noon previous Monday

Makegood Policy: The advertising manager must be notified within seven working days after publication of the advertisement for a makegood. The original copy and instructions must be clear and legible. The *University Times*' liability shall not exceed the cost of the advertisement in which the error occurred, and credit will be for the first incorrect insertion only. The *University Times* will not be responsible for copy changes made by phone. Minor spelling errors will not qualify for makegood. We reserve the right to cancel any advertisement at any time.

Cancellations: All cancellations of previously submitted advertisements must be made in writing. Cancellations must be made before ad copy deadline. They will not be accepted after that time.

Proofs are furnished upon request. Copy and art must be received 7 working days prior to publication for a proof.

Camera charges will be made for screening halftones, reductions, enlargements, reverses, veloxes and extra prints. Charges range from $5 to $10 depending on the size of the art and amount of work required.

Excessive typesetting: Rates quoted include normal typesetting. Ads requiring excessive typesetting (as determined by the Art Department) will be charged $25/hour above normal space cost.

MECHANICAL REQUIREMENTS

Column width: 1½ inches (9½ picas)
Six columns per page × 16 inches deep
Minimum display space: 4 column inches
Screen: 85% printed offset
Advertisements more than 14 inches deep will be billed for full column depth.
All fractions of an inch in display advertising will be increased to the next half inch.

APPENDIX A7-K(A)

APPENDIX A7-L

UNIVERSITY PRESS RATES FOR FLYERS AND POSTERS

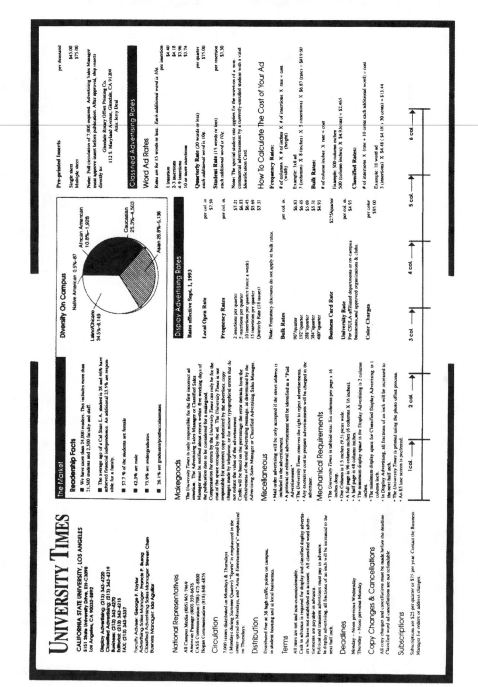

APPENDIX A7-M

SNEAK PEEK MARKETING IMPLEMENTATION SCHEDULE

Advertising
Posters
University Times ads
Flyers

Collect Data
Class schedule information
Student questionnaires

Editing
Writing
Review questionnaires
Instructor's opinion review

Promotion
Student Union table setup
New student orientation
Flyer distribution

Printing
Flyers & Posters
Guidebooks

Distribution
University bookstore
Student bookmart
Direct mailing

Spring Quarter Summer Quarter Fall Quarter
1 2 3 4 5 6 7 8 9 10 11

APPENDIX A7-N

FINANCIAL DATA

Table 1 Sneak Peek: break-even analysis

Fixed Cost per Year	Amount
Post office box	$28.00
Business license	$101.78
Wholesale license	$107.50
Ad in *University Times*	$337.00
Ad in *Schedule of Classes*	$1,080.00
Bulk rate postage permit	$60.00
Bulk rate postage fee	$60.00
Postage paid address permit	$60.00
Copyright on publication	$40.00
Answering machine	$60.00
Telephone	$30.00
Telephone/Utilities	$840.00
Typewriter	$130.00
Legal/Accounting	$2,080.00
Insurance	$1,500.00
Orientation booth	$200.00
Fliers	$140.00
Posters	$80.00
Total	$6,934.28

Variable Cost per Year	Amount
Wholesale license	$116.48
Business license	$36.40
Postage for response	$14,414.40
Transportation cost	$291.20
Postage for mail orders	$2,038.40
Printing cost	$36,400.00
Total	$1.83
	$P = $ $10,317.50
	$U = $ 2,926

$P = (U*p) - (U*V) - F$
$U = F/(p - V)$
P = profits
p = price
U = break-even quantities
V = variable cost
F = fixed cost

Table 2 Sneak Peek: five-year projected profit and loss statement

	QUARTERS AFTER STARTING BUSINESS				
	1 (Fall)	**2 (Winter)**	**3 (Spring)**	**4 (Summer)**	**Year 1**
Sales	$29,192.80	$28,100.80	$27,227.20	$27,081.60	$111,602.40
Advertising sales	$2,025.00	$3,037.50	$4,556.25	$6,834.38	$16,453.13
Cost of sales	$12,481.56	$10,170.16	$8,321.04	$6,009.64	$36,982.40
Gross profit	$18,736.24	$20,968.14	$23,462.41	$27,903.64	$91,073.13
Operating expenses					
Advertising	$619.99	$505.18	$413.33	$298.51	$1,837.00
Postage	$5,552.82	$4,524.52	$3,701.88	$2,673.58	$16,452.80
Payroll	$6,952.50	$5,665.00	$4,635.00	$3,347.50	$20,600.00
Office supplies	$624.36	$622.77	$635.67	$678.32	$2,561.11
Permit and fee	$70.20	$57.20	$46.80	$33.80	$208.00
Legal and accounting	$520.00	$520.00	$520.00	$520.00	$2,080.00
Telephone/utilities	$200.00	$170.00	$170.00	$170.00	$710.00
Licenses and taxes	$103.67	$94.11	$86.47	$76.91	$361.16
Copyright	$10.00	$10.00	$10.00	$10.00	$40.00
Insurance	$375.00	$375.00	$375.00	$375.00	$1,500.00
Other administrative and selling expenses	$1,560.89	$1,556.92	$1,589.17	$1,695.80	$6,402.78
Total operating expenses	$16,589.42	$14,100.69	$12,183.31	$9,879.42	$52,752.85
Profit	$2,146.82	$6,867.45	$11,279.10	$18,026.91	$38,320.28

	QUARTERS AFTER STARTING BUSINESS				
	5 (Fall)	**6 (Winter)**	**7 (Spring)**	**8 (Summer)**	**Year 2**
Sales	$43,789.20	$42,151.20	$40,840.80	$40,622.40	$167,403.60
Advertising sales	$3,037.50	$4,556.25	$6,834.38	$10,251.56	$24,679.69
Cost of sales	$18,722.34	$15,255.24	$12,481.56	$9,014.46	$55,473.60
Gross profit	$29,104.36	$31,452.21	$35,193.62	$41,859.50	$136,609.69
Operating expenses					
Advertising	$929.98	$757.76	$619.99	$447.77	$2,755.50
Postage	$8,329.23	$6,786.78	$5,552.82	$4,010.37	$24,679.20
Payroll	$10,428.75	$8,497.50	$6,952.50	$5,021.25	$30,900.00
Office supplies	$936.53	$934.15	$953.50	$1,017.48	$3,841.67
Permit and fee	$105.30	$85.80	$70.20	$50.70	$312.00
Legal and accounting	$780.00	$780.00	$780.00	$780.00	$3,120.00
Telephone/utilities	$300.00	$255.00	$255.00	$255.00	$1,065.00
Licenses and taxes	$155.50	$141.17	$129.70	$115.37	$541.74
Copyright	$15.00	$15.00	$15.00	$15.00	$60.00
Insurance	$562.50	$562.50	$562.50	$562.50	$2,250.00
Other administrative and selling expenses	$2,341.34	$2,335.37	$2,383.76	$2,543.70	$9,604.16
Total operating expenses	$24,884.13	$21,151.03	$18,274.97	$14,819.14	$79,129.27
Profit	$3,220.23	$10,301.18	$16,918.64	$27,040.37	$57,480.42

Table 2 continued

	QUARTERS AFTER STARTING BUSINESS				
	9 (Fall)	10 (Winter)	11 (Spring)	12 (Summer)	Year 3
Sales	$76,631.10	$73,764.60	$71,471.40	$71,089.20	$292,956.30
Advertising sales	$5,315.63	$7,973.44	$11,960.16	$17,940.23	$43,189.45
Cost of sales	$32,764.10	$26,696.67	$21,842.73	$15,775.31	$97,078.80
Gross profit	$49,182.63	$55,041.37	$61,588.83	$73,254.13	$239,066.95
Operating expenses					
Advertising	$1,627.47	$1,326.08	$1,084.98	$783.60	$4,822.13
Postage	$14,576.15	$11,876.87	$9,717.44	$7,018.15	$43,188.60
Payroll	$18,250.31	$14,870.63	$12,166.88	$8,787.19	$54,075.00
Office supplies	$1,638.93	$1,634.76	$1,668.63	$1,780.59	$6,722.92
Permit and fee	$184.28	$150.15	$122.85	$88.73	$546.00
Legal and accounting	$1,365.00	$1,365.00	$1,365.00	$1,365.00	$5,460.00
Telephone/utilities	$525.00	$446.25	$446.25	$446.25	$1,863.75
Licenses and taxes	$272.13	$247.04	$226.98	$201.90	$948.05
Copyright	$26.25	$26.25	$26.25	$26.25	$105.00
Insurance	$984.38	$984.38	$984.38	$984.38	$3,937.50
Other administrative and selling expenses	$4,097.34	$4,086.90	$4,171.58	$4,451.47	$16,807.29
Total operating expenses	$43,547.23	$37,014.31	$31,981.20	$25,933.49	$138,476.22
Profit	$5,635.40	$18,027.06	$29,607.63	$47,320.64	$100,590.73

	QUARTERS AFTER STARTING BUSINESS				
	13 (Fall)	14 (Winter)	15 (Spring)	16 (Summer)	Year 4
Sales	$107,283.54	$103,270.44	$100,059.96	$99,524.88	$410,138.92
Advertising sales	$7,441.88	$11,162.81	$16,744.22	$25,116.33	$60,465.23
Cost of sales	$45,869.73	$37,375.34	$30,579.82	$22,085.43	$135,910.32
Gross profit	$68,355.68	$77,057.91	$86,224.36	$102,555.78	$334,693.73
Operating expenses					
Advertising	$2,278.45	$1,856.52	$1,518.97	$1,097.03	$6,750.98
Postage	$15,304.96	$12,470.71	$10,203.31	$7,369.05	$45,348.03
Payroll	$25,550.44	$20,818.88	$17,033.63	$12,302.06	$75,705.00
Office supplies	$2,294.51	$2,288.67	$2,336.08	$2,492.82	$9,412.08
Permit and fee	$257.99	$210.21	$171.99	$124.22	$764.40
Legal and accounting	$1,911.00	$1,911.00	$1,911.00	$1,911.00	$7,644.00
Telephone/utilities	$735.00	$624.75	$624.75	$624.74	$2,609.25
Licenses and taxes	$380.98	$345.86	$317.77	$282.66	$1,327.26
Copyright	$36.75	$36.75	$36.75	$36.75	$147.00
Insurance	$1,378.13	$1,378.13	$1,378.13	$1,378.13	$5,512.50
Other administrative and selling expenses	$5,736.27	$5,721.66	$5,840.21	$6,232.06	$23,530.20
Total operating expenses	$55,864.47	$47,663.13	$41,372.58	$33,850.53	$178,750.70
Profit	$12,991.22	$29,394.79	$44,851.78	$68,705.25	$155,943.03

Table 2 continued

	QUARTERS AFTER STARTING BUSINESS				
	17 (Fall)	**18 (Winter)**	**19 (Spring)**	**20 (Summer)**	**Year 5**
Sales	$124,104.43	$129,088.05	$125,074.95	$124,406.10	$512,673.53
Advertising sales	$9,302.34	$13,953.52	$20,930.27	$31,395.41	$75,581.54
Cost of sales	$57,337.17	$46,719.17	$38,224.78	$27,606.78	$169,887.90
Gross profit	$96,069.60	$96,322.39	$107,780.45	$128,194.73	$418,357.17
Operating expenses					
Advertising	$2,848.07	$2,320.65	$1,898.71	$1,371.29	$8,438.72
Postage	$12,435.29	$10,132.45	$8,290.19	$5,987.36	$36,845.27
Payroll	$31,338.05	$26,023.59	$21,292.03	$15,377.58	$94,631.25
Office supplies	$2,363.14	$2,860.83	$2,920.10	$3,116.03	$11,765.10
Permit and fee	$322.48	$262.76	$214.99	$155.27	$955.50
Legal and accounting	$2,388.75	$2,388.75	$2,388.75	$2,388.75	$9,555.00
Telephone/utilities	$918.75	$780.94	$780.94	$780.94	$3,261.56
Licenses and taxes	$476.22	$432.33	$397.21	$353.32	$1,659.08
Copyright	$45.94	$45.94	$45.94	$45.94	$183.75
Insurance	$1,722.66	$1,722.66	$1,722.66	$1,722.66	$6,890.63
Other administrative and selling expenses	$7,170.34	$7,152.08	$7,300.26	$7,790.08	$29,412.75
Total operating expenses	$63,134.56	$54,122.97	$47,251.78	$39,089.20	$203,598.61
Profit	$22,934.94	$42,199.42	$60,528.67	$89,105.52	$214,768.55

Table 3 Sneak Peek: five-year cash flow projections

	Year 1	Year 2	Year 3	Year 4	Year 5
Cash Balance (beginning of year)	$8,775.14	$3,451.40	$5,966.90	$18,992.08	$34,231.84
Receipts: Sales	$111,602.40	$167,403.60	$292,956.30	$410,138.82	$512,673.53
Ad sales	$16,453.13	$24,679.69	$43,189.45	$60,465.23	$75,581.54
Total cash available	$120,377.54	$170,855.00	$298,923.20	$429,130.90	$546,905.37
Disbursements:					
Printing cost	$36,982.40	$55,473.00	$97,078.80	$135,910.32	$169,887.90
Payroll cost	$20,600.00	$30,900.00	$54,075.00	$75,705.00	$94,631.25
Advertising cost	$1,837.00	$2,755.00	$4,822.13	$6,750.00	$8,438.72
License and taxes	$361.16	$541.74	$948.05	$1,327.26	$1,659.08
Postage	$16,452.80	$24,679.20	$43,188.60	$45,348.03	$36,845.27
Insurance	$1,500.00	$2,250.00	$3,937.50	$5,512.50	$6,890.63
Legal/accounting	$2,080.00	$3,120.00	$5,460.00	$7,644.00	$9,555.00
Telephone/utilities	$710.00	$1,065.00	$1,863.75	$2,609.25	$3,261.56
Office supplies	$2,561.11	$3,841.67	$6,722.92	$9,412.08	$11,765.10
Other administrative expenses	$3,841.67	$5,762.49	$10,084.38	$14,118.12	$17,647.65
Total disbursements	$86,926.14	$130,388.10	$228,181.12	$304,336.56	$360,582.16
Cash before distribution	$33,451.40	$40,466.90	$70,742.08	$124,794.34	$186,323.21
Distribution	$30,000.00	$34,500.00	$51,750.00	$90,562.50	$135,843.75
Cash balance (end of year)	$3,451.40	$5,966.90	$18,992.08	$34,231.84	$50,479.46

Table 4 Sneak Peek: initial investment cost $18,000.00

Initial investment		
Less:		
Answering machine	$60.00	
Phone	$30.00	
Typewriter	$130.00	
Copyright	$10.00	
Telephone and utilities	$70.00	
Post office box	$28.00	
Postage permit	$120.00	
Office supplies	$270.00	
License	$208.28	
Legal/accounting	$520.00	
Insurance	$375.00	
		$ 1,821.28
Preopening expenses		$16,178.72
Postage for response	$3,603.60	
Postage paid permit	$60.00	
Advertising	$619.99	
Printing cost	$2,500.00	
Promotions	$619.99	
		$7,403.58
Cash balance—beginning of operations		$8,775.14

Table 5 Sneak Peek: balance sheet (pro forma)

	Year 1	Year 2	Year 3	Year 4	Year 5
Assets					
Current assets					
Cash	$3,451.40	$5,966.90	$18,992.08	$34,231.84	$50,479.46
Inventory	$2,500.00	$3,750.00	$6,562.50	$9,187.50	$11,484.38
Account receivables	$22,422.40	$50,450.40	$103,002.90	$127,921.41	$192,337.45
Fixed assets					
Furniture/fixture	$3,000.00	$4,500.00	$7,875.00	$7,875.00	$7,875.00
Telephone	$30.00	$60.00	$90.00	$120.00	$120.00
Typewriter	$130.00	$260.00	$520.00	$520.00	$520.00
Answering machine	$60.00	$60.00	$60.00	$60.00	
Office Supplies	$138.76	$208.14	$364.24	$509.93	$637.42
Less: Accumulated depreciation	($335.88)	($844.69)	($1,735.61)	($2,644.11)	($4,576.21)
Other asset					
Copyright	$40.00	$40.00	$40.00	$40.00	$40.00
Total Assets	$31,436.68	$64,450.75	$135,771.10	$177,821.58	$258,917.49
Liabilities and Capital					
Liabilities					
Account payable	$5,116.40	$15,150.05	$37,629.67	$14,299.62	$16,470.73
Capital					
Capital—beginning	$18,000.00	$26,320.28	$49,300.70	$98,141.43	$163,521.96
Add: Earnings	$38,320.28	$57,480.42	$100,590.73	$155,943.03	$214,768.55
Less: Distributions	($30,000.00)	($34,500.00)	($51,750.00)	($90,562.50)	($135,843.75)
Capital—ending	$26,320.28	$49,300.70	$98,141.43	$163,521.96	$242,446.76
Total liabilities and capital	$31,436.68	$64,450.75	$135,771.10	$177,821.58	$258,917.49

Table 6 Sneak Peek: selections on criteria

Accounting		No. Sec.	Instructor	Faculty
200A		13	6	1
200B		13	6	1
202		1		1
300		12	3	3
320A		7	2	1
320B		5	2	
320C		5	2	
321		3	2	
322		4	1	1
398		4		
420		3	1	
421A		2	1	
424A		3	2	
427		1	1	
433		1		1
503		1		
520		2	1	
524		1	1	
587		1		
598		4		
Total	20	86	31	9
Assuming ½ for each instructor			16	5
Assuming ¼ for each instructor			8	2

General Education	No. Sec.	Instructor	Faculty
ANTHO 250	5	2	2
ANTHO 260	4	1	3
ANTHO 265	1	1	
ARAB 100A			
ARAB 100B			
ARAB 100C			
ART 101A	2	2	
ART 101B	1	1	
ART 101C	1	1	
ART 151	1	1	
ART 152	4	2	2
ART 153	2	1	
ART 154			
ART 155	1		1
ART 156			
ART 157	1	1	
ART 158			
ART 159	3	3	
ASTRO 151	10	9	
ASTRO 152			
BIOL 155	14	2	12
BIOL 156	15	3	12
BIOL 165	2	1	1
CHEM 158	1	1	
CHEM 159	1	1	

Table 6 continued

General Education	No. Sec.	Instructor	Faculty
CHEM 160	1	1	
CHIN 100A			
CHIN 100B	1		1
CHIN 100C	1	1	
CHIN 101A			
CHIN 101B			
CHIN 101C	1	1	
CHIN 200A			
CHIN 200B			
CHIN 200C	1	1	
CHIN 201A			
CHIN 201B			
CHIN 201C			
CH S 111	4	2	2
DANC 157	4	2	2
ECON 150	2	1	1
ENGL 190	20	9	11
ENGL 225	1	1	
ENGL 250	9	4	
ENGL 258	1	1	
ENGR 250	1		1
FREN 100A	4	3	1
FREN 100B	2	1	
FREN 100C	1	1	
FREN 200A			
FREN 200B	1	1	
FREN 230			
FSCS 120	3	1	1
FSCS 250	2		2
GEOG 150	10	4	5
GEOL 150	2	2	
GEOL 151	2	2	
GEOL 152	4	2	2
GEOL 155	3	2	1
GEOL 156	3	1	2
GEOL 158	1	1	
GEOL 160			
GERM 100A			
GERM 100B	1	1	
GERM 100C	1	1	
H S 150	7	5	1
HIST 110A	1	1	
HIST 110B	1	1	
HIST 110C	1	1	
HIST 202A	10	4	3
HIST 202B	10	6	4
ITAL 100A			
ITAL 100B			
ITAL 100C	1	1	
JAPN 100A	2		2
JAPN 100B	1		1
JAPN 100C	2		2
JAPN 130			
JAPN 200A			
JAPN 200B			
JAPN 200C	1		1
LAS 150	1	1	

Table 6 continued

General Education	No. Sec.	Instructor	Faculty
LATN 100A			
LATN 100B			
LATN 100C			
LATN 222			
MICR 151	5	4	2
MUS 150	3		3
MUS 160	3	1	1
MUS 264			
PAS 101	1	1	
PAS 125	1		1
PAS 260	1	1	
PHIL 151	6	3	
PHIL 152	4	2	
PHIL 160	17	2	14
PHIL 238	1	1	
PHIL 250	4	2	2
P E 150	4	1	2
PHYS 150	3	2	
PHYS 155	1	1	
POLS 150	15	5	7
POLS 155	7	2	3
POLS 200			
POLS 250	1	1	
PSY 150	6	2	3
PSY 160	2	2	
PSY 270	1	1	
RELS 200	5	2	2
RUSS 101A			
RUSS 101B			
SOC 201	12	5	5
SOC 202	6	3	2
SOC 263	1	1	
SPAN 100A	10	7	3
SPAN 100B	2	2	
SPAN 100C	2	1	1
SPAN 105	2	2	
SPAN 130			
SPAN 200A	1	1	
SPAN 200B	1	1	
SPAN 200C	1	1	
SPAN 205A	1	1	
SPAN 205B			
SPAN 230			
SPCH 150	26	4	17
SPCH 176	3	2	
T.A. 152	1	1	
URBA 101	2		2
Total 128	357	168	149
Assuming ½ for each instructor		84	75
Assuming ¼ for each instructor		42	37

Table 6 continued

Business core requirements		No. Sec.	Instructor	Faculty
ACCT 200 A		13	7	1
ACCT 200 B		13	7	1
ACCT 300		12	5	3
CIS 294		15	4	5
CIS 301		10	6	
ECON 201		7	3	3
ECON 202		8	4	3
ECON 209		10	5	4
ECON 303		9	2	4
ECON 309		9	4	4
ECON 310		8	2	5
ECON 391		9	2	5
FIN 205		8	4	
FIN 303		10	8	
MATH 242		7	3	3
MGMT 306		11	4	4
MGMT 307		9	3	2
MGMT 308		9	7	
MGMT 497		10	10	
MKT 304		7	4	
OSBE 301		13	8	2
Total	21	207	102	49
Assuming ½ for each instructor			51	25
Assuming ¼ for each instructor			28	12

Biology	No. Sec.	Instructor	Faculty
BIOL 101	5	1	4
BIOL 102	2	2	
BIOL 103	2	2	
BIOL 302	3	1	
BIOL 315	3	1	
BIOL 330	3	1	2
BIOL 357	1	1	
BIOL 360	2	1	
C S 290	3		3
CHEM 101	9	3	
CHEM 102	8	3	3
CHEM 103	8	2	3
CHEM 122	3	1	
CHEM 123	3	1	
CHEM 201	1	1	
CHEM 301A	1	1	
CHEM 301B	1		1
CHEM 301C	2	2	
CHEM 302A	2		1
CHEM 302B	3	1	1
CHEM 302C	1	1	
CHEM 319	1	1	
CHEM 360	1	1	
CHEM 401	1	1	

Table 6 continued

Biology	No. Sec.	Instructor	Faculty
CHEM 402	1	1	
CHEM 403	1	1	
CHEM 412A	1	1	
CHEM 412B	1	1	
CHEM 419	1	1	
CHEM 462	1	1	
MATH 206	4	1	3
MATH 207	4	3	1
MATH 208	5	3	2
MATH 209	4	4	
MATH 215	4	4	
MATH 225	1	1	
MATH 230	1	1	
MATH 401	1	1	
PHYS 101	4	2	
PHYS 102	4	2	
PHYS 103	4	2	
PHYS 121	1	1	
PHYS 122	1	1	
PHYS 123	1	1	
PHYS 201	7	7	
PHYS 202	8	5	
PHYS 203	11	7	
PHYS 204	4	2	
PHYS 205	1	1	
PHYS 206	2	1	
Total 49	147	86	24
Assuming ½ for each instructor		43	12
Assuming ¼ for each instructor		22	6

Upper Division Themes	No. Sec.	Instructor	Faculty
ANTH 350	1	1	
ANTH 400	1	1	
ANTH 444	6	2	2
ANTH 450	1	1	
ANTH 438	1	1	
ART 341	1	1	
ART 350	1	1	
ART 357	3	1	
ART 381	1	1	
ART 455	1	1	
ART 456	1	1	
ART 485	1	1	
BCST 466	1	1	
BIOL 319	1	1	
BIOL 321	1	1	
BIOL 350	1	1	
BIOL 353	1	1	
BIOL 361	1	1	
BIOL 484	1	1	

Table 6 continued

Upper Division Themes	No. Sec.	Instructor	Faculty
BIOL 486	1	1	
CHEM 350	1	1	
CHEM 358	1	1	
CHEM 380	1		1
DANC 357	3	2	
ECON 460	1	1	
EDAD 480	1	1	
ENGL 350	1	1	
ENGL 358	1	1	
ENGL 381	1	1	
ENGL 383	1	1	
ENGL 385	1	1	
ENGL 387	1	1	
ENGL 392	1	1	
ENGL 399	1	1	
ENGR 352	2		2
FSCS 300	4	1	3
FSCS 450	6	2	4
FSCS 451	1		1
FL 389	1	1	
GEOG 421	1	1	
GEOG 433	1	1	
GEOG 476	1	1	
GEOL 350	1	1	
GEOL 420	2	2	
HIST 311	1	1	
HIST 350	1	1	
HIST 380	1		1
HIST 456	1	1	
HIST 459	1	1	
LAS 435	1	1	
LAS 442	1	1	
LAS 460	1	1	
LBS 300A	1	1	
LBS 300B	1	1	
LBS 300C	1	1	
MICR 363	1	1	
MUS 355	1	1	
MUS 357	3	1	2
MUS 455	1	1	
MUS 456	1	1	
NUR 307	1	1	
NUR 455	1	1	
PAS 427	1		1
PAS 442	1	1	
PAS 460	1	1	
P E 300	4	3	
PHIL 321	1	1	
PHIL 350	1	1	
PHIL 412	1	1	
PHIL 418	1	1	
PHIL 461	1	1	
PHIL 491	1	1	
PHYS 350	1	1	
PHYS 358	1	1	
PHYS 363	1	1	
PHYS 452	1	1	

Table 6 continued

Upper Division Themes	No. Sec.	Instructor	Faculty
PSY 307	1	1	
PSY 323	1	1	
PSY 462	1	1	
PSY 488	1	1	
POLS 458	1	1	
POLS 459	1	1	
REL 425	1	1	
SOC 400	1	1	
SOC 425	1	1	
SOC 430	1	1	
SOC 441	1	1	
SOC 442	1	1	
SOC 450	1	1	
SOC 483	1	1	
SPCH 385	1	1	
SPCH 489	2	1	1
SW 455	1	1	
SW 462	1	1	
T A 357	3	3	
T A 457	2	2	
Total	96 125	101	18
Assuming ½ for each instructor		51	9
Assuming ¼ for each instructor		25	5

Table 7 Sneak Peek: ratio analysis

	Year 1	Year 2	Year 3	Year 4	Year 5
Return on investment	44%	45%	47%	52%	61%
Profit margin	30%	30%	17%	12%	10%
Debit equity ratio	19%	31%	28%	9%	7%
Working capital ratio	6	4	3	12	15

RDI = Net profit/total investment
PM   = Net profit/net sales
DER = Total liabilities/total assets
WCR = Current asset/current liabilities

APPENDIX

B

SOURCES OF SECONDARY RESEARCH

Following are more than 100 sources. Some are based on bibliographies originally put together by Lloyd M. DeBoer, then Dean of the School of Business Administration at George Mason University, Fairfax, Virginia, and the Office of Management and Training of the SBA and published by the Small Business Administration as a part of two booklets, *Marketing Research Procedure, SBB 9,* and *National Directories for Use in Marketing SSB 13.* Others were compiled more recently by the author and my research assistant, Misty Iwatsu.

U.S. GOVERNMENT PUBLICATIONS

The publications in this section are books and pamphlets issued by federal agencies and listed under the issuing agency. Where availability of an individual listing is indicated by the Government Printing Office (GPO), the publication may be ordered from the Superintendent of Documents, U.S. Government Printing Office, Washington, DC 20402. When ordering a GPO publication, give the title and series number of the publication, and name of agency. You can also order by phone by calling (202) 783-3238. Contact the GPO for current prices.

Publications should be requested by the title and any number given from the issuing agency. Most libraries have some listings to identify currently available federal publications. Some keep a number of selected government publications for ready reference through the Federal Depository Library System.

American Statistics Index: A Comprehensive Guide and Index to the Statistical Publications of the United States Government. Washington, DC. Congressional Information Service, 1973–. Monthly, with annual cumulations. This is the most comprehensive index to statistical information generated by the federal agencies, committees of Congress, and special programs of the government. Approximately 7,400 titles of 500 government sources are indexed each year. The two main volumes are arranged by issuing breakdown, technical notes, and time period covered by publication. Separate index volume is arranged by subject and title and also includes the SIC code, the Standard Occupation Classification, and a list of SMSAs (standard metropolitan statistical areas).

Bureau of the Census, Department of Commerce, Washington, DC 20233

Contact the Public Information Office for a more complete listing of publications. The following is a sample.

Catalog of United States Census Publications.   Published monthly with quarterly and annual cumulations. A guide to census data and reports. This catalog contains descriptive lists of publications, data files, and special tabulations.

Census of Agriculture.   Performed in years ending in 4 and 9. Volumes include information on statistics of county; size of farm; characteristics of farm operations; farm income; farm sales; farm expenses; and agricultural services.

Census of Business.   Compiled every five years (in years ending in 2 and 7).

Census of Construction Industries.   Information from industries based on SIC codes. Included is information about number of construction firms; employees; receipts; payrolls; payments for materials; components; work supplies; payments for machinery and equipment; and depreciable assets.

Census of Governments.   Done in years ending 2 and 7. This is the most detailed source for statistics on government finance.

Census of Housing.   Provides information on plumbing facilities, whether a unit is owned or rented, value of home, when built, number of bedrooms, telephones, and more.

Census of Manufacturers.   Compiled every five years (in years ending in 2 and 7). Reports on 450 different classes of manufacturing industries. Data for each industry include: information on capital expenditures, value added, number of establishments, employment data, material costs, assets, rent, and inventories. Updated yearly by the *Annual Survey of Manufacturers.*

Census of Mineral Industries.   Covers areas of extraction of minerals. Information on employees, payroll, work hours, cost of materials, capital expenditures, and quantity and value of materials consumed and products shipped.

Census of Population.   Compiled every 10 years (in years ending in zero). Presents detailed data on population characteristics of states, counties, SMSAs, and census tracts. Demographics data reported include: age, sex, race, marital status, family composition, employment income, level of education, and occupation. Updated annually by the *Current Population Report.*

Census of Retail Trade.   This report presents statistics for more than 100 different types of retail establishments by state, SMSAs, counties, and cities with populations over 2,500. It includes data on the number of outlets, total sales, employment, and payroll. Updated each month by *Monthly Retail Trade.*

Census of Selected Services.   Provides statistics similar to those reported by the *Census of Retail Trade* for retail service organizations such as auto repair centers and hotels. Does not include information on real estate, insurance, or the professions. Updated monthly by *Monthly Selected Service Receipts.*

Census of Transportation. Information on four major phases of United States travel. (1) National Travel Survey, (2) Truck Inventory and Use of Survey, (3) Commodity Transportation Survey, and (4) Survey of Motor Carriers and Public Warehousing.

Census of Wholesale Trade. Statistics for more than 150 types of wholesaler categories. The data detail the number of establishments, warehouse space, expenses, end-of-year inventories, legal form of organization, and payroll. Updated each month by *Monthly Wholesale Trade.*

Statistical Abstract of the United States. Published annually. This is a useful source for finding current and historical statistics about various aspects of American life. Contents include statistics on income, prices, education, population, law enforcement, environmental conditions, local government, labor force, manufacturing, and many other topics.

State and Metropolitan Area Data Book. A *Statistical Abstract* supplement. Presents a variety of information on states and metropolitan areas in the United States on subjects such as area, population, housing, income, manufacturers, retail trade, and wholesale trade.

Country and City Databook. Published every five years, this supplements the *Statistical Abstract.* Contains 144 statistical items for each county and 148 items for cities with a population of 25,000 or more. Data are organized by region, division, states, and SMSAs. Standard demographics are contained in addition to other harder-to-find data.

County Business Patterns. Annual. Contains a summary of data on number and type (by SIC number) of business establishments as well as their employment and taxable payroll. Data are presented by industry and country.

Bureau of Economic Analysis, Department of Commerce, Washington, DC 20230

Business Statistics. This is the biennial supplement to the *Survey of Current Business* and contains data on 2,500 series arranged annually for early years, quarterly for the last decade, and monthly for the most recent five years.

Bureau of Industrial Economics, Department of Commerce, Washington, DC 20230

United States Industrial Outlook. Projections of sales trends for major sectors of the United States economy including business services; consumer services; transportation; consumer goods; and distribution.

Domestic and International Business Administration, Department of Commerce, Washington, DC 20230

County and City Data Book. Published every other year, supplements the *Statistical Abstract.* Using data taken from censuses and other government publications, it provides breakdowns by city and county for income, population, education, employment, housing, banking, manufacturing, capital expenditures, retail and wholesale sales, and other factors.

Measuring Markets: A Guide to the Use of Federal and State Statistical Data. Government Planning Office. Provides federal and state government data on population, income, employment, sales, and selected taxes. Explains how to interpret the data to measure markets and evaluate opportunities.

Selected Publications to Aid Business and Industry. Listing of federal statistical sources useful to business and industry.

Statistics of Income. Annual. Published by the Internal Revenue Service of the Treasury Department. This publication consists of data collected from tax returns filed by corporations, sole proprietorships and partnerships, and individuals.

State Statistical Abstract. Every state publishes a statistical abstract, almanac, or economic data book covering statistics for the state, its counties and cities. A complete list of these abstracts is in the back of each volume of the *Statistical Abstract* and *Measuring Markets.*

International Trade Administration, Department of Commerce, Washington, DC 20230

Country Market Survey. These reports describe market sectors and the markets for producer goods, consumer goods, and industrial material.

Global Market Surveys. Provides market research to verify the existence and vitality of foreign markets for specific goods as well as Department of Commerce assistance to U.S. business to help in market penetration.

Foreign Economic Trends. Prepared by U.S. embassies abroad. Each volume has a table of "Key Economic Indicators" and other data on the current economic situation and trends for the country under discussion.

Overseas Business Reports. Analysis of trade opportunities, marketing conditions, distribution channels, industry trends, trade regulations, and market prospects are provided.

Trade Opportunity Program (TOP). On a weekly basis indexes trade opportunities by product as well as type of opportunity.

U.S. Small Business Administration, Washington, DC 20416

The SBA issues a wide range of management and technical publications designed to help owner–managers and prospective owners of small business. For general information about the SBA office, its policies, and assistance programs, contact your nearest SBA office.

A listing of currently available publications can be obtained free from the Small Business Administration, Office of Public Communications, 409 Third St., SW, Washington, DC 20416 or call 1-800-U-ASK-SBA toll-free. The SBA offers 51 publications currently. One particular publication, *Basic Library Reference Sources,* contains a section on marketing information and guides to research. Get the latest *Directory of Publications* by writing or calling the 800 number. You can also obtain a free booklet, *Your Business and the SBA,* which gives you an overview of all SBA services and programs.

Management Aids (3- to 24-page pamphlet). This series of pamphlets is organized by a broad range of management principles. Each pamphlet in this series discusses a specific management practice to help the owner–manager of a small firm with management problems and business operations. A section on marketing covers a wide variety of topics from advertising guidelines to marketing research to pricing.

PERIODICALS

Business America: The Magazine of International Trade. United States. International Trade Administration. Biweekly. Activities relating to private sector or the Department of Commerce are covered including exports and other international business activities.

Business Conditions Digest. United States. Department of Commerce. Bureau of Economic Analysis. Washington, DC: Government Printing Office. Monthly. Title includes estimates on forecasts for recent months. Very useful for data not yet published elsewhere.

Economic Indicators. United States. Council of Economic Advisors. Washington, DC: Government Printing Office. Monthly. Statistical tables for major economic indicators are included. Section on credit is useful for marketers. Statistics quoted annually for about six years and monthly for the past year.

Federal Reserve Bulletin. United States. Board of Governors of the Federal Reserve System. Washington, DC: Government Printing Office. Monthly. Contains official statistics on national banking, international banking, and business.

Monthly Labor Review. United States. Bureau of Labor Statistics. Washington, DC: Government Printing Office. Monthly. This publication covers all aspects of labor including wages, productivity, collective bargaining, new legislation, and consumer prices.

Survey of Current Business. United States. Department of Commerce. Bureau of Economic Analysis. Washington, DC: Government Printing Office. Monthly, with weekly supplements. The most useful source for current business statistics. Each issue is divided into two sections. The first covers general business topics; the second "Current Business Statistics," gives current data for 2,500 statistical series or topics. Also, indexed in *Business Periodicals Index.*

Treasury Bulletin. United States. Department of the Treasury. Washington, DC: Government Printing Office. Monthly. Statistical tables are provided on all aspects of fiscal operations of government as well as money-related activities of the private sector. Useful for consumer background or from a monetary view.

DIRECTORIES

The selected national directories are listed under categories of specific business or general marketing areas in an alphabetical subject index.

When the type of directory is not easily found under the alphabetical listing of a general marketing category, such as "jewelry," look for a specific type of industry or outlet, for example, "department stores."

Apparel

American Sportswear & Knitting Times—Buyers Guide Issue. Annual. Lists manufacturers and suppliers of knitted products, knit goods, materials, supplies services, etc. National Knitting & Sportswear Assoc., 386 Park Ave. S., New York, NY 10016, 212-683-7520, Fax: 212-532-0766, E-mail: nksa@pop.interport.net.

Hat Life Directory. Annual. Includes renovators, importers, classified list of manufacturers, and wholesalers of men's headwear. Hat Life Directory, 66 York St., Jersey City, NJ 07302-0000, 201-434-8322, Fax: 201-434-8277.

Nationwide Directory of Men's & Boys Wear Buyers (exclusive of New York metropolitan area). Annually in August. More than 20,000 buyers and merchandise managers for 6,100 top department, family clothing, and men's and boys' wear specialty stores. Telephone number, buying office, and postal zip code given for each firm. Also available in individual state editions. Salesman's Guide, 121 Chanlon Rd., New Providence, NJ 07974-0000, 908-464-6800, Toll-free: 800-521-8100, Fax: 908-665-2894. Also publishes *Metropolitan New York Directory of Men's and Boys' Wear Buyers.* Semiannually in May and November. (Lists same information for the metropolitan New York area as the nationwide directory.)

Nationwide Directory of Women's & Children's Wear Buyers (exclusive of New York metropolitan area). Annually in October. Lists more than 25,000 buyers and divisional merchandise managers for about 6,100 leading department, family clothing, and specialty stores. Telephone number and mail zip code given for each store. Also available in individual state editions. Salesman's Guide, 121 Chanlon Rd., New Providence, NJ 07974-0000, 908-464-6800, Toll-free: 800-521-8100, Fax: 908-665-2894.

Appliances Household

Appliance Dealers—Major Household Directory. Annual Lists manufacturers and distributors in home electronics, appliances, and kitchens. Gives complete addresses and phone. Compiled from Yellow Pages. American Business Directories Inc., American Business Information Inc., 5711 S. 86th Circle, PO Box 27347, Omaha, NE 68127, 402-593-4600, Toll-free: 800-555-6424, Fax: 402-331-5481, E-mail: directory@abii.com, Web site:. abii.com.

Automatic Merchandising (Vending)

NAMA Directory of Members. Annually in June. Organized by state and by city, lists vending service companies that are NAMA members. Gives mailing address, telephone number, and products vended. Also includes machine manufacturers and suppliers. National Automatic Merchandising Assoc., 20 N. Wacker Dr., Chicago, IL 60606, 312-346-0370, Toll-free: 888-337-8363, Fax: 312-704-4140, Web site: vending.org.

Automotive

Automotive Service Industry Assoc.—Guide to Manufacturer's Representatives. Irregular. A geographical listing of about 300 representatives including name, address, telephone number, territories covered, and lines carried. Automotive Service Industry Assoc., 25 Northwest Point, No. 425, Elk Grove Village, IL 60007-1035, 847-228-1310, Fax: 847-228-1510, E-mail: asiaassistankmktusa.org.

Automotive Warehouse Distributors Association Membership Directory. Annually in April. Includes listing of manufacturers, warehouse distributors, their products, personnel, and territories. Automotive Warehouse Distributors Assoc., 9140 Ward Pkwy, Kansas City, MO 64114, 816-44-3500, Fax: 816-444-0330, Web site: awda.org.

Aviation

World Aviation Directory. Published twice a year in March and September. Gives administrative and operating personnel of airlines, aircraft, and engine manufacturers and component manufacturers and distributors, organizations, and schools. Indexed by companies, activities, products, and individuals. Aviation Week—McGraw Hill, Inc., 1200 G. St. NW, Ste 900, Washington, DC 20005, 202-383-2484, Toll-free: 800-551-2015, Fax: 202-383-2478, E-mail: wad@mcgraw-hill.com, Web-site: wadaviation.com.

Bookstores

Book Trade Directory, American. Annually in June. Lists more than 25,000 retail and wholesale booksellers in the United States and Canada. Entries alphabetized by state (or province), and then by city and business name. Each listing gives address, telephone numbers, key personnel, types of books sold, subject specialties carried, sidelines and services offered, and general characteristics. For wholesale entries gives types of accounts, import–export information and territory limitations. Cahners Business Info., 121 Chanlon Rd., New Providence, NJ 07974-0000, 908-464-6800, Toll-free: 800-521-8100, Fax: 908-665-2894, E-mail: info@bowker.com.

Business Firms

D&B Million Dollar Directory—Top 50,000 Companies. Annually in March. Lists about 50,000 top corporations. Arranged alphabetically. Gives business name, state of incorporation, address, telephone number, SIC numbers, function, sales volume, number of employees, and name of officers and directors, principal bank, accounting firm, and legal counsel. Dun & Bradstreet, 3 Sylvan Way, Parsippany, NJ 07054-3896, 973-605-6442, Toll-free: 800-526-0651, Fax: 973-605-6911, E-mail: dnbmdd@dnb.com, Web site: dnbmdd.com.

China and Glassware

American Glass Review—Glass Factory Directory Issue. Glass Factory Directory Issue. Annually in March. Issued as part of subscription (13th issue) to *American Glass Reviews.* Lists companies manufacturing flat glass, tableware glass, and fiberglass, giving corporate and plant addresses, executives, type of equipment used. Doctorow Communications, Inc., 1011 Clifton Ave., Clifton, NJ 07013-0000, 973-779-1600, Fax: 973-779-3242.

City Directories Catalog

Municipal Yearbook (US). Annual. Contains a review of municipal events of the year, analyses of city operations, and a directory of city officials in all the states. International City/Council Mgmt. Assoc., 777 N. Capitol St. NE, Ste. 500, Washington, DC 20002-4201, 202-962-6700, Toll-free: 800-745-8780, Fax: 202-962-3500, Web site: icma.org.

College Stores

Directory of College Stores. Annual. Published every two years. Lists about 3,000 college stores, geographically with manager's name, kinds of goods sold, college name, number of students, whether men, women, or both, whether the store is college owned or privately owned. B. Klein Publications, PO Box 6578, Delray Beach, FL 33482, 407-496-3316, Fax: 407-496-5546.

Confectionery

Candy Buyer's Directory. Annually in January. Lists candy manufacturers, importers and U.S. representatives, and confectionery brokers. Manufacturing Confectioner Publishing Co., 175 Rock Rd., Glen Rock, NJ 07452-0000, 201-652-2655, Fax: 201-652-3419, web site: themc@gomc.com.

Construction Equipment

Construction Equipment Buyer's Guide. Annually in November. Lists 1,500 construction equipment distributors and manufacturers; includes company names, names of key personnel, addresses, telephone numbers, branch locations, and lines handled or type of equipment produced. Cahners Business Info., 1350 E. Touhy Ave., Des Plaines, IL 60018, 847-635-8800, Toll-free: 800-446-6551, Fax: 847-299-8622, Web site: coneq.com.

Conventions and Trade Shows

Directory of Conventions—Regional Edition. Annually in January. Contains more than 18,000 cross-indexed listings of annual events; gives dates, locations, names and addresses of executives in charge, scope, and expected attendance. Bill Communications, 355 Park Ave. S., New York, NY 10010-1789, 212-592-6505, Toll-free: 800-266-4712, Fax: 212-592-6650.

Dental Supply

Hayes Directory of Dental Supply Houses. Annually in August. Lists wholesalers of dental supplies and equipment with addresses, telephone numbers, financial standing, and credit rating. Edward N. Hayes Publisher, PO Box 3436, Mission Viejo, CA 92690-1436.

Department Stores

Sheldon's Retail. Annual. Lists 1,500 large independent department stores, 600 major department store chains, 150 large independent and chain home-furnishing stores, 700 large independent women's specialty stores, and 450 large women's specialty store chains alphabetically by states. Gives all department buyers with lines bought by each buyer, and addresses and telephone numbers of merchandise executives. Also gives all New York, Chicago, Dallas, Atlanta, and Los Angeles buying offices, the number and locations of branch stores, and an index of all store/chain headquarters. Todd Publications, PO Box 635, Nyack, NJ 10960, 914-358-6213, Toll-free: 800-747-1056, Fax: 914-358-1059, E-mail: toddpub@aol.com.

Discount Stores

Directory of Discount & General Merchandise Stores. Annual. Lists headquarters address, telephone number, location, square footage of each store, lines carried, leased operators, names of executives and buyers (includes Canada). Also special section on leased department operators. Chain Store Guide Information Services, 3922 Coconut Palm Dr., Tampa, FL 33619, 813-627-6800, Toll-free: 800-927-9292, Fax: 813-627-6882, E-mail: info@csgis.com, Web site: csgis.com.

Drug Outlets—Retail and Wholesale

Chain Drug Stores Guide, Hayes. Annually in September. Lists headquarters address, telephone numbers, number and location of units, names of executives and buyers, wholesale drug distributors. Edward N. Hayes Publisher, PO Box 3436, Mission Viejo, CA 92690-1436.

Drug Store Market Guide. Annually in March. Lists about 53,000 retail and 700 wholesale druggists in the United States, giving addresses, financial standing, and credit rating. Also publishes regional editions for one or more states. Computerized mailing labels available. Melnor Publishing Inc., 1739 Horton Ave., Mohegan Lake, NY 10547, 914-528-7147, Fax: 914-528-1369, E-mail: melnor@prodigy.net.

National Wholesale Druggists' Association Membership and Executive Directory. Annually in January. Lists 800 American and foreign wholesalers and manufacturers of drugs and allied products. National Wholesale Druggists' Assoc., 1821 Michael Faraday Dr., Ste. 400, Reston, VA 20190, 703-787-0000, Fax: 703-787-6930.

Redbook (Drugs & Pharmaceuticals). Annually in March. Gives information on wholesale drug companies, chain drugstores' headquarters, department stores maintaining toilet goods or drug departments, manufacturers' sales agents, and discount houses operating toilet goods, cosmetic, proprietary medicine or prescription departments. Medical Economics Co., 5 Paragon Dr., Montvale, NJ 07645-1725, 201-358-7500, Toll-free: 800-223-0581, Fax: 201-573-8999, E-mail: customer service@medec.com.

Electrical and Electronics

ECN's Electronic Industry Telephone Directory. Annually in August. Contains more than 22,890 listings of manufacturers, representatives, distributors, government agencies, contracting agencies, and others. Cahners Business Info., 201 King of Prussia Rd., Radnor, PA 19087-5114, 610-964-4000, Fax: 610-964-4273, E-mail: ecninfo@chilton.net, Web-site: ecnmag.com/eitd.

Electrical Wholesale Distributors, Directory of. Detailed information on 3,400 companies with more than 7,630 locations in the United States and Canada, including name, address, telephone number, branch and affiliated houses, products handled, etc. Intertec Publishing Corp., 9800 Metcalf Ave, Overland Park, KS 66212, 913-341-1300, Toll-free: 800-262-1954, Fax: 800-633-6219, Web site: ecmbook.com.

Electrical Utilities

Electrical Power Producers, Electrical World, Directory of. Annually in November. Complete listings of electric utilities (investor-owned, municipal, and government agencies in the United States and Canada) giving their addresses and personnel and selected data on operations. UDI/McGraw Hill Co., 1200 G. St. NW, Ste. 250, Washington, DC 20005, 202-942-8788, Toll-free: 800-486-3660, Fax: 202-942-8789, Web site: electrical-world.com/enestore.

Embroidery

Annual Laces & Embroideries Directory. Annually in November. Alphabetical listing with addresses and telephone numbers of manufacturers, merchandisers, designers, cutters, bleacheries, yam dealers, machine suppliers, and other suppliers to the Schiffli lace and embroidery industry. Schiffli Lace & Embroidery Manufacturers Assoc., 596 Anderson Ave., Ste. 203, Cliffside Park, NJ 07010-1828, 201-943-7757, Fax: 201-943-7793.

Export and Import

American Export Register. Annually in September. Includes more than 30,000 importers and exporters and products handled. Thomas Publishing Co., International Division, 5 Penn Plaza, New York, NY 10001, 212-629-1177, Fax: 212-629-1140.

Canadian Trade Directory, Fraser's. Annually in May. Contains more than 42,000 Canadian companies. Also lists more than 14,000 foreign companies that have Canadian representatives. Fraser's Trade Directories Co. Ltd., 777 Bay St., Toronto, ON., Canada MSW 1A7, 416-596-5086, Fax: 416-593-3201.

Flooring

Flooring Buying & Resource Guide Issue. Annually in October. Reference to sources of supply, giving their products and brand names, leading distributors, manufacturers' representatives, and associations. Douglas Publications, Inc., 2807 N. Parham Rd., Ste. 200, Richmond, VA 23294, 804-762-9600, Fax: 804-217-8999.

Food Dealers—Retail and Wholesale

Food Brokers Directory. Annually in July. Arranged by states and cities, lists member food brokers in the United States and Europe, giving names and addresses, products they handle, and services they perform. American Business Information Inc., 5711 S. 86th Circle, PO Box 27347, Omaha, NE 68127, 402-593-4600, Toll-free: 800-555-6124, Fax: 402-331-5481, E-mail: directory@abii.com, Web site: abii.com.

Food Industry Register, Thomas'. Annually in May. *Volume 1:* Lists supermarket chains, wholesalers, brokers, frozen food brokers, exporters, warehouses. *Volume 2:* Contains information on products and services; manufacturers, sources of supplies, importers. *Volume 3:* A–Z index of 48,000 companies. Also, a brand name/trademark index. Thomas Publishing Co., 5 Penn Plaza, New York, NY 10001, 212-696-0500, Fax: 212-290-7206, E-mail: ortertr@thomasregister. com, Web site: tfir.com.

National Frozen Food Association Directory. Annually in January. Lists packers, distributors, supplies, refrigerated warehouses, wholesalers, and brokers; includes names and addresses of each firm and their key officials. Contains statistical marketing data. National Frozen Food Assoc., Inc., 4755 Linglestown Rd., Ste. 300, Harrisburg, PA 17112, 717-657-8601, Fax: 717-657-9862, E-mail: info@nffa.org, Web site: nffa.org.

Uker's International Tea & Coffee Directory & Buyers Guide. Annual. Includes revised and updated lists of participants in the tea and coffee and allied trades. Lockwood Trade Journal, Inc., 130 W. 42d St., 10th Fl., New York, NY 10036, 212-391-2060, Fax: 212-827-0945, E-mail: teacof@aol.com.

Gas Companies

Brown's Directory of North American & International Gas Co. North American and International. Annually in November. Includes information on every known gas utility company and holding company worldwide. Energy Publications Division, Advanstar Communications, 7500 Old Oak Blvd., Cleveland, OH 44130-3369, Web site: advanstar.com.

LP/Gas-Industry Buying Guide Issue. Annually in March. Lists suppliers, supplies, and distributors. Advanstar Communications, 131 W. First St., Duluth, MN 55802, Toll-free: 800-346-0085, E-mail: fulfill@superfil.com.

Gift and Art

Gift, Housewares & Home Textile Buyers, Nationwide Directory of. Annually with semiannual supplement. For 7,000 types of retail firms, lists store name, address, type of store, number of stores, names of president, merchandise managers, and buyers, etc., for giftwares and housewares. State editions also available. Salesman's Guide, 121 Chanlon Rd., New Providence, NJ 7974, 908-464-6800, Toll-free: 800-521-8110, Fax: 908-665-2894.

Gift Shops Directory. 66,291 listings. American Business Information Inc., 5711 S. 86th Circle, PO Box 27347, Omaha, NE 68127, 402-593-4600, Toll-free: 800-555-6124, Fax: 402-331-5481, E-mail: directory@abii.com, Web site: abii.com.

Home Furnishings

Home Fashions—Buyer's Guide Issue. Annually in December. Lists names and addresses of manufacturers, importers, and regional sales representatives. Fairchild Publications, Capital Cities Media, Inc., 7 W. 34th St., New York, NY 10003, 212-630-4784, Toll-free: 800-247-2160, Fax: 212-630-4796.

Interior Decorator's and Designer Supplies. Semiannually in spring and fall. Published expressly for decorators and designers, interior decorating staff of department and furniture stores. Lists firms handling items used in interior decoration. American Business Information Inc., 5711 S. 86th Circle, PO Box 27347, Omaha, NE 68127, 402-593-4600, Toll-free: 800-555-6124, Fax: 402-331-5481, E-mail: directory@abii.com, Web site: abii.com.

National Antique & Art Dealers Assoc. of America—Membership Directory. Annual. Lists 35,636 dealers with name, address, and phone number as well as size of advertisement and first year advertised in Yellow Pages. National Antique & Art Dealers Assoc., 12 East 56th St., New York, NY 10022, 212-826-9707, Fax: 212-319-0471.

Hospitals

Hospitals, Directory of. Annually in January. Lists 12,173 hospitals, with selected data. SMG Marketing Group Inc., 875 N. Michigan Ave., Chicago, IL 60611, 312-642-3026, Toll-free: 800-678-3026, Fax: 312-642-9729, Web site: smgusa.com.

Hotels and Motels

Hotels and Motels Directory. Annually. Lists more than 62,465 hotels and motels. American Hospital Publishing Inc., 737 N. Michigan Ave., Ste. 700, Chicago, IL 60611-2615, 312-440-6800, Toll-free: 800-621-6902, Fax: 312-951-8491.

OAG Business Travel Planner (North America). Quarterly. Lists more than 26,000 hotels in the United States. Also lists 14,500 destination cities, etc. Reed Travel Group-OAG Travel Services Div., 2000 Clearwater Dr., Oak Brook, IL 60521, 630-574-6000, Toll-free: 800-Dial-OAG, Fax: 630-574-6090, E-mail: info@oag.com, Web site: oag.com.

Housewares

MHMA Membership Directory. Annually in June. Compilation of resources of the housewares trade; includes listing of their products, trade names, and a registry of manu-facturers' representatives. National Housewares Manufacturing Assoc., 6400 Shafer St., Ste. 650, Rosemont, IL 60018, 847-292-4200, Fax: 847-292-4211.

Jewelry

Jewelers' Circular/Keystone—Jewelers' Directory Issue. Annual in June. Lists manufacturers, importers, distributors, and retailers of jewelry; diamonds, precious, semi-precious, and imitation stones; watches, silverware; and kindred articles. Includes credit ratings. Cahners Business Info., 201 King of Prussia Rd., Radnor, PA 19087-5114, 610-964-4000, Fax: 610-964-4273, E-mail: marketaccess@cahners.com.

Liquor

Wine and Spirits Wholesalers of America—Member Roster and Industry Direc-tory. Annually in January. Lists names of 700 member companies; includes parent house and branches, addresses, and names of managers. Also, has register of 2,200 suppliers, and gives state liquor control administrators, national associations, and trade press directory. Wine & Spirits Wholesalers of America Inc., 805 Fifteenth St. NW, Ste. 430, Washington, DC 20005, 202-371-9792, Fax: 202-789-2405, Web site: wswa.org.

Mailing List Houses

Mailing List, Directory of. Lists 1,800 firms, brokers, compilers, and firms offering their own lists for rent; includes the specialties of each firm. Arranged geographically. American Business Information Inc., 5711 S. 86th Circle, PO Box 27347, Omaha, NE 68127, 402-593-4600, Toll-free: 800-555-6124, Fax: 402-331-5481, E-mail: directory@abii.com, Web site: abii.com

Manufacturers

MacRae's Blue Book (manufacturers). Annually in March. In three volumes: Volume 1, Corporate Index lists company names and addresses alphabetically, with 40,000 branch and/or sales office telephone numbers. Volumes 2 and 3, companies listed by product classifications. MacRae's OEM Mart. Inc., 65 Bleecker St., New York, NY 10012-2420, 212-673-4700, Toll-free: 800-622-7237, Fax: 212-475-1791, Web site: dnet.com/macraes.

Manufacturers, Thomas' Register of American. Annual. Volume 1–14 products and services; suppliers of each product category grouped by state and city. Vols. 15–16 contain company profiles. Vols. 17–23 manufacturers' catalogs. More than 150,000 firms are listed under 50,000 product headings. Thomas Publishing Co., 5 Penn Plaza, New York, NY 10001, 212-696-0500, Fax: 212-290-7206, E-mail: ortertr@thomasregister.com, Web site: tfir.com.

Manufacturer's Sales Representatives

Manufacturers Agents National Assoc. Directory of Manufacturers Sales Agencies. Annually in May/June. Contains individual listings of manufacturers' agents throughout the United States, Canada, and several foreign countries. Listings cross-referenced by alphabetical, geographical, and product classification. Manufacturing Agents National Assoc. (MANA), 23016 Mill Creek Rd., PO Box 3467, Laguna Hills, CA 92654, 949-859-4040, Fax: 949-855-2973, E-mail: askmana@aol.com, Web site: manaonline.org.

Metalworking

Metalworking Directory, Dun & Bradstreet—Industrial Guide. Annually in June. Lists about 78,000 metalworking and metal-producing plants with 20 or more production employees. Arranged geographically. Dun & Bradstreet, 3 Sylvan Way, Parsippany, NJ 07054-2896, 973-605-6442, Toll-free: 800-526-0651, Fax: 973-605-6911, E-mail: dnbmdd@dnb.com.

Military Market

Military Market Magazine—Supply Bulletin Directory. Annually in January. Lists manufacturers and suppliers of products sold in military commissaries. Also lists manufacturers' representatives and distributors. Army Time Publishing Co., 6883 Commercial Dr., Springfield, VA 22159-0001, 703-750-8197, Toll-free: 800-368-5718, Fax: 703-658-8314.

Order Businesses

Mail Order Business Directory. Lists 10,000 names of mail-order firms with buyers' names, and lines carried. Arranged geographically B. Klein Publications, PO Box 6578, Delray Beach, FL 33482, 407-496-3316, Fax: 407-496-5546.

Paper Products

Sources of Supply Buyers' Guide. Lists 1,700 mills and converters of paper, film, foil, and allied products, and paper merchants in the United States alphabetically with addresses, principal personnel, and products manufactured. Also lists trade associations, brand names, and manufacturers' representatives. Wm. O Dannhausen Corp., PO Box 795, Parkridge, IL 60068, 847-823-3145, Fax: 847-696-3445, E-mail: wmdann@compuserve.com, Web site: dannhausen.com.

Physicians' Supply Houses

Hayes Directory of Medical Supply Houses. Annually in August. Listings of 1,850 U.S. wholesalers doing business in physician, hospital, and surgical supplies and equipment; includes addresses, telephone numbers, financial standing, and credit ratings. Edward N. Hayes Publisher, PO Box 3436, Mission Viejo, CA 92690-1436.

Premium Sources

Incentive Directory Issue. Annually in February. Contains classified directory of suppliers and list of manufacturers' representatives serving the premium field. Also lists associations, clubs, and trade shows. Bill Communications, 355 Park Ave. S., New York, NY 10010-1787, 212-592-6505, Toll-free: 800-266-4712, Fax: 212-592-6650.

Purchasing Government

US Government Purchasing & Sales Directory. Irregularly issued. Booklet designed to help small business receive an equitable share of government contracts. Lists types of purchases for both military and civilian needs, catalogs procurement offices by state. Lists SBA regional and branch offices, Office of Government Contracting, Small Business Administration, 409 3rd. St. SW, Washington, DC 20416, 202-205-6460.

Refrigeration and Air Conditioning

Air Conditioning, Heating & Refrigeration News—Directory Issue. Annually in January. Lists 1,900 manufacturers and 3,000 wholesalers and factory outlets in refrigeration, heating, and air-conditioning. Business News Publishing Co., 755 W. Big Beaver Rd., Ste. 1000, Troy, MI 48084, 248-362-3700, Fax: 248-362-5103, E-mail: peruccae@bnp.com, Web site: bnp.com/the-news.

Selling Direct

Direct Selling, World Directory. Annually in April. About 40 direct selling associations and 750 associated member companies. Includes names of contact persons, company product line, method of distribution, etc. World Federation of Direct Selling Assoc., 1666 K. St. NW, Ste. 1010, Washington, DC 20006, 202-293-5760, Fax: 202-463-4569, E-mail: info@wfdsa.org, Web site: wfdsa.org.

Shopping Centers

Shopping Center Directory. Annual. Alphabetical listing of 34,000 shopping centers, location, owner/developer, manager, physical plant (number of stores, square feet), and leasing agent. National Research Bureau, 330 W. Wacker Dr., Ste. 900, Chicago, IL 60606, 312-541-0100, Toll-free: 800-456-4555, Fax: 312-541-1492.

Specialty Stores

Women's Apparel Stores, Phelon's. Lists more than 7,000 women's apparel and accessory shops with store headquarters name and address, number of shops operated, New York City buying headquarters or representatives, lines of merchandise bought and sold, name of principal and buyers, store size, and price range., Phelon, Sheldon, & Marsar, Inc., 330 Main St., Ridgefield Park, NJ 07660-0000, 201-440-9096, Toll-free: 800-234-8804, Fax: 201-440-8568.

Sporting Goods

Sporting Goods Buyers, Nationwide Directory of. Including semiannual supplements. Lists more than 7,500 top retail stores with names of buyers and executives, for all types of sporting goods, athletic apparel and athletic footwear, hunting, and fishing, and outdoor equipment. Salesman's Guide, 121 Chanlon Rd., New Providence, NJ 07974, 908-464-6800, Toll-free: 800-521-8110, Fax: 908-665-2894.

Textiles

Textile Blue Book, Davison's.   Annually in March. Contains more than 8,400 separate company listings (name, address, etc.) for the United States and Canada. Firms included are cotton, wool, synthetic mills, knitting mills, cordage, twine, and duck manufacturers, dry goods commission merchants, converters, yam dealers, cordage manufacturers' agents, wool dealers and merchants, cotton merchants, exporters, brokers, and others. Davison Publishing Co. Inc., PO Box 1289, Concord, NC 28026, 704-785-8700, Toll-free: 800-328-4766, Fax: 704-785-8701, E-mail: textiles@davisonbluebook.com, Web site: davisonbluebook.com.

Toys and Novelties

Playthings—Buyers Guide.   Annually in June. Lists manufacturers, products, trade names, suppliers to manufacturers, supplier products, licensors, manufacturers' representatives, toy trade associations, and trade show management. Geyer-McAllister Publications, Inc., 51 Madison Ave., New York, NY 10010-1603, 212-689-4411, Fax: 212-683-7929.

Small World—Directory Issue.   Annually in December. Lists 200 wholesalers, manufacturers, manufacturers' representatives of toys, games, and hobbies for children and infants. Earn Shaw Publications, Inc., 225 W. 34th St., Rm. 1212, New York, NY 10122, 212-563-2742, Fax: 212-629-3249.

Trailer Parks

Campground Directory, Woodall's.   Annual. Lists and star-rates public and private campgrounds in North American continent alphabetically by town with location and description of facilities. Also lists more than 800 RV service locations. Regional editions available. American Business Information Inc., 5711 S. 86th Circle, PO Box 27347, Omaha, NE 68127, 402-593-4600, Toll-free: 800-555-6124, Fax: 402-331-5481, E-mail: directory@abii.com, Web site: abii.com.

Trucking

Trucksource: Sources of Trucking Industry Information.   Annually in November. Includes more than 700 sources of information on the trucking industry, classified by subject. American Trucking Assoc. Inc. (ATA), 2200 Mill Rd., Alexandria, VA 22314-4677, 703-838-1700, Toll-free: 800-282-5463.

Variety Stores

General Merchandise, Variety & Specialty Stores, Directory of.   Annually in March. Lists headquarters address, telephone number, number of units and locations, executives, and buyers. American Business Information Inc., 5711 S. 86th Circle, PO Box 27347, Omaha, NE 68127, 402-593-4600, Toll-free: 800-555-6124, Fax: 402-331-5481, E-mail: directory@abii.com, Web site: abii.com.

Warehouses

Affiliated Warehouse Companies—Directory. Annually in July. Lists leading public warehouses in the United States and Canada, as well as major truck lines, airlines, steamship lines, liquid and dry bulk terminals, material handling equipment suppliers, ports of the world and railroad piggyback services and routes Affiliated Warehouse Co. Inc., 54 Village Ct., PO Box 295, Hazlet, NJ 07730, 732-739-2323, Fax: 732-739-4154, E-mail: sales@awco.com.

OTHER IMPORTANT DIRECTORIES

The following business directories are helpful to those persons doing marketing research. Most of these directories are available for reference at the larger libraries. For additional listings consult the *Guide to American Directories* at local libraries.

Bradford's Directory of Mkt. Research Agencies & Mgmt. Consultants in the US & the World. Gives names and addresses of more than 2,400 marketing research agencies in the United States, Canada, and abroad. Lists service offered by agency, along with other pertinent data, such as date established, names of principal officers, and size of staff. Bradford's Directory, PO Box 2300, Centreville, VA 20122, 703-631-1500, Fax: 703-830-5303.

Consultants & Consulting Organizations Directory. Contains 16,000 entries. Guides reader to appropriate organization for a given consulting assignment. Entries include names, addresses, phone numbers, and data on services performed. Gale Research, 27500 Drake Rd., Farmington Hills, MI 48331-3535, 248-699-gale, Toll-free: 800-877-gale, Fax: 248-699-8069, E-mail: galeord@gale.com.

Research Centers Directory. Lists more than 11,000 nonprofit research organizations. Descriptive information provided for each center, including address, telephone number, name of director, data on staff, funds, publications, and a statement concerning its principal fields of research. Has special indexes. Gale Research, 27500 Drake Rd., Farmington Hills, MI 48331-3535, 248-699-gale, Toll-free: 800-877-gale, Fax: 248-699-8069, E-mail: galeord@gale.com.

Thomas' Food Industry Register. Annually in May. Lists in two volumes wholesale grocers, chain-store organizations, voluntary buying groups, food brokers, exporters and importers of food products, frozen-food brokers, distributors and related products distributed through grocery chains. Thomas Publishing Co., 5 Penn Plaza, New York, NY 10001, 212-696-0500, Fax: 212-290-7206, E-mail: ortertr@thomasregister.com, Web site: tfir.com.

Thomas' Register of American Manufacturers. Annually in February. In 23 volumes. Volumes 1–14 contain manufacturers arranged geographically under each product, and capitalization or size rating for each manufacturer, under 50,000 product headings. Volumes 15 and 16 contain company profiles and a brand or trade name section with more than 112,000 listings. Volumes 17–23 are catalogs from more than 1,500 firms. Thomas Publishing Co., 5 Penn Plaza, New York, NY 10001, 212-696-0500, Fax: 212-290-7206, E-mail: ortertr@thomasregister.com, Web site: tfir.com.

INTERNET SOURCES

AMERICAN BUSINESS INFORMATION
http://www.abii.com/
Order in-depth profile on any business. Get the address and phone number of any business.

AMERICAN DEMOGRAPHICS
http:www.demographics.com
Demographics of special interest to marketers.

AMERICAN EXPRESS SMALL BUSINESS EXCHANGE
http://www.americanexpress.com/smallbusiness/
Information on creating a business plan, managing a business, and expert advice on small business problems.

BUSINESS ESSENTIALS LIBRARY
http://pasware.com/
Sections on business planning including sample plans, information on financing, and marketing, plan outline, answers questions, etc.

COMMERCIAL SERVICES OF THE U.S. DEPARTMENT OF COMMERCE
http://www.ita.doc.gov/uscs/
Numerous programs having to with export, including trade statistics abroad.

DUN AND BRADSTREET
http://www.dbisna.com/dbis/market/hmenu.htm
Tips for creating a marketing plan and more.

FORTUNE 500
http://pathfinder.com/@@nEp5NAYAo1fNhn6/fortune/1997/ specials/f500/index.html
Statistics and data on Fortune 500 companies.

FREE MARKETING MAGAZINE FOR CONSULTANTS
http://wwwhansommarketing.com
Online help for consultant, marketing tips, and more.

HOOVERS ONLINE
http://www.hoovers.com/
Company information and profiles on more than 2,700 companies, both public and private.

THE INTERNET INVENTION STORE
http://www.catalog.com/impulse/invent.htm
Information on new products.

INTERNET LINKS TO FREE ADVERTISING
http://www.portal.ca/~direct/biz/free1.htm

KENNEDY INFORMATION RESEARCH GROUP
http://www.kennedyinfo.com
General information on consulting, trends, fees, etc.

LINKEXCHANGE
http://www.linkexchange.com
Banner exchange, starting, promoting, and managing a Web site. Selling online, and more.

THE MARKET RESEARCH CENTER
http:www.airsearch.com
Links to any product or service category. Good source for information on competitive sites.

MCNI
http://www/mcni.com
Forums, free consultant listing, search service, bookstore, and more.

PROMOTION CLINIC
http://www.promotion-clinic.ppa.org
Ideas, products, and promotion campaigns

SMALL BUSINESS ADVISOR
http://www.isquare.com/
Advice and short reports for small businesses.

SMARTAGE
http://www.smartage.com
Graphics programs to create Web sites and banners, information on free advertising, building and selling an online store, and more.

STATISTICAL ABSTRACT OF THE UNITED STATES
Numerous sites—Use a search engine and look up Statistical Abstract Of The United States.
Demographics of all types.

TRADE SHOW CENTRAL
http://www.tscentral.com:80/html/ven_fac.html
Search directory for 33,000 trade shows worldwide.

U.S. SMALL BUSINESS ADMINISTRATION
http://www.sbaonline.sba.gov/
Information on starting a business, expanding one, local small business administration resources, shareware, and more.

WORLD INVENTORS TRADE ASSOCIATION
http://www.inventnet.com.au/invent/prod.htm
Information on new products from 35 countries.

WORLD TRADE DIRECTORIES SOURCES
http://www.net-promote.com/wholesale-directories.html
Sources of trade directories for purchase.

APPENDIX C

EXAMPLES OF SIMPLE RESEARCH AND A MARKETING RESEARCH CHECKLIST

The kind of marketing research you do is limited only by your imagination. Some research can be done, even of the primary type, at very little cost except for your time. Here are some examples of simple research done by small businesses, which greatly increased sales. These ideas were suggested by J. Ford Laumer, Jr., James R. Hams, and Hugh J. Guffey, Jr., all professors of marketing at Auburn University of Auburn, Alabama, in their booklet *Learning about Your Market,* published by the Small Business Administration.

1. *License Plate Analysis.* In many states, license plates give you information about where car owners live. Therefore, simply by taking down the numbers of cars parked in your location and contacting the appropriate state agency, you can estimate the area from which you draw business. Knowing where your customers live can help you in your advertising or in targeting your approach to promotion. By the same method you can find who your competitors' customers are.

2. *Telephone Number Analysis.* Telephone numbers can also tell you the areas in which people live. You can obtain customers' telephone numbers from sales slips, credit card slips, or checks. Again, knowing where they live will give you excellent information about their lifestyles.

3. *Coded Coupons.* The effectiveness of your advertising vehicle can easily be checked by coding coupons that can be used for discounts or inquiries about products. You can find out the areas that your customers come from, as well as which vehicle brought them your message.

4. *People Watching.* Simply looking at your customers can tell you a great deal about them. How are they dressed? How old are they? Are they married or single? Do they have children or not? Many owners use this method intuitively to get a feel about their customers. However, a little sophistication with a tally sheet for a week can provide much more accurate information simply, easily, and without cost. It may confirm what you've known all along, or it may completely change your picture of your typical customer.

CHECKLIST FOR APPRAISAL OF YOUR RESEARCH STUDY

1. Review of research objectives:
   a. In relation to the problem.
   b. In relation to previous research.
   c. In relation to developments subsequent to initiation of research.

2. Overall study design:
   a. Are the hypotheses relevant? Consistent?
   b. Is the terminology relevant and unambiguous?
   c. Is the design a logical bridge from problem to solution?
   d. Are there any biases in the design that may have influenced the results?
   e. Was care taken to preserve anonymity, if needed?
   f. Were proper ethical considerations taken into account?
   g. Was the study well administered?

3. Methods used:
   a. Were the right sources used (populations sampled)?
   b. Do any of the data collection methods appear to be biased?
   c. What precautions were taken to avoid errors or mistakes in data collection?
   d. If sampling was used, how representative is the sample? With what margin of error?
   e. Were the data processed with due care? What precautions were taken to assure good coding?
   f. Are the categories used in tabulation meaningful?
   g. Were any pertinent tabulations or cross-classifications overlooked? On the other hand, are the tabulations so detailed as to obscure some of the main points?
   h. Do the analytical (statistical) methods appear to be appropriate?
   i. Is the report well executed in terms of organization, style, appearance, etc?

4. Review of interpretations and recommendations:
   a. Do they follow from the data? Are they well supported?
   b. Are they comprehensive? Do they relate to the whole problem or only part of it?
   c. Are they consistent with the data? With existing information, other studies, executives' experiences, etc.?
   d. Were any relevant interpretations overlooked?

5. Responsibility for action and follow-up:
   a. Will information receive due consideration from all those concerned?
   b. What are the implications of the results for action? Will all action possibilities be considered? (How do the results affect aspects of total operation outside the scope of the report?)
   c. Is an action program necessary? Will it be formulated?
   d. Is further information needed? If so, along what lines?
   e. Is responsibility for follow-up clearly assigned?
   f. Should a time be set for reevaluation of the action program (e.g., to reevaluate an innovation, or test a new package after introduction)?

APPENDIX

HOW TO LEAD A TEAM

One of the most important and difficult challenges you face in developing a marketing plan is working on a team. Teamwork is never easy. You must work with different personalities, having different work schedules, different priorities, different motivation, and different ways of approaching the project. Further, someone may or may not be assigned as team leader. You may think that teamwork is something that you only need to be concerned with as a student. You may be under the impression that once you graduate, you need never be concerned with teamwork again. You would be very much mistaken. Most companies of all sizes use teams to accomplish work to some extent or another. Over the last 10 years, there has been a dramatic increase in the use of team structures in companies due to the quality movement and the use of process action teams. Process action teams focus on improving the process of getting some type of work accomplished. But long before the quality movement, teams had already made important contributions in industry. In fact, back in 1987, management guru Tom Peters stated, "…the power of the team is so great that it is often wise to violate apparent common sense and force a team structure on almost anything."[1]

To understand just how powerful teams are, try to identify what kind of work has all of the following characteristics:

- The workers work very hard physically, including weekends, with little complaint.
- The workers receive no money and little material compensation for their services.
- The work is dangerous, and workers are frequently injured on the job.
- The work is strictly voluntary.
- The workers usually have very high morale.
- There are always more volunteers than can be used for the work.
- The workers are highly motivated to acheive the organization's goals.
- Not only is the work legal, but many community organizations encourage it.

Turn the page to identify this work. The work which has all of these characteristics is…

---

[1] Tom Peters, *Thriving on Chaos* (New York: Knopf, 1987), p. 306.

A HIGH SCHOOL FOOTBALL TEAM

WHAT'S SO GREAT ABOUT A TEAM?

Yes, all of the characteristics of the football team are true. The operative word here is *TEAM.* Can you begin to see just how powerful and unique a team can be? Yet the basic concept of a team is very simple. A team is simply two or more individuals working together to reach a common goal.

Teams in industry have achieved incredible goals. One of General Electric's plants in Salisbury, North Carolina, increased its productivity by 250 percent compared to other General Electric plants making the same product, but without teams. General Mills' plants with teams are 40 percent more productive than plants without teams. Westinghouse Furniture Systems increased productivity 74 percent in three years with teams. Using teams, Volvo's Kalimar facility reduced defects by 90 percent.

A number of scientists have observed that when geese flock in a V formation to reach a destination, they are operating as a team. Their common goal is their destination. And by teaming, they extend their range by as much as 71 percent! Flocking also illustrates some other important aspects of effective teaming. One goose doesn't lead all the time. The lead position at the point of the V varies. Note that this is also true in football. On different plays, the leadership role varies. Also, at different times in football, different individuals may assume important leadership roles. At any given time, the head coach, line coach, team captain, quarterback, or someone else may have the most important leadership role on the team.

Getting back to our flock of geese, should a single goose leave formation, he or she soon returns because of the difficulty in flying against the wind resistance alone. Should a goose fall out of formation because it is injured, other "team members" will drop out and attempt to assist their teammate. You may have thought that the honking noise that geese make in formation serves no useful purpose. But scientific investigation found that honking was all part of their teamwork. The honking was the cheering which encouraged the leader to maintain the pace. Flocks of geese, football teams, and teams of students developing a marketing plan share the following characteristics if they are to be effective:

- They demonstrate coordinated interaction.
- They are more efficient working together than alone.
- They enjoy the process of working together.
- Responsibility rotates either formally or informally.
- There is mutual care, nurturing, and encouragement among team members and especially between leaders and followers.
- There is a high level of trust.
- Everyone is keenly interested in everyone else's success.

As you might expect, when you have a group acting together toward a common goal showing these characteristics, you see some very positive results. It becomes not just a team, but a winning team. The team members have a degree of understanding and acceptance not found outside the group. They produce a greater number of ideas, and these ideas are of higher quality than if they thought up some ideas individually and met to make a list of the total. Such a team has higher motivation and performance levels which offset individual biases, and cover each other's "blind spots."

If you saw the picture *Rocky,* you may remember the scene where Rocky's girlfriend's brother demands to know what Rocky sees in his sister. "She fills spaces," answers Stallone, playing the role of Rocky. "Spaces in me, spaces in her." With fewer "blind spots" and performing together in such a way as to emphasize each member's strengths and make his or her weaknesses irrelevant, an effective team is more likely to take risks and innovative action that lead to success.

When a flock of geese becomes a winning team, they get to their destination quicker than other flocks. They get the most protective nesting areas which are located closer to sources of food and water. Their gooslings are bigger, stronger, and healthier. They have a much better chance of survival and procreation. We see the winning football teams in the Super Bowl. And a winning marketing planning team? In class, this is the team that gets the "A," and has a lot of fun doing it. In real life, the winning team developing a marketing plan gets the resources needed, and goes on to build a multi-billion dollar success in the marketplace.

WHO GETS TO BE THE TEAM LEADER?

Sometimes you will be assigned the position of team leader; sometimes not. Sometimes no team leader assignment will be made. However, you may be the only graduate student on a team with undergraduate students. Moreover, in your "other life," you are a company president. You are confident that your fellow team members will follow your lead. You go to several meetings and attempt to take charge. Guess what? Your teammates reject you in favor of someone else who isn't one-tenth as qualified. What do you do?

My advice is this: If you are assigned or selected as team leader by your teammates, do the job to the best of your ability. If you are not assigned or selected as team leader by your teammates, support whoever is team leader to the best of your ability. Never let your ego get in the way of your doing the best you can for your team. Not only will this help your team become a winning team, but you will earn the respect of your teammates and maintain your own self-respect as well. A good leader can both lead and follow. He or she doesn't need to be the leader in order to make a major contribution to the team.

HOW DO I LEAD IF I AM THE LEADER?

There is no way of telling you how to be a leader in 25 words or less. There are volumes written about leadership. I should know. I wrote a couple. These were recommended by leaders from Mary Kay Ash, CEO Emeritus of Mary Kay Cosmetics, and CEOs of major corporations to Senator Barry Goldwater, and General H. Norman Schwarzkopf. I highly recommend these books to you.[2]

I will point out one critical fact. There is no question that as team leader, you have a major responsibility for the ultimate marketing plan that is produced. There is an old say-

---

[2] William A. Cohen, *The New Art of the Leader* (Paramus, NJ: Prentice-Hall, 2001) and *The Stuff of Heroes: The Eight Universal Laws of Leadership* (Marietta, GA: Longstreet, 1998).

ing that it is better to have an army of lambs led by a lion than an army of lions led by a lamb. This emphasizes the extreme importance of the leader in getting the job done. There is no such thing as an excuse that "all my team members were lambs." A leader who says this is really saying that "I am a lamb." We really don't know what the team members were. They could have all been lions and still failed with a lamb as a leader.

Although I can't make you an expert leader in a few pages of suggestions, there are specific things I can tell you which you need to know about being a *team* leader. Psychologists and researchers in leadership found that teams progress through four stages of development. Each stage not only has different characteristics, but members of teams tend to ask different questions in each stage. Partly because the concerns of the team tend to be different in each stage, the leader's focus, actions, and behavior must be different in each stage as well. This is extremely important because what might be the correct actions in one stage would be counterproductive and incorrect in another. For example, in the second stage of development members actually tend to be committed, and even obedient. The leader's focus during this stage must be on building relationships and facilitating tasks. But look out! In the next stage, members tend to challenge each other and even their leader. You've got to focus on conflict management and examining key work processes to make them better. If you are stuck in stage two while your team is in stage three, you may lose your moral authority as leader.

So, as a team leader, you must first identify what stage the team is in. Then, pay attention to your focus and take actions to answer the concerns of your team while you help move them toward completing the project. With this in mind, here are the four stages of team development:

- Stage 1: Getting Organized
- Stage 2: Getting Together and Making Nice-Nice
- Stage 3: Fighting It Out
- Stage 4: Getting the Job Done

Now let's look at each in turn.

STAGE 1: GETTING ORGANIZED

When you first get together as a team, you're going to find that many of your team members may tend to be silent and self-conscious, unless they have known one another previously. This is because they are uncertain. They don't know what is going to happen, and they may be worried about what is expected of them. The questions that may occur to your fellow team members at this time include: Who are these other guys? Are they going to be friendly or to challenge me? What are they going to expect me to do? What's going to happen during this process? Where exactly will we be headed and why? What are our precise goals? Where do I fit in? How much work will this involve? Is this project going to require me to give up time that I need to put in elsewhere?

As the team leader, your primary focus during stage 1 is just as the stage is named: to organize the team. Your actions should include making introductions; stating the mission of the team; clarifying goals, procedures, rules, expectations; and answering questions. The idea is to establish a foundation of trust right from the start. You want an atmosphere of openness with no secrets. Although members may disagree with each other or with you, everyone gets his or her say and everyone's opinion is listened to and considered.

To do this, you must model these expected behaviors yourself. If you aren't open, no one else will be. If you don't treat the opinions of others with respect, neither will anyone else. If you listen carefully, so will everyone else. If you argue and try to shout down others, so will those you are attempting to lead.

You may be interested in characteristics of high-performance teams as distinguished from those that performed less well.[3] Keep these in mind as you organize your team.

- Clear goals
- Goals known by all
- Goals achieved in small steps
- Standards of excellence
- Feedback of results
- Skills and knowledge of everyone used
- Continuous improvement expected
- Adequate resources provided
- Autonomy
- Performance-based rewards
- Competition
- Praise and recognition
- Team commitment
- Plans and tactics
- Rules and penalties
- Performance measures

Remember, in stage 1, your principal focus is on getting organized. At the same time, you are laying the foundations of trust and openness for the stages that follow.

STAGE 2: GETTING TOGETHER AND MAKING NICE-NICE

Congratulations! You did a great job of getting your marketing planning team together at the first meeting. Now you have a different challenge. Members tend to ignore disagreements and conform obediently to the group standards and expectations, as well as your directions as leader. There is heightened interpersonal attraction, and at the end, everyone will be committed to a team vision. All of this is what you want.

Of course, team members still wonder and ask themselves questions. What are the team's norms and expectations? How much should I really give up and conform to the group's ideas? What role can I perform on this team? Where can I make a contribution? Will I be supported in what I suggest, or will others "put me down"? Where are we headed? How much time and energy should I commit to this project?

During this stage, you have several major challenges:

- Facilitating role differentiation

---

[3] F. Petrock, "Team Dynamics: A Workshop for Effective Team Building," Presentation at the University of Michigan Management of Managers Program, 1991.

- Showing support
- Providing feedback
- Articulating and motivating commitment to a vision

To facilitate role differentiation, you need to continue to build relationships among your team members. You want your team members to contribute according to their strengths where they are most needed. You also want to assist them in whatever tasks they are working on. You can do this by asking about their strengths, and preferences for tasks that need to be done. As they proceed, it is your responsibility to ensure they have the resources to do the job. When there are disagreements between team members, as leader it is your responsibility to resolve the situation. As a task facilitator, you yourself may function in a variety of roles. At times you may give direction, or at least suggestions. You are sometimes an information seeker, and at others, an information giver. You must monitor, coordinate, and oversee everything that is going on. Avoid blocking others from contributing, and don't let anyone else block either. People try to block others in a variety of ways, including fault-finding, overanalyzing, rejecting out of hand, dominating, stalling, and some others we might never anticipate. Don't let them do it!

Show support for others by building people up every chance you get. Build on their ideas, but give them credit for being the first to think them up. And as indicated earlier, let everyone be heard. Don't let someone who is more articulate, powerful, or popular block the ideas of some other team member who is less so.

Providing effective feedback is not easy. You must indicate what is going to work, and what won't. To do this without offending, so this person maintains his or her self-respect and continues to contribute is the real challenge. To best accomplish this, talk about behavior, not about personalities. Make observations, not inferences. Be as specific as possible. Share ideas and information. Don't set yourself up as a "know-it-all" who gives advice. Learn the art of the possible. It is possible to give too much feedback at one time, especially if the feedback is more critical than congratulatory. In fact, critical feedback is always difficult. Look for ways of doing this that remove the "sting" of criticism. Former President Ronald Reagan gave a small statue of a foot with a hole in it to his Secretary of the Interior when the secretary made a major public gaffe. The statue was the "Shoot Yourself in the Foot" Award. There was a lot of laughter and good humor as President Reagan presented it. Still, it was criticism. You might establish a pot where people have to put in a dollar if they show up late to a team meeting. The money could go toward a team party or for some other team purpose. Finally, remember you give feedback for value to the team—not for personal emotional release; not to show who's boss and not to show how clever you are.

Finally, you must focus on articulating and motivating commitment to a vision. A vision is sort of a mental picture of the outcome of the mission. Maybe the vision is to submit the best marketing plan in the class. Maybe it is to win a prize with the plan. Maybe it is to develop a plan for someone who is actually going to implement it. In any case, you should sell the outcome, the good things that will happen as a result of the team's work in precise terms. Motivating your team means making your vision, their vision also. To do this, you must get them involved. Ask their opinions. Modify your vision as necessary. Ground the vision in core values. Also, people don't sacrifice to do small tasks. They sacrifice only for big tasks. So if you are preparing a marketing plan for a medical product that can be very beneficial, emphasize building a better world more than profitability. If you can get people involved with suggestions and ideas about the vision and how to achieve it, you will have attained two essential ingredients: public commitment and ownership. Get those, and you've gone a long way to building a winning team.

STAGE 3: FIGHTING IT OUT

When you enter stage 3, the good news is that you have a team fully committed to a vision, and fighting to get a first-class marketing plan developed, printed, and bound. Unfortunately, because individuals have so much of themselves invested, members in this stage can become polarized, may form cliques, become overly competitive, and may even challenge your authority as leader.

Clearly, you have your work cut out for you. Your focus during this stage must be on conflict management, continuing to ensure that everyone gets to express his or her ideas, examining key work processes to make them better, getting team members working together rather than against each other, and avoiding groupthink. All of these are pretty straightforward except for groupthink. What is groupthink?

Groupthink has to do with adopting some idea or course of action simply because the group seems to want it, and not because it is a particularly good idea that has been throughly discussed and thought through. The most conspicuous example of group-think has been popularized as a "Trip to Abilene." In a "Trip to Abilene," a family makes a miserable two-hour trip to Abilene and returns to a ranch in west Texas. The trip is made in a car without air-conditioning on a hot, humid, summer day on the suggestion of one of the family members. All members agreed on the trip, although later it turns out that they did so simply "to be agreeable." Whereupon, the member who suggested the idea states that he didn't want to go either. He simply suggested the idea to make conversation.

To avoid groupthink, all ideas should be crtically evaluated. You should encourage open discussion of all ideas on a routine basis. Some more sophisticated ideas can be better evaluated by calling in outside experts to listen or even rotating assignment of a devil's advocate to bring up all the reasons against any proposed action. One idea that helps many teams avoid groupthink is a policy of second-chance discussions. With this technique, all decisions made at a meeting have their implementations deferred until one additional confirmation discussion at a later date.

During this stage, the questions raised by your fellow team members will include: How will we handle disagreements? How do we communicate negative information? Can the composition of this team be changed? How can we make decisions even though there is a lot of disagreement? Do we really need this leader? You may wish that your fellow team members were not asking themselves these questions, especially the last. However, better to be forewarned so you can deal with these issues, than to be surprised.

There are a number of actions you can take to help your team during this stage. You can think up ways to reinforce and remotivate commitment to the vision. You can turn your fellow team members into teachers, helping others with problems they may be having. In fact, you should know that using others as teachers, or leaders, for subareas in the project helps to generate their public commitment. You might think up ways to provide individual recognition, such as a small prize for the most accomplished during the previous week. As arguments arise, you can work on being a more effective mediator. You can look for win/win opportunities and foster win/win thinking, where both sides of an argument or an issue, benefit. One way to increase feelings of cohesion in the group is to identify a common "enemy." Other class teams competing for "best marketing plan" might constitute one such "enemy."

There are plenty of challenges for you as a leader in this stage. You will learn a tremendous amount about leading groups. Do it right, and your team enters the final stage looking, acting, and performing like a real winner.

STAGE 4: GETTING THE JOB DONE

Of course your team is getting the job done during all four stages. But if you've done things right, when you get to stage 4, you are really on a roll. How soon your team reaches this stage varies greatly. Clearly, it is to your advantage to get to this stage as soon as you can, and to spend the bulk of your time working on your marketing plan in this stage. During this stage, team members show high mutual trust and unconditional commitment to the team. Moreover, team members tend to be self-sufficient and display a good deal of initiative. The team looks like an entrepreneurial company. As team leader, your focus during this final stage should be on innovation, continuous improvement, and emphasizing and making most of what your team does best, its core competencies.

Team members' questions reflect this striving for high performance. How can we continuously improve? How can we promote innovativeness and creativity? How can we build on our core competencies? What further improvements can be made to our processes? How can we maintain a high level of contribution to the team?

As team leader, your actions are in direct line with these questions. Do everything you can to encourage continuous improvement. Celebrate your team's successes. Keep providing feedback on performance on an ongoing basis. Sponsor and encourage new ideas and expanded roles for team members. And most important, help the team avoid reverting back to earlier stages.

WHEN GOOD TEAM MEMBERS DO BAD THINGS

As you progress through the four stages, you will occasionally be surprised by team members you considered first rate, doing things to hurt the team. When that happens, you'll have to take some kind of action. You might also consider the root cause. Why did this productive team member go wrong? Here are some of the more common reasons that good team members err:

- Inequity of effort.
  When one or more members of the team fail to work up to a certain standard of effort, you will soon find that others will do likewise. The erring team member thinks "If this other person isn't working up to his effort, why should I?" This is one reason why you cannot allow one of the team members to goof off and do less than his or her fair share. You must stop inequity of effort before it starts.

- No accountability.
  This occurs when members are allowed to "freewheel," and no feedback occurs. Since no one else seems to care, the member feels insignificant and unimportant. This can lead to general inequity of effort.

- Same reward to everyone.
  This, too, is related to inequity of effort. The team member wonders why he or she should work harder than other team members when all get the same reward. You want every member striving to contribute to the maximum extent possible. Same reward can lead to everyone trying to do the minimum. The solution is to set up a reward system, even if the "reward" is a simple public recognition of an above-the-call-of-duty or a successful accomplishment.

- Coodination problems.

  There is no getting around it—the more people involved, the more coordination required. That can mean waiting for the work of others, having to get others' approval, and other delays. For someone who has always worked successfully alone, the inefficiencies are frustrating and painfully obvious. As already noted, however, the loss in efficiency of the individual can be more than made up by the synergistic effect. Team members can not only help one another, but cheer them on and rejoice in another individual's success. As team leader, you must make certain this happens. You must make it efficient and fun to be part of the team. Do this, and all members will see that they can accomplish more as a member of a group than they ever could individually.

SUMMARY

The focus of this book is how to put together a marketing plan. You will learn a lot from doing this. It is a skill that is worth a great deal to any corporation. You may get to work on a team. If so, you are going to learn a great deal from this also. It is an invaluable experience. If you are really lucky, you will have the responsibility of team leader. You have achieved a triple whammy. You are going to learn more than anyone else. It's not going to be easy. You will face the stiffest challenges and the most difficult work. You will bear the heaviest responsibility. It can also be one of the most rewarding experiences of your life. The material in this appendix can help you, but only you can determine how to apply the information. Your success is up to you. Good luck!

Index